ARTIFICIAL INTELLIGENCE
A PRACTICAL APPROACH

ARTIFICIAL INTELLIGENCE

A PRACTICAL APPROACH

- Concepts
- Principles
- Case Studies
- Experiments
- Projects
- LISP & PROLOG Programming

[For the Students of B.E./B.Tech. Computer Science Engineering and Information Technology [CSE/IT]

Er. RAJIV CHOPRA

Asst. Prof. (CSE/IT)

BE(CSE); M.I.T; M.Tech(IT)–USIT, GTBIT, GGSIPU, Delhi

CCEH —Crezone Certified Ethical Hacker

S Chand And Company Limited

(ISO 9001 Certified Company)

S Chand And Company Limited

(ISO 9001 Certified Company)

Head Office: D-92, Sector–2, Noida – 201301, U.P. (India), Ph. 91-120-4682700

Registered Office: A-27, 2nd Floor, Mohan Co-operative Industrial Estate, New Delhi – 110 044, Phone: 011-49731800

www.**schandpublishing.com**; e-mail: **info@schandpublishing.com**

Marketing Offices:

Chennai	:	Ph: 23632120; chennai@schandpublishing.com
Guwahati	:	Ph: 2738811, 2735640; guwahati@schandpublishing.com
Hyderabad	:	Ph: 40186018; hyderabad@schandpublishing.com
Jalandhar	:	Ph: 4645630; jalandhar@schandpublishing.com
Kolkata	:	Ph: 23357458, 23353914; kolkata@schandpublishing.com
Lucknow	:	Ph: 4003633; lucknow@schandpublishing.com
Mumbai	:	Ph: 25000297; mumbai@schandpublishing.com
Patna	:	Ph: 4011400; patna@schandpublishing.com

First Edition 2012

Second Revised Edition 2013; Reprints 2020, 2022, 2023, 2024, 2025

Reprint 2026

ISBN: 978-81-219-3948-5 **Product Code:** H3AIN50COMP10ENAB14O

PRINTED IN INDIA

By Shri Shyamlal Printing Press Private Limited, Plot 20/4, Site-IV, Industrial Area Sahibabad, Ghaziabad – 201 010 and Published by S Chand And Company Limited, A-27, 2nd Floor, Mohan Co-operative Industrial Estate, New Delhi – 110 044.

ACKNOWLEDGEMENT

Writing a good book which gives practical exposure also is not an easy job. It requires sincere efforts, hard work and blessings of omnipresent God and others who all motivated me to write this book.

I gratefully acknowledge the support given by CMD of S. Chand & Company Ltd. as well as Mr. Navin Joshi (Executive V.P), Mr. Amit Gupta (CEO), Mr. S. Bhatnagar (Pre-Press Manager) and the entire team of S. Chand for publishing the book on time and with a nice format.

I am also thankful to my wife Mrs. Shakti Chopra, my twin babies — Arjeesh (son) and Arshitha (daughter) for their constant support and patience and also the encouragement given by my parents, Dr. J.R. Chopra (Ex. Prof. of Physics) and Mrs. Sushma Chopra (Ex. Principal).

Er. RAJIV CHOPRA

PREFACE

Many books on AI are available in market but they tend to be very formal and dry. My attempt is to make AI very simple so that a student thinks as if a teacher is sitting behind him and guiding him. AI has two main goals — building intelligent machines and understanding the nature of intelligence. Expert systems are computer-based systems that use knowledge often acquired from human experts to solve problems reading such expertise as in medical diagnosis, legal advising, tax planning, image interpretation and engineering design. AI and ES are linked via Knowledge Engineering (KE). KE is concerned with reducing a large body of knowledge to a set of facts and rules of a knowledge base and the inference procedures required for utilizing that knowledge for problem solving. KE is concerned with the task of building expert systems using appropriate tools.

This text is bolstered with many solved and unsolved problems, CASE STUDIES, experiments of AI in LISP and PROLOG programming of all Indian Universities. Every effort has been made to alleviate the treatment of the book for easy flow of understanding of students as well professors alike.

Any suggestions to enhance the quality of the book will be highly acknowledged and welcomed.

e-mail: raj_74chopra2004@yahoo.com

Er. RAJIV CHOPRA

GGSIPU B.TECH (CSE/IT) (SEM VIII)

Paper: Artificial Intelligence 2010-11

Code No.: ETCS 402 | **L T C**
Paper: Artificial Intelligence | **3 1 4**

Instructions to Paper Setters:

1. Question No. 1 should be compulsory and cover the entire syllabus. This question should have objective or short answer type questions. It should be of 25 marks.
2. Apart from question No. 1, rest of the paper shall consist of four units as per the syllabus. Every unit should have two questions. However, students may be asked to attempt only 1 question from each unit. Each question should be of 12.5 marks.

UNIT-1

Scope of AI: Games, theorem proving, natural language processing, vision and speech processing, robotics, expert systems, AI techniques-search knowledge, abstraction.

Problem Solving (Blind): State space search: production systems, search space control; depth-first, breadth-first search.

Heuristic Based Search: Heuristic search, Hill climbing, best-first search, branch and bound, problem reduction, constraint satisfaction end, means-end analysis.

[No. of Hrs: 12]

UNIT-II

Game Playing: Game tree, minimax aLgorithm, alpha beta cutoff, modified minimax algorithm, horizon effect, futility cut-off.

Knowledge Representation: Predicate Logic: Unification, modus Ponens, modus tolens, resolution in predicate logic, conflict resolution, forward chaining, backward chaining, declarative and procedural representation, rule-based systems.

Structured knowledge representation: semantic nets: slots, exceptions and default frames, conceptual dependency, scripts.

[No. of Hrs.: 12]

UNIT-III

Handling Uncertainty: Non-monotonic reasoning, probabilistic reasoning, use of certainty factors, fuzzy logic.

Natural language processing: introduction, syntactic processing, semantic processing, pragmatic Processing.

[No. of Hrs.: 10]

UNIT-IV

Learning: Concept of learning, learning automation, genetic algorithm, learning by inductions, neural nets.

Expert systems, need and justification for expert systems, knowledge acquisition, case studies: MYCIN, RI.

[No. of Hrs.: 10]

GGSIPU B.TECH (CSE/IT) (SEM VIII)

Academic Plan for VIII Semester (For Year 2011-12)

Subject: Artificial Intelligence **Code No.: ETCS 402 Total**

Teaching weeks in semester: 14 weeks **Total number of lecturers: 40**

Total number of tutorials: 16

S. No.	Topics to be covered	Total no. of lectures	Total no. of tutorials
	First Term		
	Scope of AI: Games, theorem proving, natural language processing, vision and speech processing, robotics, expert systems, AI techniques-search knowledge, abstraction.	3	3
	Problem Solving (Blind): State space search; production systems, search space control; depth-first breadth-first search.	1	
	Heuristic Based Search: Heuristic search, Hill climbing, best-first search, branch and bound, problem reduction. constraint satisfaction end, means-end analysis.		
	Knowledge representation: predicate logic: unification, modus ponens, modus tolens, resolution in predicate logic, conflict resolution, forward chaining, backward chaining, declarative and procedural representation, rule-based systems.	4 2 6	2 2
	Structural knowledge representation: semantic nets: slots, exceptions and default frames, conceptual dependency, scripts.	2	1
	Second Term:		
	Game Playing: Game Tree, minimax algorithm, alpha beta cutoff, modified minimax algorithm, horizon effect, futility cut-off.	4	2
	Handling Uncertainty: Non-Monotonic reasoning, probabilistic reasoning, use of certainty factors, fuzzy logic.	4	
	Expert System: Need and justification for expert systems, knowledge acquisition, case studies: MYCIN, RI.	5	2
	Learning: Concept of learning automation, genetic algorithm, learning by inductions, neural nets.	5	2
	Third Term		
	Natural language processing: introduction, syntactic processing, semantic processing, pragmatic processing.	4	2

CONTENTS

CHAPTER

INTRODUCTION TO AI

1.0 INTRODUCTION

We need to develop some paradigms or algorithms that cause our machines to perform tasks that otherwise require cognition or perception when performed by humans. Any artificially intelligent system must possess three essential components:–

1. A means for representation of diverse kinds of knowledge

Knowledge may be generic and domain specific, implicit and at different levels of abstraction. The representation mechanism that we opt must be able to handle this knowledge in any form. **Please note that a representational structure enforces certain limitations on the nature of inferences that can be drawn from the embedded knowledge.**

2. A framework for reasoning

We need to have some control mechanisms to constrain the search through a Knowledge Base (KB) and the means of arriving at conclusions.

3. A mechanism for learning

An artificial intelligent system must have a method of learning new data, storing it in the existing structures internally with minimal or no disturbances to them.

Classical AI or Good Old Fashioned AI is **symbolic** and **top-down** in its approach.

What is AI exactly?

According to Patterson, "AI is a branch of computer science that deals with the study and the creation of computer systems that exhibit some form of intelligence." By '**intelligence**' we mean

(*a*) Systems that learn new concepts and tasks;

(*b*) Systems that can reason and draw useful conclusions about the world around us;

(*c*) Systems that can understand a natural language or perceive and comprehend a visual scene; and

(*d*) Systems that perform other types of feats that require human types of intelligence.

Many other definitions of AI have been given:

1. **General definition:** "An understanding of AI requires an understanding of related terms such as intelligence, knowledge, reasoning, thought, cognition, learning and solving problems."
2. **By Advert:** "AI is the part of computer science concerned with designing intelligent computer systems *i.e.* systems that exhibit characteristics that we associate with intelligence in human behavior."
3. **By heuristic (i.e., Rule of Thumb):** "AI is the branch of computer science that deals with the ways of representing knowledge using symbols rather than numbers and with the rules of thumb for processing information."

4. **Modern definition: "AI is defined as the branch of computer science dealing with symbolic and non-algorithmic method of problem solving."**

NOTE: AI works with "*pattern-matching*" methods which attempt to describe object, events and process in terms of their qualitative nature and logical and combinational relationship.

Please understand that "**intelligence**" is a catchy word here. **Intelligence** means an integrated sum of all knowledge and facts, acquired through study and experience. **Also note that the food for this intelligence is knowledge.**

AI task domain

Basically, AI covers three types of tasks:

(*a*) Mundane tasks

(*b*) Formal tasks

(*c*) Expert tasks

Let us understand these tasks now.

I. Mundane tasks

AI has some mundane tasks also like,

(*a*) Perception of vision and speech.

(*b*) Natural language understanding.

(*c*) Common sense reasoning.

(*d*) Robotics.

II. Formal tasks

AI formal tasks include:

(*a*) Game playing, e.g., chess, 8-queens problems, water-jug problem etc.

(*b*) Mathematics — geometry, calculus, etc.

III. Expert tasks

It includes:

(*a*) Engineering field.

(*b*) Scientific analysis.

(*c*) Medical and financial analysis.

What AI is NOT?

1. **AI is not the study and creation of conventional computer systems.**

All programs exhibit some degree of intelligence and an AI program must go beyond this degree of intelligence also. This is not the case. Remember that human beings are more intelligent than our intelligent systems also as we only have created them.

2. **AI is not the study of mind, nor of body, nor of languages, as found in fields of psychology physiology, cognitive science or linguistics.**

Although there is some overlap between these fields and AI, yet the goal of AI is to develop a computer system that is capable of performing intelligent tasks effectively and efficiently.

So, what AI will include? It includes areas like:

(*a*) Robotics

(*b*) Memory organization

(*c*) Knowledge representation

(*d*) Storage and recall

(*e*) Learning models

(*f*) Inference techniques

(*g*) Common sense reasoning

(*h*) Decision making.

(*i*) Pattern recognition

(*j*) Searching

(*k*) Speech recognition

(*l*) Speech synthesis.

History of AI

Let us see the history of AI in 1950s, 1960s, 1970s, 1980s and 1990s in a tabular form now.

Year	Developments made
1950s	❍ Birth of AI
	❍ First Neural Net Simulator (Minsky)
	❍ GPS—General Purpose Problem Solver (Simon)
	❍ GTP—Geometry Theorem Prover—(Gelertber), input diagrams, backward reasoning.
	❍ SAINT—Symbolic integration
1960s	❍ ANALOGY—could solve IQ test puzzle
	❍ STUDENT—could solve algebraic word problems
	❍ SHRDLU—could manipulate blocks using robotic arm
	❍ STRIPS—a problem solver planner
	❍ Minsky and Papert—demonstrated the limitations of neural nets
1970s	❍ Conceptual Dependency theory (Shank)
	❍ Frames (Minsky)
	❍ Machine Learning: ID3 (Quinlan), AM (Lenat)
	❍ Expert system got success
	❍ DENDRAL by Feigenbaum— to identify molecular structure.
	❍ MYCIN by Shortliffe and Buchanan – to diagnose infectious blood diseases
1980s	❍ Cheaper computing, so AI Software a feasible success, neural nets revisited
	❍ XCON (by McSermott)—saved $ 40m per year
	❍ Neural computing—back propagation (Werbos), associative memory (Hopfield), logic programming developed and used
1990s	❍ Embedded intelligent systems, agents
	❍ Hybrid approaches: logic + neural nets + genetic algorithms + fuzzy logic
	❍ CYC (by Lenat)—a far-reaching project to capture common sense reasoning
	❍ Society of Mind (Minsky)—Intelligence is a product of complex interactions of simple agents
	❍ Deep Blue (formerly Deep Thought)—defeated Kasparov in speed chess in 1997

Let us see the entire history now, from 1941 to 1991.

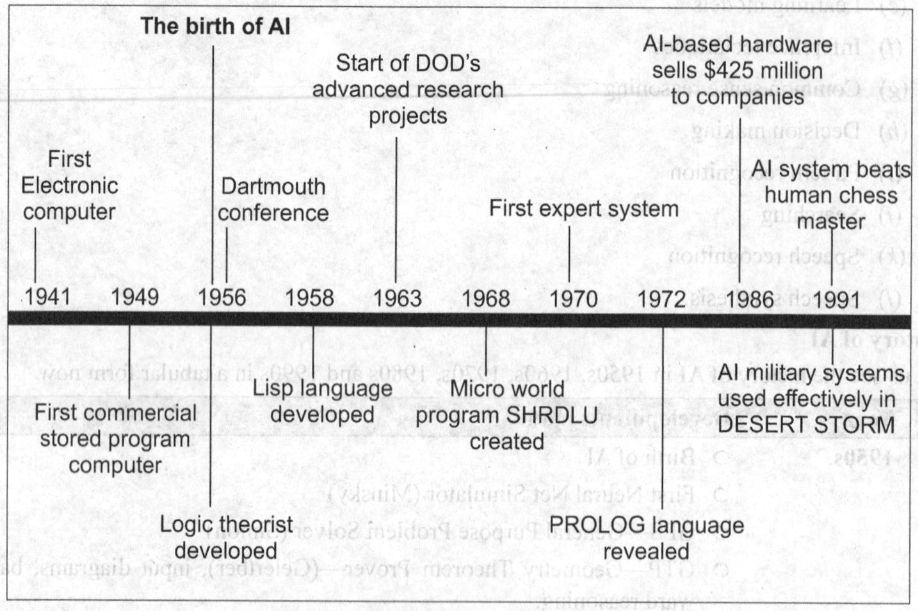

Fig. 1.1 History of AI.

1.1 SCOPE OF AI

AI has a very wide scope. Some of its applications are discussed below:

1.1.1 Games

According to Newell and Simon (1976), **the essential basis for human problem solving is to systematically explore a space of problem states, i.e., successive and alternative stages in the problem solving.** For example, the different board configurations in a chess game or intermediate steps in a reasoning process. This space is called as **state space**. This space of alternative solutions is then searched to find a final answer.

Please understand that games can generate extremely large search spaces. So, we need powerful techniques to search for our solution in this space. **These techniques are called as heuristics. Also note that intelligence resides in heuristics only.** So, AI helps here.

1.1.2 Theorem Proving

It is a formal system wherein logic lends itself to automation. A large variety of problems can be solved by using logical axioms and treating problem instances as theorems to be proved. Theorem proving has devised powerful solution heuristics and reduced the complexity of the search space. **For example,** design and verification of logic circuits, control of complex systems etc., will respond to such an approach.

Many modern theorem provers function as '**intelligent assistants**'. By this we mean that it allows humans to do the task of decomposition of large problems into subproblems and devising heuristics for searching the space of possible proofs. On the other hand, the **theorem prover** then performs the simpler but still demanding task of proving lemmas, verifying smaller guesses and completing the formal aspects of a proof outlined by the humans.

1.1.3 Natural Language Processing (NLP)

It is a subfield of AI which deals with the methods of communicating with a computer in one's own natural language. This will fill the gap between the humans and the machines. So, now one need not be computer literate to communicate with it.

1.1.4 Vision and Speech Processing

Computer vision is a computation intensive process. It involves multiple transformations. This relies more on classical AI methods of symbolic processing.

Speech understanding requires recognition of basic speech patterns. These patterns are matched against lexicon patterns for recognition. Developing systems that understand speech has been a continuing goal of AI researchers.

1.1.5 Robotics

According to the Robot Institute of America (RIA) — **"A robot is a reprogrammable, multifunctional, manipular that is designed to move materials, parts, tools or specialized devices through various programmed motions for the performance of a variety of tasks."**

Today, we need intelligent Robots to make them smaller devices. So, intelligence needs to be embedded into it. So, now vision is very essential. These intelligent robots as well as AI promise us to solve our complex problems easily.

1.1.6 Expert Systems (ES)

They are knowledge intensive programs that solve problems in a domain that needs a good technical expertise. As per the definition given by British Computer Society's Committee of the Specialist Group on Expert Systems—

"The embodiment within a computer of a knowledge-based component from an expert skill in such a form that the machine can offer intelligent advice or take an intelligent decision about a processing function. A desirable additional characteristic which many would regard fundamental, is the capability of the system on demand to justify its own line of reasoning in a manner directly intelligible to the inquirer. The style adopted to attain these characteristics is rule-based programming."

So, we find from this definition that an AI specialist or a knowledge engineer or expert system designers are responsible for implementing knowledge in a program, both effectively and intelligently.

For example,

1. **DENDRAL** — developed at Stanford University in late 1960s. It was designed to infer the structure of organic molecules from their chemical formulas and mass spectrographic information about the chemical bonds present in the molecules. As these organic molecules tend to be very large, so the number of possible structures for these molecules tend to be huge. DENDRAL addresses this problem of a large search space by applying the heuristics knowledge of expert chemists to the structure elucidation problem.

   DENDRAL used domain specific knowledge for this.

2. **MYCIN** — It uses the expert medical knowledge to diagnose and prescribe treatment for spinal meningitis and bacterial infections of the blood. It was developed at Stanford in mid-1970s. It provides clear and logical explanations of its reasoning. It uses a control structure appropriate to the specific problem domain.

3. **PROSPECTOR** — A program for determining the probable location and the type of ore deposits based on geological information about a site.

   Please note that most expert systems have been written for relatively specialized expert level domains.

1.2 AI TECHNIQUES

I. Search Knowledge

Knowledge can be defined as the body of facts and principles accumulated by humankind or the act, fact or state of knowing. For example, in **biological organisms**, knowledge is stored as complex structures of interconnected neurons. The structures correspond to symbolic representations of the knowledge possessed by the organism, the facts, rules and so on. **Please note that an average human brain weighs about 3.3 pounds and contains an estimated number of 10^{12} neurons. Also note that these neurons and their interconnection capabilities provide about 10^{14} bits of potential storage capacity.** On the other hand, in computers knowledge is stored as symbolic structures but in form of collections of magnetic spots and voltage states.

Knowledge is of three types as shown below:

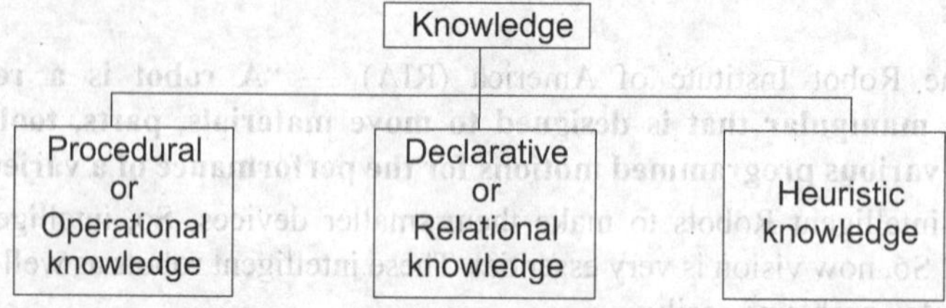

Fig. 1.2 Types of knowledge

Let us define these types now.

1. Procedural or Operational Knowledge

It is defined as a compiled knowledge related to the performance of some task. For example, steps to solve a quadratic equation are expressed as a procedural knowledge.

2. Declarative or Relational Knowledge

It is a passive knowledge expressed as statements of facts about the world. For example, personnel data in a database. Such data are explicit pieces of independent knowledge.

3. Heuristic Knowledge

Heuristics means using some rules of thumb or tricks or some strategies to simplify the solution to problems. We acquire this after much experience.

Some terminologies related to knowledge

We define certain terms that will be used again and again here. They are as follows:

1. **Knowledge and data:** A doctor has both **knowledge** as well as **data**. Here, **data** is the patient's record whereas **knowledge** is what he has learned in his medical college. This was explained by Feigenbaum and McCorduck.
2. **Belief:** It is defined as essentially any meaningful and coherent expression that can be represented. It may be true or false.
3. **Hypothesis:** It is defined as a justified belief that is not known to be true. It is backed up with some supporting evidences but it may still be false.
4. **Knowledge:** It is a true justified belief.
5. **Meta knowledge:** It is the knowledge about the knowledge.
6. **Epistemology:** It is the study of the nature of knowledge.

AI technique is a method that exploits knowledge that should be represented in such a way that:

1. It captures generalizations.
2. It can be understood by people who must provide it.

3. It can be easily modified to correct errors and to incorporate changes.
4. It can be used many situations even if it is not totally accurate or complete.
5. It can be used to help overcome its own sheer bulk by helping to narrow the range of possibilities that must usually be considered.

Please note that it is possible to solve AI problems without using AI techniques but the solutions would be inefficient. Also it is possible to apply AI techniques to the solution of non-AI problems and this will be a good thing for those problems that possess same characteristics as AI problems have.

Those systems that depend on a rich base of knowledge to perform difficult tasks are known as knowledge-based systems.

A knowledge-based system (KBS) consists of three main components as shown in Fig. 1.3.

Fig. 1.3 Components of a KBS

Explanation: KBSs get their power from the expert knowledge that has been coded into facts, rules, heuristics and procedures. The knowledge is stored in a knowledge base only. Since it is stored separately (from I/O unit and Inference CU) so we can easily add new knowledge to this knowledge base or refine existing knowledge without recompiling the control and inferencing programs. So, now the construction as well as the maintenance of KBS becomes very simple.

Knowledge-base is different from database. **Let us tabulate the differences between them now.**

Data Base (DB)	Knowledge Base (KB)
1. It is defined as a collection of data representing facts.	1. It has information at a higher level of abstraction.
2. It is larger than a KB.	2. It is smaller than a DB.
3. Changes are fast.	3. Changes are gradual.
4. All information needs to be stated explicitly.	4. It has the power of inferencing.
5. It is mainttained for operational purposes.	5. It is used for data analysis and planning.
6. Knowledge is represented by relational, network or hierarchical model.	6. Knowledge is represented by logic or rules.

Knowledge may be represented at various levels as shown in Fig. 1.4.

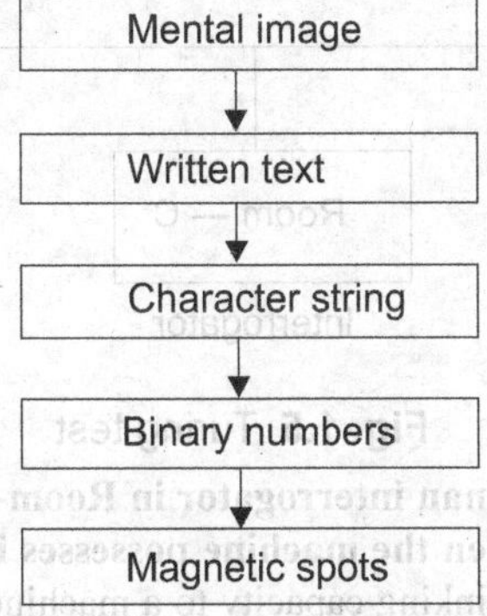

Fig. 1.4 Levels of knowledge representation

Please note, however, that any choice of representation will depend on the type of problem to be solved and the inference methods available.

Not only this, knowledge organization in memory is also very vital. The KBS discussed in Fig. 1.3 may require several (tens of thousands) of facts and rules to perform their intended tasks. So, now it is mandatory to easily search, locate and retrieve appropriate facts and rules from this KB. We use indexings to speed up searches — we can form groups of knowledge of similar type and then make a pointer to point to this group. So, now instead of searching for an entire KB, only a small portion of it may be accessed.

We need to manipulate this knowledge also. Usually, the user gives some input and thus, initiates a search for a **goal** or **decision. Please understand that this requires that known facts in the KB be located, compared (matched) and altered somehow. Also note that this process may set up some sub-goals which requires some more inputs and so on until a final solution is found.** This requires a form of inference or deduction using the knowledge and inferring rules. Please note here that all forms of reasoning require certain amount of searching and matching. Also note that searching and matching both consume the maximum time of computation in AI systems. So, we need to have the best searching technique today so that we can avoid this combinatorial explosion problem during searching.

Now, the question is **how to acquire knowledge?** Knowledge may be acquired from sources like textbooks, references, reports, technical research papers and so on and to be **useful**, it should be accurate, complete, inconsistent and so on. Our KBS depends on a high quality knowledge for their success.

1.3 ALAN TURING MACHINE

In 1950, Alan Turing published an article in the "Mind Magazine" which triggered a controversial topic — **"Can machines think?"** So, the **Turing test is —"A computer is programmed well enough to have a conversation with an interrogator and passes the test if the interrogator cannot discern if there is a computer or human at the other end."**

It means that in this imitation game there are three actors —

(*a*) a male,

(*b*) a female, and

(*c*) an interrogator.

That is,

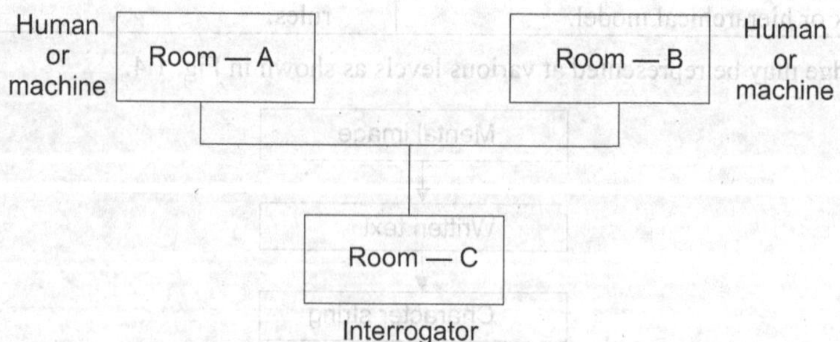

Fig. 1.5 Turing test

Turing proposed that if a human interrogator in Room-C (Fig. 1.5) is not able to identify who is in Room-A or Room-B, then the machine possesses intelligence. Turing considered this as a sufficient test for attributing thinking capacity to a machine. This test is not that easy as given here because we know that humans are far more superior in common sense and reasoning. But, even today this Turing test is the ultimate test that a machine must pass in order to be called as intelligent.

So, the full Turing test is — to consider a machine to be intelligent we need to test that —

"Can machines think?" ↔ "Can machines behave intelligently?"

So, for this imitation game above, the Turing test needs an operational definition of intelligence. For this the computer needs to possess the following —

(*a*) Natural Language Processing (NLP)

It is required to communicate with Room-A or Room-B.

(*b*) Knowledge Representation

It is required to store and retrieve information provided before or during interrogation.

(*c*) Automated Reasoning

It is used to access stored information to answer queries and to draw new conclusions.

(*d*) Machine Learning

It is needed to adapt to new conditions and to detect and extrapolate patterns.

(*e*) Vision

It is required for total Turing test – to reeognize interrogator's actions above.

(*f*) Motor Control

It is to act upon objects as requested.

(*g*) Senses

For total Turing test, these are needed like smell, touch, etc.

Please understand that for a program to pass this Turing test, it needs to pass and exhibit these capabilities.

Limitations of Turing Test

Turing test has certain drawbacks which are given below—

1. Say, a machine has passed the Turing test. Now, the question is as to what level of proficiency it has achieved? We can say that it is the level of programmer only, that is, its proficiency. In fact, a machine demonstrates the intelligence of human brains only.
2. What happens if a machine passes this Turing test, is intelligent, manipulates all formal symbols but lacks understanding.
3. Turing test is not reproducible, constructive and amenable to mathematical analysis.
4. It does not consider about the physical interaction with the interrogator and the environment.

1.4 CHARACTERISTICS OF AI PROBLEMS

1. Almost all AI problems have a **combinatorial explosion** of solutions.

   For example, in case of a chess game, the number of possible positions has been estimated to about 35^{100}, which is too large. So, our conventional computers cannot handle this huge solution space. Thus, we need AI programs.
2. AI programs manipulate symbolic information, on the other hand conventional computers (or programs) deal with numeric processing.
3. An AI program needs a large KB, whereas a conventional program needs a large DB.
4. An AI program has an ability to learn. Conventional systems have not achieved that level till now.
5. An AI program needs an imprecise knowledge whereas a conventional program needs a precise knowledge.

Let us tabulate the differences between the two now.

AI Program	Conventional Program
1. It manipulates symbolic information.	1. It manipulates numeric information.
2. It uses heuristic search method.	2. It uses algorithmic search method.
3. It seeks for satisfactory answers.	3. It seeks for optimal answers.
4. It involves large KB.	4. It involves large DB.
5. It involves frequent modifications.	5. It involves rare modifications.

1.5 INTELLIGENT AGENTS

These are software programs which work in the background to carry out specific, repetitive, predictable task for an individual user. Alan Turing suggested that a system or agent can be said to be **intelligent** when the agent's performance cannot be distinguished from that of a human performing the same task. Thus, we define now. **An intelligent agent is a software entity which senses its environment and then carries out some set of operations on behalf of a user with some amount of autonomy and to do so, it employs some knowledge or representation of the end-user's goal. Please note that an agent is different from a program.** An **agent** need not be a program at all. It may be a robot or a college professor. Also note that Software agents are by definition programs but a program must measure up to several marks to be an agent.

For example, humans, animals, autonomous mobile robots or softbots calculators are **real-world agents. Software agents** live in system's O.S.

Please understand that systems are agents or not with respect to some environment. AI is about the design and implementation of intelligent agents. The concept is shown below in Fig. 1.5.

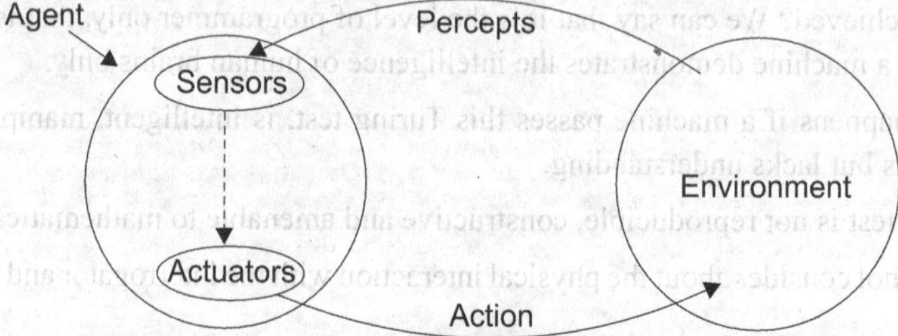

Fig. 1.6 Role of an agent

As shown in Fig. 1.6, an **agent** perceives its environment through sensors. It then acts upon that environment through **actuators.**

For examples—

1. A human agent has eyes, ears, nose etc. as sensors while hands, legs, mouth are actuators.
2. Software agent receives keystrokes, files, packets are sensory inputs and acts on the environment by displaying on the screen, writing files and sending packets over a network.

Characteristics of Agents

Agents have some features which are listed below:

1. They are **autonomous,** i.e., can work on their own.
2. They are **persistent** over a prolonged time period.
3. They are **adaptive,** i.e., adjust to changes.

4. They are **mobile,** i.e., can be transported over networks.
5. They have ability to **learn**.

Applications of Intelligent Agents (IA)

There are some major applications of IA and are given below—

1. IAs are used to access and navigate information using different search engines.
2. IAs help in decision-making by the knowledge workers.
3. IA like **voice-activated interface agent** reduces the user's task of explicitly commanding the computer.
4. IAs perform the time-consuming and combersome tasks of searching databases, doing retrievals and filtering of information and sending the result-sets back to the user, in distributed environments.
5. IAs can be used to assist managers to do their job. Some management-oriented tasks that an agent can do are— advising, alter, browse, distribute, enlist, explain, filter, guide, match, monitor, navigate, negotiate, organize, query, report, remind, retrieve, schedule, search, secure, store, suggest, summarize, reach, translate and watch.

SUMMARY

The word '**Artificial**' means making, a copy of something natural and '**Intelligence**' means the ability to gain and apply knowledge and skills. Kurzweil, in 1990, defined AI as the art of creating machines that perform functions that require intelligence when performed by people. **But please remember that humans are much more intelligent than AI system** as we (humans) only program these AI applications (called as AI programs now). Also, we found that the idea of AI originated from a historic experiment called as Turing Test.

MULTIPLE CHOICE QUESTIONS [MCQ]

1. The branch of computer science dealing with symbolic and non-algorithmic method of problem solving is called as—

(*a*) Knowledge (*b*) AI (*c*) Meta-knowledge (*d*) None of there

2. Robotics is a type of —

(*a*) Mundane task (*b*) Formal task (*c*) Expert task (*d*) None of there

3. The birth of AI took place in —

(*a*) 1950s (*b*) 1960s (*c*) 1970s (*d*) 1980s

4. Which of the following expert systems was designed to infer the structure of organic molecules from their chemical formulas ?

(*a*) DENDRAL (*b*) MYCIN (*c*) PROSPECTOR (*d*) None of there

5. An average human brain has

(*a*) 10^{10} neurons (*b*) 10^{11} neurons (*c*) 10^{12} neurons (*d*) None of there

6. The steps to solve a quadratic equation are expressed as a —

(*a*) Procedural knowledge (*b*) Relational knowledge

(c) Heuristics knowledge (*d*) None of there

7. Feigenbaum and Mc-Corduck differentiated between —

(*a*) Intelligence and AI (*b*) AI and IA

(*c*) Knowledge and data (*d*) None of there

8. The study of the nature of knowledge is called as —

(*a*) Epistemology (*b*) Ontology (*c*) Agent (*d*) None of there

9. Which of the following is larger?

(*a*) KB (*b*) DB (*c*) Student database (*d*) None of there

10. The idea of AI originated from —

(*a*) Turing Test (*b*) Chemical Test

(*c*) Biological Test (*d*) None of there

11. Agents are —

(*a*) autonomous (*b*) adaptive (*c*) Both 'a' and 'b' (*d*) None of there

12. The problems that AI tackles have —

(*a*) Very little amount of solutions

(*b*) Same number of solutions as our conventional programms have

(*c*) Combinatonia explosion of solutions

(*d*) None of the above

13. An AI program uses a technique —

(*a*) Binary Search (*b*) Heuristic Search

(*c*) Algorithmic Search (*d*) None of there

14. A set of all possible states for a given problem is known as —

(*a*) State space (*b*) Table space (*c*) Reduction space (*d*) None of there

15. Which of the following are more intelligent?

(*a*) Humans (*b*) AI systems (*c*) Expert systems (*d*) None of there

ANSWERS

1. (*b*)	2. (*a*)	3. (*a*)	4. (*a*)	5. (*c*)
6. (*a*)	7. (*c*)	8. (*a*)	9. (*b*)	10. (*a*)
11. (*c*)	12. (*c*)	13. (*b*)	14. (*a*)	15. (*a*)

CONCEPTUAL SHORT QUESTIONS WITH ANSWERS

Q. 1. Differentiate between Intelligence and Artificial Intelligence.

Ans. Let us tabulate the differences between the two —

Intelligence	Artificial Intelligence
1. It is a natural process.	1. It is programmed by humans.
2. It is actually hereditary.	2. It is not hereditary.
3. Good knowledge is required for intelligence.	3. KB is required to generate output.

4. No electricity from outside is required.	4. We need electrical energy to get output.
5. No human is an expert. We may get better solutions from other humans.	5. Expert systems are made which aggregate many persons experiences and ideas.

Q. 2. How is strong AI different from weak AI?

Ans. Let us tabulate the differences between them —

Strong AI	Weak AI
1. A strong AI claims that computers can be made to think on a level at least equal to humans.	1. A weak AI claims that some "thinking like" features are added to computer to make them more useful tool.
2. It deals with the creation of some form of computer-based AI that can truly reason and solve problems.	2. It deals with the creation of some form of computer-based AI that can reason and solve problems in a limited domain.
3. In strong AI, the programs are themselves the explanations.	3. A machine need not possess true intelligence.
4. "*Doing*" is sometimes referred to as strong AI.	4. "*Helping*" is called as weak AI.
5. We have still to achieve the objectives of strong AI.	5. We have already reached the objectives of weak AI.

Q. 3. Define what is a rational agent.

Ans. A rational agent is a type of agent that acts to achieve the best outcome or when there is uncertainty then to achieve the best expected outcome.

Q. 4. Define the following terms:

(*a*) **Fuzzy Logic**

(*b*) **Planning**

(*c*) **Problem Space.**

Ans. (*a*) **Fuzzy Logic**

A logic in which the truth values are real values in the closed interval [0 .....1] is called as a fuzzy logic. It uses the definitions of boolean operators to fit this continuous domain.

(*b*) **Planning**

A field of AI concerned with systems that construct sequences of action to achieve goals in real world like environments.

(*c*) **Problem Space/State Space**

The formulation of an AI problem into states and operators. We have a start state and a goal state. The problem space is searched to find a solution.

Q. 5. What are the major components of an AI system?

Ans. Any AI system has four main components and are shown in Fig. 1.7.

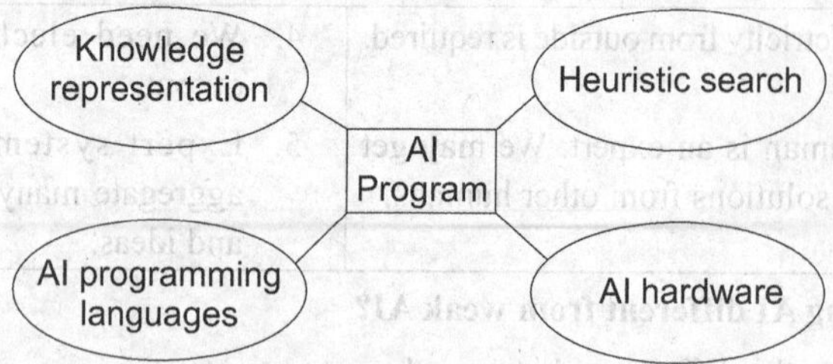

Fig. 1.7

Please understand that in AI system the quality of result depends upon how much knowledge the system possesses. The knowledge so available is to be represented in an efficient manner. The inferencing process has to be best. AI programs are written in specialized languages like Turbo-Prolog and LISP. **Also note that most of the AI programs are implemented on conventional Von Neumann machines only.** Today, even dedicated workstations have also emerged for AI programming.

Q. 6. What an agent comprises of?

Ans. We simply put it in an equation form, i.e.,

Agent = architecture + program

The **architecture** makes the percepts from the sensors available to the program, runs the program and feeds the program's action choices to the actuators as they are generated. So, the program we choose has to be one that is appropriate for the architecture.

Q. 7. What are the various task environments?

Ans. Basically, 6 types of task environments can be found for various problems.

(*a*) Fully observable v/s partially observable.

(*b*) Deterministic v/s stochastic.

(*c*) Episodic v/s sequential.

(*d*) Static v/s Dynamic.

(*e*) Discrete v/s Continuous.

(*f*) Single agent v/s multi-agent.

I. Fully observable v/s Partially observable

A task environment is fully observable if an agent's sensor gives it a complete access to the state of environment at each point of time. **For example,** a chess with a clock is fully observable environment.

On the other hand, an environment is partially observable because of noisy and inaccurate sensors. **For example,** an automated taxi cannot see what other drivers are thinking.

II. Deterministic v/s Stochastic

If the next state of the environment is completely determined by the current state and the action is executed by the agent then the environment is **deterministic** else it is **stochastic** environment. **For example,** Image analysis provides a deterministic environment whereas Taxi driving is a stochastic case.

III. Episodic v/s Sequential

In episodic task environment, the agent's experience is divided into atomic episodes. Each episode consists of the agent perceiving and then performing a single action. **For example,** image analysis would give episodic environment, while in sequential environments the current decision could affect all future decisions. **For example,** chess and taxi driving are sequential. **Please note that episodic environments are much simpler than sequential environments because the agent does not need to think ahead.**

IV. Static v/s Dynamic

If the environment can change while an agent is deliberating, then we say the environment is **dynamic** for that agent else it is **static. For example,** Taxi driving is dynamic. Crossword puzzles are static. Chess with clock is semi-dynamic.

V. Discrete v/s Continuous

A discrete or continuous distinction can be applied to the state of the environment and to the percepts and actions of the agent. **For example,** Taxi driving is continuous state problem whereas chess with a clock is discrete.

VI. Single Agent v/s Multiagent

These environments are easy to distinguish. **For example**, an agent solving a crossword puzzle by itself is clearly in a single agent environment, whereas playing chess with a clock is a multiagent environment.

EXERCISE QUESTIONS

Q. 1. (*a*) If the Turing Test is passed, does this show that computer exhibits Intelligence? State reasons.

(*b*) How declarative knowledge is different from procedural knowledge?

(*c*) Discuss the importance of heuristics in problem solving.

[GGSIPU, B.Tech (CSE)—8th sem., May-June 2009]

Q. 2. Compare knowledge representation to data representation in a database.

[GGSIPU, B.Tech (CSE)—8th sem., May-June 2009]

Q. 3. What is Turing's Test? Explain its significance.

[GGSIPU, B.Tech (CSE)—8th sem., May 2008]

Q. 4. Define AI. List important task domains of AI.

[GGSIPU, B.Tech (CSE)—8th sem., Sept. 2005]

Q. 5. What is AI? What are its application areas? **[GGSIPU, B.Tech (IT)—7th sem., 2007-08]**

Q. 6. What do you mean by knowledge acquisition?

[GGSIPU, B.Tech (IT)—8th sem., 2nd Internal Test, April 2008]

Q. 7. What is the role of Heuristics in AI? **[GGSIPU, MCA—4th sem., June 2001]**

Q. 8. Write different approaches of knowledge representation.

[GGSIPU, MCA—4th sem., May 2002]

Q. 9. "An AI system must contain a lot of knowledge if it is to handle anything but trivial problems but with the growth of knowledge it becomes harder to access appropriate information." Discuss this dilemma as encountered in AI systems.

[GGSIPU, MCA—4th sem., May 2003]

Q. 10. Term 'AI' is a misnomer. Comment. **[GGSIPU, MCA—4th sem., May 2004]**

Q. 11. In what context did Turing suggest his well-known test? Explain the Turing Test. **[GGSIPU, MCA—4th sem., May 2005]**

Q. 12. Define AI. What are its application areas? **[GGSIPU, BCA—5th sem., Dec. 2001]**

Q. 13. Write short notes on application of AI. **[GGSIPU, BCA—7th sem., Dec 2001]**

Q. 14. Can a system engaged in purely numeric computation be called an intelligent system? Explain with suitable arguments. **[IGNOU, MCA—3rd sem., June 2004]**

Q. 15. Explain the difference between the following terms — Knowledge and data. **[DU-DCE, ME (CS), 2005]**

Q. 16. What is AI? Briefly explain KBS? **[KUD, BE. (CSE)—8th sem., Ist Internal Test, March 1997]**

Q. 17. Describe knowledge representation and knowledge acquisition? **[KUD, B.E. (CSE)—8th sem., 1996]**

Q. 18. Define and describe the difference between knowledge, hypothesis, belief and data. Also discuss the differences between declarative and procedural knowledge. **[KUD, B.E. (CSE)—8th sem, 1997]**

Q. 19. What is AI? Write various areas of AI. **[UPTU, B.Tech (CSE)—8th sem., 2006-07]**

Q. 20. (*a*) How does AI solve problems for which no practically feasible algorithm exists?

(*b*) Discuss the scope of AI applied to various categories of problems. **[GGSIPU, B.Tech (CSE)—8th sem., May 2011]**

CHAPTER 2

AI APPROACHES

2.0 INTRODUCTION

A problem solving agent firstly formulates a goal and a problem to solve. Then the agent calls a search procedure to solve it. It then uses the solution to guide its actions. It will do whatever the solution recommends as the next thing to do and then remove that step from the sequence. Once the solution has been executed, the agent will formulate a new goal. **Please note that in intelligent agents case, a KB corresponds to the environment, operators correspond to sensors and the search techniques are the actuators.**

The KB describes the current task domain and the goal (or state). Operators manipulate this KB. And the control strategy decides what operators to apply and where to apply them. **Also note that the aim of any search technique is the application of an appropriate sequence of operators to an initial state to achieve the goal.** A problem solving agent (system) uses either forward or backward reasoning. Each of its operator works to produce a new state in the KB.

Forward reasoning or bottom-up or data-driven reasoning means applying operators to those structure in the KB that best describes the task domain in order to produce a modified state. On the other hand, **backward reasoning** will break down the goal (problem) statement into subgoals (problems) which are easier to solve and these sub-solutions are sufficient to solve the original problem as a whole.

2.1 PROBLEM SOLVING

2.1.1 Problem Specification

Problem domain formulation is a very important task. This problem definition must be unambiguous and clear. So, we define an abstract problem in terms of real workable states which are clearly understood.

Please understand that these states are operated upon by a set of operators. The overall control strategy decides which operator is to be used. To formulate any problem, **four components** are defined in a very formal way. These four components are —

(1) The initial state (or **starting state**).

(2) **State space** i.e., a description of all possible states reachable from the initial state. **Please note that this state space forms a graph in which the nodes are states and the arcs represent actions.**

(3) ***Goal test*** that determines whether a given state is a goal state.

(4) ***Path cost*** is a function that assigns a numeric cost to each path.

Please note here that solution to a problem is a path from the initial state to a goal state. Also note that the quality of the solution is measured by the path cost function and obviously, an optimal solution has the lowest path cost among all solution.

So, these four components will do problem formulation. To achieve our objective, we use **operationalization**. **The process of creating a formal description of a problem using the knowledge about the given problem, so as to create a program for solving a problem is called as operationalization.** Thus, in general, any problem can be solved using the following steps—

Step-1: **Define a state space** which contains all possible configurations of the relevant objects. You can even include some impossible states.

Step-2: **Identify initial states** i.e., one or more such states from our search space that would describe possible situations from where problem solving may start.

Step-3: **Specify goal states** i.e., specify one or more states which would be acceptable as solutions to our problem.

Step-4: **Specify set of rules** i.e., give a set of rules which describe the actions (operators) available and a control strategy to decide the order of application of these rules.

At the **core heart** of many intelligent processes lies the process of **search.**

Search can be characterized as finding a path through a graph or tree structure. This requires moving from node to node after successively expanding and generating connected nodes. Node generation is accomplished by computing the identification or the representation code of children nodes from a parent node. Once this is done, a child is said to be *generated* and the parent is said to be *explored.* **The process of generating all of the children of a parent is also known as expanding the node. A search procedure is a strategy for selecting the order in which nodes are generated and a given path selected.**

Search problems may be classified as:

1. Blind or uninformed search: In this search technique, no preference is given to the order of successor node generation and selection. The path selected is blindly or mechanically followed. No information is used to determine the preference of one child over another. For e.g. DFS, DFS, bidirectional searchs.

2. Informed or directed search: In this search technique, some information about the problem space is used to compute a preference among the children for exploration and expansion. For e.g. Heuristic search.

2.1.2 State Space Search With Examples

We define the state space as a set of all possible sates of a given problem. A state space representation allows for the formal definition of a problem which makes the movement from initial state to the goal state quite easy. In a way, we can also say that various problems like planning, learning, discoveries in science, theorem proving etc. are all essentially search problems only.

Advantages and Disadvantages of state-space representations

Advantages: This representation is very useful in AI because it provides a set of all possible states, operations and goals. If the entire state-space representation for a problem is given then it is possible to trace the path from the initial to goal state and identify the sequence of operators required for doing it.

Disadvantage(s): It is not possible to visualize all states for a given problem. Also, the resources of the computer system are limited to handle huge (combinational) state-space representation.

We are now in a position to describe some search space problems.

EXAMPLE 1: The eight tile puzzle problem formulation.

Problem formulation

The eight tile puzzle consists of a 3-by-3 (3*3) square frame board which holds eight (8) movable tiles numbered as 1 to 8. One square is empty, allowing the adjacent tiles to be shifted. The objective of the puzzle is to find a sequence of tile movements that leads from a starting configuration to a goal configuration, as shown in Fig. 2.1 below.

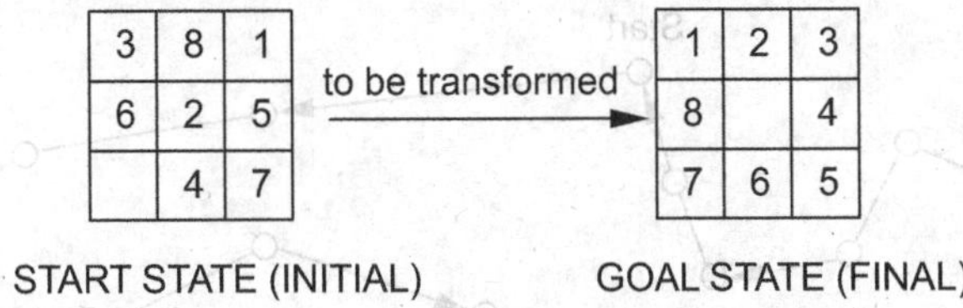

Fig. 2.1 Initial and final states of 8-puzzle problem.

The states of the 8-tile puzzle are the different permutations of the tiles within the frame.

Please note that an optimal solution is the one that maps an initial arrangement of tiles to the goal state with the smallest (minimum) number of moves. Also note that the root node can be any random starting state.

Let us do a *standard formulation* of this problem now.

States: It specifies the location of each of the 8-tiles and the blank in one of the nine squares.

***Initial state*:** Any state can be designated as the initial state.

Goal: Many goal configurations are possible one such is shown in Fig. 2.2.

***Legal moves (or states)*:** They generate legal states that result from trying the four actions—

(*a*) blank moves left.

(*b*) blank moves right.

(*c*) blank moves up.

(*d*) blank moves down.

Path cost: Each step costs 1, so the path cost is the number of steps in the path.

The tree diagram showing the search space is shown in Fig. 2.2.

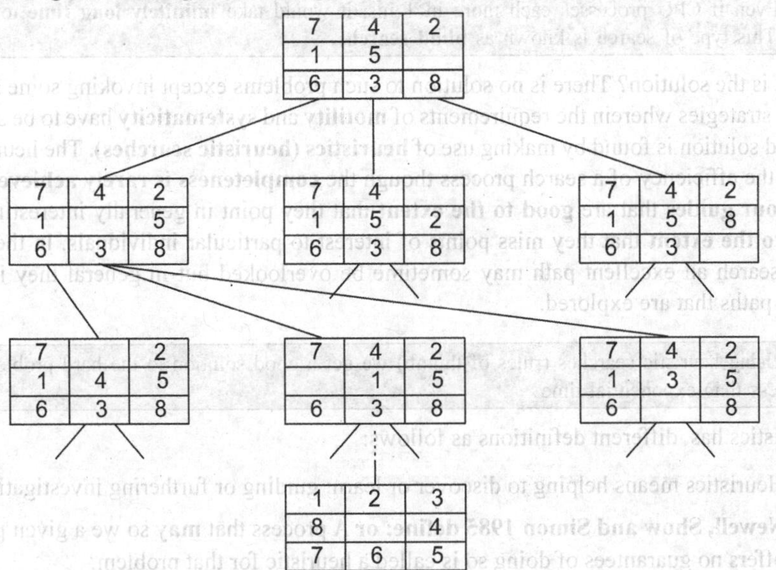

Fig. 2.2 Tree diagram (search space) of 8-puzzle problem.

EXAMPLE 2: The Traveling Salesman Problem

Problem formulation

"It involves n-cities with paths connecting the cities. A tour is any path which begins with some starting city, visits each of the other cities exactly once and returns to the starting city". A typical tour is depicted here, in Fig. 2.3.

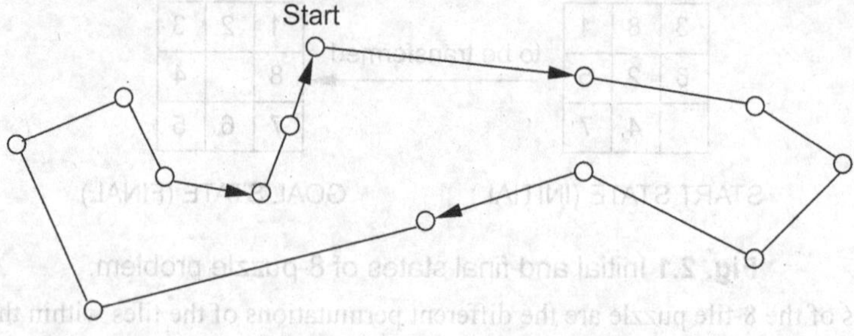

Fig. 2.3 TSP

The objective of a TSP is to find a minimal distance tour. To explore all such tours requires an exponential amount of time. As long as n is small, this approach works but it breaks down quickly as number of cities grow. If there are N-cities then the number of different path among them is 1.2… (N–1) or (N–1)! The time to examine a single path is proportional to N. So the total time required to perform this search is proportional to N! i.e., it requires O(N!) transverses through the graph, an exponential number.

TSP: This is a classical problem in graph theory. It has no closed, analytic and algorithmic solution. This problem is soluble for smaller number (n) of cities-But it breaks down as number of cities grow.

If there are n-cities, the number of different paths among them is $(n-1)!$. **Please note that the time to examine a single path is proportional to n. So, the total time to search is $n!$. Also note that if n is large then the time taken is also large. This phenomenon is known as combinatorial explosion.**

NOTE: Even if CPU processes each more in 1 ms, it would take **infinitely long time** to arrive at a solution. This type of search is known as **blind search,**

What is the solution? There is no solution to such problems except invoking some special type of control strategies wherein the requirements of **motility** and **systematicity** have to be sacrificed. A guaranteed solution is found by making use of **heuristics (heuristic searches).** The heuristic search improves the efficiency of a search process though the **completeness is rarely achieved.** They are just like t**our guides** that are **good to the extent** that they point in generally interesting direction and **bad to the extent** that they miss points of interest to particular individuals. In the process of heuristic search an excellent path may sometime be overlooked but in general they improve the quality of paths that are explored.

NOTE: Using heuristic searches (rules of thumb) we get a good solution to the hard problem (such as TSP) in less than exponential time.

Heuristics has different definitions as follows:

(*a*) Heuristics means helping to discover or learn; guiding or furthering investigation.

(*b*) **Newell, Show and Simon 1985 define: or** A process that **may** so we a given problem but offers no guarantees of doing so is called a heuristic for that problem.

(*c*) **Marvin Merisky (1963) define:** " A heuristic is any method or trick used to improve the efficiency of a problem-sowing program and that heuristic methods are related to improving problem – sowing performance."

(*d*) **Feigenbaum and Feldmen (1963) define:** "A state heuristic (heuristic rule, heuristic method) is a rule of thumb, strategy, trick, simplification or any other kind of device that drastically limits search for solutions in large problem spaces. Heuristics do not guarantee optimal solutions, in fact, they do not guarantee any solution at all that can be said for a useful heuristic is that it offers solutions that are good enough most of the time."

(*e*) **Judea Pearl (1983) define:** "It is the nature of good heuristics both that they provide a simple means of indicating which among several courses of action is to be preferred and that they are not necessarily guaranteed to identify the most effective course of action, but do so sufficiently often. It is often said that heuristic methods are unpredictable, they work wonders most of the time but may fail miserably some of the time."

Thus, heuristic programming differs significantly from algorithmic programming even though heuristic programs themselves must be expressed in algorithmic form.

Heuristics in TSM problem: A significant improvement is seen if TSP is sowed using heuristic. Now the time required is proportional to N^2 instead of $N!$

For example, if $n = 5$ then

(*a*) **Case 1:** If combinational explosion is used, then paths to be examined are 5! = **120**

(*b*) **Case 2:** If nearest neighbour heuristic is used, then number of paths to be examined are $5^2 = 25$ only.

This is a significant improvement.

Conclusions: A well designed heuristic function can play an important part in efficiently guiding a search/process towards a solution. **Please understand the sometimes very simple heuristic function can provide a fairly good estimate of whether a path is any good or not. Also understand that more complex heuristic functions may be difficult.**

It's **standard formulation** is as follows—

States: Location specified by city.

Actions: Driving along the roads between cities.

Goal: City B.

Path cost: Total distance or expected travel time.

EXAMPLE 3. Water Jug Problem

Problem formulation:

The problem domain is as follows "**We are given two jugs, a four-gallon one and a three-gallon one. Neither has any measuring markers on it. There is a pump which can be used to fill the jugs with water.** How can we get exactly two gallons of water into the four-gallon jug?" This is shown in Fig. 2.4.

The *state space* for this problem can be described as the set of ordered pairs of integers (x, y) such that $x = 0, 1, 2, 3$, or 4 and $y = 0, 1, 2$, or 3. Here x is the number of gallons of water in the four-gallon jug and y is the quantity of water in the three-gallon jug. **Please note that the start state is (0, 0) and the goal state is (2, *n*) for any value of *n*, as the problem does not specify how many gallons need to be filled in the three-gallon jug (0, 1, 2, 3). Also note that the problem has one initial state and many goal states.** Some problems may have many initial states and one or many goal states.

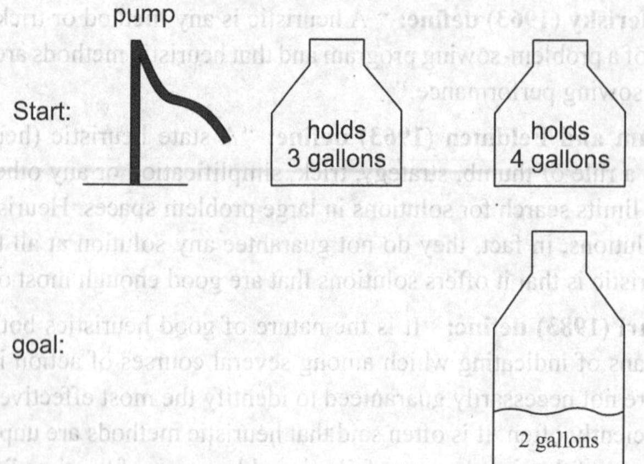

Fig. 2.4 A water jug problem.

The **operators** to be used to solve the problem is shown in table-1 below—

Table 1: Production rules (or operators) for the water jug problem

Rule	Action
1. $(x, y) \to (4, y)$ if $x < 4$	Fill the 4-gallon jug
2. $(x, y) \to (x, 3)$ if $y < 3$	Fill the 3-gallon jug
3. $(x, y) \to (x - d, y)$ if $x > 0$	Pour some water out of the 4-gallon jug
4. $(x, y) \to (x, y - d)$ if $y > 0$	Pour some water out of 3-gallon jug
5. $(x, y) \to (0, y)$ if $x > 0$	Empty the 4-gallon jug on the ground
6. $(x, y) \to (x, 0)$ if $y > 0$	Empty the 3-gallon jug on the ground
7. $(x, y) \to (4, y - (4 - x))$ if $x + y \geq 4$ and $y > 0$	Pour water from the 3-gallon jug into the 4-gallon jug until the 4-gallon jug is full

Problem formulation

States: Amount of water in both jugs.

Actions: Empty large, empty small, pour from small to (empty) large, pour from large to (empty) small.

Goal: Specified amount of water in both jugs.

Path cost: Total number of actions applied.

Solution to Water Jug Problem

We also need a **control structure** which loops through a simple cycle in which some rule whose left side matches the current state is chosen, the appropriate change to the state is made as described in the corresponding right side and the resulting state is checked to see if it corresponds to a goal state. The loop continues as long as it does not lead to the goal. **Please note that the speed with which the problem is solved depends upon the mechanism control structure, which is used to select the next operation. Also note that there are several sequences of operators which will solve the problem.** Two such possible solutions are shown in Fig. 2.5 (*a*) and Fig. 2.5 (*b*).

Water in four-gallon jug (x)	Water in three-gallon jug (y)	Rule applied (control strategy)
0	0	
0	3	2
3	0	9
3	3	2
4	2	7
0	2	5 or 12
2	0	9 or 11

Fig. 2.5 (*a*) One solution to water jug problem.

The 2nd solution can be —

Water in four-gallon jug (x)	Water in three-gallon jug (y)	Rule applied (control strategy)
0	0	
4	0	1
1	3	8
1	0	6
0	1	10
4	1	1
2	3	8

Fig. 2.5 (*b*) Another solution to water jug problem.

Thus, we find that how an informal problem state has been converted to a formal problem state. But the rules should be stated explicitly and not written because they are allowable. **For example,** rule-1 in table-1 states that— "Fill the four-gallon jug", but it should have been— "if the four gallon jug is not already filled completely". However, the rule as stated in its first-form is not wrong as there is no condition that the already filled jug cannot be filled. So, in order to increase the efficiency of problem solving program, it is imperative to encode some constraints in the left side of the rules so that the rules should lead to a solution. Thus, rules should be made more general.

Water jug problem is a simple example of solving a problem through state space search.

Even these approaches may not be exhaustive. So, we go with another method of problem-reduction techniques.

2.1.3. Problem Reduction

The process of decomposing (or breaking) up of a complex problem into a set of primitive sub-problems, finding the sub-solutions for these sub-problems and then integrating all these sub-solutions to get the solution of the given complex problem (as a whole) is known as problem reduction.

Practically, our space search is said to be good if a solution to a problem is naturally expressed in terms of either a final state or a path from an initial state to the final state. **Please note that we should be able to** define rules for transforming one state to another based on the available actions in the domain. Problem reduction is better if it is easy to decompose a problem into independent **sub-problems. Also note that we have to define rules to do this.** Here, searching will be less. We will discuss about it in detail a bit later.

2.1.4 Production Systems

These systems were proposed by Emil Post in 1943. They are also known a **inferential systems**, **Rule-based systems** or **simply productions**. For describing and performing the search operation in AI programs it is useful to structure them. The process of solving the problem can usefully be modeled as a production system. If one adopts a system with **production rules** and a '*rule-interpreter*', then the system is known as a **production system.** In these systems, the working memory of the system models human *short-term memory* while the productions are part of **long-term memory**. On each cycle of operation, productions are matched against the working memory of facts. And a production whose conditions are satisfied can add or delete facts in the working memory. **Please note that this is opposite to the situation in databases.** These production systems often have many rules and relatively fewer facts.

Rules of production systems.

Rule-1: Production systems represent both knowledge as well as action.

Rule-2: Production system provide a language in which the representation of expert knowledge is very natural.

Rule-3: Production systems provide a heuristics model for human behaviour.

Rule-4: Production systems model strong data-driven nature of intelligent action. Whenever new inputs enter the database, the behaviour of the system changes.

Rule-5: Production systems allow us to add new rules easily without disturbing the rest of the system.

Let us now see the architecture of a production system. It is shown in Fig. 2.5(c). It comprises of three main components—

1. Rule base.
2. Global database
3. Control structure.

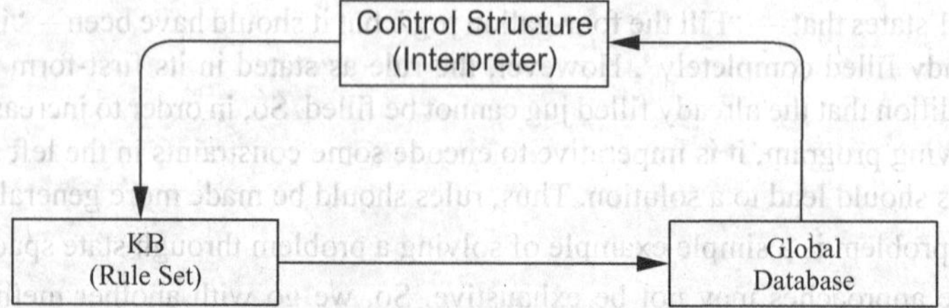

Fig. 2.5(c) Parts of a production system.

The process of transforming a problem statement into these components of the production system is called as problem representation. Selection of a good representation is an art in AI to solve practical problems and that there are many ways to represent a problem. **Please note that a good problem solution requires an efficient control strategy, good representations for problem states, moves and goal conditions.** The effort that is required to solve a problem in AI depends on the problem representation scheme. **Also note that we select those representations which need small state spaces.** If the state space is not less then we can even reduce or combine certain rules also. If these simple transformations do not work then we can even reformulate our problem but our ultimate goal is to be achieved i.e., of small state space.

Let us now see these various components of a production system.

I Rule Base

Production rules are extremely popular knowledge representation (KR) structure today. They are conditional IF-THEN branches only. These rules apply on the global database. Each rule may have a **Precondition.** If the precondition of the rule is satisfied then only the corresponding rule is applied to a state. It is only after the application of rule that the problem's state changes. The KR in production systems is decoded in a declarative (not procedural) form which comprises of a set of rules which are of this form—

Solution → action

Such problem situation-action rules are often called as production-rules or IF-THEN rules. And a system which uses this form of knowledge is called as a production system. Each of the IF condition is called as clause (s). A set of clauses joined by logical ANDs is called as a **Horn clause.** Each production rule constitutes a chunk of knowledge Practically speaking, to achieve modularity, the entire knowledge is broken down into fragments. **The ACTION part of one production rule becomes the CONDITION part for another production rule and this is known as the production-rule-chain or networking of rules.**

For example, the University's grading system might be reasoned as follows—

IF the marks obtained are less than 75
THEN declare the student as in First Class.

Associated with these production rules are **certainty factors/probability factors.**

For example,

IF Car doesn't work
THEN battery is down OR battery connection are poor.

In this scenario, we can use an certainty factor also and say that there is a strong evidence (0.9) that the battery is down. This factor of probability can also be used here. The range of this factor is from 0 to 1 as $0 \leq \text{probability} \leq 1$. This type of reasoning is also called as **inexact reasoning**. This example shows that human reasoning consists of IF-THEN rules with certainty factor attached with it. The syntax of these rules is—

```
IF      <antecedent–1>
        <antecedent–2>
             ⋮
        <antecedent–n>
THEN
        <consequence 1>|(with certainty C1)
        <consequence 2>|(with certainty C2)
             ⋮
        <consequence n>|(with certainty Cn)
```

The antecedent part is also called as a condition part or left hand side (LHS). The consequence part of a production rule is also called as the action part or right hand side (RHS). When LHS matches then the designated condition in the production rule (action) will be executed. **Please note here that the application of rule changes the database.**

Many systems like our earlier water jug problem, OPS5 (a production system language), expert systems, SOAR (general problem solving architecture) etc. provide an overall architecture of a production system described above. It allows the programmer to write rules which define particular problems to be solved.

II Global database

It is a **central data structure** used by the production system. This database may be as simple as a small matrix of numbers or as complex as a large relational indexed file structure. **Please note, however, that this database is not the same as database of DBMS.** The global database can be accessed by all the rules. **Also remember that no part of the database is local to any of the rules in particular.** Each rule has a precondition which is either satisfied or not by the global database. If the precondition is satisfied, the rule can be applied. **Since the application of rules changes the database, so it is also called as a dynamic structure** (continuously changing due to the operation of production rules) or working memory **or short-term memory**.

III Control Structure/Strategy

It means an interpreter program to control the order in which the production rules are fixed. Also it resolves the conflicts if more than one rule becomes applicable simultaneously. **Please note that this structure applies the rules to the database, again and again, until a description of the goal state is produced. Also note that this process of identifying the rules which are tried until some sequence of them is found which produced a database satisfying the termination condition (goal) is called as a searching process.**

Efficient control strategies means enough knowledge about the problem to solve so that the rule or the sequence of rules, so selected has a good chance of being the most appropriate. The control strategies are of two types—

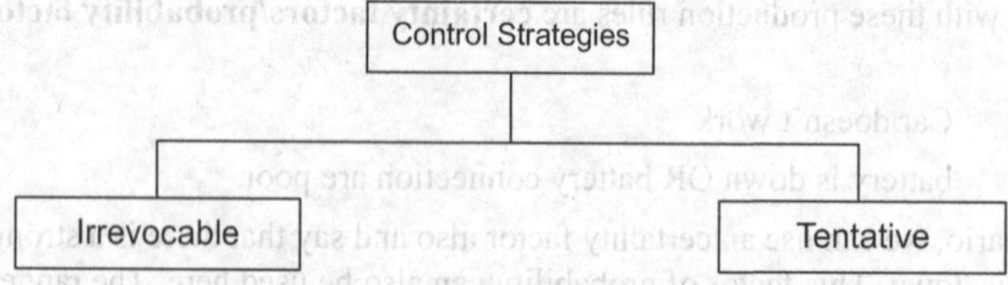

Fig. 2.6 Types of control strategies.

Let us define and explain them now, one by one.

Irrevocable Control

Here in, an acceptable rule is selected and applied irrevocably without provision for reconsideration later.

Tentative control

Herein, an applicable rule is selected arbitrarily or based on some good reason, then it (rule) is applied but with an option to return to this point in the computation to apply some other rule.

We can use two methods here. They are as follows—

(*a*) Back-tracking.

(*b*) Graph search control.

Back-tracking is a process in which the control strategy can be tentative. In this method, a rule is selected and if it does not lead to a solution, then the intervening steps are forgotten and instead another rule is selected. This back tracking technique can be used regardless of how much or how little knowledge is available for choice of rules. **Please note that if no knowledge is available, rules can be selected according to some arbitrary scheme.** Finally, the control will back track to select the appropriate rule. To reduce the frequency of back tracking to select suitable rules can be reduced and made more efficient if good rule-selection knowledge can be used.

Graph Search Control makes a provision for keeping track of the effects of several sequences of rules simultaneously. As we know that graphs (or trees) are very useful data structures to keep track of the effects of several sequences of rules. We can keep track of the various rules applied and the database produced by a structure called as a *search* trees. **At the root of the tree is a description of the initial configuration. The links or arcs (directed) show various rules that can be applied.** It represents the states which can be reached by just one move from the initial state. This strategy keeps on generating a tree till a database is produced which satisfies the termination condition. **Please note that this strategy is inefficient as the resulting tree grows too rapidly. This happens because we show all applicable rules being applied to every state description. Also note that an intelligent control strategy would grow a tree much narrower using its special knowledge to focus the growth of the tree towards the goal.**

However, the control strategy has certain characteristics. These characteristics are as follows—

1. **It should cause motion from the initial state that must lead to a solution.**

   For example, consider the following problem.

   Problem: Water-jug problem.

   Control strategy: Start each time at the top of the list of applicable rules and apply it.

   What happens with this control strategy?

   We will continue filling indefinitely the four-litre jug with water in the first operator.

   Will this give us a solution?

   No, it doesn't give any solution as this does not cause motion from the initial state.

2. **It should be systematic**

   If in our water-jug problem, we apply the appropriate rules at random in our solution, instead of starting every time from the first rule, again and again then with the application of this **control strategy,** a tree is generated. This **control strategy** is better than the first one and leads to solution eventually. The tree gets expanded at more and more levels and needs many steps for expansion. This happened because this control strategy has been selected taking into view the local motion only i.e., considering one step at a time. It does not consider global motion i.e., taking into account a collective view of many steps. The tree is expanded continuously until the goal is reached. Now, we call this control strategy as breadth-first search (BFS). In BFS, the new states so generated at each level are put at the end of the queue which generated them. A bfs works like this—

Please note here that these strategy examples are the nodes for goal at the nth level before going to $(n + 1)^{th}$ level. The algorithm for bfs is as follows—

Step-1: Create a variable called START-LIST and set it to the initial state.

Step-2: Until a goal state is found or START-LIST is empty do:

2.1 Remove the first node (element) from the START-LIST and call it a. If START-LIST is empty, quit.

2.2 For each way that each rule can match the state described in a do:

2.2.1 Apply the rule to generate a new state i.e., if node a has successors then generate all of them.

2.2.2 If the new state is a **goal state**, quit and return this state i.e., terminate search.

2.2.3 Otherwise add the new list to the end of START-LIST.

Step-3: Goto step-2.

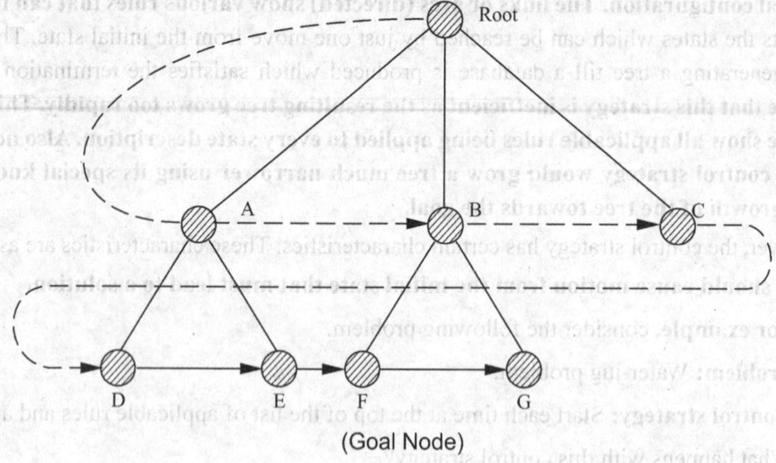

Fig. 2.7 Search tree after two levels of search.

Control strategy for putting new states in front of queue: As we already know that a queue works on a LIFO principle i.e., last-in, fist-out. Herein, a single branch of the tree is traversed until it finds a solution or until a decision to terminate the path is made. **Please note that this means that if two states A1 and A2 are produced by applying operators to a state A, then every state reachable from A1 will be examined before any state reachable from A2. Also note that if there are an infinite number of states reachable from A1, then A2 will never be examined.** So, what should be done?

In such a case, we need to impose some kind of **depth cut-off. It is defined as the maximum length of operator application-sequence.** Hence, the search tree or path is terminated when it reaches dead-end, produces previous state or it becomes larger then futility limit. **Please understand that back-tracking occurs, to the most recent created state from which alternate moves are available. A chronological backtracking** is one in which the order in which the steps are undone will depend only on the temporal sequence in which the steps were originally created. Another variant of backtracking is **dependency directed backtracking** which involves truth maintenance which uses non-monotonic reasoning and will be discussed later on. This search procedure is called as Depth-First Search (DFS). A DFS, in general, will look like this—

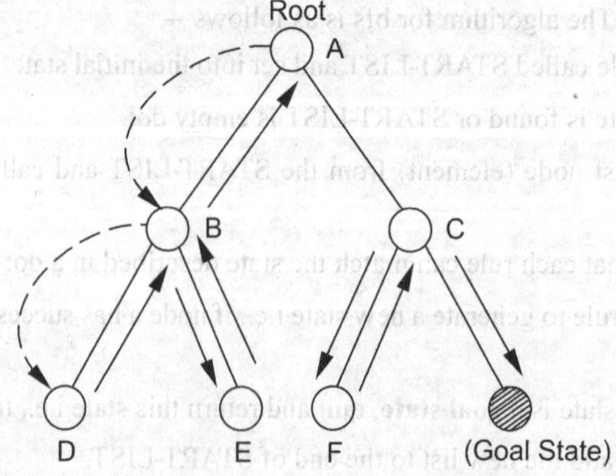

Fig. 2.8 Search tree using DFS.

We can generate such a tree for our water-jug problem also, as shown below in Fig. 2.9.

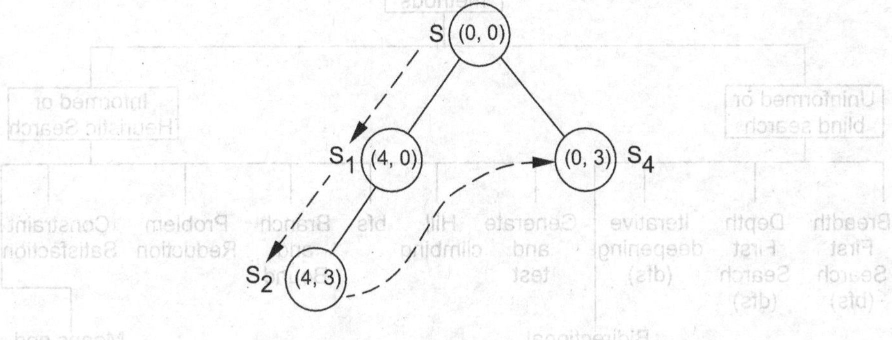

Fig. 2.9

The algorithm of dfs, in general is as follows:

Step-1: Put the initial node on a list, START-LIST.

Step-2: If (START-LIST is empty) or (START-LIST = GOAL), terminate search.

Step-3: Remove the first node from START. Call this node a.

Step-4: If (a = GOAL) terminate search with success.

Step-5: Else if node a has successors, generate all of them and add them at the beginning.

Step-6: Goto step-2.

Chronological back tracking, used in DFS involves lot of time and is not efficient also. In real problems, this can even make a problem-solving system impractical.

Non-chronological or dependency directed back tracking, those choice are withdrawn on which the dead-end depends. Herein, time does not determine which choices are to be withdrawn as it happens in chronological back tracking.

2.2 SEARCHING TECHNIQUES

As we have already discussed that searching our state space forms the core heart of AI problem solving. Once a problem is formulated, we then need to solve it. We can use this technique in many areas like theorem proving, game playing, expert systems, natural language processing etc. This involves the tasks like deduction, inferencing, planning, common sense reasoning, fuzzy logic etc.

2.2.1 Types of Searching

As we known that in a search method or technique or strategy, we firstly select one option and leave other options if this option is our final goal, (solution) else we continue selecting, testing and expanding until either a solution is found or there are no more states to be expanded. This will be determined by the search method. So, we need many different types of search algorithms. Basically, there are 2-types of searches—

1. Uniformed or blind search or unguided.
2. Informed or heuristic search or guided.

But, please note that all search techniques are distinguished by the order in which nodes are expanded. Various search strategies are shown in Fig. 2.10.

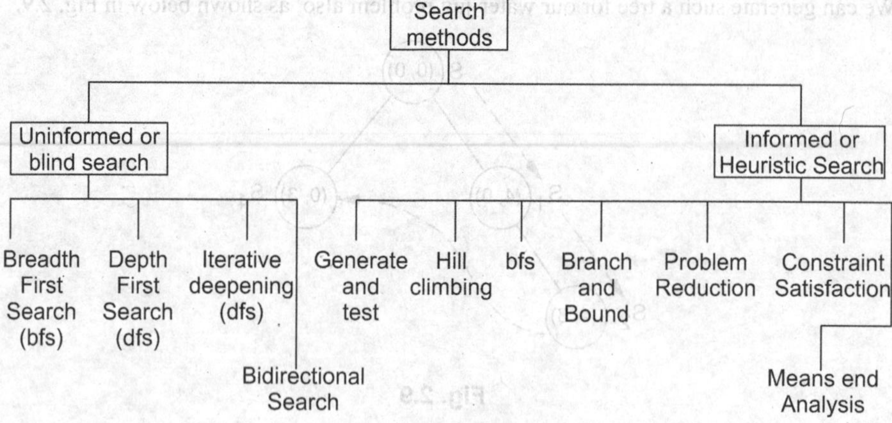

Fig. 2.10 Types of searching.

Let us now discuss these strategies one by one in detail.

2.2.2 Uniformed/Blind/Brute Force/Exhaustive Search

As we know that the state-space is a directed graph in which each node is a state and each arc shows the application of an operator transforming a state to a successor state. **But please note that a node is different from a state. A node is a data structure used to represent the search tree. However, a state corresponds to a configuration of the world**. So, nodes are on some particular paths always. They are defined by the parent node pointer. On the other hand, states are not on some particular paths. **Also note here that two different nodes can contain the same world state if that state is generated via two different search paths.** And a solution is a path from the initial or start state to a goal state. These goal states may be defined explicitly or as a set of states satisfying a given predicate. **In blind or uniformed search,** these is no order in which the solution paths are considered i.e., it uses no domain specific information to search a solution in the search space. **Again, the state space is combinational** , so this type of search is actually **impracticable for the nontrivial problems**. It is called as brute-force search as it examines every node in the tree until a goal is found. These algorithms make some assumptions:—

1. A **procedure** must be there to find all successors of a given node i.e., all states are **reachable** from the current state and that too by a single operator application.
2. The state-space graph is a **tree**. It means that there is only one start state (i.e., root of tree) and that the path from the start node to any other node is unique.
3. Whenever a node is expanded, creating a node for each of its successors, the successor nodes contain pointers back to the parent node. Finally, when a goal node is generated, the path from the root to the goal can be easily found.

So, blind search algorithms uses only the initial state, search operators and a test for a solution. It proceeds systematically by exploring nodes either randomly or in some predetermined order.

2.2.2.1 Breadth-First Search (BFS)

It is the most simple form of blind search. In this technique the root node is expanded first, then all of its successors are expanded and then their successors and so on. **In general, in bfs, all nodes are expanded at a given depth in the search tree before any nodes at the next level are expanded.**

It means that all immediate children of nodes are explored before any of the children's children are considered. The search tree generated by bfs is shown below in Fig. 2.11.

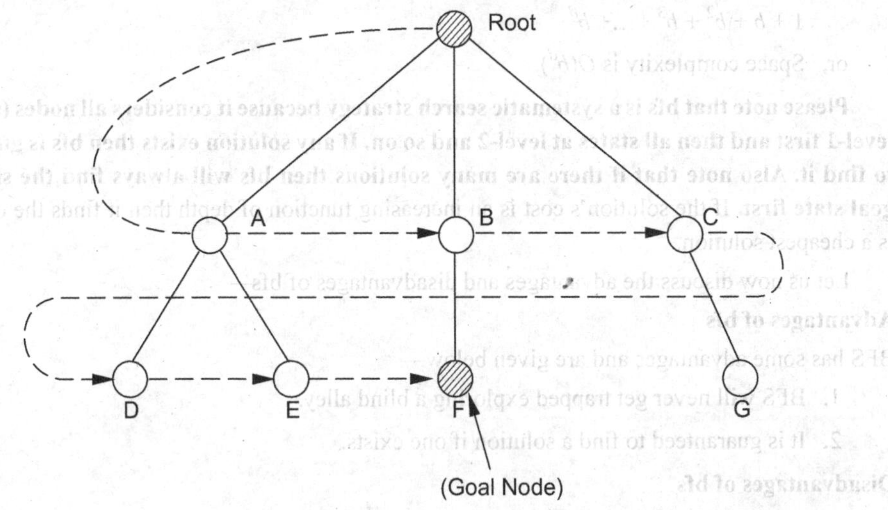

Fig. 2.11 Search tree for bfs.

Please note here that we are using the convention that the alternatives are tried in the left-to-right order. Also note that bfs is a brute-search so it generates all the nodes for identifying the goal. The breadth-first method expands nodes in order of their proximity to the start node measured by the number of arcs between them.

In general, it considers every possible sequences of length n before any sequence of length $n + 1$. Although this search may be an extremely long yet it is guaranteed eventually to find the minimum or shortest path length (possible solution sequence) solution, if any solution exists. A bfs algorithm uses a data structure-queue that works on FIFO principle. This queue will hold all generated but still unexplored nodes. **Please remember that the order in which nodes are placed on the queue for removal and exploration determines the type of search.** The bfs algorithm is as follows—

Step-1: Put the start (initial) node on a list, called OPEN of unexplored nodes. If the start node is a goal node, a solution has been found.

Step-2: If (OPEN is empty) or (OPEN = GOAL), no solution exists, so terminate search.

Step-3: Remove the first node, a, from OPEN and place it in a list called CLOSED, of expanded nodes.

Step-4: Expand node, a. If it has no successor then goto step-2.

Step-5: Place all successors of node, a, at the end of OPEN.

Step-6: If any of the successors of node, a, is a goal state then solution is found.

Time and Space complexity of bfs algorithm

The amount of time taken for generating these nodes is proportional to the depth, d and branching factor, b and is given by —

$$1 + b + b^2 + b^3 + \ldots + b^d$$

$\therefore$ Time complexity is $O(b^d)$.

Now, bfs has to remember each and every node it has generated. So, the space-complexity will also depend upon the function of depth, d and the branching factor, b.

So, space complexity is given by

$1 + b + b^2 + b^3 + \ldots + b^d$

or, Space complexity is $O(b^d)$.

Please note that bfs is a systematic search strategy because it considers all nodes (states) all level-1 first and then all states at level-2 and so on. If any solution exists then bfs is guaranteed to find it. Also note that if there are many solutions then bfs will always find the shallowest goal state first. If the solution's cost is an increasing function of depth then it finds the one which is a cheapest solution.

Let us now discuss the advantages and disadvantages of bfs—

Advantages of bfs

BFS has some advantages and are given below—

1. BFS will never get trapped exploring a blind alley.
2. It is guaranteed to find a solution if one exists.

Disadvantages of bfs

BFS has certain disadvantages also. They are given below—

1. Time complexity and space complexity are both $O(b^d)$ i.e. exponential type. This is a very big hurdle.
2. All nodes are to be generated in bfs. So, even unwanted nodes are to be remembered (stored in queue) which is of no practical use of the search.

2.2.2.2 Depth-first Search (DFS)

DFS begins by expanding the initial node i.e. by using an operator, generate all successors of the initial node and test them. It (dfs) is characterized by the expansion of the most recently generated or deepest node first. DFS needs to store the path from the root to the leaf node as well as the unexpanded nodes. It is neither complete nor optimal. If dfs goes down an infinite branch (depth cut-off point) will not end till a goal state is found. Even if it is found, there may be a better solution at a higher level. This **depth cut-off (d)** introduces many problems also. If *d* is set too shallow, goal may be missed. If *d* is set too deep then extra computation may be performed. The dfs algorithm is as follows—

Step-1: Put the initial node on a list, START-LIST.

Step-2: If (START-LIST is empty or (START = GOAL) then terminate (end) search.

Step-3: Remove the first node from START-LIST. Call this node, a.

Step-4: If (a = GOAL) then terminate search with success.

Step-5: Else if node a has successors, generate all of these and add them at the beginning of START-LIST.

Step-6: Goto step-2.

So, the search tree for dfs is as shown in Fig. 2.12.

Time and space complexities for dfs

The amount of time taken for generating these nodes is proportional to the depth, *d* and branching factor, *b* and is given by

$1 + b + b^2 + b^3 + \ldots b^d$

$\therefore$ Time complexity = $O(b^d)$.

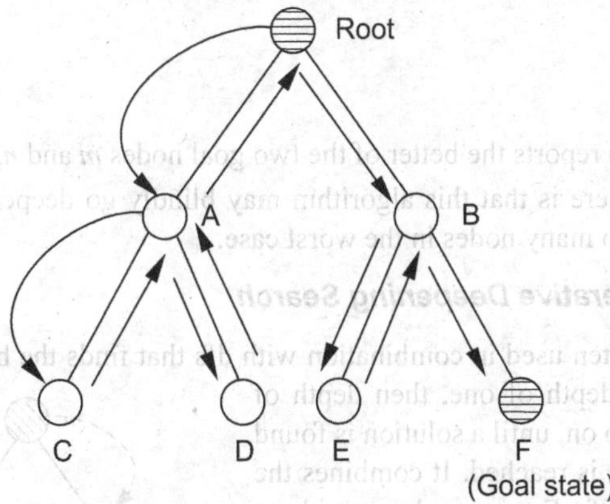

Fig. 2.12 Search tree for dfs.

Also note that dfs stores only the current path it is pursing. So, the space complexity will be a linear function of depth, *d*. So,

Space complexity = $O(d)$.

The value of cut-off depth (d) is important here as then otherwise the search will go on and on. Two cases arise—

1. If *d* is small, solution may not be found.
2. If *d* is large, time complexity will be more.

Advantages of DFS

DFS has some advantages. They are given below—

1. Memory requirements in dfs are less as only nodes on the current path are stored.
2. By chance, dfs may find a solution without examining much of the search space of all.

Disadvantages of DFS

This type of search can go on and on, deeper and deeper into the search space and thus, we can get lost. This is referred to as **blind alley**.

Depth first: Branch and Board

The Branch and Bound control strategy generates one path at a time. It also keeps track of the best path so found. This value is used as a bound on future candidates. As paths are constructed one at a time, the algorithm examines each partially completed path. If the algorithm determines that the best possible extension to a path branch will have greater cost than the board, it eliminates that partial path and all of its possible extensions. This reduces search considerably but still leaves an **exponential number** of paths.

This variation of depth-first, guarantees **optimal solution.** All other variations of dfs experience the undesirable property that obtained (if at all) is NOT guaranteed to be optimal. This is so because all these algorithms discontinue search once a solution is found. But this algorithm (in general) does not stop searching immediately after finding the first solution.

```
//Unbounded Dfs – Branch – and – Bound.
UDFBB(n){
if f(n) > cost (solution) then return;
if n is a goal node then
                    solution: = superior(m, n);
```

for each n_i of n do

UDFBB (n_i);

return; }

Here, superior (m, n) reports the better of the two goal nodes m and n, in terms of cost.

The **disadvantage** here is that this algorithm may blindly go deeper into some unpromising paths and thus generate to many nodes in the worst case.

2.2.2.3 Depth-First Iterative Deepening Search

It is a general strategy often used in combination with dfs that finds the best depth limit. It begins by performing dfs to a depth of one, then depth of two, depth of three and so on, until a solution is found or some maximum depth is reached. It combines the benefits of both bfs and dfs. For example, consider a tree as shown.

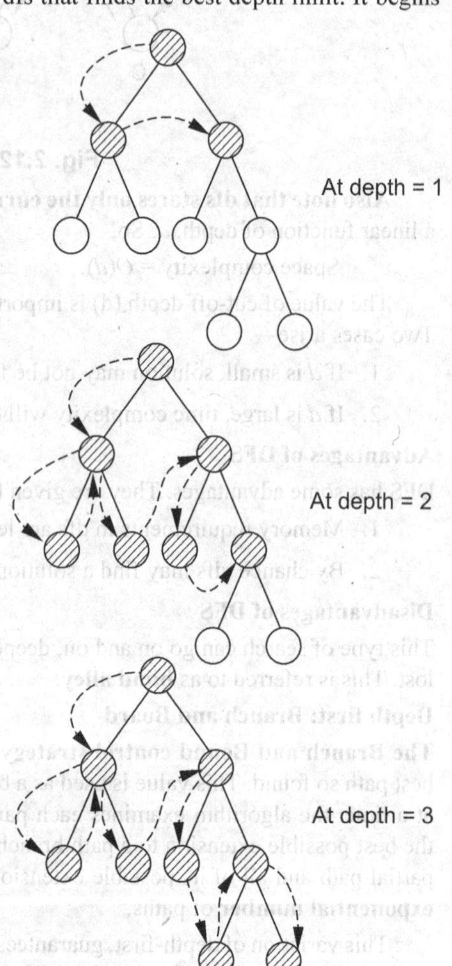

We have shown 3-stages of iterative—deepening search. **Please note here that the number of nodes expanded by iterative-deepening search is not much more than that would be using bfs.** Next we write an algorithm for depth first iterative deepening search—

Step-1: Start

Step-2: Initialize $d \leftarrow O$

Step-3: do

$d \leftarrow d + 1$;
DFID (root, d);
Until SUCCESS;

Step-4: End.

This algorithm starts with the smallest d = 1. It then increments d in a loop on encountering FAILURE until a SUCCES is found.

This search also guarantees to find a shortest path solution as it expands all nodes at a given depth before expanding nodes at a greater depth. **Also note that it performs wasted computations before reaching the goal depth.**

Time and space complexities

The time and space complexities of this search algorithm are also $O(b^d)$ and $O(d)$ respectively.

It can be shown that depth first iterative deepening is **asymptotically optimal**, among brute force tree searches, in terms of time, space and length of the solution. In fact, it is linear in its space complexity like dfs and is asymptotically optimal to bfs in terms of the number of nodes expanded. **Please note that in general, iterative deepening is preferred uninformed search method when there is a large search space and the depth of the solution is unknown. Also note that iterative deepening search is analogous to bfs in that it explores a complete layer going to the next layer.** It is better to develop an iterative analog to uniform – cost search, inheriting the depth –

first's guarantee to find a solution and avoiding its memory requirements. The basic **idea** is to use increasing path – cost limits instead of increasing depth limits. The resulting algorithm called iterative lengthening search, incurs substantial overhead as compared to uniform – cost search.

Advantages of Depth-first Iterative Deepening Search

1. It is guaranteed to find a shortest path solution.
2. It is a preferred uniformed search method when the search space is large and the depth of the solution is not known.

Disadvantages of Depth-first Iterative Deepening Search

1. It performs wasted computations before reaching the goal depth.
2. The time complexity is $O(b^d)$ i.e., exponential type only.

Is this search bfs or dfs?

This search is similar to both bfs as well as dfs.

How bfs? It is similar to bfs in that it explores a complete layer of new nodes at each iteration before going to the next layer.

How dfs? It is similar to dfs for a single iteration.

Why is it called as iterative?

This search terminates at the depth, *d* on each iteration if no goal has been found, removes all nodes from the queue, increments d by one and initiates the search again. Hence, it is called as an **iterative search**.

2.2.2.4 Bidirectional Search

This search is used when a problem has a single goal state that is given explicity and all the node generation operators have inverses. Searching is done by searching forward from the initial node and backward from goal node simultaneously. So, the program must save (store) the nodes so generated on both search frontiers until a common node is found. Both dfs and bfs can be modified slightly to perform this search.

Time and Space Complexities of bidirectional Search

To perform this search to a depth of *k*, the search is made from one direction and the nodes at depth k are stored. At the some time, a search to a depth of *k* and $k + 1$ is made from the other direction and all nodes generated are matched against the nodes stored from the other side. This process is repeated for lengths $k = 0$ to $d/2$ from both the directions. So, its **time and space complexities are both $O(b^{d/2})$ when node matching is done in constant time per node.**

Advantages of bidirectional search

1. It is used to solve the 8-puzzle problem.
2. Only slight modification of dfs and bfs can be done to perform this search.

Disadvantages of bidirectional search

1. Since the number of nodes increases as b^d with depth *d*, so such problems becomes intractable for large depths.
2. All node generation operators must have inverses also as only then this type of search can be used.

2.2.2.5 Beam Search

1. It is like Bfs in that it progresses level by level.
2. But beam search **moves downward** only through the best, *W* nodes at each level by applying heuristics, the other nodes are ignored.

3. Consequently, the number of nodes explored remains manageable even if there is a great deal of branching and the search is deep.
4. Whenever beam search is used, there are only *W* nodes under consideration at any depth rather than the exponentially explosive number of nodes as is done in bfs.
5. The **width of the beam** is fixed and whatever be the depth of the tree, the number of alternatives to be scanned is the product of the width of the beam and the depth.

2.2.3 Informed/Heuristic Search

The term **heuristic** is used for algorithms which find solutions among all possible ones. Recall that heuristic is a rule of thumb or judgment technique that leads to a solution but provides no guarantee of success. Still heuristic play an important role in searching process because of the exponential nature of most of the problems. **Please note that they help to reduce the number of alternatives from an exponential number to a polynomial number.**

So, we get a solution in a reasonable amount of time. The additional information about the properties of the specific domain which is built into the state and operator definitions is called as **heuristic information.**

And a search using this heuristic information is called as a **heuristic or informed search. A heuristic function determines a number which determines how good or bad a node can be.** If ev(n) is a best solution state and ev(n, p) is a best path then a heuristic is any information which shows how good or bad that path is likely to be so, we can expand that good node and can generate only its children. There is no blind expansion. So, pruning of the search tree occurs. In nutshell, the heuristics needed to solve problems are expressed as a heuristic function which maps the problem states into numbers. These numbers are then appropriately used to guide search. Heuristic search methods use some general purpose search techniques. The most simplest is the generate And-Test method which is discussed next.

2.2.3.1 Generate-And-Test Algorithm

It is a weak method meaning that it helps usually but not always.

It may or may not overcome the combinational explosion problem of AI. This algorithm works in two modules—

(*a*) Generator module: It creates the possible solutions.

(*b*) Tester module: It tests (or evaluates) each of the proposed solution either accepting or rejecting that solution.

Please understand that here an action may stop when one acceptable solution is found or action may continue until all possible solutions are found. Let us develop its algorithm now—

Step-1: **Generate** a possible candidate solution which can either be a point in the problem space or a path from the initial state.

Step-2: **Test** to see if this possible solution or candidate solution is a real solution by comparing the state reached with the set of goal states.

Step-3: If it is a real, acceptable solution then return, success else repeat from step-1 again (as it is a failure).

This algorithm is basically a dfs procedure only as complete solutions must be created before testing. **Please note that when it is used in a systematic form then it is simply an exhaustive search of the problem space.** It can also operate by generating solutions randomly and hence is often called as a **British Museum method.** However, in this method also there will be no guarantee that a solution will ever be found. So, we need a heuristic to sharpen the search. But this is useful for simple problems and is in efficient for problems having large state space search.

2.2.3.2 Hill climbing

It is so called because of the way the nodes are selected for expansion. At each point in the search path, a successor node that appears to lead most quickly to the top of the hill (goal) is selected for exploration. In this method of searching, the generate-and-test method is augmented by a heuristic foundation which measures the closeness of the current state to the goal state. Hill climbing can be employed if the path to the goal does not matter. It is a local search method in which we consider the state space landscape. This is shown in Fig. 2.12.

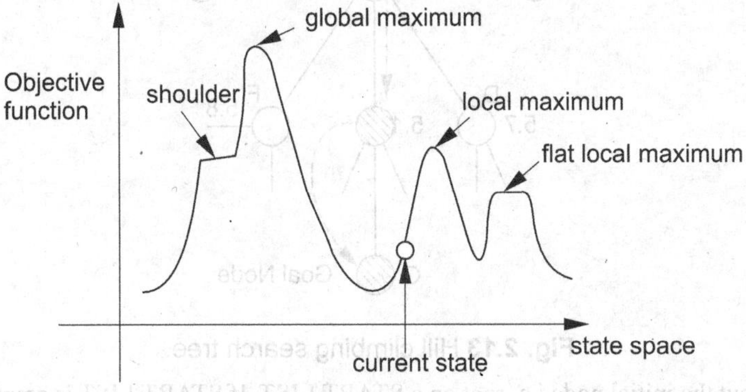

Fig. 2.12 State space landscape for local search.

A landscape has both "location" (defined by the state) and "elevation" (defined by the value of the heuristic cost function or objective function). The aim is to find **global minimum** (lowest valley) if the elevation corresponds to heuristic cost function and if the elevation corresponds to the objective function then the aim will be to find the highest peak or **global maximum.**

NOTE: You can convert from one to the other just by inserting a minus sign.

Local search algorithm explores this landscape. A **complete local search algorithm** always finds a goal if one exists. An **optimal algorithm** always finds a global minimum/maximum. Hill climbing search modifies the current state to try to improve it. This is shown in Fig. 2.12 by an arrow. It is in this way that the cost function provides a task-specific knowledge into the control process.

So, a search tree is generated with the help of heuristic function. As explained earlier also, **hill climbing is like dfs** where the most promising child is selected for expansion. When the children have been generated, alternative choices are evaluated using the heuristic function. The path that appears most promising is then chosen. No further reference to the parent or other children is retained. **Please note that there is practically, no difference between hill-climbing and dfs except that the children of the node that has been expanded are sorted by the remaining distance.** Let us now write an algorithm for hill-climbing—

Step-1: Put the initial node on a list, START-LIST.

Step-2: If (START-LIST is empty) or (START-LIST is GOAL) then terminate search.

Step-3: Remove the first-node from the START-LIST. Call this node, n.

Step-4: If (n = GOAL) then terminate search with SUCCESS.

Step-5: Else if node, *n*, has successors then generate all of them. Find how far they are from the goal node. Sort them by the remaining distance from the goal and add them to the beginning of START-LIST.

Step-6: Goto step-2.

Let us consider a tree and apply our algorithm now.

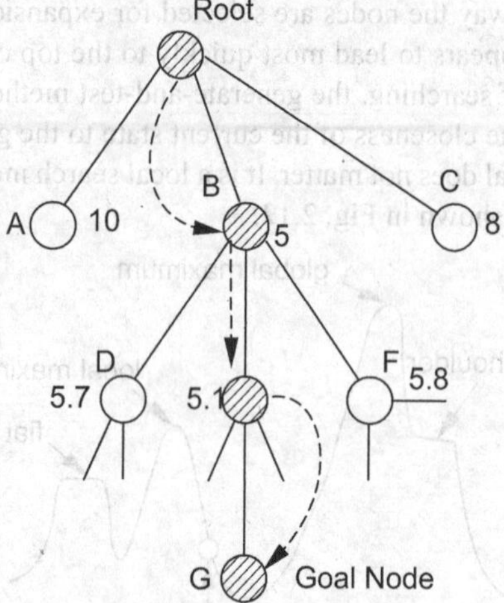

Fig. 2.13 Hill climbing search tree.

Here, we put the initial node i.e. root on a START-LIST. If START-LIST is empty or if START-LIST is our goal itself then the search terminates. Else we remove this node (n) from the START-LIST and generates its successors. We sort this START-LIST on the basis of the distances from the goal (see figure) and keep on repeating this process till a goal is found. **Please note that a new state has to be better, meaning that if we consider the cost function then it means a lower value and if we consider the objective function then it means a higher value.** If the algorithm is constantly following the direction which gives the fastest rate of increase then it is called as the **steepest ascent hill climbing**. But if the lowest cost is best then it is a **down hill algorithm. Also note that this algorithm is called as a steepest rise with back-tracking search method because it is prepared to back up and try a different path if the steepest one leads to a dead end.** Hill climbing is sometimes called as a **greedy local search** because it grabs a good neighbour state without thinking ahead about where to go next. But hill climbing suffers from following problems—

I Local maximum

It is a state which is better than all of its neighbours but is not better than some other states which are farther away. **Please note that at local maxima, all moves appear to make the things worse.** They are sometimes frustrating also as they often occur almost within slight of a solution. They are also called as **foot-hills.** It is shown in Fig. 2.14.

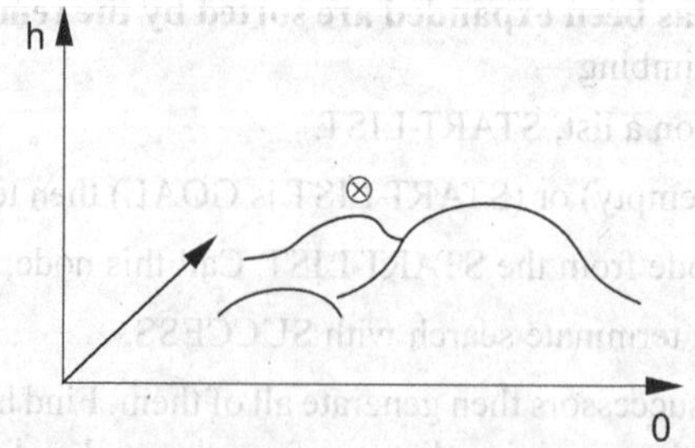

Fig. 2.14 Local maximum or (foot hill).

Solution to this problem

1. One possible solution is **backtracking.**

   We can backtrack to some earlier node and try to go in a different direction to attain the global peak. We can maintain a list of paths almost taken and go back to one of them if the path that was taken leads to a dead end.

2. Another solution can be a list of promising plan.

II Plateau

It is a flat area of the sarch space in which a whole set of neighbouring states (nodes) have the same value. On a plateau, it is not possible to determine the best direction in which to move by making local comparisons. Actually, plateau is an area of the state space landscape where the evaluation function is flat. It can be a **flat local maximum** (from which no uphill exist exists) or a **shoulder** from which it is possible to make progress. A plateau is shown in Fig. 2.15.

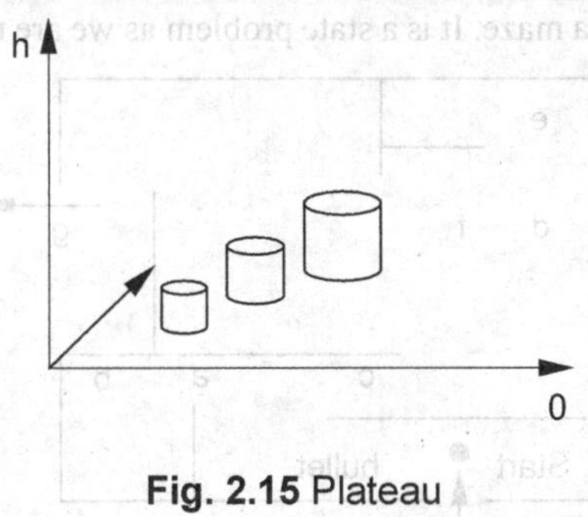

Fig. 2.15 Plateau

Solution to this problem

1. A **big jump** in some direction can be done in order to get to a new section of search space. This method is recommended as in a plateau all neighbouring points have the same value.
2. Another solution is to apply small steps several times in the same direction. This depends on the rules available.

III Ridge

It is a special kind of local maximum. It is an area of the search space which is higher than the surrounding areas and that itself has a slope. This is shown in Fig. 2.16.

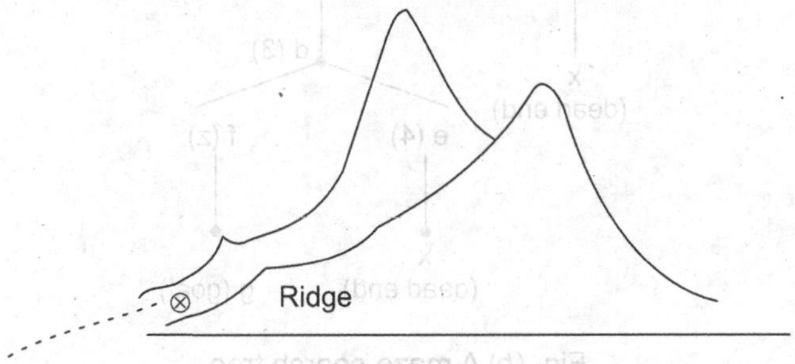

Fig. 2.16 Ridge.

We cannot travel the ridge by single moves as the orientation of the high region compared to the set of available moves makes it impossible.

Solution to Ridge problem

1. Trying different paths at the same time is a solution. We can apply two or more rules before doing the test. This corresponds to moving in several directions at once.

2. Bidirectional search can be useful here.

Advantages of Hill climbing

It can be used in continuous as well as discrete domains.

Disadvantages of Hill climbing

1. It is not an efficient method.
2. It is not suited to problems where the value of the heuristic function drops off suddenly when the solution may be in sight.
3. It is a local method as it looks at the immediate solution and decides about the next step to be taken rather than exploring all consequences before taking a move.

We are in a position to solve some examples now.

EXAMPLE 1. Consider a bullet-maze problem.

The figures below shows a maze. It is a state problem as we are not keen in the shortest path but in the goal state only.

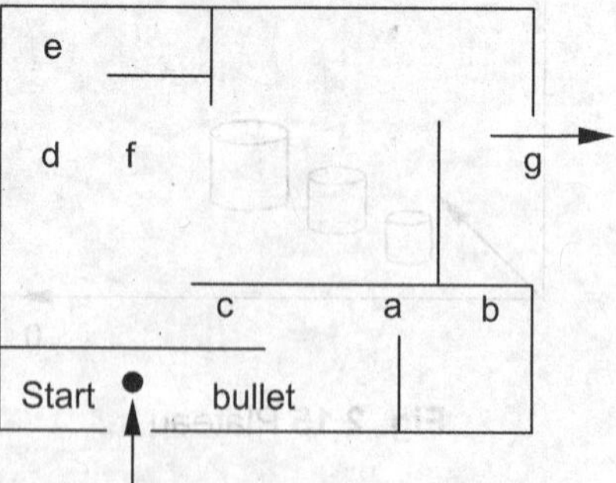

Fig. (*a*) Maze

You are also given a maze-search tree as follows—

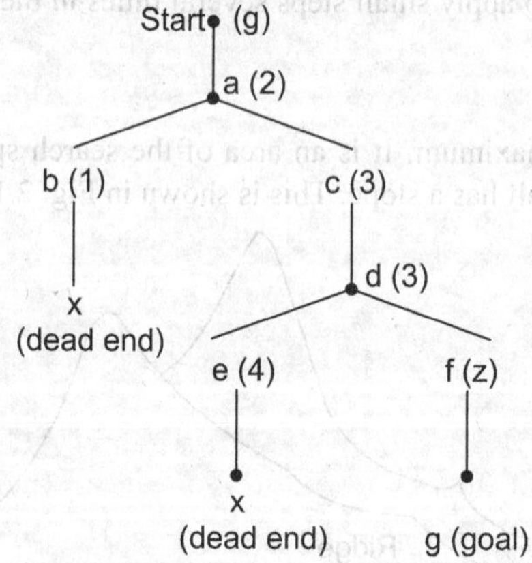

Fig. (*b*) A maze-search tree.

(Fig. a)—The start is marked with a bullet and the exist (goal state) is marked as g. Other letters mark the choice points in the maze.

(Fig. b)— The numbers in brackets show the heuristic evaluation function for each node.

The evaluation function chosen is the distance measured from the node to the goal.

Explain how it leads to dead ends?

Which node is local minima? Is there a plateau problem?

SOLUTION 1. At node 'a' (fig. b) it appears at first that 'b' is the most promising direction. But this leads to a dead end.

From node 'b', whatever path we take, takes us away from the goal. Hence, 'b' is called as **local minimum**. A simple search will stop at 'b' and never reach the goal state (g) which is global minimum.

The value of heuristic function does not change between 'c' and 'd'. That is, it is 3. So, there is no progress. What if our search space is large? There may be a whole area of the search space with no change of heuristic. When this happens, our heuristic fails to give any guidance about possible direct path.

EXAMPLE 2. Consider the **block-world problem**. It has 8 blocks, A to H which are similar and equal to each other. There initial state and final state (or goal state) are as follows:

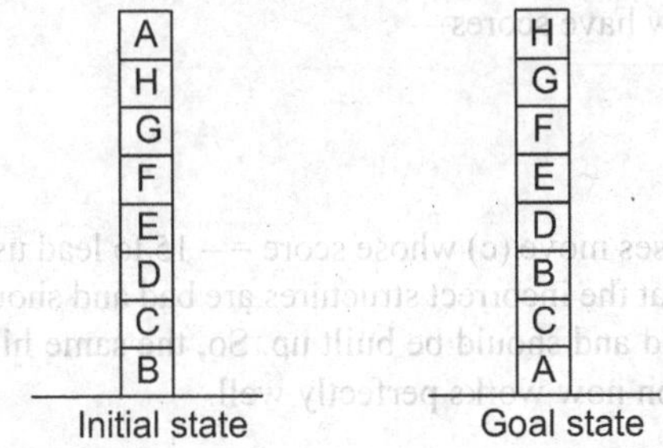

Also the following two operators are given —

01 : Pick up one block and put it on table.

02 : Pick up one block and put it on another.

Let the heuristic function be—Add one point for every block which is resting on the thing it is supposed to be resting on. Subtract one point for every block which is sitting on the wrong thing.

Correspondingly, the initial state has a score of 4. Goal state has a score of 8. **What problems can be faced if this problem is solved? Can you define the heuristic function globally taking the whole structure of block as a single unit?**

SOLUTION 2. The most natural move could be to move block-A onto the table. This is an intermediate state and is shown below—

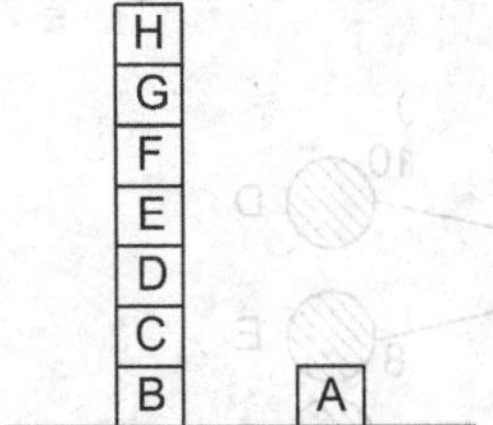

Moving A on table from the initial state (above fig.) has a score of 6. This move is allowed and this state produces three states as shown below with scores of 4 each (using our operators—01 and 02)

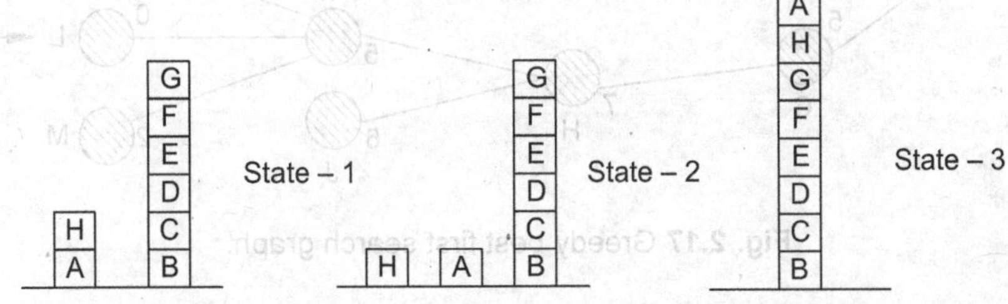

Now, hill climbing will stop because all these states have the same score. **Please note that they have a produced a score of 4 which is less than that of the intermediate state with score of 6** (from where these states arised).

We say now that the process has reached a local maxima. Our problem is that the current state appears to be better than any of its successor states as more blocks rest on the correct objects. To solve this problem, we disassemble a good local structure as it is wrong in the global context. This fault is inherent in our heuristic function now—A global heuristic function is defined which takes the whole structure of blocks as a single unit.

For each block which has the correct support structure i.e., if the complete structure below it is exactly as it should be then add one point for every block in the support structure. For each block which has an incorrect support structure, subtract one point for every block in the existing support structure. So, now the goal state has a score = – 28. The initial state has the score = – 21. The three states produced from this now have scores—

$a = -28$

$b = -16$

$c = -15.$

Thus, hill climbing chooses move (c) whose score = – 15 to lead us to a solution. This modified heuristic function assumes that the incorrect structures are bad and should not be accepted. And that the correct structures are good and should be built up. So, the same hill-climbing procedure which failed earlier heuristic function now works perfectly well.

2.2.3.3. *Best-First Search/Greedy Search*

Actually, best-first search is a combination of depth-first (dfs) and breadth-first (bfs) search methods. The approach used here is to select that single path at a time which is more promising one than the current path. The most promising node is chosen for expansion i.e., all of its successors are generated. Again the most promising node is chosen. **Please note that this changes the search from dfs to bfs. Also note that if we find that after the expansion, no node is more promising then we can backtrack.** This search uses again a heuristic function called as an **evaluation function** which is an indicator of how far a node is from the goal node.

Please remember that the goal nodes have an evaluation function value of zero.

Let us take an example to understand best-first search now.

EXAMPLE. Consider the following search graph, given in Fig. 2.17.

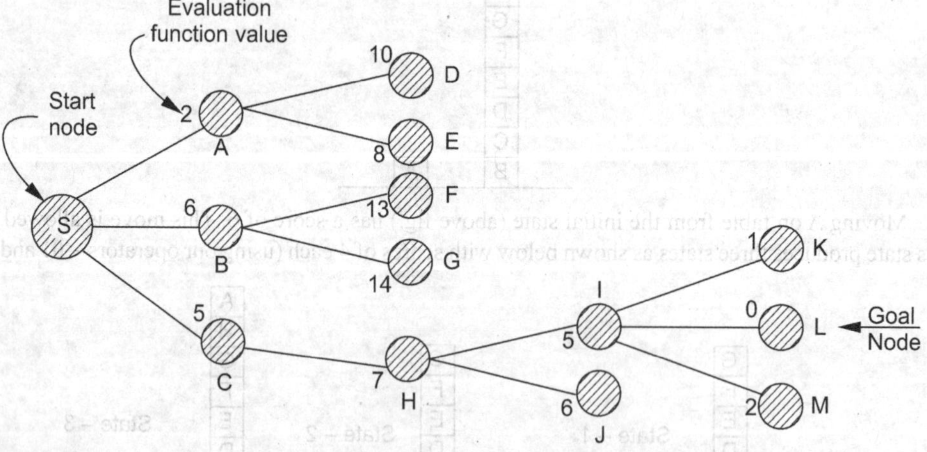

Fig. 2.17 Greedy best first search graph.

Working: We start with a start-nodes, S. Now, S has three children i.e., A, B and C with their heuristic function values 2, 6 and 5 respectively. These weights show approximately, how far they are from goal node. So, we write, children of S are —

(A : 2), (B : 6), (C : 5)

Out of these, the node with minimum value is (A : 2). So, we select A and its children are explored (or generated).

It's children are—

(D : 10) and (E : 8)

The search process now has four nodes to search for, namely—

(B : 6), (C: 5), (B: 10) and (E : 8)

Out of these, node-C has the minimal value of 5. So, we select it and expand. So, we get (H : 7) as its child. Now, the nodes to search are as follows—

(B : 6), (D: 10, (E: 8) and (H : 7)

Out of these, node-B is minimal so, we choose it and expand it to get its children—

(F : 13) and (G : 14)

At this point of time, the nodes available are :

(D : 10), (E : 8), (H : 7), (F : 13), (G : 14)

Out of these, minimum is (H : 7). So, we select it and expand to get—

(I : 5) and (J : 6)

So, nodes available for search now are —

(D : 10), (E : 8), (F :13), (G : 14), (I : 5), (J : 6)

Out of these, minimum is (I : 5), so we expand it now.

It's children are—(K : 1), (L : 0) and (M : 2).

So, available nodes are—

(D : 10), (E : 8), (H : 7), (F : 13), (G : 14)
(J : 6), (K : 1), (L : 0) and (M : 2)

Out of these, minimal is (L : 0) which is our goal-node. So, search stops here. Let us tabulate this in a tabular form now.

Step	Node being expanded	Children (on expansion)	Available nodes (to search)	Node Chosen
1.	S	(A : 2), (B : 6), (C : 5)	(A : 2), (B : 6), (C : 5)	(A : 2)
2.	A	(D : 10), (E: 8)	(B : 6), (C : 5), (D : 10), (E : 8)	(C : 5)
3.	C	(H : 7)	(B : 6), (D : 10) , (E : 8), (H : 7)	(B : 6)
4.	B	(F : 13), (G : 14)	(D : 10), (E : 8), (H : 7), (F : 13), (G : 14)	(H : 7)
5.	H	(I : 5), (J : 6)	(D : 10), (E : 8), (F : 13) (G : 14), (I : 5), (J : 6)	(I : 5)
6.	I	(K : 1), (L : 0), (M : 2)	(D : 10), (E : 8), (H : 7), (F : 13), (G : 14), (J : 6),(K : 1), (L : 0), (M : 2)	Goal node is found. So, search stops now.

Please note that in the best-first search, we 'jump all around' in the search graph to identify the node with minimal evaluation function value (indicated in braces). Also note that

the paths found by this search algorithm are likely to give faster solutions because it expands a node that seems to be closer to the goal. But there is no guarantee on this.

Comparison of hill climbing and best-first searches

In hill climbing search, we sort the children of the first node being generated. On the other hand, in **best-first search**, we have to sort the entire list to identify the next node to be expanded. Unlike hill climbing, this search retains all estimates computed for previously generated nodes and makes solution based on the best among them all.

Comparison of Best-first search and depth-first search

Best-first search resembles depth-first search in the way it prefers to follow a single path all the way to goal but will back up when it hits a dead end. It suffers from the same defects as depth first search i.e., it is non-optimal and is incomplete because it can go all along an infinite path and will never return to try other path possibilities.

We develop an algorithm for Best-first search now.

1. Place the starting node S (initial state) on the queue.
2. If the queue is empty, return failure and stop.
3. If the first element on the queue is a goal node g, return success and stop. Otherwise,
4. Remove the first element from the queue, expand it and compute the estimated goal distances for each child. Place the children on the queue (at either end) and assign all queue elements in ascending order corresponding to goal distance from the front of the queue.
5. Return to step 2.

We are in a position to solve some examples now.

EXAMPLE 1. Consider the search tree given below—

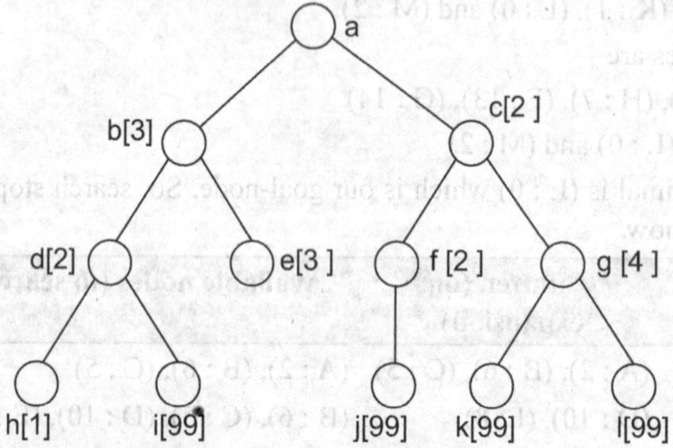

Show how the following searches are performed—

(*a*) **Hill climbing**

(*b*) **Best-first search?**

SOLUTION 1.

(*a*) **Using Hill Climbing**

The heuristic function value is an estimate of the distance to the goal and is shown in brackets. **Please note that lesser is its value, the better it is**

Using hill climbing we get—

1. Start at a (start-node)
2. Children of a = [b(3), c(2)]

3. Out of these best child is c(2).
4. Children of c = [f(2), g(4)]
5. Best child is f(2) now.
6. Children of f = [j(99)]—not a goal.
7. Backtrack to g through c.
8. Children of g = [k(99), l(3)]
9. Best child, *l* is goal node.

(*b*) Using Best-first search

1. Start at a, the start node
2. Children of a [b(3), c(2)]
3. Best-first = c
4. Children of c = [f(2), g(4)]
5. Consider [f(2), g(4), b(3)]
6. Best-first = [f(2)]
7. Children of f = [j(99)]
8. Consider [j(99), g(4), b(3)]
9. Best first = b(3)
10. Children of b = [d(2), e(3)]
11. Consider [d(2), e(3), j(99), g(4)]
12. Best first = d(2)
13. Children of d = [h(1), i(99)]
14. Consider [h(1), i(99), e(3), j(99), g(4)]
15. Best-first-h, is a good node

Example 2. Using search tree given below, list the elements of the queue just before the next node is expanded. Use best first search where the numbers correspond to estimated cost-to-goal for each corresponding node.

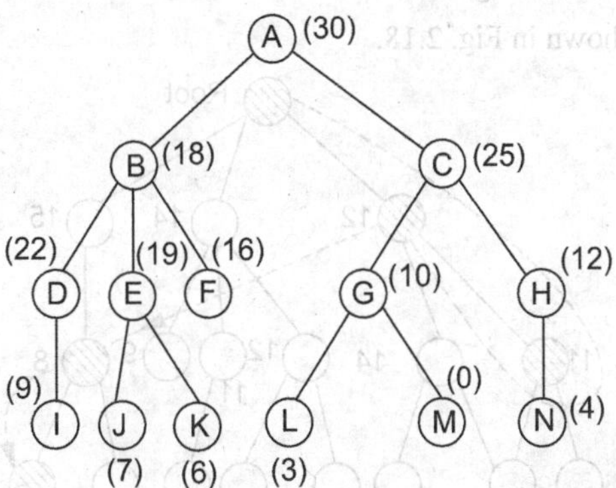

Solution 2. The table shows the cost from the initial node to the goal node

From Node	To Node	Cost of Node	Possible Dueue	Cost so far	Final Best First Dueue
A	B	30	A – B	48	✓
	C	30	A – C	55	×
B	D	18	A – B – D	70	×
	E	18	A – D – E	97	×
	F	18	A – D – F	64	✓
F	Next Node	16	A – B – F – Next Node	64	✓

The path is A – B – F – Next node in the given trce.

2.2.3.4 Branch and Bound Search

This strategy applies to problems having a **graph search space where more than one alternative path may exist between two nodes**. This strategy saves all path lengths (or costs) from a node to all generated nodes and chooses the shortest path for further expansion. It then compares the new path lengths with all old ones and again chooses the shortest path for expansion. In this way, any path to a good node is certain to be a minimal length path.

The time required depends on the order in which the paths are explored. But this method is inadequate for solving larger problems.

It's **algorithm** is as follows—

1. Form a queue of partial paths. Let the initial queue be of zero-length, zero-step path from the root node to no where.
2. Until (queue is empty) or (goal is found) find if the first path in the queue reaches the goal node.
   (*a*) If the first path reach the goal node, do nothing.
   (*b*) If the first path does not reach the goal node then.
      (*i*) Remove the first path from the queue.
      (*ii*) Form new path from the removed path by extending one step.
      (*iii*) Sort the queue in increasing order of the cost accumulated so far.
3. If the goal has been found then return SUCCESS else return FAILURE.
4. End Branch-and-Bound algorithm.

The search graph is shown in Fig. 2.18.

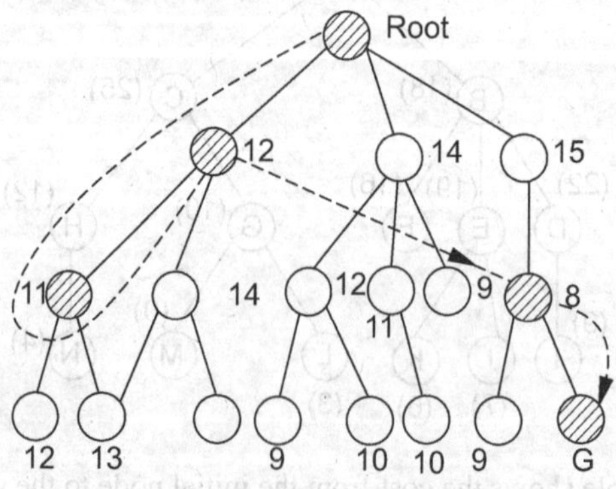

Fig. 2.18 Branch-and-bound search.

Using Branch-and-Bound on Traveling Salesman Problem (TSP)

Let us assume that there are a number of cities to be visited. From the starting city, the algorithm will begin generating complete paths. But it has to keep track of the shortest path found so far. **Please note that no further exploration of any path will be done if its partial length becomes greater than the shortest path found so far.** This technique still guarantees a shortest path for our TSP problem.

2.2.3.5 A* Algorithm

Basic principle—"Sum the cost and the evaluation function values for a state to get its "goodness" worth and use this as a yardstick instead of the evaluation function value in best first search. The sum of the evaluation function value and the cost along the path leading to that state is called as a fitness number." Before discussing about the fitness number, let us see what is **evaluation function value** and the **cost functions.** In best-first search, we use **evaluation function value** i.e., a value that estimates how far a particular node is from the goal. On the other hand, **cost functions** show how much resources like time, energy, money etc. have been spent in reaching a particular node from the start. While evaluation function values deal with the future, cost function's values deal with the past. **However, please note that the cost function values are more concrete than the evaluation function values as the cost function values are really expanded. Also note that if it is possible to obtain both, the evaluation function values and the cost function values then A* algorithm can be used.**

What is a fitness number?

A fitness number, $f'(n)$, is a heuristic function that estimates the merits of each node that we generate. So, this algorithm can search more promising paths first. **Dash** in the function indicates that it is an approximation to a function, $f(n)$, that gives the actual or true evaluation of the node. It is given as follows—

$$f'(n) = g'(n) + h'(n) \quad \ldots(1)$$

where $f'(n)$ – is the estimated cost of the cheapest solution through n.

$h'(n)$ – is an estimate of the additional cost of getting from the current node to a goal state.

$g'(n)$ – is an estimate of getting from the initial node to the current node.

The corresponding true values are $f(n)$, $g(n)$ and $h(n)$ of $f'(n)$, $g'(n)$ and $h'(n)$ respectively.

For state space tree problems,

$$g'(n) = g(n) \quad \ldots(2)$$

Because there is only one path and the distance $g'(n)$ will be known to be true minimum from the start to the current node n. In case of graphs, there can be alternate paths from the start node to n. So, for state space tree problem, we can also represent the heuristic function as —

$$f'(n) = g(n) + h'(n) \quad \text{(from equation –1 and 2)}$$

How to select $h'(n)$ and $g(n)$?

The function $g(n)$ lets us choose which node has to be expanded next not only on the basis of how good the node itself looks [as measured by $h'(n)$] but also on the basis of how good the path to the node was. By introduction of $g(n)$ into $f'(n)$ we will not be always choosing the node to expand that appears to be closest to the goal. This is important in cases where we care about the path we find if our concern is only getting to a solution by any means we can define $g(n) = 0$. In this way we will be choosing the node that seems closest to the goal. On the other hand, if we want to find a path involving lowest number of steps, then we can set the cost of going from a node to its successor as a constant (usually 1). In this way A* algorithm can be used whether we want to find a **minimal-cost overall path or simply any path as quickly as possible.**

h′(*n*) is a measure of the cost of getting from the node to a solution. **Therefore, good nodes get low values and bad nodes get high values.** Hence, minus sign has to judiciously placed. This is opposite to that *g*(*n*) which has to be non-negative. If *g*(*n*) has a negative value then paths that traverse cycles in the graph will appear to get better as they get longer. Now, if *h*′(*n*) estimates *h*(*n*) perfectly, then A* will converge immediately to the goal with no search. If it is always zero, the search strategy will be random. If the value of *g*(*n*) is always one, the search will be breadth first. Now a question comes to our mind that what happens if *h*′(*n*) is neither perfect nor zero. There are two possibilities. One is that overestimates *h*(*n*) and the other is that it underestimates *h*(*n*). Let us now examine what happens in both the cases.

Case I: *h*′(*n*) underestimates *h*(*n*)

Consider the situation as shown in Fig. 2.19. Assuming that the cost of all arcs is 1, Fig. 2.19 (a) shows that initially all nodes except A are on OPEN. For each node, *f*′(*n*) is indicated as the sum of *h*′(*n*) and g (*n*). From the figure we observe that node B has the lowest *f*′(*n*) which is 4. So it is expanded first. Suppose B has only one successor E and appears to be three moves away from a goal. Now *f*′(*E*) is 5 which is same as *f*′(*C*). Suppose we decide to allow the same path which we are currently following. Then, we will expand *E* next. Suppose it too has a single successor *F* which is three moves from the goal. This has been shown in Fig. 2.19 (*b*), i.e., the situation two steps later after *B* and *E* have been expanded. Now, *f*′(*F*) = 6 which is greater than *f*′(*C*). So we will expand *C* next. Thus, we see that by underestimating *h*′(*B*) we have wasted some effort. Thus, we find that B was farther away than we initially thought and we go back to try another path.

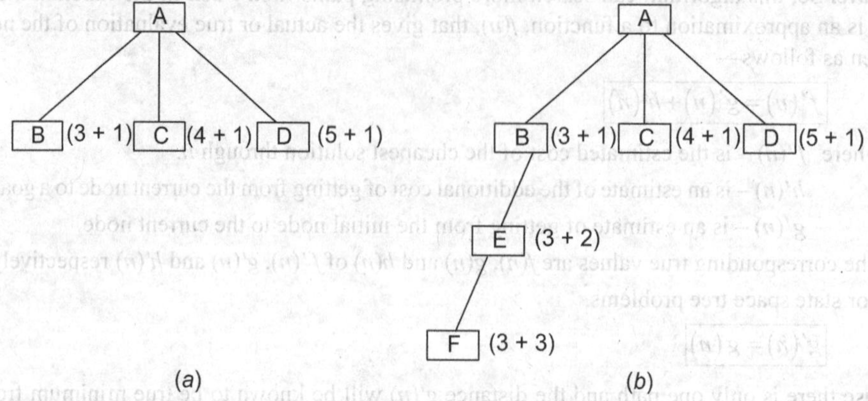

Fig. 2.19 *h*′(*n*) overestimates *h*(*n*).

Case II: *h*′(*n*) overestimates *h*(*n*)

Now consider the situation shown in Fig. 2.20.

Here also we expand *B* in the first step. At the second step, we again expand *E*. At the next step we expand *F* and finally we generate *G*. The solution path has length 4. But suppose if there was a direct path from *D* to a solution giving a path of length 2, we will never find it. Thus, by overestimating *h*′(*D*) we make *D* look so bad that we may find some other solution which is worse without even expanding *D*.

In general, we can say that if *h*′(*n*) overestimates *h*(*n*), we cannot be guaranteed of finding the cheapest path solution unless we expand the entire graph until all paths are longer than the best solution.

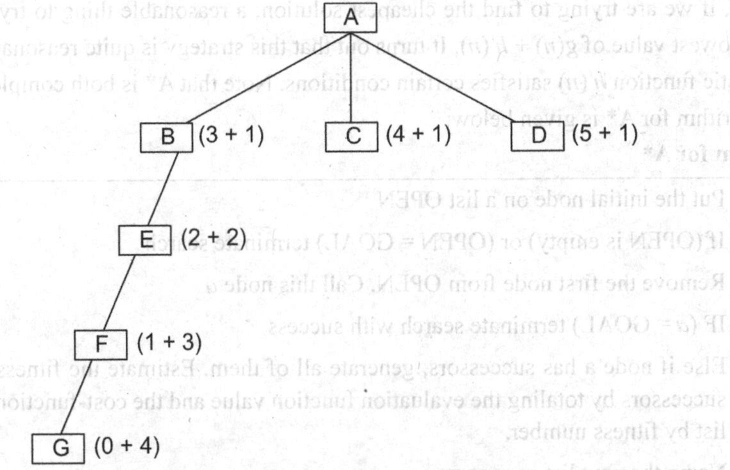

Fig. 2.20 $h'(n)$ overestimates $h(n)$.

Now we will see how the $f'(n)$ function is evaluated in A* search. Consider Fig. 2.21 again with the same evaluation function values as in Fig. 2.17. Now associated with each node are three numbers, **the evaluation function value, the cost function value and the fitness number.**

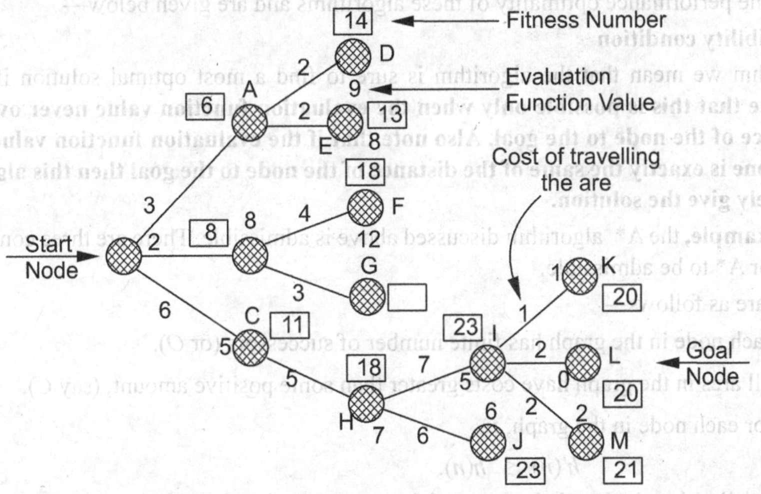

Fig. 2.21 A sample tree with fitness number used for A* search.

The fitness number, as stated earlier, is the total of the evaluation function value and the cost-function value. For example, for node K the fitness number is 20, which is obtained as follows:

(Evaluation function of K) + (cost function involved from start node S to node K)

= 1 + (Cost function from S to C + Cost function from C to H + Cost function from H to I + Cost function from I to K)

= 1 + 6 + 5 + 7 + 1 = 20.

While best-first search uses the evaluation function value only for expanding the best node, A* uses the fitness number for its computation.

Thus, if we are trying to find the cheapest solution, a reasonable thing to try first is the node with the lowest value of $g(n) + h'(n)$. It turns out that this strategy is quite reasonable provided that the heuristic function $h'(n)$ satisfies certain conditions. Note that A* is both complete and optimal.

Algorithm for A* is given below:

Algorithm for A*

1. Put the initial node on a list OPEN
2. If (OPEN is empty) or (OPEN = GOAL) terminate search
3. Remove the first node from OPEN. Call this node *a*
4. IF (*a* = GOAL) terminate search with success
5. Else if node a has successors, generate all of them. Estimate the fitness number of the successors by totaling the evaluation function value and the cost-function value. Sort the list by fitness number.
6. Name the new list as CLOSED.
7. Replace OPEN with CLOSED.
8. Goto Step 2.

Let us now discuss some common properties of heuristic search algorithms. These properties evaluates the performance optimality of these algorithms and are given below—

1. Admissibility condition

By algorithm we mean that the algorithm is sure to find a most optimal solution if one exists. **Please note that this is possible only when the evaluation function value never overestimates the distance of the node to the goal. Also note that if the evaluation function value which is a heuristic one is exactly the same of the distance of the node to the goal then this algorithm will immediately give the solution.**

For example, the A* algorithm discussed above is admissible. There are three conditions to be satisfied for A* to be admissible.

They are as follows—

1. Each node in the graph has finite number of successors (or *O*).
2. All arcs in the graph have costs greater than some positive amount, (say *C*).
3. For each node in the graph, *n*,

$$h'(n) \leq h(n).$$

This implies that the heuristic guess of the cost of getting from node *n* to the goal is never an overestimate. This is known as a **heuristic condition.**

Only if these three conditions are satisfied, A* is guaranteed to find an optimal (least) cost path. **Please note that A* algorithm is admissible for any node *n* if on such path, $h'(n)$ is always less than or equal to $h(n)$.** This is possible only when the evaluation function value never overestimates the distance of the node to the goal. Although the admissibility condition requires $h'(n)$ to be a lower bound on $h(n)$, **it is expected that the more closely $h'(n)$ approaches $h(n)$, the better is the performance of the algorithm.**

If $h(n) = h'(n)$ –an optimal solution path would be found without over expanding a node off the path. We assume that one optimal solution exists.

If $h'(n) = 0$ –A* reduces to blind uniform cost algorithm or breadth-first algorithm.

Please note that the admissible heuristics are by nature optimistic because they think that the cost of solving the problem is less than it actually is because $g(n)$ is the exact cost for

each *n*. Also note that *f*(*n*) should never overestimate the true cost of a solution through n. For example, consider a network of roads and cities with roads connecting these cities. Our problem is to find a path between two cities such that the mileage/fuel cost is minimal. Then an admissible heuristic would be to use distance to estimate the costs from a given city to the goal city. Naturally, the air distance will be either equal to the real distance or will underestimate it i.e., $h'(n) \leq h(n)$.

2.2.3.6 Problem Reduction

***OR graph*:** As we have already studied Best-first search tree. It's search graph can be explored to avoid duplicate paths. In such a **directed search graph**, each **node** represents a point in the problem space.

Each node also indicates how much promising it is, a parent link (pointing back to the best node form which it came) and the list of nodes generated (or explored) from it. **Please note that the parent link will make it possible to recover the path to the goal once the goal is found.** The list of successors (explored) will make it possible if a better path is found to an already existing node and also to propagate the improvement down to its successors.

This graph is known as an OR graph.

It is so called because each of its branches represents an alternative problem solving path. The techniques that we have studied so far, all are the example of OR graph only as in them we try to find a single path to the goal. **OR graph finds a single path.**

AND-OR graph (or tree)

We already know about the **divide-and-conquer strategy** i.e., **a solution to a problem can be obtained by decomposing it into smaller sub-problems. Each of this sub-problem can then be solved to get its sub-solution. These sub-solutions can then be recombined to get a solution as a whole. This is called as decomposition or reduction.** This method generates arcs which are called as **AND arcs. Please note that one AND arc may point to any number of successor nodes, all of which must be solved in order for an arc to point to a solution.** Here also several arcs may emerge from a simple node. Each will indicate the different ways in which the original problem might be solved. This is actually called as an AND-OR graph or AND/OR tree. For example.

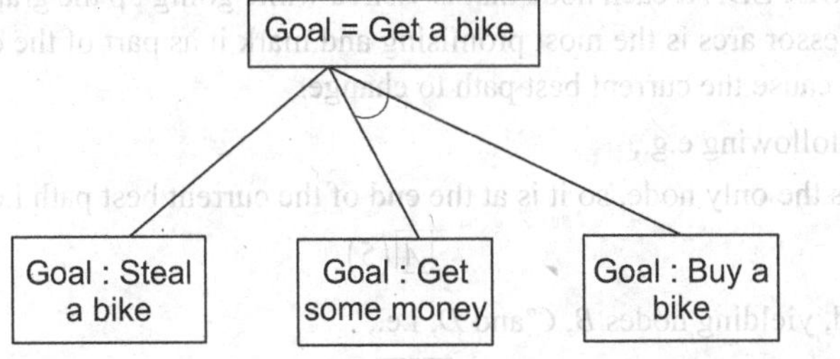

Fig. 2.22 AND/OR graph example.

Actually, best-first is not suitable for searching AND-OR graphs. Consider a small AND/OR tree shown in Fig. 2.23.

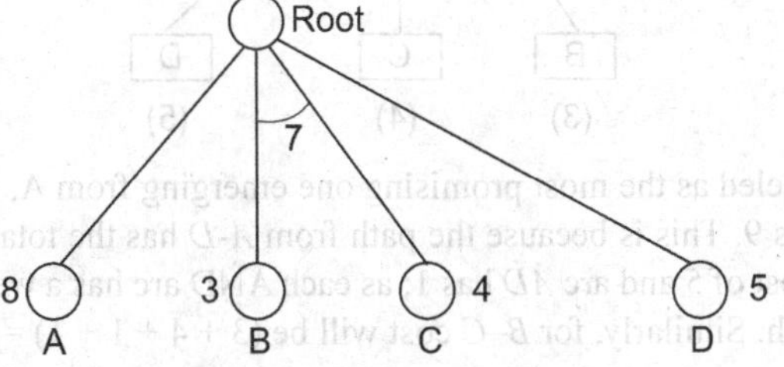

Fig. 2.23 Sample AND/OR tree.

Here, the numbers show the approximate value of the heuristic function ($f'(n)$) at that node. In Fig. 2.23, we observe that the minimal is B which has the $f'(n)$ value of 3. **But please note that B forms a part of the AND graph** and so we need to consider the other branch also of this AND tree i.e., C which has a weight of 4. So, our estimate now is (3 + 4) = 7. Now, this estimate is more costlier than that of branch D i.e. 5. So, we explore node-D instead of C as it has the lowest value. This process goes on till we search our goal node. **From this we observe that the choice of node to expand depends on it's $f'(n)$ value and also on whether that node is part of the current best path from the initial node.**

Algorithm to search AND-OR graph

In order to develop an algorithm for searching an AND-OR graph, we define a term called as **Futility**. If the estimated cost of a solution becomes greater than the value of FUTILITY, then the search is abandoned. So, futility is like a **threshold value** i.e., any solution with a cost above it, is too expensive to be practical, even if it could ever be found. Let us write an algorithm of problem reduction now.

1. Initialize the graph to the starting node.
2. Loop until the starting node is labeled SOLVED or until its cost goes above FUTILITY:
   (*a*) Traverse the graph, starting at the initial node and following the current best path and accumulate the set of nodes that are on that path and have not yet been expanded or labeled as solved.
   (*b*) Pick one of these unexpanded nodes and expand it. If there are no successors, assign FUTILITY as the value of this node. Otherwise, add its successors to the graph and for each of them compute $f'(n)$. If $f'(n)$ of any node is *O*, mark that node as SOLVED.
   (*c*) Change the $f'(n)$ estimate of the newly expanded node to reflect the new information provided by its successors. Propagate this change backward through the graph. If any node contains a successor arc whose descendants are all solved, label the node itself as SOLVED. At each node that is visited while going up the graph, decide which of its successor arcs is the most promising and mark it as part of the current best path. This may cause the current best path to change.

Consider the following e.g.,

At step 1, *A* is the only node, so it is at the end of the current best path i.e., Before step 1:

A (5)

It is expanded, yielding nodes *B*, *C* and *D*, i.e.,

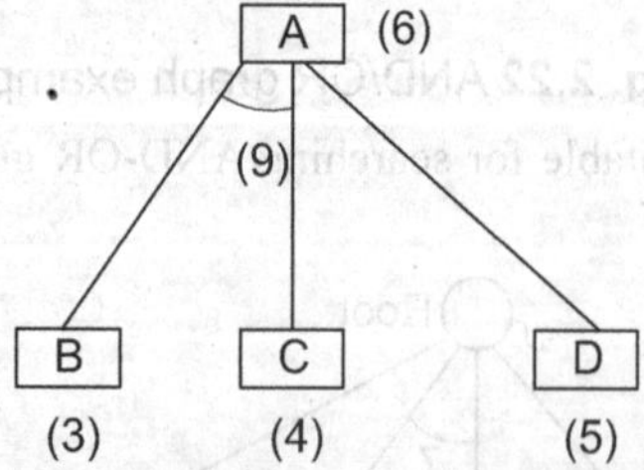

The arc to *D* is labeled as the most promising one emerging from A, since it costs 6 compared to B and C, which costs 9. This is because the path from *A-D* has the total cost of (*D* + the cost of arc *AD*). Now, *D* has cost of 5 and arc *AD* has 1; as each AND arc has a weight of one. So, total cost is 5 + 1 =6 for *A–D* path. Similarly, for *B–C* cost will be (3 + 4 + 1 + 1) = 9.

In step (2), node *D* is chosen for expansion.

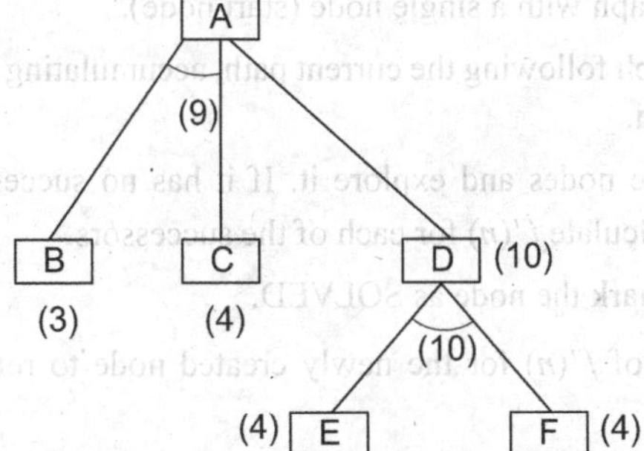

∴ Combined cost estimate of new AND-arc to E and F is 4 + 4 + 1 + 1 = 10.

So, we update the $f'(n)$ value of D to 10. Going back one more level, we see that this makes the AND arc B –C better than arc to D, so it is labeled as the current best path by arrows. **At step 3,** we traverse that arc from A and discover the unexpanded nodes B and C. Let's choose to explore B first. This generates two new arcs, the ones to G and to H i.e.,

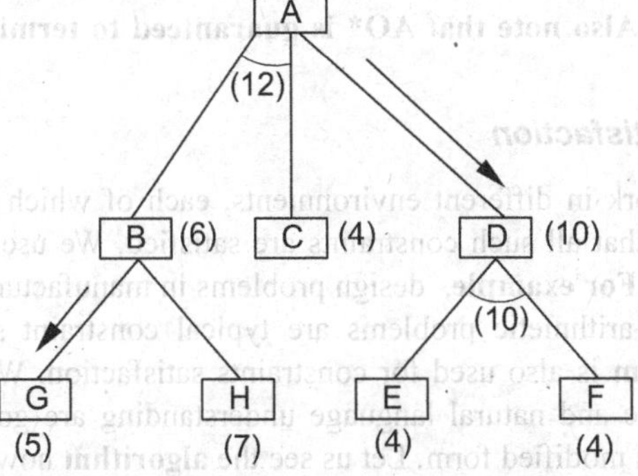

Propagating their $f'(n)$ values backward, we update $f'(n)$ of B to 6. This requires updating the cost of the AND arc $B - C$ to 12 (i.e., 6 + 4 + 2 =12). Comparing this with arc to D, which has the cost of 10, we find it is better. So, we explore D and thus either node–E or F is chosen for expansion at step-4.

This process continues until either a solution is found or all paths have led to dead ends, indicating that there is no solution.

2.2.3.7 AO* algorithm

Our real-life situations cannot be exactly decomposed into either AND tree or OR tree but is always a combination of both. So, we need an AO* algorithm where O stands for 'ordered'. Instead of two lists OPEN and CLOSED of A* algorithm, we use a single structure GRAPH in AO* algorithm. It represents a part of the search graph that has been explicitly generated so far. **Please note that each node in the graph will point both down to its immediate successors and to its immediate predecessors. Also note that each node will have some $h'(n)$ value associated with it**. But unlike A* search , $g(n)$ is not stored. It is not possible to compute a single value of $g(n)$ due to many paths to the same state. It is not required also as we are doing top-down traversing along the best-known path.

This guarantees that only those nodes that are on the best path are considered for expansion. **Hence, $h'(n)$ will only serve as the estimate of goodness of a node.**

Next, we develop an AO* algorithm.

Step-1: Create an initial graph with a single node (start node).

Step-2: Transverse the graph following the current path, accumulating nodes that have not yet been expanded or solved.

Step-3: Select any of these nodes and explore it. If it has no successors then call this value—FUTILITY else calculate $f'(n)$ for each of the successors.

Step-4: If $f'(n) = 0$; then mark the node as SOLVED.

Step-5: Change the value of $f'(n)$ for the newly created node to reflect its successors by back propagation.

Step-6: Wherever possible use the most promising routes. If a node is marked as SOLVED then mark the parent node as SOLVED.

Step-7: If the starting node is SOLVED or value is greater than FUTILITY then stop, else repeat from step-2.

Please note that AO* will always find a minimum cost solution if one exists, if $h'(n) < h(n)$ and that all arc costs are positive. The efficiency of this algorithm will depend on how closely $h'(n)$ approximates $h(n)$. **Also note that AO* is guaranteed to terminate even on graphs that have cycles.**

2.2.3.8 Constraint Satisfaction

In the real-world, we work in different environments, each of which has some constraints. Our solution should be such that all such constraints are satisfied. We use extensive domain specific and heuristic knowledge. **For example**, design problems in manufacturing, optimal tour problems and so on. Even crypta-arithmetic problems are typical constraint satisfaction problems. The term **relaxation algorithm** is also used for constraints satisfaction. Waltz algorithm for labeling line drawings in a picture and natural language understanding are good examples of constraint satisfaction algorithm in a modified form. Let us see the **algorithm** now.

1. Until a complete solution is found or until all path have led to dead ends, do:
    1. Select an unexpanded node of the search graph.
    2. Apply the constraint inference rules to the selected node to generate all possible new constraints.
    3. If the set of constraints contains a contradiction, then report that this path is a dead-end.
    4. If the set of constraints describes a complete solution, then report success.
    5. If neither a contradiction nor a complete solution has been found, then apply the problem space rules to generate new partial solutions that are consistent with the current set of constraints. Insert these partial solutions into the search graph.

To see how this algorithm works, consider the following problem.

Problem **(cryptarithematic problem)**

```
  S E N D
+ M O R E
---------
M O N E Y
```

Constraints

1. Values are to be assigned to letters from 0 to 9 only.
2. No two letters should have the same value.
3. If the same letter occurs more than once, it must be assigned the same digit each time.
4. The sum of the digits must be as shown in the problem.

Initial Problem State

S = ?	M = ?	C1 = ?
E = ?	O = ?	C2 = ?
N = ?	R = ?	C3 = ?
D = ?	E = ?	C4 = ?

Goal States: A goal state is a problem state in which all letters have been assigned a digit in such a way that all constraints are satisfied.

SOLUTION

The solution process proceeds in cycles. At each cycle, two vital things are done—

(*a*) Constraints are propagated by using rules which correspond to the properties of arithmetic. A value is guessed for some letter whose value is not yet determined, as this affects the effort involved in search.

(*b*) More constraints are added/generated due to propagating constraints.

At each cycle, there may be several choices to apply. A few useful heuristics can help to select the best rule to apply first. **For example**, if there is a letter that has only two possible values and another with six possible values then there is a better chance of guessing right on the first than on the second. This procedure can be implemented as dfs also so that a large number of intermediate positions in both the problem and the constraint spaces will not have to be stored. We can also store all constraints in one central database and also to record at each node the changes that must be undone during backtracking.

The results of first few cycles of processing of this crytarthimetic problem are shown in Fig. 2.24. Here, C1, C2, C3, C4 are the carry bits out of the columns, from right to left.

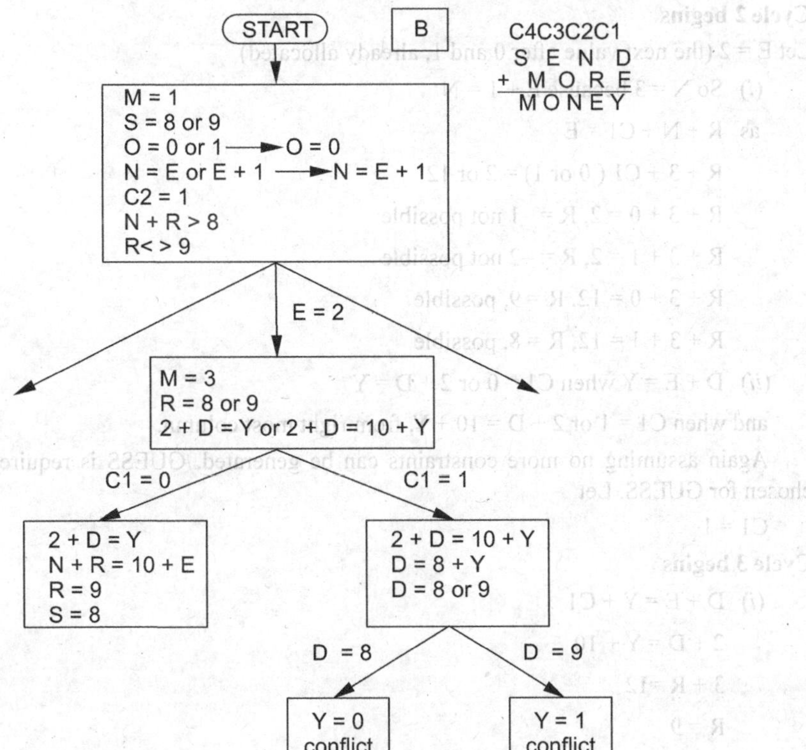

Fig. 2.24 Solution to crytarthimetic problem

Cycle 1

(*i*) M = 1 because two single digit numbers plus a carry cannot total more than 19.

(*ii*) S = 8 or 9 (minimum values) because S + M + C3 should be > 9 (to generate a carry) and M = 1, therefore S + 1 + C3 > 9 or S + C3 > 8, as C3 can be 0 or 1. So S > 8 or > 7 depending upon C3 = 0 or 1.

(*iii*) O = 0 because S + M + C3 ≤ 1.

O must be atleast 10 to generate a carry and it can be at most 11. That is O can be zero or 1. As M is already 1 and no two digit should have the same value, so O is zero (0).

(*iv*) N = E or E + 1 depending on the value of C2. But N cannot have the same value as E. So N = E + 1 and C2 = 1.

(*v*) In order for C2 to be 1, the sum of N + R + C1 must be greater tan 9, so N + R must be greater than 8.

(*vi*) N + R cannot be greater than 18, even with a carry in so, E cannot be 9.

E + O + C2 = N

When C2 = 0 and O = 0

E = N which is not possible.

At this point let's assume that no more additional constraints are generated so a GUESS is made.

Suppose value of E (which occurs the maximum number of times (3) and so interacts maximum with other letters).

Cycle 2 begins

Let E = 2 (the next value after 0 and 1, already allocated)

(*i*) So N = 3 because E + 1 = N

as R + N + C1 = E

R + 3 + C1 (0 or 1) = 2 or 12

R + 3 + 0 = 2, R = –1 not possible

R + 3 + 1 = 2, R = –2 not possible

R + 3 + 0 = 12, R = 9, possible

R + 3 + 1 = 12, R = 8, possible

(*ii*) D + E = Y when C1 = 0 or 2 + D = Y

and when C1 = 1 or 2 + D = 10 + Y, from right most column.

Again assuming no more constraints can be generated, GUESS is required and now C1 is chosen for GUESS. Let

C1 = 1

Cycle 3 begins

(*i*) D + E = Y + C1

2 + D = Y + 10

3 + R =12

R = 9

(*ii*) S = 8 because S was either 8 or 9, as now R has been allotted '9'. Now let us assign value to C1, 0 or 1.

First let us assign C1 = 10.

D + E = Y + 10 (because C1 = 1)

D + E = 10 + Y

2 + D = 10 + Y and for this to happen

Either D = 8

or D = 9

So C1 cannot be 1.

Now consider C1 = 0.

then 8 + D = Y, Y can be 0 or 1

D = – 8 (when Y = 0)

D = – 7 (when Y = 0)

So C1 cannot be 0 either.

Thus D has four values, two negative and two positive.

When D = 8

Y = 10 i.e., = 0

and when D = 9

Y = 11 i.e., 1

So Y = 0 and Y = 1

lead to conflict.

This contradiction could have been explained through another type of arguments:

Earlier S = 8 or 9 and again R = 8 from II loop and when C1 = 1, D = 8 or 9

And now D = 8 or 9 from C1 = 1.

Three letters cannot share two values, so C1 $\neq$ 1.

Comments on Constraints Propagation

The rules of the constraint propagation should not infer spurious constraints. Nor do they need to infer all legal rules

For example, we could adopt an alternative path which gives C1 = 0.

Let C1 = 1

Then E + D = Y + C1

or E + D = Y + 10

2 + D = Y + 10

D would be either 8 or 9

8 or 9 is assigned to R

is assigned to D

is assigned to S

Two values cannot be shared among three letters, so C1 cannot be 1. If this were realized earlier fruitless search could have been avoided. But the constraint propagation rules used were not that sophisticated so it took some search steps. Whether the time taken by the actual search route is more or less than the constrained method depends upon how long it takes to perform the reasoning required for constraint propagation.

We are in a position to solve a problem now.

EXAMPLE 1. Trace the constraint satisfaction procedure solving the following cryptarithmatic program:

```
  C R O S S
+ R O A D S
-----------
D A N G E R
```

SOLUTION 1.

```
  C R O S S
+ R O A D S
-----------
D A N G E R
```

(*i*) D = 1 since it is generated because of carry which at most can be 1($\because$ 9 + 9 = 18).

(*ii*) C + R = 10 or 12 to 18 depending up carry C4.

(*iii*) Since, we have no path to move on, we guess the values for S.

(*a*) C + R = A
 + 4 =

(*b*) R + O = N
 4 + =

(*c*) O + A = G

(*d*) S + D = E
 2 + 1 = 3

(*e*) S + S = R
 2 + 2 = 4

Thus we get: A C D E G N O R S
 ↓ ↓ ↓ ↓
 1 3 4 2(guess)

Now, lets say 'O' = 5 (any thing other than 1, 2, 3, 4)

if O = 0 then R + 0 = N

$\Rightarrow$ 4 + 0 = 4 (Not possible)

$\therefore$ guess O = 5

(*a*) C + R = A
 + 4 =

(*b*) R + O = N
 4 + 5 = 9

(*c*) O + A = G
 5 + =

(*d*) S + D = E
 2 + 1 = 3

(*e*) S + S = R
 2 + 2 = 4

$\therefore$ A C D E G N O R S
 ↓ ↓ ↓ ↓ ↓ ↓
 1 3 9 5 4 2
 (guess)

Here, C + R should be 10, 12, 13, 14, 16, 16 or 17 as $C_4 \neq 1$

$\therefore$ for C we can have,

for C = 6 (for total of 10) we have A = 0

and A + 0 = G i.e. 5 + 0 = 5 i.e. G = 5

$\Rightarrow$ O = G = 5 (not possible)

$\Rightarrow$ For O = 6, 7, 8 too we are not able to get values for C s.t. C + R > 10 (no value in this case can be (=O) as it will result in same value for 2 different characters) and for O = 6 we get repeating values.

$\therefore$ Our guess for S = 2 is wrong.

(*iv*) For S = 3,

(*a*) C + R = A (*b*) R + O = N (*c*) O + A = G

9 + 6 = 15 6 + 5

(*d*) S + D = E (*e*) S + S = R

3 + 1 = 4 3 + 3 = 6

$\therefore$ A C D E G N O R S

↓ ↓ ↓ ↓ ↓

5 9 1 4 6 3(guess)

Since, C + R ≥ 12

C ≠ 6, as it will give C = R = 6

C ≠ 7, as 7 + 6 = 13 $\therefore$ A = 3 $\Rightarrow$ A = S = 3

C ≠ 8, as 8 + 6 = 14 $\therefore$ A = 4 $\Rightarrow$ A = E = 4

$\therefore$ C = 9, 9 + 6 = 15 $\therefore$ A = 5

Now we need to find G, N, O.

If O = 2 then

(*a*) C + R = A (*b*) R + O = N (*c*) O + A = G

9 + 6 = 15 6 + 2 = 8 2 + 5 = 7

(*d*) S + D = E (*e*) S + S = R

3 + 1 = 4 3 + 3 = 6

$\therefore$ A C D E G N O R S

↓ ↓ ↓ ↓ ↓ ↓ ↓ ↓ ↓

5 9 1 4 7 8 2 6 3

(guess) (guess)

This solution has no repetitions thus we get—

C R O S S		9 6 2 3 3
+ R O A D S	→	+ 6 2 5 1 3
D A N G E R		1 5 8 7 4 6

2.2.3.9 Means-End Analysis (MEA)

Means-end-analysis is a special type of knowledge-rich search that allows both backward and forward searching.

Principle: "It (MEA) allows us to solve the major parts of a problem first and then go back and solve the smaller problems that arise while assembling the final solution".

Technique: It is based on the use of the operators which transform the state of the world. **The difference between the current state and the goal state is detected.**

Once such a difference is isolated, an operator that can reduce the difference has to be found. But sometimes it is not possible to apply this operator to the current state. So, we try to get a sub-problem out of it and try to apply our operator to this new state. If this also does not produce the desired goal state then we try to get second sub problem and apply this operator again. This process may be continued. **But please note here that if the difference is chosen correctly and if the operator is really effective at reducing the difference then the two sub problems are easier to solve than the original problem.**

Why is it called as Means-End-Analysis?

Given a description of the desired state of the world (**the end**) it works backwards, selecting and using operators that will achieve it (**the means**). Hence, the name, Means-End-Analysis (MEA).

MEA works incrementally

The above technique of MEA works incrementally and not as a single step. This is so because the operators are applied recursively till a goal state is achieved.

MEA works on three primary goals.

They are as follows—

(*a*) Transformation.

(*b*) Reduction

(*c*) Application

Transformation means to transform object A into object B i.e.,

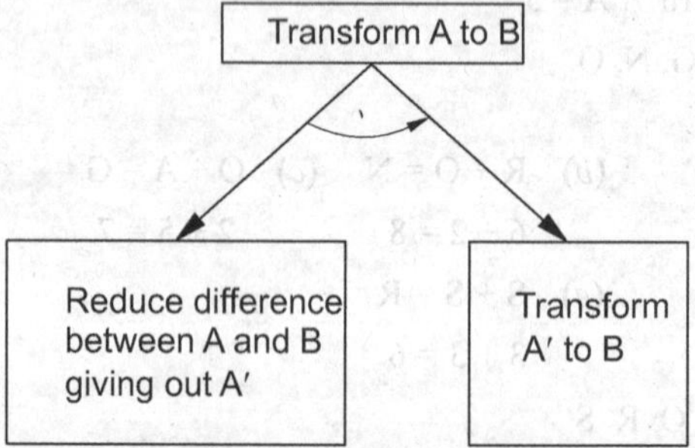

This is an AND graph which subdivides a problem into an intermediate problem and then transforms that problem into the goal state B. **Please note that this process terminates when there is no difference between A and B or we can say when the goal is reached.**

Reduction means to reduce the difference between object-A and object-B by modifying object-A i.e.,

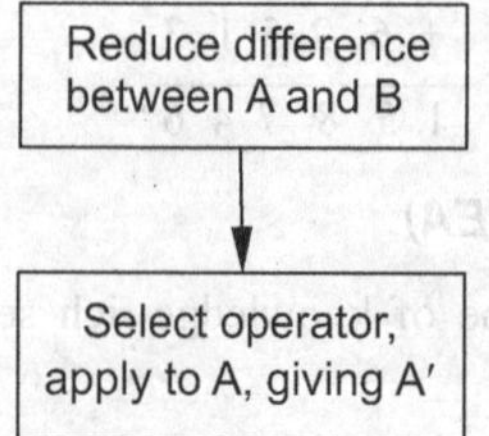

Please note that the goal of this operation is to reduce the difference between the object A and object-B by transforming object A into object-A', nearer the goal B, by means of a relevant operator (say, R).

Application means to apply the operator R to object-A. This will again be a AND graph showing the goal of reducing the difference between object-A and the pre-conditions required for the operator R, giving intermediate object A". Operator R is then applied to A", transforming it to A', which is close to the goal B. That is,

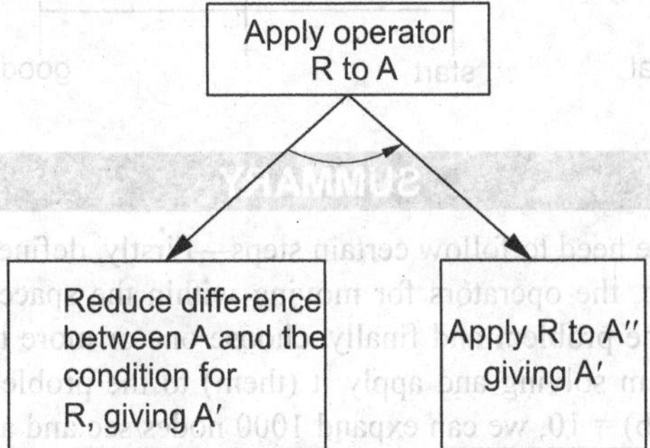

Please understand that states are described in some structured way like by predicate calculus and moves are performed by the operators. Each operator has a—

(*a*) **Pre-condition:** It puts some constraints on the states it uses.

(*b*) **Post-condition:** It says which conditions will be true when the operator has been used.

For examples —

(*a*) GPS was the first AI program to exploit MEA.

(*b*) STRIPS (A Robot Planner) is an advanced problem solver that incorporates MEA.

Algorithm for Means-End-Analysis (MEA)

We given an algorithm for MEA now.

Step-1: Until the goal is reached or no more procedures are available.

Step-2: Describe the current state, the goal state and the difference between the two.

Step-3: Use the difference between the current state and goal state, possibly with the description of the current state or goal state, to select a promising procedure.

Step-4: Use the promising procedure and update the current state.

Step-5: If goal is reached then success else it is a failure.

We are in a position to solve an example now.

Example 1. Show how Mean-End-Analysis (MEA) can be used to solve the problem of getting from one place to another. Assume that the available operators are walk, drive, take the bus, take a cab and fly.

Solution 1. Means-End Analysis—

Available Operators	Preconditions	Results
1. Walk		at (man, loc)
2. Drive	have (man, car) ^ (on obj, bus)	at (man, loc)^ at (obj, loc)
3. Take bus	On (man, bus)^ on (obj, bus)	at (man, loc)^ at (obj, loc)
4. Take cab	hire (man, cab) ^ on (obj, cab)	at (obj, loc)
5. Fly	book (man, airbus)^ on (obj, airbus)	at (man, loc) ^ at (obj, loc)

∴ **Difference Table** is as follows

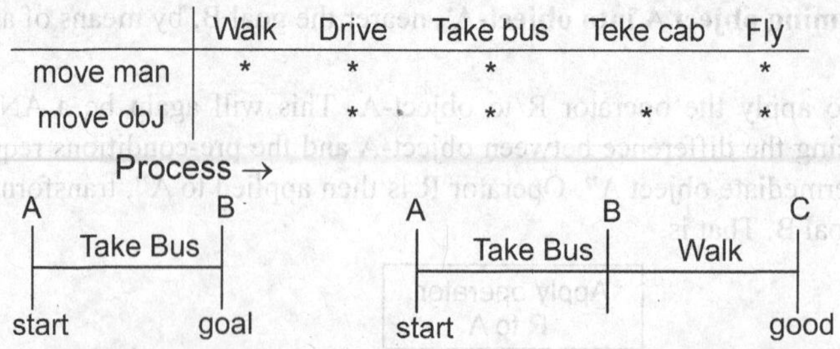

SUMMARY

To solve an AI problem we need to follow certain steps—Firstly, define the problem precisely i.e., specify the problem space, the operators for moving within the space and the starting and goal state. Secondly, analyze the problem and finally, choose one or more techniques for representing knowledge and for problem solving and apply it (them) to the problem. In BFS, if we assume that the branching factor (b) = 10, we can expand 1000 nodes/sec and also assume 100 bytes/node storage then the observe that as the depth increases, number of nodes increases and both time and memory requirement also increases. One such snapshot is given below—

Depth	Nodes	Time	Memory
0	1	1 ms	100 bytes
2	111	0.1 sec	11 KB
4	11, 111	11 secs	1 MB
6	10^6	18 min	111 MB
8	10^8	31 hrs	11 GB
10	10^{10}	128 days	1 TB
12	10^{12}	35 yrs	111 TB
14	10^{14}	3500 yrs	11, 111 TB

This table shows how memory requirements increases as the depth increases.

MULTIPLE CHOICE QUESTIONS [MCQS]

1. States are operated upon by a set of

   (*a*) Operators (*b*) Components (*c*) State space (*d*) None of the above.

2. Nodes are states and arcs represent

   (*a*) Directions (*b*) Actions (*c*) Functions (*d*) None of the above.

3. The process of creating a formal description of a problem using the knowledge about the given problem, so as to create a program for solving a problem is called as

   (*a*) Standardization (*b*) Operationalization

   (c) Generalization (*d*) None of the above.

4. A set of all possible states of a given problem is known as

   (*a*) State (*b*) Space search (*c*) State space (*d*) None of the above.

5. The process of decomposing up of a complex problem into a set of primitive sub problems, finding solutions to them and then integrating them to get a complete solution as a whole is known as

(*a*) Expansion (*b*) Problem reduction

(*c*) Production systems (*d*) None of the above.

6. Production systems were proposed by

(*a*) Foreign bank (*b*) Codd (*c*) Emit post (*d*) None of the above.

7. The maximum length of operator-application-sequence is known as

(*a*) Depth cut-off (*b*) Depth of tree

(*c*) Search path (*d*) None of the above.

8. Uniformed search is also known as a

(*a*) Heuristic search (*b*) Blind search

(*c*) Goal search (*d*) Beam search.

9. The time complexity of the bfs algorithm

(*a*) 0 (bd) (*b*) 0 (b^d) (*c*) 0 (d^b) (*d*) 0 (b + d)

10. Blind alley means

(*a*) Applying two or more searches (*b*) Search that can go on and on

(*c*) Blind search only (*d*) None of the above.

11. A heuristic is a

(*a*) Rule of thumb (*b*) Mathematics formulae

(*c*) Equation (*d*) None of the above.

12. The most common problem with all AI solution is

(*a*) Polynomial explosion (*b*) Combinational explosion

(*c*) Nuclear explosion (*d*) None of the above.

13. Which module creates the possible solutions in Generate-And-Test-Algorithm

(*a*) OS module (*b*) Kernel module

(c) Generator module (*d*) None of the above.

14. An area of the search space which is higher than the surrounding areas is a

(*a*) Ridge (*b*) Plateau (*c*) Hill (*d*) None of the above.

15. Which of the following is a greedy search

(*a*) BFS (*b*) DFS

(*c*) Best-First Search (*d*) None of the above.

16. Goal nodes have an evaluation function value of

(*a*) Zero (*b*) One (*c*) Two (*d*) Three

17. The sum of the evaluation function value and the cost along the path leading to the state is called as

(*a*) Fitness number (*b*) Whole number

(*c*) Complex number (*d*) None of the above.

18. Constraint satisfaction is also referred to as

(*a*) Divide-and-conquer algorithm (*b*) Greedy algorithm

(*c*) Relaxation algorithm (*d*) None of the above.

19. Mean-End-Analysis (MEA) allows

(*a*) Backward searching (*b*) Forward searching

(*c*) Both 'a' and 'b' (*d*) None of the above.

20. MEA works on three primary goals which are

(*a*) Transformation, scaling and rotation

(*b*) Transformation, reduction and application

(*c*) Scaling, reduction and application

(*d*) None of the above.

ANSWERS

1. (*a*)	**2.** (*b*)	**3.** (*b*)	**4.** (*c*)	**5.** (*b*)
6. (c)	**7.** (*a*)	**8.** (*b*)	**9.** (*b*)	**10.** (*b*)
11. (*a*)	**12.** (*b*)	**13.** (*c*)	**14.** (*a*)	**15.** (*c*)
16. (*a*)	**17.** (*a*)	**18.** (*c*)	**19.** (*c*)	**20.** (*b*)

CONCEPTUAL SHORT QUESTIONS WITH ANSWERS

Q. 1. What is the relationship between various search algorithms-Breadth-first, uniform cost, AO*, A* and Best-First search?

Ans. As shown in Figure, when $h'(n) = 0$ for all nodes, we have uniform-cost algorithm. When $f'(n) = g(n) = \text{depth}(n)$, we have breadth-first search which spreads out along contours of equal depth. Please note from above diagram that both the uniform-cost and breadth-first algorithms are special cases of A* (with $h'(n) = 0$), so they are both admissible.

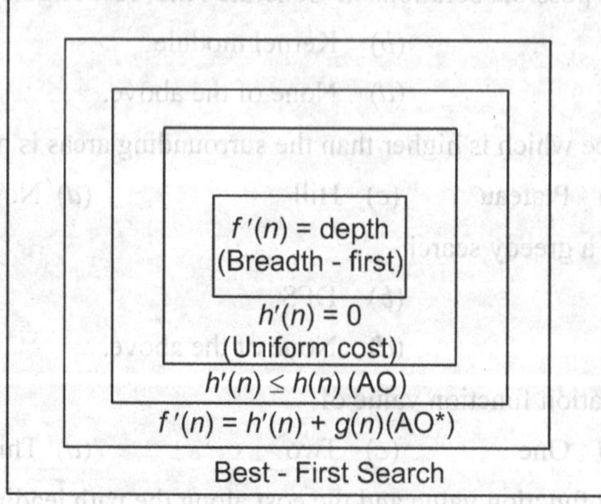

Q2. What is Search Control Knowledge?

Ans. A large KB contains thousands of rules when there are many possible paths for reasoning, it is critical that fruitless ones are not pursued. Knowledge about which paths are most likely to lead quickly to a goal state is called as a **search control knowledge.**

Q3. When would best-first search be worse than simple breadth-first search?

Ans. CASE WHEN BEST-FIRST SEARCH IS WORSE THAN BREADTH-FIRST SEARCH

Consider a graph—

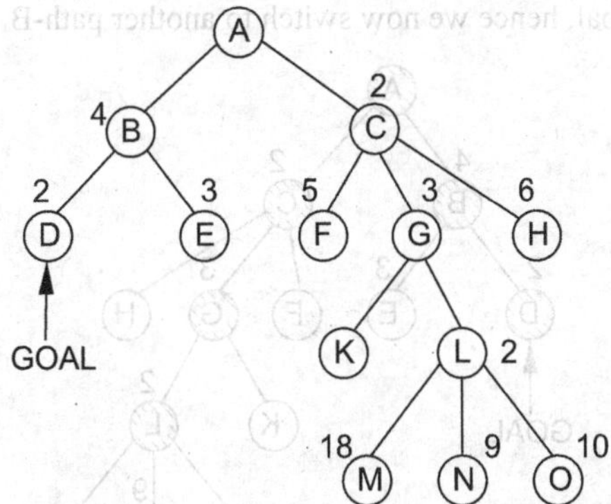

Using Breadth First Search, to reach the goal 'D' we would transverse as—

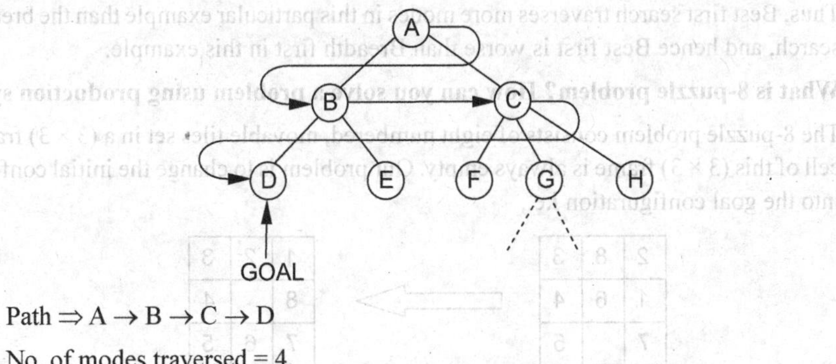

Path ⇒ A → B → C → D

No. of modes traversed = 4.

Using Best First Search, to reach the goal 'D' we would traverse as—

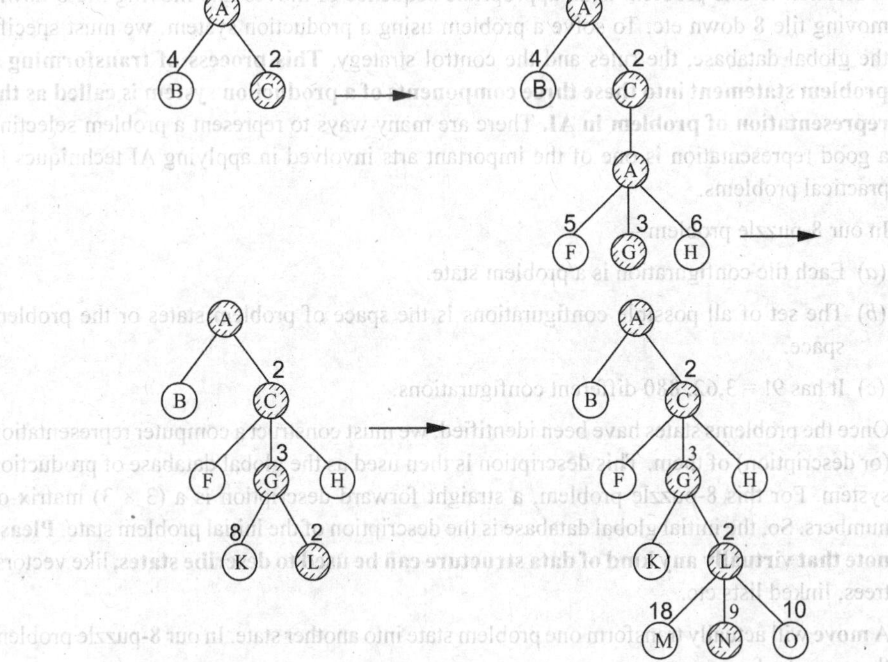

which is not the goal, hence we now switch to another path-B

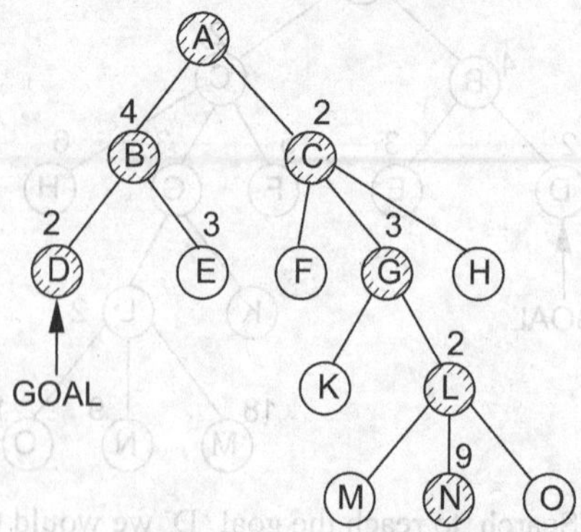

Thus, Best first search traverses more modes in this particular example than the breadth-first search, and hence Best first is worse than Breadth first in this example.

Q4. What is 8-puzzle problem? How can you solve a problem using production system?

Ans. The 8-puzzle problem consists of eight numbered, movable tiles set in a (3 × 3) frame. One cell of this (3 × 3) frame is always empty. Our problem is to change the initial configuration into the goal configuration i.e.,

2	8	3
1	6	4
7		5

(Initial State)

1	2	3
8		4
7	6	5

(Goal State)

A solution to this problem is an appropriate sequence of moves like moving tile 6 down, moving tile 8 down etc. To solve a problem using a production system, we must specify the global database, the rules and the control strategy. **This process of transforming a problem statement into these three components of a production system is called as the representation of problem in AI.** There are many ways to represent a problem selecting a good representation is one of the important arts involved in applying AI techniques to practical problems.

In our 8-puzzle problem—

(*a*) Each tile configuration is a problem state.

(*b*) The set of all possible configurations is the space of problem states or the problem space.

(*c*) It has 9! = 3,62, 880 different configurations.

Once the problems states have been identified, we must construct a computer representation (or description) of them. This description is then used as the global database of production system. For this 8-puzzle problem, a straight forward description is a (3 × 3) matrix of numbers. So, the initial global database is the description of the initial problem state. **Please note that virtually any kind of data structure can be used to describe states,** like vectors, trees, linked lists etc.

A **move** will actually transform one problem state into another state. In our 8-puzzle problem there can be four moves—

(*a*) Move empty space (blank) to the left

(*b*) Move blank up

(*c*) Move blank to right

(*d*) Move blank down.

Please note that these moves are modeled by the production rules which operate on the state descriptions in the appropriate manner. Also note that the rules have preconditions which must be satisfied by a state description in order for them to be applicable to that state description.

We have to reach our goal state. We can also specify some True/False condition on states to serve as a goal condition. It is the problem-goal condition that forms a basis for the termination condition of the production system. The control strategy repeatedly applies rules to state descriptions until a description of a goal state is produced. It also keeps track of the rules which have been applied so that it can compose them into the sequence representing the problem solution. We may add some constraints also to our solution i.e., to find an optimal (minimum) path solution (with smallest number of moves). For this, costs are associated with each move and the minimum is selected.

Q. 5. Is our 8-puzzle problem a heuristic search problem?

Ans. The 8-tile problem is a heuristic search problem. Herein, we have (8×4) possible tile moves. Most of these moves are illegal at any point. These illegal moves are visible to humans but not to our computer. A computer will simply swap it with a neighbouring tile. So, we use heuristics. The average solution cost for a randomly generated 8-tile puzzle is about 22 steps. The branching factor is about 3. This is because when the empty tile is in **middle**, there are **four** possible moves, when it is in a **corner** there are **two** and when it is on an **edge**, there are **three**. **Thus, an exhaustive search to a depth of 22 would have about** $33^{22} \approx 3.1 \times 10^{10}$ states. We can bring this down also by a factor of 1,70,000 if we keep track of repeated states. This is so because there are only—

$\frac{9!}{2}$ = 1,81,440 distinct states that are reacheable.

Heuristics used

1. Say, h_1 represents the number of misplaced tiles. If all 8-tiles are out of position then the start state would have $h_1 = 8$. Since any tile which is out of place must be moved at least once, h_1 is an admissible heuristic.

2. Say, h_2 represents the sum of the distances of the tiles from their goal positions. **Please note here that the tiles cannot move diagonally, so the distance we will count is the sum of the horizontal and vertical distances. This distance is called as the city block distance or Manhattan distance. Also note that when we move one tile, h_2 can still be applied as any move brings us one step closer to the goal.**

Q. 6. What is heuristics?

Ans. According to various AI researchers—

1. Newell, Shaw and Simon (1957)

"A process that may solve a given problem but offers no guarantees of doing so is called as a heuristic for that problem".

2. Marvin Minisky (1961)

"A heuristic is any method or trick used to improve the efficiency of a problem-solving program."

3. Feigenbaum and Feldman (1963):

"A state heuristic is rule of thumb, strategy, trick, simplification or any other kind of device which drastically limits search for solutions in large problem spaces. Heuristics do not guarantee optimal solution; in fact, they do not guarantee any solution at all. It can be said for a useful heuristic is that it offers solutions which are good enough most of the time."

Judea Pearl (1984):

"It is the nature of good heuristics both that they provide a simple means of indicating which among several course of action is to be preferred and that they are not necessarily guranteed to identify the most effective course of action, but do so sufficiently often. It is often said that heuristic methods are unpredictable, they work wonders most of the time but may fail miserably some of the time".

Q. 7. Distinguish between Heuristic algorithms and solution guaranteed algorithms?

[Cochin Univ., B. Tech (CSE) 7th Sem. Oct. 2000]

Ans. Let us tabulate the difference between the two

Heuristic Algorithms	Solution guaranteed algorithm
1. These algorithms are **non-exact algorithms** that do not guarantee that the best will be found. So, they are considered to be approximate algorithms.	1. **These algorithms are also called as exact-algorithms** as they guarantee to find an optimal solution.
2. They find solutions close to the best one.	2. They guarantee to find optimal solutions.
3. They find fast solutions.	3. They take exponential time to do so.
4. It is called as heuristic because it must prove that the best solution is the best. For e.g., Local search methods, simulated annealing etc.	4. It always finds an optimal solution. For e.g.: Branch and Bound, dynamic programming, Branch and cut etc.

Q. 8. Using the search tree given below, list the elements of the queue just before that next node is expanded. Use best first search where the number correspond to estimated cost-to-goal for each corresponding node.

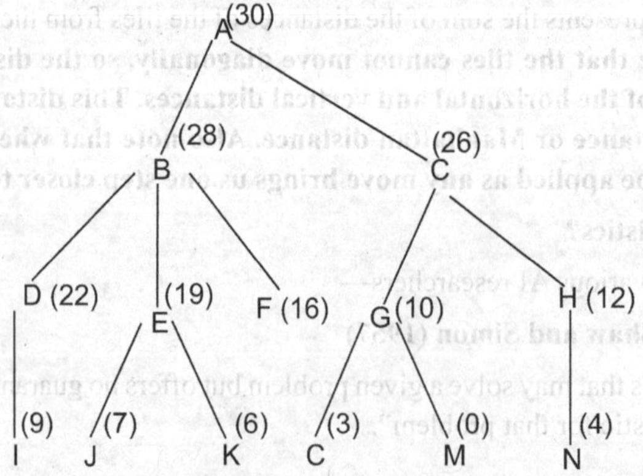

Ans. The best-first-search's cost is calculated in the following manner.

From node	To node	Cost of node	Possible Queue	Cost so far	Final best First queue
A	B	30	A-B	30	✓
	C	30	A-C	30	✓
B	D	28	A-B-D	58	×
	E	28	A-B-E	58	×
	F	28	A-B-F	58	×
C	G	26	A-C-G	56	✓
	H	26	A-C-H	56	✓
G	L	10	A-C-G-L	66	✓
	M	10	A-C-G-M	66	✓
H	N	12	A-C-H-N	68	×
L	Next node	3	A-C-G-L-Next Node	69	×
M	Next node	0	A-C-G-H-Next node	66	✓

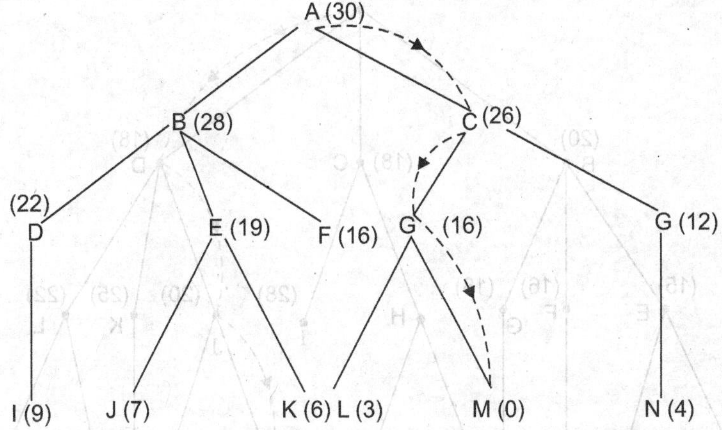

Q. 9. Using the search the given below, list the elements of the queue just before that next node is expanded. Use best-first search where the number correspond to estimated cost-to-goal for each corresponding node.

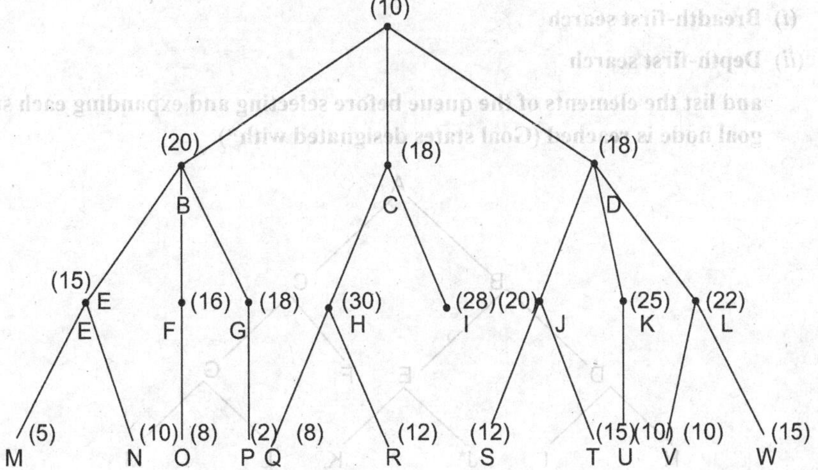

Ans. The table showing best-first search cost is as follows.

From node	To node	Cost of node	Possible queue	Cost so far	Final best First queue
A	B	10	A-B	30	×
	C	10	A-C	28	✓
	D	10	A-D	28	✓
D	J	20	A-B-J	48	✓
	K	20	A-D-K	53	×
	L	20	A-D-L	50	×
C	H	18	A-C-H	58	×
	I	18	A-C-I	56	×
D	S	20	A-D-J-S	60	✓
	T	20	A-D-J-T	63	×

The best first search has path as A-D-J-S-Next node with cost 60.

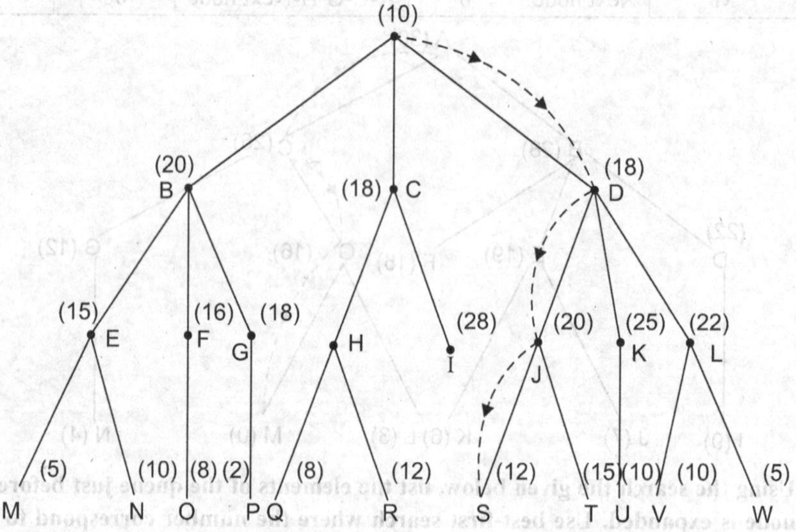

Q. 10. For the search given below, use

(*i*) Breadth-first search

(*ii*) Depth-first search

and list the elements of the queue before selecting and expanding each state until goal node is reached (Goal states designated with*).

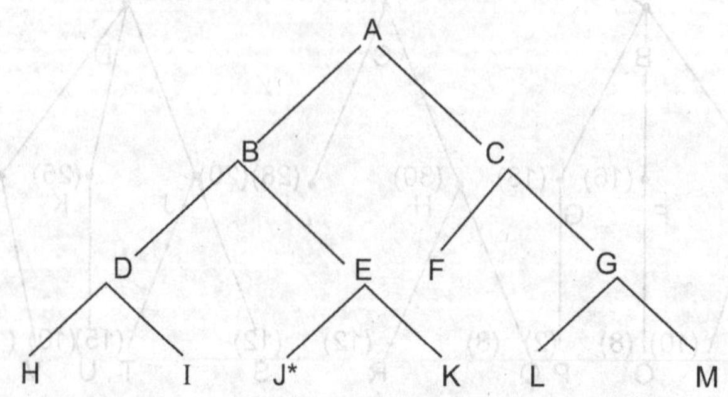

Ans. (*i*) **Breadth first search:**

The given goal is J.

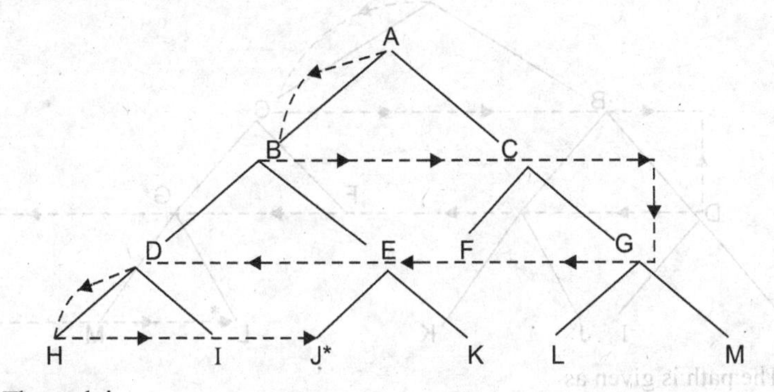

The path is

A-B-C-G-F-E-D-H-I-J.

(*ii*) **Depth-first-search:**

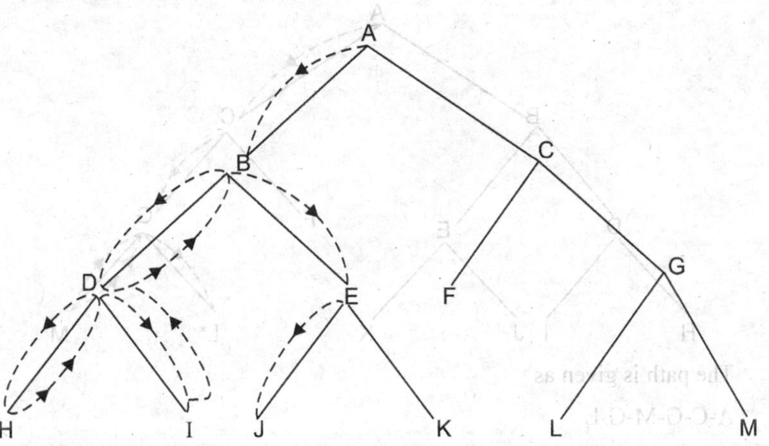

A-B-D-H-I-D-B-E-J.

Q. 11. For the search tree given below, use

(*i*) **Breadth first search.**

(*ii*) **Depth-first search.**

Goal is designed by

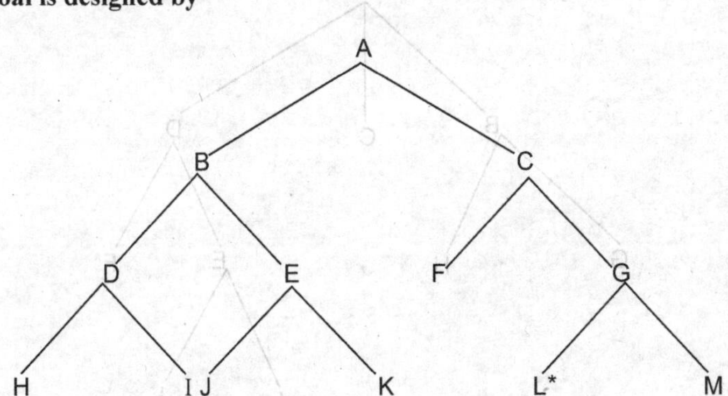

Ans. (*i*) **Breadth first search:**

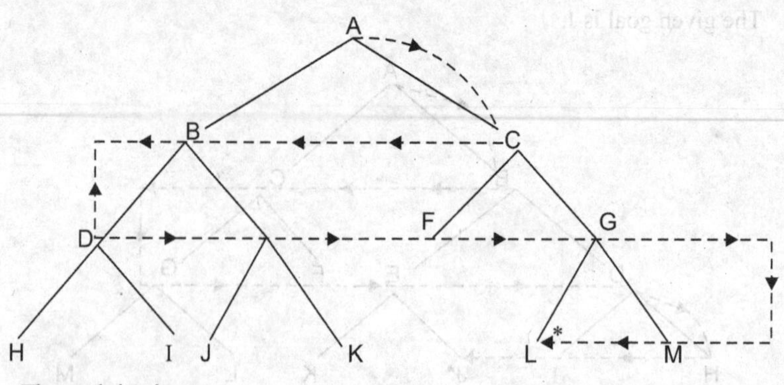

The path is given as

A-C-G-M-G-L

(*ii*) **Depth–first search:**

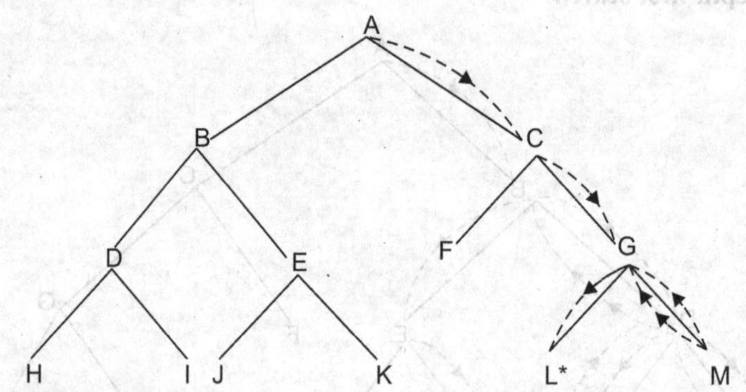

The path is given as

A-C-G-M-G-L

Q. 12. For the search tree given below, use

(*i*) **Breadth-first search**

(*ii*) **Depth first search**

Goal is shown as

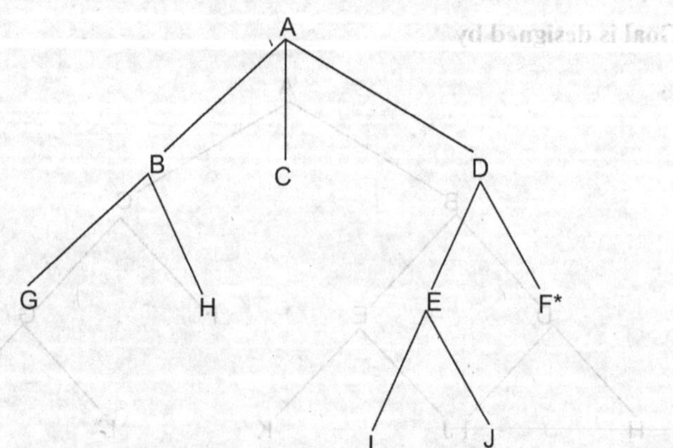

Ans. **(*i*) Breadth first search**

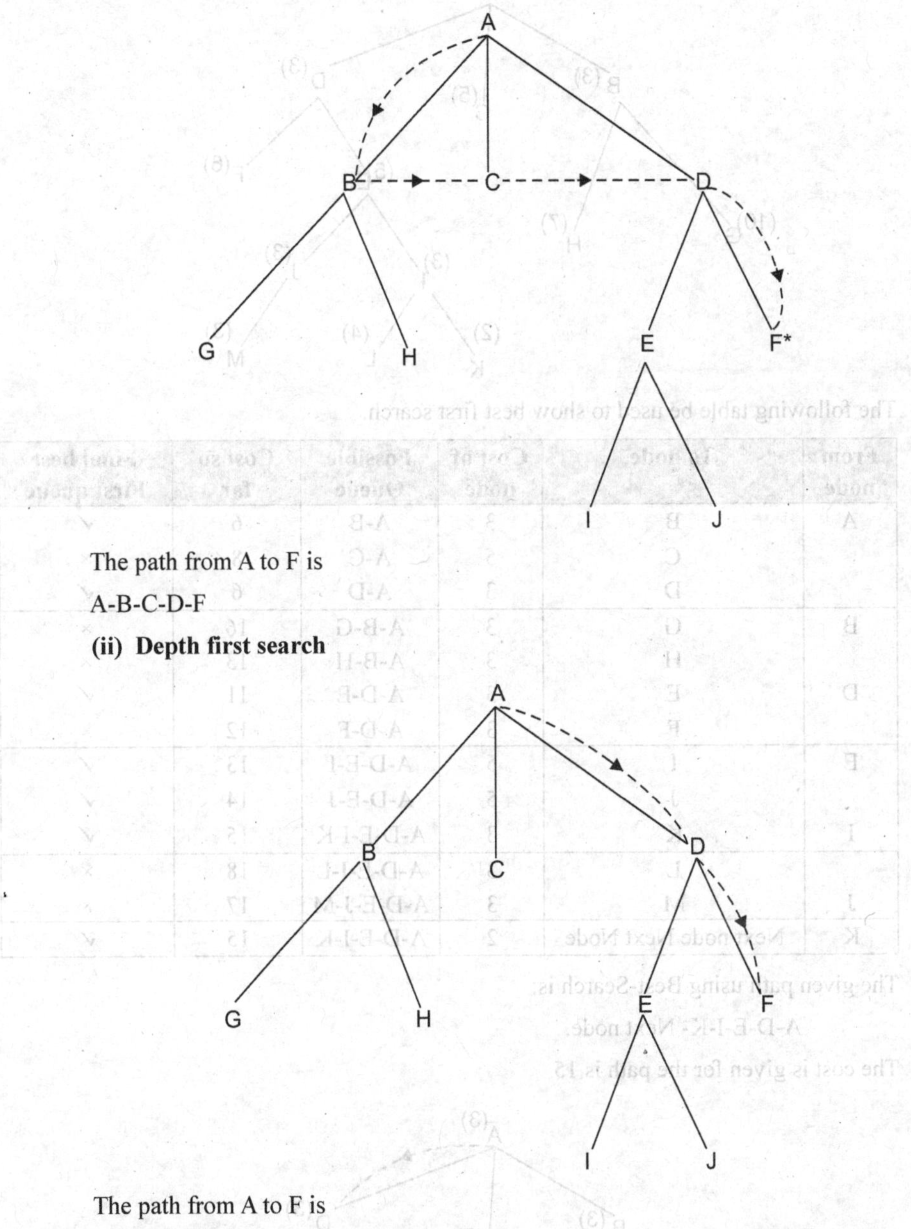

The path from A to F is

A-B-C-D-F

(ii) Depth first search

The path from A to F is

A-D-F

Q. 13. Using the search tree given below, list the elements of the queue just before next node is expanded. Use Best-first-Search where the number correspond to estimated cost-to-goal for each corresponding node.

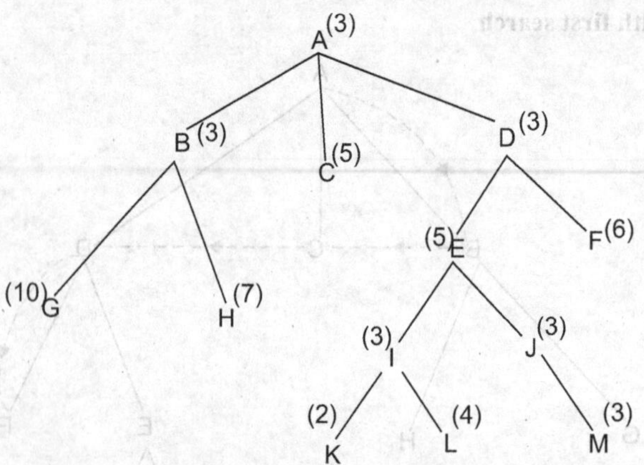

Ans. The following table be used to show best first search.

From node	To node	Cost of node	Possible Queue	Cost so far	Final best First queue
A	B	3	A-B	6	✓
	C	5	A-C	8	×
	D	3	A-D	6	✓
B	G	3	A-B-G	16	×
	H	3	A-B-H	13	×
D	E	3	A-D-E	11	✓
	F	3	A-D-F	12	×
E	I	5	A-D-E-I	13	✓
	J	5	A-D-E-J	14	✓
I	K	3	A-D-E-I-K	15	✓
	L	3	A-D-E-I-L	18	×
J	M	3	A-D-E-J-M	17	×
K	Next node Next Node	2	A-D-E-I-K	15	✓

The given path using Best-Search is:

A-D-E-I-K- Next node.

The cost is given for the path is 15

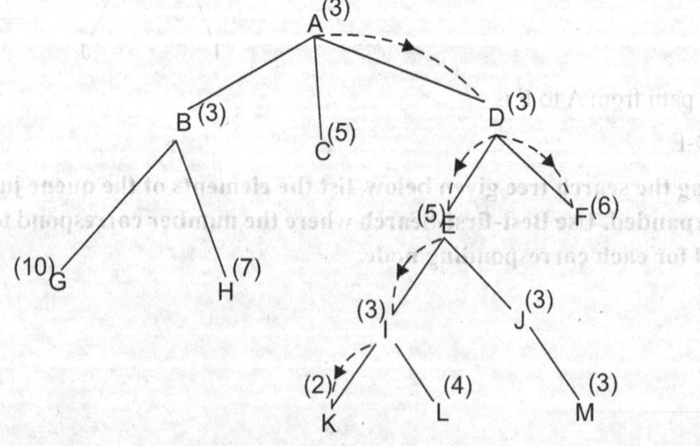

EXERCISE QUESTIONS

Q. 1. Given an example of a real world problem which can be effectively solved by "Hill climbing Algorithm. Explain the terms plateau and ridge.

[GGSIPU, B. Tech (CSE)-8th Sem., May 2008]

Q. 2. (*a*) Explain means end analysis with an example.

(b) What do you understand by admissible heuristic? Develop an admissible heuristic for any problem of your own. **[GGSIPU, B. Tech (CSE) 8th Sem., May 2009]**

Q. 3. (*a*) Compare uniformed search with informed search.

(*b*) Discuss problem reduction strategy of a problem with an example.

[GGSIPU, B. Tech (CSE)-8th Sem., May 2009]

Q. 4. (*a*) What are the problems with hill climbing and how can they be solved?

(*b*) Explain Means End Analysis Search technique with a suitable example.

(*c*) State the best first search algorithm.

(*d*) Define the following terms in reference to Steepest Ascent Hill Climbing:

(*i*) Local Maximum

(*ii*) Plateau.

(*iii*) Ridge. **[RTM, Nagpur University B.E., (IT) 7th Sem. Summer 2009]**

Q. 5. (*a*) Write the difference between :

(*i*) OR graph and AND-OR graph

(*ii*) Generate and test and hill climbing.

(*b*) How state space search work on state space of an AI problem? Explain it with the help of water jug problem.

(*c*) Explain advantages and disadvantages of dfs and bfs.

(*d*) What are various issues to be considered in the design of search problems/programs.

[RTM, Nagpur University, B.E. (C.T.)-7th Sem., Winter 2009]

Q. 6. Using a suitable example, illustrate steps of A* search. Why is A* search better than Best First Search. **[DTU (DCE)-ME (CS)-2005]**

Q. 7. Explain BFS algorithm. **[Cochin University, B.Tech (CSE)-8th Sem. Oct. 2004]**

Q. 8. (*a*) Why Hill-climbing is named so? Illustrate using an example.

(*b*) Discuss and compare Blind Search with Heuristic based search. Which one is better? Discuss using an example. **[GGSIPU, B.Tech (CSE)-8th Sem. May 2011]**

3 CHAPTER

GAMES SOLVING (ADVERSIAL SEARCH)

3.0 INTRODUCTION

Adversial search technique is a mixture reasoning and creativity. Game playing is often called as an **adversial search**. Successful game playing is generally deemed to require intelligence. Game playing is a search problem with the following components—

(*a*) Initial state of the game.

(*b*) Operators defining legal moves.

(*c*) Successor function.

(*d*) Terminal test (defines end-of-game state).

(*e*) Goal test.

(*f*) Path cost (or utility or pay-off function).

Game playing has been one of the most publicized area of AI research. With the success of **Deep Blue** (1997) another landmark was reached i.e. a computer program that could defeat the best chess player in the world. Game playing happens to be a good domain to explore machine intelligence because of two main reasons:

(*a*) They provide a structured task in which it is very easy to measure success or failure.

(*b*) They did not require large amount of knowledge. They are solvable by straight forward search from starting state to final (winning) state.

3.1 GAME PLAYING

To solve our game problems, we draw a game tree (or graphs) to show all possible game states. The nodes are linked by moves (arcs). The branches are labeled with the players who can make the choice between them. In a game tree, alternative layers will be controlled by different players.

3.1.1 Game Trees

A game tree is defined as an instance of a tree in which the root node represents the state before any moves have been made, the nodes in the tree represent possible states of the games (or positions) and arcs in the tree represent moves. We represent the moves on alternate levels of the game tree so that all edges leading from root node to the first level represent possible moves for the first player and edges from the first level to the second represent moves for the first player and edges from the first level to the second represent moves for the second player and so on. The leaf nodes in this tree represent **final states** (where the game has been won, lost or drawn). In simple games, a **goal node** might represent a state in which the computer has won but for complex games (like chess, go etc) the concept of a goal state is rarely of any use.

One method of playing a game might be for the computer to use a tree search algorithm such as dfs or bfs, searching for a goal state i.e. the final state of the game where the computer has won). **But please note that this approach does not work because there is another intelligence involved in the game.** We will consider this to be a rationally informed opponent who plays to win. Whether this opponent is human or another computer does not matter.

Iterative methods apply here because search space is too large for interesting games to search for a solution. Therefore, search will be done before each moves in order to select the best move to be made.

Adversary methods apply here because an opponent who is trying to win, makes alternate moves, not controllable by you.

Evaluation function is used to evaluate the "**goodness**" of a configuration of the game. For a computer to use game-tree to make decisions about moves in a game of tic-tac-toe, it needs to use an evaluation function which enables it to decide whether a given position in the game is good or.bad. If we use exhaustive search, then we only need a function that can recognize a win, a loss or a draw. Then the computer can treat "win" states as goal nodes and carry out search in normal way. **Also note that these evaluation functions are known as static evaluators because they are used to evaluate a game from just one static position. Since the size of the game tree is very large, so it is almost never possible to search the game tree completely.** In other words, the search will rarely reach a leaf node in the tree (at which the game is said to be either won, lost or drawn). This means that the software needs to be able to cutoff search and evaluate the position of the board at that node. Hence, an evaluation function is used to examine a particular position of the board. So, evaluation function must be efficient. This will not slow down the game play. To be effective, the evaluation function needs to give a higher score to a better position. For a chess game, this function will be very complex. These functions are usually weighted linear functions meaning that a number of different scores are determined for a given position and simply added together in a weighted fashion.

For e.g., For a **chess game**, a very **simple evaluation function might be—**

"Count the number of queens, the number of pawns, the number of bishops and so one and add them up using weights to indicate the relative value of those pieces"

That is,

$$\text{Score} = 9q + 5r + 3b + 3n + p$$

where q-number of queens.

r-number of rooks.

n-number of knights.

b-number of bishops.

p-number of pawns.

If the two computer programs were to compete with each other at a game (say checkers) and that they had

— Same processing capabilities and speeds.

— Used same algorithms for examining the search tree,

Then the game would be decided by the quality of the program's evaluation functions. In general, the evaluation functions for game playing programs do not need to be perfect but need to give a good way of comparing two positions to determine which is better. **But please understand that in complex games like chess, Nim, Othello, Checkers, Tic-Tac-Toe, Go etc. this is not an easy question as two grandmasters will sometimes differ on the evaluation of a position.** One way to develop an accurate evaluation function is to actually play games from each position and see who wins. If the play is perfect on both the sides then this will give a good indication of what the evaluation of the starting position should be.

For example, for Tic-Tac-Toe the evaluation function, f(n) is as follows—

f(*n*) = [number of 3-lengths open for me] – [number of 3-lengths open for you]

Where a 3-length is a complete row, column or diagonal.

Most evaluation functions are specified as a weighted sum of "features":

(W1 *feature 1) + (W2 *feature 2) +…+ (Wn *feature n)

Like, in a chess game, some features evaluate piece placement on board and other features describe configurations of several pieces. The need today is to develop an evaluation function that is dynamic and is able to accurately evaluate positions it has never seen before.

Most of the games considered here are **zero-sum games. It means that if the overall score at the end of a game for each player can be 1 (a win), 0 (a draw) or – 1 (a loss), then the total score for both players for any game must always be 0. This means that if one player wins, the other must lose.** The only other alternative is that both players draw. That is why, we consider the search techniques that are discussed here to be adversarial methods because each player is not only trying to win but to cause the opponent to lose. In the algorithms like minimax and Alpha-Beta (discussed next), it is important that the computer can assume that the opponent is rational and adversarial. That is, **the computer needs to assume that the opponent will play to win.**

3.1.2 Minimax Algorithm

Minimax search procedure is a depth-first search procedure. When evaluating game trees, it is usual to assume that the computer is attempting to maximize some score that the opponent is trying to minimize. Normally, we would consider this score to be the result of the **evaluation function** for a given position, so we would usually have a **high positive score means a good position for the computer, a score of 0 means a neutral position and a high negative score means a good position for the opponent.**

Principle: The basic principle behind minimax is that a path through the tree is chosen by assuming that at its turn (a max node), the computer will choose the more that will give the highest eventual static evaluation and that at the human opponent's turn (a min node), he or she will choose the move that will give the lowest static evaluation.

The Minimax algorithm is used to choose good moves. It is assumed that a suitable static evaluation function is available, which is able to give an overall score to a given position. In applying Minimax, the static evaluator will only be used on leaf nodes. The values of the leaf nodes will be filtered up through the tree, to pick out the best path that the computer can achieve. This is done by assuming that the opponent will play rationally and will always play the move that is best for him or her and thus worst for the computer. So, the computer's aim is to maximize the lowest possible score that can be achieved.

As an example, consider a simple game tree. Fig. 3.1 shows how minimax works on it.

Please note that the best result that max can achieve is a score of 6. If max chooses the left branch as its first choice then min will choose the right branch, which leaves max a choice of 1 or 3. In this case, max will choose a score of 3. If max starts by choosing the right branch, min will have a choice between a path that leads to a score of 7 or a path that leads to a score of 6. Therefore, it will choose the left branch, leaving max a choice between 2 and 6. Fig. 3.1 shows how Minimax can use dfs to traverse the game tree. The arrows start from the rest node at the top and go down to the bottom of the left branch. This leads to a max node, which will get a score of 5. The value 5 is, hence, passed up to the parent of this max node. Following the right path

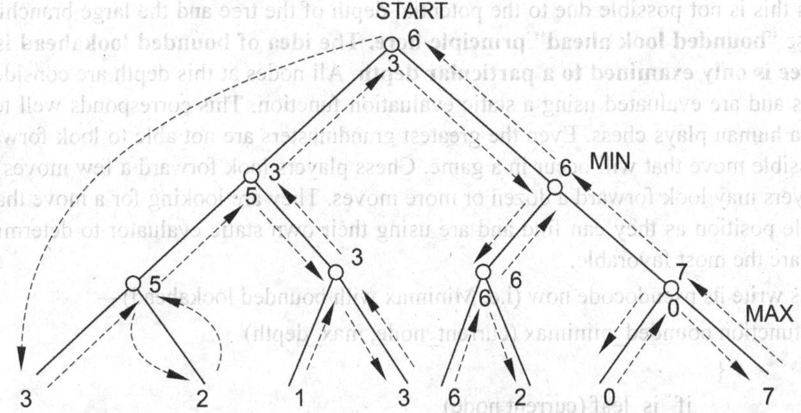

Fig. 3.1 A minimax example.

from this min node leads to another max node, this time getting a score of 3. **Also note that the arrows show the order in which the nodes are examined by the algorithm and the values that are passed through the tree.** This comes back up to the min node which now chooses the minimum of 3 and 5 and selects 3. Eventually, having traversed the whole tree, the best result for max comes back upto the root node (6).

Let us write its psendo-code now—

```
function minimax (current-node)
{
    if  is-leaf (current-node)
        return static-evaluation (current-node);
    if  is-min-node (current-node)
        return min (minimax (children-of (current-node)));
    if  is-max-node (current-node)
        return max (minimax (children-of (current-node)));
}
```

The else part is never required as every node must be a leaf node, a min node or a max node only.

We also observe that this is a **recursive function** because to evaluate the scores for the children of the current node, this algorithm must be applied recursively to those children until a leaf node is reached. **Also understand that Minimax can be done non-recursively, starting at the leaf nodes and going up the tree in a recursive breadth first search.**

Limitations of Minimax:

1. The effectiveness of Minimax is limited by the depth of the game tree which is itself limited by the time needed to construct and analyze it. The time increases exponentially with the depth of the tree.
2. A rapid tie between the assigned and actual value to static evaluation function fails to decide the expansion of game tree.

3.1.3 Horizon Effect Problem

Minimax algorithm is unsuitable for use in many games like chess where the game tree is very large. The problem is that in order to run Minimax, the entire game tree must be examined and for games like chess this is not possible due to the potential depth of the tree and the large branching factor. So, we use "**bounded look ahead" principle here. The idea of bounded lookahead is that the search tree is only examined to a particular depth.** All nodes at this depth are considered to be leaf nodes and are evaluated using a static evaluation function. This corresponds well to the way in which a human plays chess. Even the greatest grandmasters are not able to look forward to see every possible move that will occur in a game. Chess players look forward a few moves and good chess players may look forward a dozen or more moves. They are looking for a move that leads to a favorable position as they can find and are using their own static evaluator to determine which positions are the most favorable.

Let us write its pseudocode now (i.e. Minimax with bounded lookahead)—

```
function bounded_minimax (current_node, max_depth)
    {
        if  is_leaf (current node)
            return static-evaluation.(current-node);
        if  (depth-of (current-node) = = max-depth)
            return static-evaluation (current-node);
        if  (is-min-node (current-node))
            return min (minmax (children-of (current-node)));
        }
```

Actually, it is not reasonable to apply a fixed cut-off point for search. A bounded cut-off at a particular node can leave any one of the opponent in a problem. One way of avoiding this problem is to cut-off search at positions that are deemed to be **quiescent**. **Please note that a quiescent position is one where the next move is unlikely to cause a large change in the relative positions of the two players. Also note that a position where a piece of chess can be captured without a corresponding recapture is not quiescent.**

This bounded Minimax Search has another problem—**the horizon effect,** coined by Berliner in 1977.

Horizon effect: This problem involves an extremely long sequence of moves that clearly lead to a strong advantage for one player, but where the sequence of moves, although potentially obvious to a human player, takes more moves than is allowed by the bounded search. Hence, the significant end of the sequence has been pushed over the horizon. This problem occurs in a checkers playing program named as Chinook.

What is the solution?

There is **no universal solution** to the horizon problem but one method to minimize its effect is to always search a few ply deeper when a position is found that appears to be particularly good. The **singular-extension heuristic** is defined as follows:

"If a static evaluation of a move is much better than that of other moves being evaluated, continue searching."

It is possible for the nodes or positions to have same heuristic scores. This means that they lie on a **plateau** as in case of hill climbing. They tell nothing about the movement of the game. The better estimate of the score for each position is obtained beyond plateau. This is a **horizon effect**.

In 1975, Donald knuth and R.W. Moore introduced a **negmax procedure** which uses the same function (as used in minimax function) to evaluate each node in backing up from the successor nodes. Say, the evaluation function for the jth terminal node in a complete tree is as follows—

$$\left.\begin{aligned} f_j &= -1 \quad \text{(for loss)} \\ f_j &= 0 \quad \text{(for draw)} \\ f_j &= +1 \quad \text{(for win)} \end{aligned}\right\}$$

Then, the negmax evaluation function $F(j)$ is given by

$$F(j) = f_j \text{ for terminal nodes}$$

$$F(j) = \text{MAX } \{-F(i1), -F(i2), \ldots -F(\text{in})\}$$

for successor states $i1$ to in.

This formalism states that the best move for either player is that which maximizes F(j). By simply selecting the move which maximizes the negative of the successor position's evaluation function, the negmax formation implements the minimax heuristic.

3.1.4 Alpha-Beta Cutoff (Pruning)

Bounded lookahead makes our game tree smaller to examine. In some cases, it is extremely useful to be able to prune (cut) sections of the game tree. It is possible to remove sections of the game tree that are not worth examining, to make searching for a good move more efficient.

Principle: If a move is determined to be worse than another move that has already been examined, then further examining the possible consequences of that worse move is pointless. Consider a partial game tree as shown in Fig. 3.2.

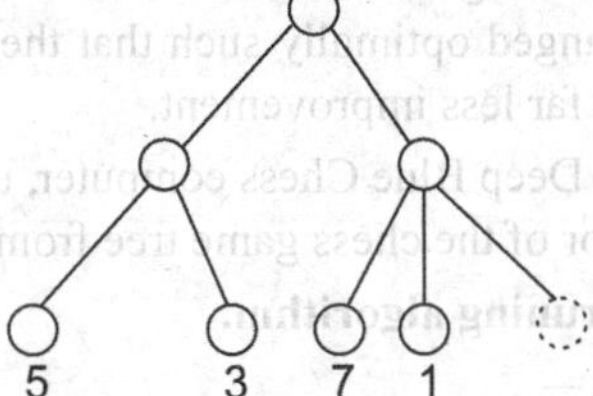

Fig. 3.2 A partial game tree.

This is a tree with five leaf nodes. The top arc represents a choice by the computer and so is a maximizing level. That is, the top node is a **max node**. After calculating the static evaluation function for the first four leaf nodes, it becomes unnecessary to evaluate the score for the fifth node (shown as a dotted circle). Let us see why?

In choosing the left-hand path from the root node, it is possible to achieve a score of 3 or 5. Because this level is a minimizing level, the opponent can be expected to choose the move that leads to a score of 3. So, by choosing the left-hand arc from the root node, the computer can achieve a score of 3. By choosing the right-hand arc, the computer can achieve a score of 7 or 1 or a mystery value. Because the opponent is aiming to minimize the score, he or she could choose the position with a score of 1, which is worse than the value the computer could achieve by choosing the left-hand path. So, the value of the right most left node doesn't matter. The computer must not choose the right-hand arc because it definitely leads to a score of at best 1, assuming the opponent does not irrationally choose the 7 option.

In this example, alpha-beta pruning removes only one leaf node from the tree. But in larger game trees, it can result in a valuable reductions in tree size. In 1993, Winston showed that it will not necessarily remove large positions of a game tree. But infact, in worst case, alpha-beta pruning will not prune any searches from the game tree but even in this case it will compute the same result as Minimax and will not perform any less efficiently.

Analysis of Alpha-Beta Pruning

Alpha-Beta Pruning method provides its best performance when the game tree is assigned such that the best choice at each level is the first one (i.e., the left most choice) to be examined by the algorithm using alpha-beta cut-off will examine a game tree to double the depth that a Minimax algorithm without alpha-beta pruning would examine in the same number of steps. How? If a game tree is arranged optimally, then the number of nodes that must be examined to find the best move using alpha-beta pruning can be derived as found—

$$S = \begin{cases} 2b^{d/2} - 1 & \text{if } d \text{ is even.} \\ b^{(d+1)/2} + b^{(d-1)/2} - 1 & \text{if } d \text{ is odd.} \end{cases}$$

where b–branching factor of game tree.

d–depth of game tree

S–number of nodes that must be examined.

$\therefore$ $S \approx 2b^{d/2}$

Without alpha-beta pruning, where all nodes must be examined:

$$S = b^d$$

$\therefore$ We find that using alpha-beta pruning reduces the effective branching factor from b to $\sqrt{b}$ meaning that in a fixed period of time, Minimax with alpha-beta pruning can look twice as far in the game tree as Minimax without pruning. This represents a significant improvement. For e.g., in chess it reduces the effective branching factor from 38 to 6. But it must be remembered that it assumes that the game tree is arranged optimally such that the best choice is always the leftmost choice. In reality, it might provide far less improvement.

For e.g., In implementing the Deep Blue Chess computer, use of alpha-beta method did in fact reduce the average branching factor of the chess game tree from 38 to around 6.

Implementation of alpha-beta pruning algorithm.

Let us write its algorithm first—

S1: The game tree is traversed in depth-first order. At each non-leaf node, a value is stored. For **max nodes,** this value is called alpha and for **min nodes** the value is **beta**.

S2: An **alpha value** is the **maximum** (best) **value** found so far in the max node's descendants.

S3: A **beta value** is the **minimum** (best) **value** found so far in the min node's descendants.

We write the function alpha-beta now.

```
function alpha-beta (current-node)
    {
        if is-leaf (current-node)
            return static-evaluation (current-node)
        if is-max-node (current-node) and
            alpha-value of (current-node)>=
            beta-value-of (min-ancestor-of (current-node)
            then cut-off-search-below (current-node);
        if is-min-node (current-node) and
            beta-value-of (current-node) <=
            alpha-value-of (max-ancestor-of (current-node) then
            cut-off-search-below (current-node);
    }
```

Instead of searching back up the tree for ancestor values, we propagate values down the tree as follows:

(*a*) **For each max node**, the minimum beta value for all its **min node ancestors** is stored as **beta**.

(*b*) **For each min node,** the maximum alpha value for all its **max node ancestors** is stored as **alpha**.

(*c*) Hence, each **non-leaf node** will have a beta value and an alpha value stored.

(*d*) Initially, the root node is assigned an alpha value of negative infinity and a beta value of infinity.

The above alpha-beta function can be modified also wherein we use another variable, say '**children**' to represent all of the children of the current node. We add the following statement now—

alpha = max (alpha, alpha-beta (children, alpha, beta))

If means that alpha is set to the greatest of the current value of alpha and the values of the current node's children are calculated by recursively calling alpha-beta ( ).

```
// Modified alpha-beta function using
// recursion.
function alpha-beta (current-node, alpha, beta)
{
    if is-root-node (current-node)
    {
    alpha = – infinity
    beta = infinity
    }
if is_leaf (current_node)
    return static_evaluation (current_node);
if is_max_node (current_node)
    {
    alpha = max(alpha, alpha-beta (children, alpha, beta));
    If alpha >= beta
        cut_off_search_below (current_node);
    }
if  is_min_node (current_node)
    {
    beta = min (beta, alpha_beta (children, alpha, beta));
    if beta <=alpha
        cut-off-search-below (current_node);
    }
}
```

We are in a position to solve an example now.

EXAMPLE. For the given game tree, apply alpha-beta pruning procedure—

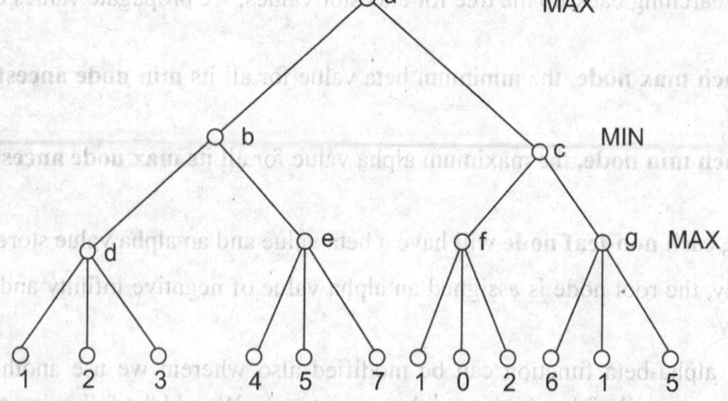

Solution. If it is my turn to move then the root is labeled as "**MAX**" node indicating it is **my turn** otherwise if is labeled as "**MIN**" node to indicate it is my **opponent's turn**. Here, we assume that the static evaluation function returns large values to indicate good situations for us. So, our goal is to **maximize** the value of the static evaluation function of the next board position. **Please note that acrs represent the possible legal moves for the player that the arcs emanate from.** Because moves alternate so each level of the tree has nodes that are all MAX or all MIN. **Also note that the nodes at level i are of the opposite kind from those at level (i + 1).**

With these assumptions, let us try to solve this problem now.

The non-terminal (or non-leaf) nodes in the tree are labeled from a to g. Terminal (or leaf nodes) nodes have scores assigned to them by static evaluation i.e.,

a is MAX node (i.e., my turn)

b and c are MIN nodes (i.e., opponent's turn)

d, e, f and g are MAX nodes (i.e., my turn)

Now, we follow the tree by depth-first search. The **first-step** is to follow the path a, b, d, and then to the three children of d i.e.,

Path 1 : $a \rightarrow b \rightarrow d \rightarrow (1 \rightarrow 2 \rightarrow 3)$

This gives an alpha value for 'd' as 3. This is passed up to 'b' which now has the beta value of 3 and an alpha value that has been passed down from 'a' of negative infinity.

Now, the first child of 'e' is examined and has score of 4. In this case, clearly, there is no need to examine the other children of 'e' because the minimizing choice at node 'b' will definitely do worse by choosing 'e' rather than 'd' so, cutoff is applied here and nodes with score of 5 and 7 are never examined. Let us show this in a tabular form now.

S. No.	Node	Alpha	Beta	Meaning
1.	a	$-\infty$	∞	Alpha starts at $-\infty$ Beta starts at ∞
2.	b	$-\infty$	∞	
3.	d	$-\infty$	∞	
4.	d	1	∞	
5.	d	2	∞	
6.	d	3	∞	Upto this point, we have examined the three children of d. We get an alpha value of 3, which is passed back upto node b.
7.	b	$-\infty$	3	At this MIN node, we get a score of 3 or better (lower). Now we need to examine the children of 'e' to see if we can geta lower score.

S. No.	Node	Alpha	Beta	Meaning
8.	e	–∞	3	
9.	e	4	3	A score of 4 can be obtained from the first child of 'e'. MIN will do better if chosen rather than 'e' because if he chooses 'e' max can get atleast 4, which is worse for min than 3. Hence, we can ignore of ther children of 'e'. A CUT-OFF occurs.
10.	a	3	∞	The value of 3 has been passed back up to the root node. Hence, MAX now knows that he can score atleast 3. He now needs to see if he can do better.
11.	c	3	∞	
12.	f	3	∞	We now examine the three children of f and find that none of them is better than 3. So, we pass back a value of 3 to c.
13.	c	3	3	MAX has already found that by taking the left hand branch, he can achieve a score of 3. Now it seems that if he chooses the right-hand branch, MIN can choose 'f' which means he can only achieve a score of 2. So, cut-off can now occur because there is no need to examine it or its children.

Result: Thus, out of 12 leaf nodes in the tree, this algorithm needed to examine only 7 to conclude that the best move for MAX is 'b', so MIN will choose 'd' and MAX will choose the right hand node, ending with a static evaluation of 3.

Please note that at this stage, this is the right answer because if MAX chooses 'c' then MIN will clearly choose f, resulting in MAX being able to achieve a score of only 2.

∴ Optimized game tree (using our algorithm) is as shown in Fig.

Herein, the minimax algorithm with alpha—beta cut-off will need to examine only five of the eight leaf nodes.

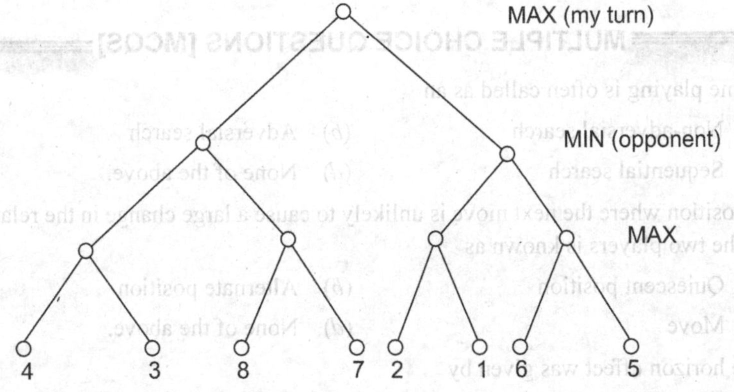

3.1.2 Futility cut-off

The Alpha-Beta procedure discussed above can also be used to cutoff additional paths that provide only slight improvements over paths which have already been explored.

For e.g.: Consider a Minimax tree below—

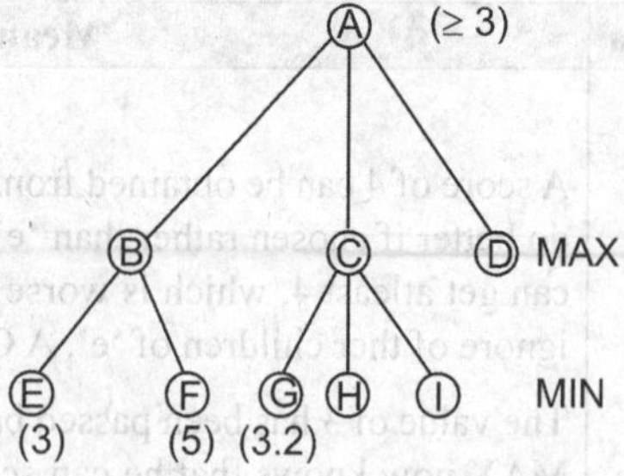

Fig. 3.5 Shows futility cutoff.

After examining node G, we can say that if the move is along C, the value of static evaluation function is 3.2 but the move towards B has a guaranteed score of 3. Because 3.2 is just slightly better than 3 (in the scale of 0-10), we should terminate exploration of C. Thus, we can devote more time in exploring other parts of the tree which could be more useful. **This limit of the static evaluation function is called as futility cutoff limit.** It helps in terminating the exploration of a **subtree** which offers little possibility for improvement over other known paths.

SUMMARY

Minimax Search procedure is a depth-first, depth limited search procedure. We start at the current position and use the plausible move generator to generate the set of possible successor positions. We can apply the static evaluation function to those positions and simply choose the best one. After doing so we can back that value upto the starting position to represent our evaluation of it. **Root node** represents the configuration of the board at which a decision must be made as to what is the best single move to make next. We assume that the static evaluation function returns large values to indicate good situations for us. So, our goal is to maximize the value of the static evaluation function of the next board position. This process of backing up values gives the optimal strategy that both players would follow given that they both have the information computed at the leaf nodes by the evaluation function.

MULTIPLE CHOICE QUESTIONS [MCQS]

1. Game playing is often called as an

(*a*) Non-adversial search (*b*) Adversial search

(*c*) Sequential search (*d*) None of the above.

2. A position where the next move is unlikely to cause a large change in the relative positions of the two players is known as

(*a*) Quiescent position (*b*) Alternate position

(*c*) Move (*d*) None of the above.

3. The horizon effect was given by

(*a*) Berliner (*b*) Boehm (*c*) Jacobson (*d*) None of the above.

4. Most evaluation functions are specified as a weighted sum of features given by the formula

(*a*) (W1*feat1) * (W2*feat2) *…* (Wn*featn)

(*b*) (W1+feat1) * (W2*feat2) *…* (Wn*featn)

(*c*) (W1*feat1) * (W2*feat2) *…* (Wn*featn)

(*d*) None of the above.

5. When we say that if one player wins, the other loose then it is a

(*a*) Zero-sum game (*b*) Two-sum game

(c) Four-sum game (*d*) Eight sum game.

ANSWERS

1. (*b*) **2.** (*a*) **3.** (*a*) **4.** (*c*) **5.** (*a*)

CONCEPTUAL SHORT QUESTIONS WITH ANSWERS

Q. 1. MIN/MAX strategy uses two rules. What are they?

[MDU, B.E. (CSE)-6th Sem. May 2009]

Ans. Two rules that are used in MIN/MAX strategy are as follows—

1. For maximizer, if static evaluation function value found at any node is less than the α-value, reject it.
2. For minimizer, if static evaluation function value found at any node is more than β-value, reject it.

Q. 2. What is plausible move generator?

Ans. These are certain moves that are unproductive (or dangerous) because they obviously lead away from engagement or to an immediate loss of a piece with no hope of trapping the after player. These moves are avoided by the substitution of a plausible move generator in place of the legal move generator. The plausible move generator is equivalent to a beam search in which only a limited number of promising nodes are expanded.

For e.g. In a chess game, the average branching from a node in chess could be cut from 30 to 10 by means of a plausible move generator.

Q. 3. What is an agent? How is it related to architecture and program? How agent should act? Name some agent types and their goals and environment descriptions.

[UPTU, B.Tech (CSE) 6th Sem. 2006-07]

Ans. An agent is anything that can be viewed as perceiving its environment through **sensors** and acting upon that environment through **effectors.**

For e.g. (*a*) A **human agent** has eyes, ears, etc for sensors and hands, legs, mouth, etc. for effectors.

(*b*) A **robotic agent** subsitutes cameras and infrared range finders for sensors and various motors for effectors.

(*c*) A **software agent** has encoded bit strings as it percepts.

AI designs an **agent program** i.e., a function that implements the agent mapping from percepts to actions. This program will work on some sort of architecture—which might be a plain computer. In general, the architecture makes the percepts from the sensors available to the program, runs the program and feeds the program's action choices to the effectors as they are generated. The relationship among agents, architectures and programs is—

Agent = Architecture + Program

A rational agent is one that does the right thing. The right action is one that will cause the agent to be most successful. That leaves us with the problem of deciding 'how' and 'when' to evaluate the agent's success.

The term '**performance measure**' is used for how the criteria that determine how successful an agent is?

An **omniscient agent** knows the actual outcome of its actions and can act accordingly but omniscience is impossible in reality.

An **ideal rational agent** is one which, for each possible percept sequence, should do whatever action is expected to maximize its performance measures on the basis of the evidence provided by the percept sequence and whatever inbuilt knowledge the agent has.

For example Software robots (or softbots) is a software agent.

We list some agents, their percepts, actions, goals and their environment descriptions—

Agent Type	Percepts	Action	Goals	Environment
1. Refinery pressure	Temperature, pressure, readings	Open/close valves, adjust temperatures	Maximize purity	Refinery
2. Medical diagnosis system	Symptons, findings, patient's answers	Questions, tests, treatments	Healthy patients, minimize costs	Patient, hospital

Q. 4. Explain the following statement— "Exhaustive searching of game trees is not possible."

Ans. Exhaustive searching on game trees is not possible bcasue typically trees have very high braching factors and often will be very deep.

For E.g.1, a game tree of a chess game has an average branching factor of 38. A tree can have an infinite depth.

E.g.2 a tic-tac-toe game has maximum depth of 9 and a maximum braching factor of 9 meaning that it has nearly $9 \times 8 \times 7 \times \ldots \times 2 \times$ nodes in the tree i.e., more than 350,000 nodes to examine.

EXERCISE QUESTIONS

Q. 1. Explain why and how AI methods are suitable for game playing. Are there any limitations?

[RTM Nagpur University, BE (IT) 7th Sem., Summer 2003]

Q. 2. Explain Minimax search with reference to game playing.

[RTM Nagpur University, BE (IT) 7th Sem., Summer 2003, 2004, 2005, 2007, 2009]

Q. 3. Write short notes on - minimax search procedure. **[DTU (DCE)-ME (CS) 2005]**

Q. 4. Why game playing problems are considered as AI problems?

[Coachin University, B.Tech (CSE) 8th Sem., OCT 2000]

Q. 5. Explain the Mini-Max with α, β cut offs game playing strategy.

[MDU, B.E. (CSE) 6th Sem., 2008-2009 & Dec. 2009]

Q. 6. (*a*) What is a state space search? Give any example of a Game which happens to be a problem of state space search and justify your answer properly.

(*b*) Perform minimax on the following tree—

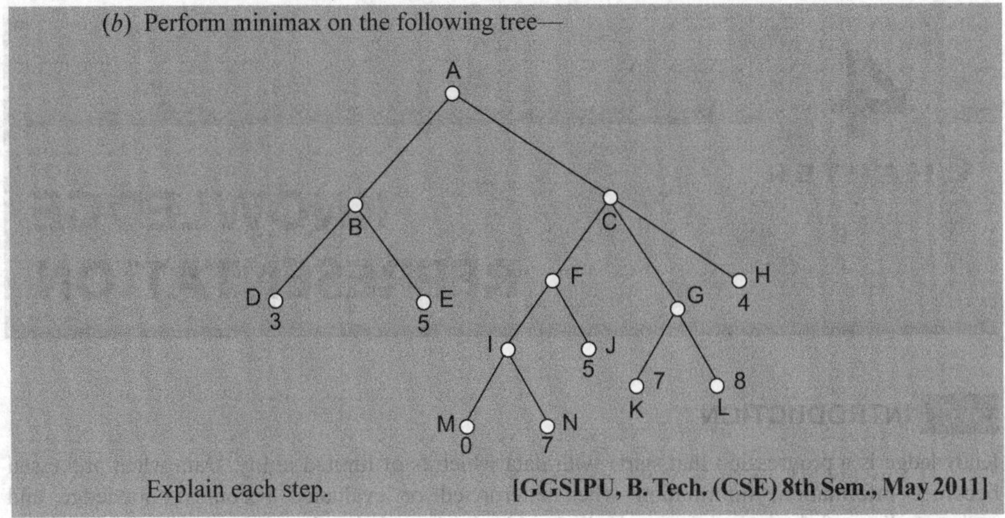

Explain each step. **[GGSIPU, B. Tech. (CSE) 8th Sem., May 2011]**

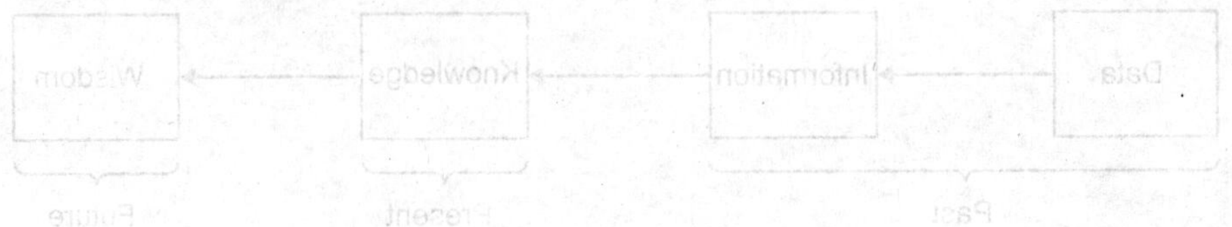

4

CHAPTER

KNOWLEDGE REPRESENTATION

4.0 INTRODUCTION

Knowledge is a progression that starts with data which is of limited utility. Data when processed becomes information, information when interpreted or evaluated becomes knowledge and understanding of the principles embodied with the knowledge is wisdom. This is shown in Fig. 4.1 in knowledge, lies the power.

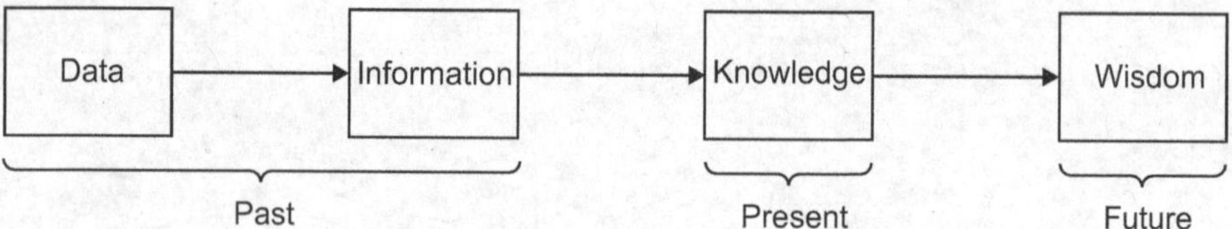

Fig. 4.1 Relationship between data, information, knowledge and wisdom.

A good knowledge representation system should possess the following properties:-

1. **Representational adequacy:** It is defined as an ability to represent the required knowledge.
2. **Inferential adequacy:** It is defined as an ability to manipulate the knowledge represented to produce new knowledge corresponding to that inferred from the original.
3. **Inferential Efficiency:** It is defined as an ability to direct the inferential mechanisms into the most productive directions by string appropriate guides.
4. **Acquisitioned Efficiency:** It is defined as an ability to acquire new knowledge using automatic methods where possible rather than reliance on human intervention.

Please understand that information is static while knowledge is dynamic as it lies within us. Even our expert systems (to be discussed later) are **knowledge-based systems**. These systems are used by **knowledge engineers.** and the process of development building and maintaining knowledge based systems is the domain of **Knowledge Engineering. Knowledge is central to A.I. An A.I**. system must be capable of doing three things:

(*a*) Store knowledge.

(*b*) Apply the knowledge stored to solve problems.

(*c*) Acquire new knowledge through experience.

Also note that any AI system has 3 key components Representation, Reasoning and Learning.

In A.I. different types of knowledge needs to be represented.

(1) Objects: Facts about objects in our world domain need to be represented

For example: Guitars have strings. The fact associated with the object guitar is that they have strings. We need to store and represent this fact.

(2) Events: Actions that occur in real world.

For example: Arjun played guitar in boys band group.

(3) Performance: A behavior. For example, playing a guitar involves knowledge about how to do things.

(4) Meta-knowledge: It is the knowledge about what we know.

For example: A Robot to manage your moods.

So to solve problems in A.I. we must represent knowledge. There are two entities involved here.

(*a*) **Facts:** Are data or instance that are specific and unique. These are the truths about the real world. It is also considered as a **knowledge level.**

(*b*) **Representation of facts:** We usually define the representation in terms of symbols that can be manipulated by programs. It is also called as a **symbol level.**

Knowledge Types

Major classification of knowledge is as follows:

Tacit (or procedural) knowledge and Explicit or declarative knowledge

Let us tabulate the differences between them now.

Tacit Knowledge or Procedural	Explicit Knowledge or Declarative
1. It is an *embodied* knowledge that exists *within* a human being.	1. It is an *embedded* knowledge that exists *outside* the human being.
2. It is difficult to articulate formally.	2. It can be easily articulated formally.
3. It is difficult to share or communicate this knowledge.	3. This knowledge can be shared, copied, processed and stored.
4. This knowledge is drawn from experience, action, subjective insight.	4. This knowledge is drawn from artifact of some type as principle, procedure, process and concepts.
5. It is a procedural knowledge about how to do something.	5. It is a declarative knowledge that something is true or false.
6. It focuses on tasks that must be performed to reach on particular objective and goal.	6. It refers to the representations of objects and events, knowledge about facts and relationships.
Examples: Procedures, rules, strategies, agendas, models.	**Examples:** concepts, objects, facts, propositions, assertions, semantic nets, logic and descriptive models.
7. It is hard to debug	7. It is easy to validate.
8. Process oriented.	8. Data oriented.
9. Representations in form of set of rules.	9. Representation in form of production system.

Other sources of knowledge also exist –

(*a*) **Inheritable knowledge**

We can inherit certain type of knowledge also. **For example:**

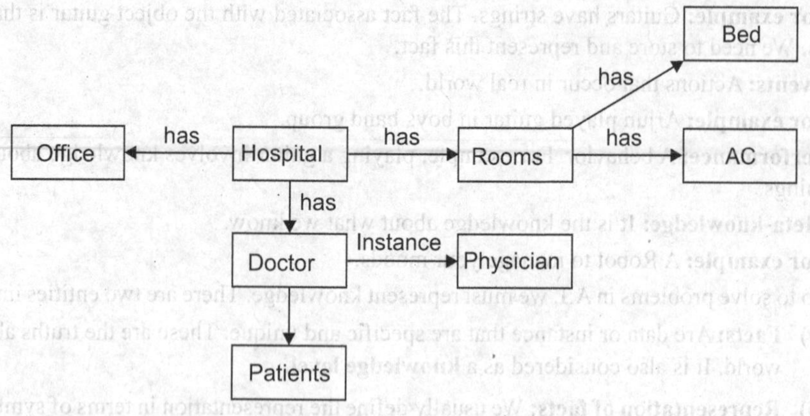

Fig. 4.2 Hospital attribute representation.

The 'hospital' object has certain features like it will have rooms, doctors, office etc. Furthermore, Rooms have bed, AC etc. Doctor has patients and so on. Here, the relationship 'has' indicates the salient features or **property or attributes.** The physician is an instance of Doctor. This is known as **property inheritance** which we shall study a bit later.

(*b*) Inferential knowledge

The knowledge representation method which can use inference mechanism to use this knowledge is called as inferential knowledge. The inferential knowledge requires an inference mechanism for the purpose of exploiting it. Many inference procedures like Resolution will be discussed a bit later. **For example:** Predicate logic.

(*c*) Relations knowledge

This knowledge is represented in of relations/tables in DBMS, form example. the knowledge regarding EMPLOYEE may be represented as

EMPNO	ENAME	EADDR	EPHONE
1.	Vineet	MAIT	852136
2.	Mayur	IITM	526521
3.	Ankit	ITM	921211
4.	Karan	GTBIT	912110
5.	Vijay	VIPS	891929

It can be used to answer simple queries like 'What is the phone number of Vineet'. But this representation cannot store any semantic information like it cannot answer queries like 'Is Vineet a good employee'?.

(*d*) Heuristic knowledge

Heuristics means **'rule of thumb.'** Guessing is the way of making conclusions. It is a form of judgemental information. For example. say, if TV is not working. The guess would be that either tube is not working or probably power is OFF. This is heuristic knowledge.

(*e*) Commonsense knowledge

A knowledge gained by our experience about any general phenomenon.

For example. In order to differentiate human from other animals, the presence of commonsense knowledge plays a vital role.

(*f*) Explicit knowledge

A knowledge which an individual gains explicitly is called as explicit knowledge.

For example: two raised to three is eight ($2^3 = 8$) is a kind of explicit knowledge.

This knowledge can be easily communicated, easily processed by computers and sent electronically.

(g) Uncertain knowledge

Today, we are surrounded by many uncertainties. These uncertainties need to be considered as they also provide some sort of knowledge.

For example : If it is cloudy, it will rain.

We use a reasoning process on the available knowledge to draw conclusions. We need such a system which can handle these uncertainties.

> **Do you know?** In human brain, knowledge is stored in form of neurons whereas in computers knowledge is stored as symbolic structures.

Knowledge is a collection of "facts" from some domain. We need a representation of facts that can be manipulated by a program. English cannot be used directly to draw inferences. We need some symbolic representation. **Please note that we must be able to map facts-to-symbols and vice versa using forward and backward representation mapping.** The basic knowledge representation of facts is shown in Fig. 4.3. Consider an English sentence.

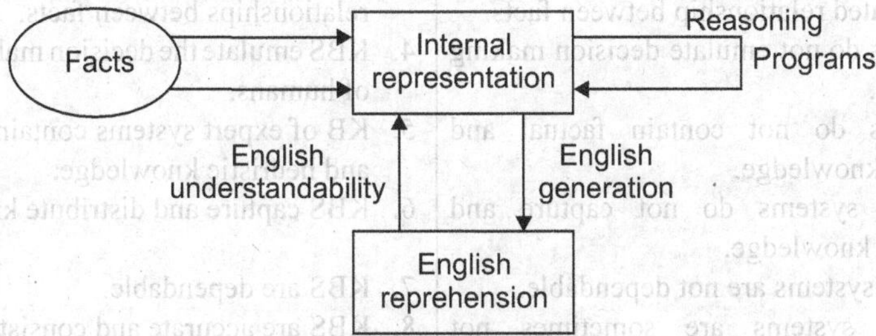

Fig. 4.3 Basic knowledge representation of facts (an English sentence)

For example : consider a 'fact' represented in **'English'** as follows —

'Joe is a father'

Using forward mapping function, the above fact is represented in logic as —

Father (Joe)

On the other hand, **if we use backward mapping function,** then we can generate that English statement back again, i.e., we get –

'Joe is a father'

What are those forward and backward representations?

Forward and Backward representations are shown in Fig. 4.4

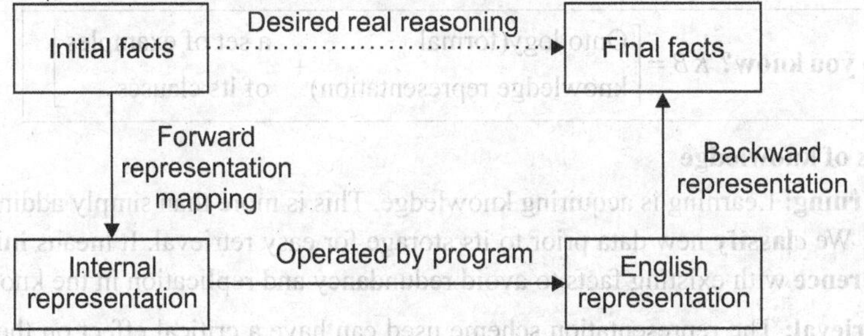

Fig. 4.4 Forward v/s backward representations.

Please note the dotted line on the top. It shows the abstract reasoning process that a program is intended to model. The solid lines on bottom indicate the concrete reasoning process that the program performs.

How to store knowledge?

Collected and stored knowledge is called as **a knowledge base (KB).** A KB is a set of files that stores the knowledge for **knowledge management.** It may be a machine readable as a human readable KB (like articles, papers, user marvels. etc.).

Let us tabulate the differences between database and knowledge base now.

Database (DB)	Knowledge Base(KB)
1. Database stores data that is simple and flat (relational).	1. Knowledge base can be used to store cause and effect information and imprecise and probabilistic information.
2. Database does not consist of fuzzy facts.	2. Knowledge base may consist of fuzzy facts. There is a mechanism which manipulates uncertain information.
3. Databases do not contains more sophisticated relationship between facts.	3. KB contains more sophisticated relationships between facts.
4. Databases do not emulate decision making processes.	4. KBS emulate the decision making processes of humans.
5. Databases do not contain factual and heuristic knowledge.	5. KB of expert systems contains both factual and heuristic knowledge.
6. Database systems do not capture and distribute knowledge.	6. KBS capture and distribute knowledge.
7. Database systems are not dependable.	7. KBS are dependable.
8. Database systems are sometimes not consistent.	8. KBS are accurate and consistent.
9. Database systems are sometimes not profitable.	9. KBS are profitable.
10. A database expert is needed to update databases.	10. An expert knowledge of the domain is needed for updating KB.

Characteristics of a good KB

1. A good KB must be rich in both quality and quantity.
2. It should have carefully written articles.
3. It should be updated regularly.
4. It should have an excellent search engine for easier accessibility.
5. It should have a very good design of the content format.

$$\textbf{Do you know? } KB = \begin{bmatrix}\text{Onto logy(formal} \\ \text{knowledge representation)}\end{bmatrix} + \begin{bmatrix}\text{a set of examples} \\ \text{of its clauses}\end{bmatrix}$$

Applications of knowledge

1. **Learning:** Learning is acquiring knowledge. This is more than simply adding new facts to KB. We **classify** new data prior to its storage for easy retrieval. It means **interaction and inference** with existing facts to avoid redundancy and replication in the knowledge.
2. **Retrieval:** The representation scheme used can have a critical effect on the **efficiency** of the method. Humans are very good at it. Many AI methods have tried to modal a human.

3. **Reasoning:** It means to infer facts from existing data.

4.1 PROPOSITIONAL LOGIC AND ITS RESOLUTION

A logic is defined as a formal system in which the formulae or sentences have true or false values. In 1976, Robert Kowalski came up with an equation

Algorithm = Logic + Control

The **logic component** specifies the knowledge to be used in solving problems.

The **control component** determines the problem solving strategies by means of which that knowledge is used.

Please note that the logic component determines the meaning of the algorithm whereas the control component only affects its efficiency. In reasoning about truth values, we use a number of operators like

Operator	Meaning
$\wedge$	and
$\vee$	or
$\neg$	not
$\rightarrow$	implies
$\leftrightarrow$	iff (if and only if)

It is useful to represent these logical operators using truth table showing the possible values that can be generated by applying an operator to truth tables.

Let us now see various truth tables (for these operators).

1. **Not ($\neg$) operator:** It is a **unary operator** i.e. it is applied only to one variable

   Its truth table is as follows –

A	$\neg A$
true	false
false	true

2. **and ($\wedge$) operator**: It is a **binary operator,** i.e. it acts on two variables. It is also called as **conjunctive operator.** Its truth table is as follows:

A	B	$A \wedge B$
false	false	false
false	true	false
true	false	false
true	true	true

NOTE: that $A \wedge B$ is true if both A and B are true else it is False. A and B can be any statement or proposition.

3. **or ($\vee$) Operator:** It is again a **binary operator** and is also known as **disjunctive operator**.

   Its truth table is a follows –

A	B	$A \vee B$
false	false	false
false	true	true
true	false	true
true	true	true

So, $A \vee B$ is true for all cases except for $A = B =$ false. This table represents an **inclusive or operator**. An exclusive or would have been 'false' in the final row.

4. Implies (→) Operator: Its truth table is as follows–

A	B	$A \rightarrow B$
false	false	true
false	true	true
true	false	false
true	true	true

This type of implication is also called as **material implication**. Also note that in statement,

$A \rightarrow B$

'A' is known as **antecedent.**

and 'B' is known as **consequent.**

$A \rightarrow B$ is real as 'A implies B' or 'if A then B' or 'if A is to B then B is true'

We can also construct complex truth tables like for $A \vee (B \vee C)$ the truth table is as follows—

A	B	C	$A \wedge (B \vee C)$
false	false	false	false
false	false	true	false
false	true	false	false
false	true	true	false
true	false	false	false
true	false	true	true
true	true	false	true
true	true	true	true

for $n = 3$ (i.e., 3 variables A, B and C) these are 8 outputs. **In general, for n inputs there will be 2^n outputs. Please note that the use of brackets is very important because $A \wedge (B \vee C) \neq (A \wedge B) \vee C$. Also note that to avoid ambiguity, these logical operators are assigned precedence.** The order of precedence is as follows –

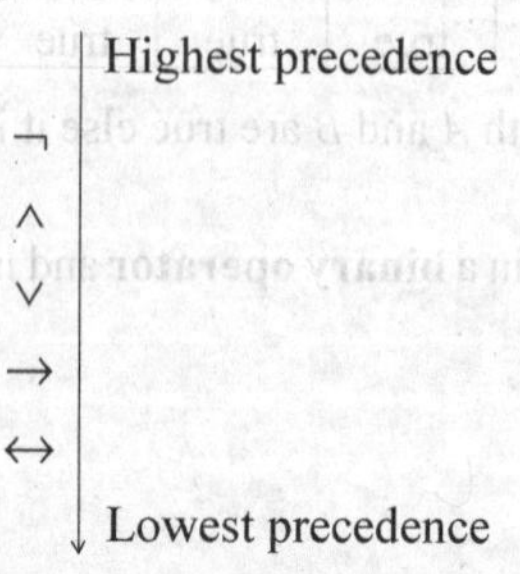

This means that $\neg A \vee B = (\neg A) \vee B$

Tip: Use braces whenever an expression becomes ambiguous.

5. **Tautology:** Consider the following truth table –

A	$A \vee \neg A$
false	true
true	true

This truth table has a property, that is, the value of expression is always true irrespective of the value of A. **Such an expression that is always true is known as tautology.** If A is a tautology, we write —

$\models A$

A logical expression that is tautology is often described as being valid. A **Valid expression** is defined as being one that is true under any interpretation. In other words, no matter what meanings and values we assign to variables in a valid expression, it will still be true. If an expression is false in any interpretation, it is described as being contradictory. The following expressions are contradictory:

(*a*) $A \wedge \neg A$

(*b*) $(A \vee \neg A) \rightarrow (A \wedge \neg A)$

It does not matter what A means in these expressions. The result cannot be time.

Some expressions are **satisfactory** but **not valid.** This means that they are true under some interpretation but not under all interpretations. The following expressions are satisfactory —

(*a*) $A \vee A$

(*b*) $(A \wedge B \vee \neg C) \rightarrow (D \wedge E)$

Please note that a contradictory expression is clearly not satisfactory and so is described as being unsatisfactory.

Tip: Logic is studied as knowledge representation language in A.I.

Logics are of different types —

(*a*) Propositional logic.

(*b*) Predicate logic.

(*c*) Temporal logic.

(*d*) Modal logic.

(*e*) Description logic. etc.

Out of these propositional logic and predicate logic are fundamental to all logic.

Propositional logic

Propositions are statements used in mathematics. A proposition or sentence is classified as declarative sentence whose value is either 'true' or 'false'.

For example. —

(*a*) The sky is blue.

(*b*) Snow is white.

(*c*) 4 * 4 = 16

Propositions are of two types —

(*a*) Atomic propositions.

(*b*) Molecular propositions.

Atomic propositions are single propositions. The above given examples are all propositions.

Molecular propositions are formed by combining two or more atomic propositions.

For example. —

"Lata Mangeshkar is a singer and Rajiv Chopra is an author".

Propositions are 'sentences' either true or false but not both. A sentence is the smallest unit in propositional logic. If proposition is 'time', then truth value is 'time'. If proposition is 'false' then truth value is 'false'.

> **NOTE:** Propositional logic is also called as Propositional Calculus or Sentential Calculus or Boolean Algebra.

Please understand that propositional logic tells the ways of joining and/or modifying entire propositions, statements or sentences to form more complicated propositions, statement or sentences as well as the logical relationships and properties that are derived from the methods of combining or altering statements. Also note that the process used for performing manipulation of the symbols is according to some rules and laws.

A BNF (Backus Naur Form) grammar of Sentences in Propositional logic is as follows —

Sentence → Atomic sentence |complex sentence|

Atomic sentence → true |false| symbol

Symbol → $P|Q|R\ldots$

Complex sentence → ¬ sentence

| (Sentence ∧ Sentence)

| (Sentence □ Sentence)

| (Sentence → Sentence)

| (Sentence ↔ Sentence)

Some terminologies in Propositional Logic

1. **Statement:** A statement is a sentence that is TRUE or FALSE. These statements have some properties:–

   (*a*) **Satisfiability:** A statement is satisfiable if there is some interpretation for which it is true.

   (*b*) **Contradiction:** A sentence is contradictory (unsatisfiable) if there is no interpretation for which it is true. **For example,** Japan is capital of India.

   (*c*) **Validity:** A sentence is valid if it is true for every interpretation.

   For example, the sentence $P \vee \neg P$ is valid. Valid sentences are also called as tautologies.

   (*d*) **Logical Equivalence:** Two sentences are logically equivalent if they have the same truth table under every interpretation, written as $P \leftrightarrow Q$.

   For example, $P \wedge Q$ and $Q \wedge P$ are logically equivalent and this can be shown using truth tables given earlier.

2. **Connective or operator:** The connectives join simple statements into compound statements and joins compound into larger compound statements.

For example : 6 basic connectives and their symbols

Connectives	Symbols	Meaning
Assertion	P	'P is true'
Negation	$\neg P$, ~, !, not	'P is false'
Conjunction	$p \wedge g$, AND, &	'Both p and q are true'
Disjunction	$p \vee q$, i, OR	'Either p is true or q is true or both'
Implication	$p \to q$, ⊃, ⇒, if then	'if p is true from q is also true' (i.e., p implies q)
Equivalence	↔, ≡, ⇔, if and only if	'P and q are either both true or both false'

NOTE: Both propositions and connective are the basic elements of propositional logic.

3. **Truth value:** The truth value of a statement is its TRUE or False value.

   For example

   (*a*) q is either TRUE or FALSE.

   (*b*) $\sim q$ is either TRUE or FALSE.

   (*c*) $q \to p$ is either TRUE or FALSE.

NOTE: Use 'T' or '1' to mean TRUE & 'F' or '0' to mean FALSE

For example.

p	q	$\neg p$	$\neg q$	$p \vee q$	$p \to q$
T	T	F	F	T	T
T	F	F	T	T	F
F	T	T	F	T	T
F	F	T	T	F	T

4. **Tautologies:** A proposition that is always true is called as a tautology.

   For example: $(p \vee \neg p)$ is always true irrespective of the value of p.

5. **Contradictions:** A proposition that is always false is called as a contradiction.

   For example: $(q \vee \neg g)$ is always false regardless of the truth value of the proposition.

6. **Contigencies:** A proposition is called as a contigency, if that proposition is neither a tautology nor a contradiction.

   For example : $(p \vee q)$ is a contingency

7. **Antecedent and consequent:** In the conditional statements, $p \to q$, 'p' is the 'if-clause' and is called as **antecedent** whereas 'a' is the 'then clause' and is known as **consequent.**

8. **Argument:** Any argument can be expressed as a **compound statement. If we take all premises, conjoin them and make that conjunction the antecedent of a conditional and make the conclusion the consequent then this implication statement is called as the corresponding conditional of the argument.**

Please remember the following points here:

1. Every **argument** has a **corresponding condition.**
2. Every **implication statement** has a **corresponding argument.**

3. Because the corresponding condition of an argument is a statement, it is therefore **either a tautology or a contradiction or a contingency.**
4. An argument is **valid** "if and only if" its corresponding conditional is a **tautology.**
5. Two statements are **consistent** 'if and only if' their **conjunction is not a contradiction.**
6. Two statements are **logically equivalent** "if and only if" their truth table columns are identical or "if and only if" the statement of their equivalence using "≡" is a **tautology.**

NOTE: Truth tables are used to test validity tautology, contradiction, contingency, consistency and logical equivalence.

A logical system is defined in terms of its syntax, its semantics and a set of rules of deduction for proving.

An expression is referred to as a well formed formula (WFF) if it is constructed correctly according to the rules of the syntax of propositional calculus. We define a sentence recursively in terms of other sentences.

More formally **a WFF consists of atomic symbols joined with connectives.**

$\therefore\ P, P \wedge \neg P, P \wedge Q, P \vee Q, P \rightarrow Q, P \leftrightarrow Q$ are WFFs.

A WFF is defined recursively as —

1. An atom (say *P*) is a WFF.
2. If *P* is a WFF then $\neg p$ *is a WFF.*
3. If *P* and *Q* are WFF, then $(P \vee Q)$, $(P \wedge Q)$, $(P \rightarrow Q)$ and $(P \leftrightarrow Q)$ are WFF.
4. A string of symbols is a WFF if and only if it is obtained by using above rule 1 to rule 3

Also note the following points about WFF:

1. A WFF is not a proposition but if we substitute a proposition in place of a propositional variable, we get a proposition.

   For example : $\neg(P \vee Q) \wedge (Q \wedge R) \rightarrow (\neg Q \wedge R)$
2. The WFF is also simply called as a formula.
3. WFF are conveniently represented as **truth tables.**
4. A WFF for all true entries is called as a tautology.
5. Two WFFs, say α and β in propositional variables $p_1, p_2 \cdots p_n$ are equivalent if the formula $\alpha \rightarrow \beta$ is a tautology then, the equivalent statements are represented as $\alpha \equiv \beta$.
6. **Please understand that** $\alpha \leftrightarrow \beta$ **and** $\alpha \equiv \beta$ **are different as** $\alpha \leftrightarrow \beta$ **is a formula** whereas $\alpha \equiv \beta$ is not a formula but a relation between α and β.

The semantics (meaning) of the operators of propositional calculus can be defined in terms of truth tables. If our knowledge is represented in form of propositional logic then it is very easy for a computer to do reasoning on this knowledge. The set of inference rules and laws that are used for reasoning are given below:

Rule 1: Idempotency Rule

(*a*) $P \vee P = P$

(*b*) $P \wedge P = P$

Rule 2: Commutative Law

(*a*) $P \vee Q = Q \vee P$

(*b*) $P \wedge Q = Q \wedge P$

(*c*) $P \leftrightarrow Q = Q \leftrightarrow P$

Rule 3: Associative Law

(*a*) $(P \vee Q) \vee R = P \vee (Q \vee R)$

(*b*) $(P \wedge Q) \wedge R = P \wedge (Q \wedge R)$

Rule 4: Distributive Law

(*a*) $P \wedge (Q \vee R) = (P \wedge Q) \vee (P \wedge R)$

(*b*) $P \vee (Q \wedge R) = (P \vee Q) \wedge (P \vee R)$

Rule 5: De Morgan's rule

(*a*) $\sim (P \vee Q) = \sim P \wedge \sim Q$

(*b*) $\sim (P \wedge Q) = \sim P \vee \sim Q$

Rule 6: Implication Removal

$P \leftrightarrow Q = \sim P \vee Q$

Rule 7: Biconditional elimination

$P \leftrightarrow Q = (P \rightarrow Q) \wedge (Q \rightarrow P)$

Rule 8: Absorption Law

(*a*) $P \vee (P \wedge Q) \equiv P$

(*b*) $P \wedge (P \vee Q) \equiv P$

Rule 9: Contrapositive

$P \Rightarrow Q \equiv \neg Q \Rightarrow \neg P$

Rule 10: Double negation

$P \equiv \neg (\neg P)$

Rule 11: Fundamental identities

(*a*) $P \vee \neg P \equiv T$

(*b*) $P \wedge \neg P \equiv F$

(*c*) $P \vee \neg T \equiv T$

(*d*) $P \vee T \equiv P$

(*e*) $P \vee F \equiv P$

(*f*) $P \vee F \equiv F$

(*g*) $(F \neg Q) \wedge (P \Rightarrow \neg Q) = \neg P$

(*h*) $P \Rightarrow Q \equiv (\neg P \vee Q)$

Rule 12: AND (∧) rule (Introduction)

Given P and Q. We deduce $P \wedge Q$ i.e.

$$\frac{P \quad Q}{P \wedge Q}$$

This follows from the definition of $\wedge$.

Rule 13: AND ($\wedge$) rule (Elimination)

Given P and Q. We deduce P and Q i.e. separately i.e.

(*a*) $P \wedge Q \rightarrow P$

(*b*) $P \wedge Q \rightarrow Q$

This also follows from the definition of $\wedge$.

Rule 14: OR ($\vee$) rule (Introduction)

Given P and Q, We deduce P and Q i.e. separately i.e.

(*a*) $A \rightarrow A \vee B$

(*b*) $B \rightarrow A \vee B$

i.e. from A we can deduce the disjunction of A which any expression.

Rule 15: Modus Ponens

From given two statements P and $P \rightarrow Q$, infer Q i.e.,

$$\begin{array}{l} P \\ \underline{P \rightarrow Q} \\ \therefore\ Q \end{array}$$

> **NOTE:** In implication form, this rule is written as
>
> $(P \wedge (P \rightarrow Q)) \rightarrow Q$

For example.

Given: Rajiv is intelligent

and: Rajiv is intelligent $\rightarrow$ Rajiv is author.

Conclude: Rajiv is author.

Rule 16: Modus Tollens

From the given two statements, $\neg Q$ and $(P \rightarrow Q)$, infer $\neg P$ i.e.

$$\begin{array}{l} \neg P \\ \underline{P \rightarrow Q} \\ \therefore\ \neg Q \end{array}$$

For example :

Given: Ajay is not a religious person.

and: Ajay goes to temple daily implies Ajay is a religious person

Conclude: Ajay does not go to temple daily.

> **NOTE:** In implication form, this rule is written as
>
> $(\neg Q \wedge (P \rightarrow Q)) \rightarrow \neg Q$

Rule 17: Chain Rule/Hypothetical syllogism

From $(P \rightarrow Q)$ and $Q \rightarrow R)$, infer $(P \rightarrow R)$ i.e.

$$\begin{array}{l} P \rightarrow Q \\ \underline{P \rightarrow Q} \\ \therefore\ (P \rightarrow R) \end{array}$$

For example :

Given: It is raining → must take umbrella

and: Must take umbrella → There is no sun

Conclude: There is no sun.

> **NOTE:** In implication form, this rule is written as
> $((P \to Q) \wedge (Q \to R)) \to (P \to R)$

Rule 18: Reductio Ad Absurdum

This rule states that if we assume that *A* is false ($\neg A$) and this leads to a contradiction ($\perp$) then we say that *A* is true. This is known as proof by contradiction. This is

$$\begin{array}{l} \neg A \\ \vdots \\ \perp \\ \hline \therefore\ A \\ \hline \end{array}$$

Here, the symbol $\perp$ is called as **falsumn** which is used to indicate an absurdity or a contradiction.

For example., $\perp$ can be deduced from $A \wedge \neg A$.

Rule 19: Disjunctive syllogism

From two given sentences, $\neg P$ and $(P \vee Q)$, infer Q i.e.,

$$\begin{array}{l} \neg P \\ P \vee Q \\ \hline \therefore\ Q \\ \hline \end{array}$$

> **NOTE:** In implication form, this rule is written as
> $(\neg P \wedge (P \vee Q)) \to Q$

Rule 20: Constructive and Destructive dilemma

From given two sentences

$$\begin{array}{l} (P \to Q) \wedge (R \to S) \\ \text{and} \qquad (P \vee R) \\ \hline \therefore\ (Q \vee S) \\ \hline \end{array}$$

(Constructive dilemma)

Also,

$$\begin{array}{l} (P \to Q) \wedge (R \to S) \\ \neg(P \vee R) \\ \hline \therefore\ (Q \vee S) \\ \hline \end{array}$$

(Destructive dilemma)

> **NOTE:** In implication form, this rule is written as
> $((P \to Q) \wedge (R \to S)) (\neg Q \wedge S) \to (P \vee R)$.

We are in a position to solve some examples now.

EXAMPLE 1: Given P and Q, prove that

$((P \to Q) \to P) \to P$ is tautologous.

SOLUTION: We draw its truth table —

P	Q	$((P \to Q) \to P) \to P$		
T	T	T	T	T
T	F	F	T	T
F	T	T	F	T
F	F	F	F	T

Hence, $((P \to Q) \to P) \to P$ is tautologous.

EXAMPLE 2: Find the equivalent expression of

A (& $(A \vee B)$) using truth table

SOLUTION:

A	B	$(A \vee B) = C$ (say)	$A \& C$
t	t	t	t
f	f	f	f
t	f	t	t
f	t	t	f

$\therefore$ A (& $(A \vee B)) = A$ $[\because AB' + AB = A(B' + B) = A]$

EXAMPLE 3: Prove that $(A \wedge B) \to A \vee B$.

SOLUTION: Given $A \wedge B$ (assumption)

$\to A$ (by $\wedge$ elimination)

$\to A \vee B$ (by $\vee$ introduction)

Hence Proved.

EXAMPLE 4: Prove that —

$((P \wedge Q) \to R) \vee (\sim Q \to \sim R)$ is valid.

SOLUTION: Let us denote this statement by Q

Q: $((P \wedge Q) \to R) \vee (\sim Q \to \sim R)$

We draw its truth table now:

P	Q	R	$P \wedge Q$	$P \wedge Q \to R$	$\sim Q \to \sim R$	Q
T	T	T	T	T	T	T
T	T	F	T	F	T	T
T	F	T	F	T	F	T
T	F	F	F	T	T	T
F	T	T	F	T	T	T
F	T	F	F	T	T	T
F	F	T	F	T	F	T
F	F	F	F	T	T	T

∵ Q is true under all interpretations.

∴ It is a valid statement.

EXAMPLE 5: Show that the set of statements "I will be wet if it rains and I go out of the house. It is raining now. I go out of the house. I will not be wet" are inconsistent.

SOLUTION: W : I will be wet.

R : It rains.

G : I go out of the house.

∴ A set of formulae corresponding to given word problem is —

$\{(R \wedge G) \rightarrow W, R, \sim W\}$

It can be shown using truth table that

$((R \wedge G) \rightarrow W) \wedge R \wedge G \wedge \sim W$ is false under all interpretations and hence is inconsistent.

EXAMPLE 6: Determine whether each of following is

(*a*) Satisfiable. (*b*) Contradictory. (*c*) Valid.

$S_1 : (P \,\&\, Q) \vee \sim (P \,\&\, Q)$

$S_2 : (P \,\&\, Q) \rightarrow (R \vee \sim Q)$

$S_3 : (P \,\&\, Q) \rightarrow (R \vee \sim Q)$

$S_4 : (P \vee Q) \,\&\, (P \vee \sim Q) \vee P$?

SOLUTION: $S_1 : (P \,\&\, Q) \vee \sim (P \,\&\, Q)$

Its truth table is —

G : I go out of the house.

P	Q	$P \& Q = A$	$\sim(P \& Q) = B$	$A \vee B$
t	f	f	t	*t*
f	t	f	t	*t*
f	f	f	t	*t*
t	t	t	f	*t*

∴ It is satisfiable.

∴ It is not contradictory

∴ It is valid as sentence is true for every interpretation.

Consider $S_2 : (P \,\&\, Q) \rightarrow (R \vee \sim Q)$

P	Q	R	$P \& Q = X$	$\sim Q$	$R \vee \sim Q = Y$	$X \rightarrow Y$
f	f	f	f	t	t	f
f	f	t	f	t	t	f
f	t	f	f	f	f	t
f	t	t	f	f	t	f
t	f	f	f	t	t	f
t	f	t	f	t	t	f
t	t	t	t	f	t	t

∴ It is satisfiable

It is not contradictory

It is not valid.

$S_3 : (P \& Q) \rightarrow (R \vee \sim Q)$

Its truth table is —

P	Q	R	$P \& Q = X$	$\sim Q$	$R \vee \sim Q = Y$	$X \rightarrow Y$
f	f	f	f	t	t	f
f	f	t	f	t	t	f
f	t	f	f	f	f	t
f	t	t	f	f	t	f
t	f	f	f	t	t	f
t	f	t	f	t	t	f
t	t	f	t	f	f	f
t	t	t	t	f	t	t

∴ It is satisfiable

It is not contradictory

It is not valid.

$S_4 : (P \vee Q) \& (P \vee \sim Q) \vee P$

P	Q	$P \vee Q = X$	$\sim Q$	$P \vee \sim Q = Y$	$Y \vee P = Z$	$X \& Z$
t	t	t	f	t	t	t
f	t	t	f	f	f	f
t	f	t	t	t	t	t
f	f	f	t	t	t	t

∴ It is satisfiable

It is not contradictory

It is not valid.

Normal Forms in Propositional Logic

There are two major normal forms of statements in propositional logic. They are Conjunctive Normal Form (CNF) and Disjunctive Normal Form (DNF).

Any formula can be converted into its normal form by substituting it by its equivalent formulae. Two formulas P and Q are equivalent if and only if the truth values of P and Q are same for all values of P and Q. We have already discussed some widely used equivalent formulae in table III.

A formula P is said to be in CNF if it is of the form

$$P = P_1 \wedge P_2 \wedge P_3, \ldots, \wedge P_n; n \geq 1$$

where each $P_1, P_2, P_3, \ldots, P_n$ is a disjunction of an atom or negation of an atom.

A formula P is said to be in DNF if it has the form

$$P = P_1 \vee P_2 \vee P_3, \ldots, \vee P_n; n \geq 1$$

where each $P_1, P_2, P_3, \ldots, P_n$ is a conjunction of an atom or negation of an atom.

Conversion Procedure to Normal Form

Step 1: Eliminate implication and biconditionals. We use the following laws

$$(P \rightarrow Q) = \neg P \vee Q$$

$$(P \leftrightarrow Q) = (P \rightarrow Q) \wedge (Q \rightarrow P)$$

$$= (\neg P \vee Q) \wedge (\neg Q \vee P)$$

Step 2: Reduce the NOT symbol by the formula $(\neg(\neg P)) = P$ and apply De Morgan's theorem to bring negations before the atoms.

$$\neg(P \vee Q) = \neg P \wedge \neg Q$$
$$\neg(P \vee Q) = P \vee \neg Q$$

Step 3: Use Distributive laws and other equivalent formula given in table III to obtain the normal form

$$P \wedge (Q \vee R) = (P \wedge Q) \vee (P \wedge R)$$
$$P \vee (Q \wedge R) = (P \vee R) \wedge (P \vee R)$$

Conjunctive Normal Form

The resolution rule applies only to disjunction of literals. So it would seem to be relevant only for knowledge bases and queries consisting of such disjunctions. How can then it lead to a complete inference procedure for all of propositional logic? **The answer is that every sentence of propositional logic is logically equivalent to a conjunction of disjunctions of literals. A sentence expressed as a conjunction of disjunctions of literals is said to be in a conjunctive normal form (CNF).** Every sentence can be transformed into a CNF sentence using the following steps making use of table 6.2

1. Eliminate $\leftrightarrow$ replacing $P \leftrightarrow Q$ with $(P \rightarrow Q) \wedge (Q \rightarrow P)$
2. Eliminate $\rightarrow$ replacing $P \rightarrow Q$ with $\neg P \wedge Q$.
3. CNF requires $\neg$ should appear only in literals, so we move $\neg$ inwards by repreated application of following equivalences to Table 6.2

$$\neg(\neg P) \equiv \text{Double-negation elimination}$$
$$(P \wedge Q) \equiv (\neg P \wedge \neg Q) \text{ de Morgan}$$
$$\neg(P \vee Q) \equiv (\neg P \vee \neg Q) \text{ de Morgan}$$

4. We now apply distributivity law, distributive $\vee$ over $\wedge$. whenever the sentence contains nested $\vee$ over $\wedge$ operators applied to literals.

EXAMPLE 1: Convert $((P \rightarrow Q) \rightarrow R)$ into CNF

SOLUTION: $((P \rightarrow Q) \rightarrow R)$

$$= \neg(P \rightarrow Q) \vee R$$
$$= \neg(\neg P \vee Q) \vee R$$
$$= (P \vee \neg Q) \wedge (\neg Q \vee R)$$
$$= (P \vee R) \wedge (\neg Q \vee R)$$

Hence, $(P \vee R) \wedge (\neg Q \vee R)$ is the CNF of $((P \rightarrow Q) \rightarrow R)$

We are in a position to solve some examples now.

EXAMPLE 2: Convert $(P \rightarrow Q) \rightarrow R$ to CNF?

SOLUTION: Given: $(P \rightarrow Q) \rightarrow R$

$$= (\sim P \vee Q) \rightarrow R$$
$$= \sim(\sim P \vee Q) \vee R \qquad [\because P \rightarrow Q = \sim P \vee Q]$$
$$= (P \,\&\sim Q) \vee R \qquad \text{[De Morgan's law]}$$
$$= (P \vee R) \,\&\, (\sim Q \vee R) \qquad \text{[By distributive law]}$$

Example 3: Convert $\sim (P \& Q) \& (P \vee Q)$ **to DNF?**

Solution: $(\sim P \vee \sim Q) \& (P \vee Q)$ [De Morgan's law]

$= ((\sim P \vee \sim Q) \& P) \vee ((\sim P \vee \sim Q) \& Q)$ [By distributive law]

$= (\sim P \& P) \vee (\sim Q \& P) \vee (\sim P \& Q) \vee (\sim Q \& Q)$

Example 4: Convert $\sim (P \vee \sim Q) \& (R \rightarrow S)$ **to DNF?**

Solution: $(\sim P \& Q) \& (\sim R \vee S)$ [De Morgan's law]

$= \sim (\sim ((\sim P \& Q) \& (\sim R \vee S)))$ [Negative 2 times]

$= \sim ((P \vee \sim Q) \vee (R \& \sim S))$

Example 5: Convert $P \rightarrow ((Q \& R) \leftrightarrow S)$ **to DNF?**

Solution: $F \rightarrow G = \sim F \vee G$

$\therefore$ We have —

$= (\sim P) \vee ((Q \& R) \rightarrow S$

$= (\sim P) \vee (\sim (Q \& R) \vee S) \& (\sim S \vee (Q \& R))$ [$\because P \leftrightarrow Q = (\sim P \vee Q) \& (\sim Q \vee P)$]

$= (\sim P) \vee (((\sim Q \vee \sim R) \vee S) \& ((\sim S \vee Q) \& (\sim S \vee R)))$ [Distributive law?]

$= (\sim P) \vee ((\sim Q \vee \sim R) \vee S) \& ((\sim S \vee Q) \& (\sim S \vee R)))$

Example 6: Convert $(\sim P \& Q) \vee (P \& \sim Q) \& S$ **to CNF?**

Solution: $(\sim P \& Q) \vee P \& (\sim Q \& S)$ (Associativity)

$= ((\sim P \vee P) \& (Q \vee P) \& (\sim Q \& S))$ [Distributive law]

Resolution in Propositional Logic [By Robinson]

Resolution is the process of producing proofs by refutation or contradiction. It is a procedure used for **theorem proving.** It is the rule of **inference. The procedure of resolution is as follows:**

1. Assume that the negation of the theorem which we want to prove is time.
2. Show that the axioms and the assumed negation of the theorem together cannot be true.
3. Conclude that the assumed negation of the theorem cannot be true because it leads to contradiction.
4. Conclude that the theorem must be true as the assumed negation of the theorem is not true.

Resolution is applicable only on the facts represented in clausal form. A clause is a special formula expressed as disjunction of literals. If a clause contains only one literal then it is called as a **visit clause. Please note that CNF representation of a formula is of the form** $(C_1 \wedge C_2 \wedge \ldots \wedge C_n)$ **where each** $C_k (1 \leq k \leq n)$ **is a clause**

If two clauses C_1 and C_2 contain a complementary pair of literals $\{L, \sim L\}$ then these clauses may be resolved together by deleting L from C_1 and $\sim L$ from C_2 and constructing a new clause by the disjunction of the remaining literals in C_1 and C_2. The new clause thus generated is called as **resolvent of** C_1 and C_2. Here, C_1 and C_2 are called **parents** of resolved clause. The parents can contain more than one set of complementary pair of literals. All complementary pair of literals are removed and resolvent is constructed, by the disjunction of the remaining literals in the parents.

For example : Consider two clauses

C_1 with literal $L1$ and $\sim L2$

& C_2 with literal $\sim L1$ and $L2$

i.e., $C_1 = L1 \vee \sim L2 \vee C_1'$

& $C_2 = \sim L1 \vee \sim L2 \vee C_2'$

where C_1' and C_2' are disjunction of remaining literals in C_1 and C_2 respectively

After resolving C_1 and C_2 we get

An inverted binary tree is generated with the last node of the binary tree to be a **resolvent. This is known as a Resolution tree. Resolved literals are underlined for more clarity.**

For example : Consider two clauses as

$$C_1 = P \vee Q \vee \sim R$$

& $$C_2 = \sim Q \vee W$$

$\therefore$ $P \vee \underline{Q} \vee \sim R$ $\qquad$ $\sim \underline{Q} \vee W$

$$P \vee \sim R \vee W$$

$\therefore$ Resolvent $(P \vee Q \vee \sim R, \sim Q \vee W) = P \vee \sim R \vee W$

Now, consider another example with three clauses —

$$C_1 = P \vee Q \vee R$$

$$C_2 = \sim Q \vee W$$

and $$C_3 = \sim P \vee \sim W$$

$\therefore$ $P \vee \underline{Q} \vee R$ $\qquad$ $\sim \underline{Q} \vee W$

$\underline{P} \vee \sim R \vee \underline{W}$ $\qquad$ $\sim \underline{P} \vee \sim \underline{W}$

$$R$$

∴ Resolvent R = (C_1, C_2, C_3)

Please note that the order of clauses taken for resolution is immaterial, we have to identify two clauses with complementary literals and resolve them. Take the current resolvent and try to find another clause yet not been resolved having complementary literal proceed till all the clauses have been resolved. *Also note that the resolved clauses are not used in resolution process further.*

In a similar manner, in the big system, where there are multiple clauses, all pairs of resolvable clauses are identified and resolved.

Resolution Rule: The resolution of clauses

$(A \vee B)$ and $(\neg B \vee C)$ is $A \vee C$.

Resolution works on the principle of **refutation,** i.e., it presumes that the statement to be proved is not true and then it proves that whatever we have assumed is not true and hence the original statement is true. Now let us resolve the following clause —

$\{(\neg A, B)\ (\neg A, \neg B, C), A \neg C\}$

We start by resolving the first clause with the second clause, thus eliminating B and $\neg B$ to get

$\{(\neg A, C), A, \neg C\}$

$= \{C, \neg C\}$

$= \bot$ (i.e., falsum).

∴ This resolution has resulted in a **falsum** meaning that the original clauses were inconsistent. Thus, we have refutated the original clauses using resolution.

Refutation (RR)

∴ We say that

$\{(\neg A, B), (\neg A, \neg B, C), A \neg C\} = \bot$

after *RR*.

This is how refutation helps in logical inferencing.

Let us now write an algorithm for Resolution using Propositional Logic —

Algorithm : Resolve (P, F)

Step 1: Convert all propositions of F to clausal form.

Step 2: Negate P and convert the result to clausal form. Add it to the set of clauses obtained in step 1.

Step 3: Repeat until either of the contradictions is found or no progress can be made.

(*a*) Select two clauses (called as parent clauses).

(*b*) Resolve them together to create the resolvent.

(*c*) If the resolvent is the empty clause, then a contradiction has been found.

If it is not, then add it to the set of clauses available.

Application of Resolution

Resolution cannot be used to solve **combinational search** problems but it can help us by telling whether the solution to such a problem exists or not.

For example.: **Consider a three coloring problem "Given a map, it is possible to color the countries using three colors such that no two countries that are next to each other have the some color."**

We can represent this search in form of clauses and their satisfiability can be tested using resolution. This method tells us that if a solution exists but does not tell us what that solution is. **We are in a position to solve some problems now.**

EXAMPLE 1: "If it is hot, then it is humid. If it is humid then it will rain. It is hot." Show that "It will rain".

SOLUTION: Let us denote these statements

H : It is humid

R : It will rain.

O : It is hot.

$\therefore$ Formulae corresponding to given sentences are —

If it is hot, then it is humid i.e., $O \rightarrow \mathrm{H} \cong \sim O \vee H$

If it is humid, then it will rain i.e., $H \rightarrow \mathrm{R} \cong \sim Q \vee R$

Construct a set, S, of clauses from above set of statements as given below —

$$S = \{\sim O \vee H, \sim H \vee R, O\}$$

Include negation of "It will rain (say R)" to the set, S.

$$\therefore \quad S' = \{\sim O \vee H, \sim H \vee R, O, \sim R\}$$

Now, we can show that S' *is* unsatisfiable, i.e., from S' one can deduce empty clause, then we can infer or conclude that 'It will rain'.

$\therefore$ The resolution tree is —

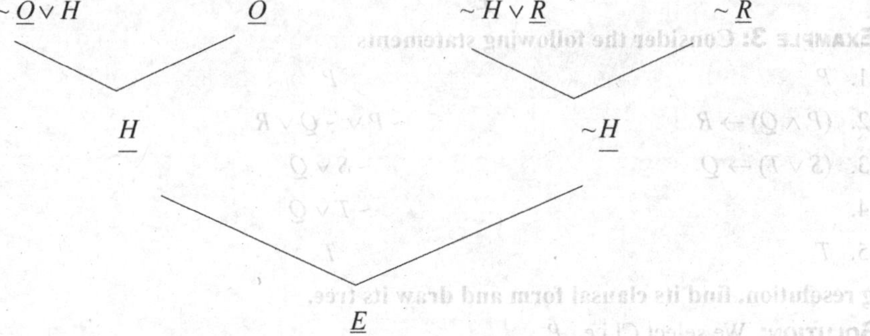

$\therefore$ an empty clause (E) is deduced from a set, S', "It will rain" is concluded from S.

EXAMPLE 2: Consider the following statements —

$$A \rightarrow B$$
$$B \rightarrow C$$
$$C \rightarrow D$$
$$\mathrm{D} \rightarrow EVF$$
$$A \rightarrow F.$$

Using resolution, find its clausal from and draw its tree.

SOLUTION: Firstly, we negate the conclusion

$A \rightarrow F$, i.e., we get $\neg(\mathrm{A} \rightarrow F)$.

Next, $D \rightarrow E \vee F$

$\equiv \neg D \vee (E \vee F)$

& $\neg(A \rightarrow F) \equiv \neg(\neg A \vee F)$

$\equiv A \wedge \neg F$

$\therefore$ Our clauses are, $\mathrm{S} = \{(\neg A, B), (\neg B, C), (\neg C, D), (\neg \underline{D}, E, F), (A \neg F)\}$

and our proof in tree form will be —

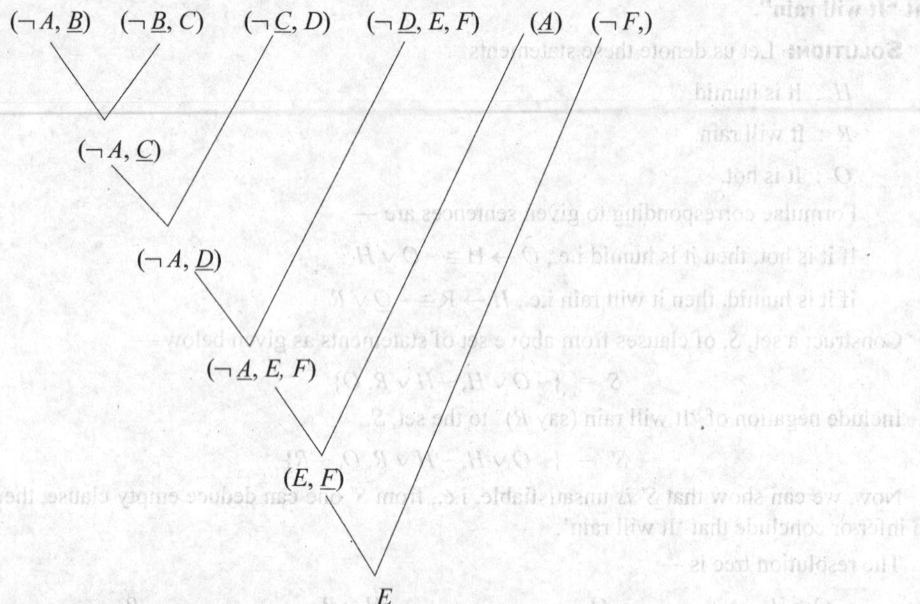

EXAMPLE 3: Consider the following statements

1. P	P
2. $(P \wedge Q) \rightarrow R$	$\sim P \vee \sim Q \vee R$
3. $(S \vee T) \rightarrow Q$	$\sim S \vee Q$
4.	$\sim T \vee Q$
5. T	T

Using resolution, find its clausal form and draw its tree.

SOLUTION: We select Cl i.e., P

and then negate $\sim R$.

Now select ($C2$) clauses as

$\sim P \vee \sim Q \vee R$.

∴ We have two clauses as—

$C1 : \sim \text{R}$

$C2 : \sim P \vee \sim Q \vee R$

∴ Resolvent will be $\sim P \vee \sim Q$.

Here, we have proved R. We should always select those pairs that can be resolved very easily. Now, prove P. We negate $\sim P$ to P.

$C1 : \sim P \vee \sim Q$

$C2 : P$

Resolvent is $\sim Q$.

Now prove T. Select $\sim T \vee R$

$C1 : \sim Q$

$C2 : \sim T \vee Q$

∴ Resolvent is $\sim T$.

At last we have $C1$ as T and $C2$ as $\sim T$. It is left empty which is a contradiction.

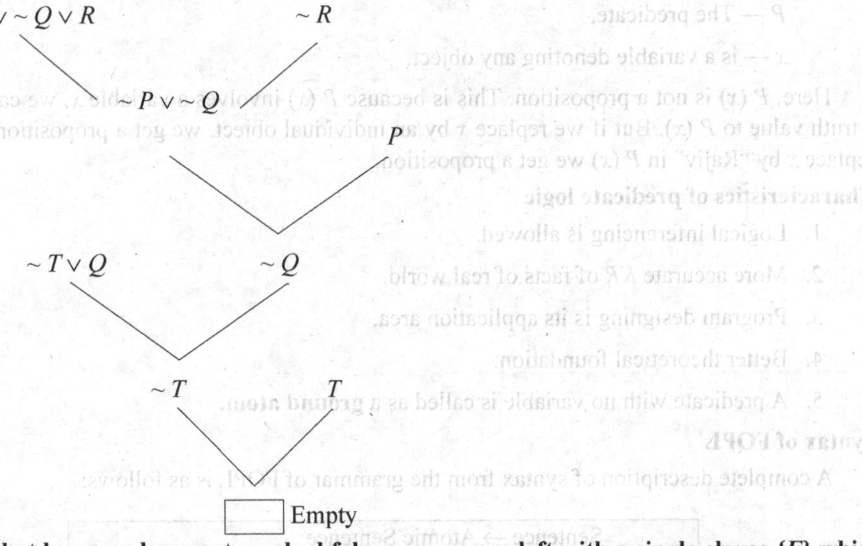

Note that here, we have not reached falsum as we are left with a single clause {*E*} which cannot be resolved with anything now. Hence, we can conclude that our original conclusion was not valid.

Limitations of Propositional Logic

A very serious limitation of propositional logic is that common elements within propositions cannot be used to make inference.

For example.,

Consider the following statements in propositional logic.

S_1 : Rajiv is an author of 12 books.

S_2 : Rajiv is assistant professor.

S_3 : All professors are authors

Now, from S_1, S_2 and S_3 we cannot conclude that all professors are authors because this method of representation fails in capturing the relationship between any individual. Propositional logic lacks in expressiveness which is very vital for good KR. Propositional logic is too coarse to easily describe properties of objects. We cannot make generalized statements.

So, we go to predicate logic.

4.2 PREDICATE LOGIC & ITS RESOLUTION

We are interested in a form of predicate logic called as **first order predicate logic.** FOPL allows the quantified variables to refer to object domain and not to predicates or functions. If the quantification is over first order predicates and functions then it becomes **second order predicate.** Similarly, third order predicate allows quantification over predicates and function of second order and so on. A.I. researchers have found that FOPL is most suitable for KR.

Every complete sentence contains two parts — **a subject** and a **predicate.**

Subject: The subject is what (or whom) the sentence is about.

Predicate: It tells something about the subject.

For example. In the sentence, 'Rajiv is an author' subject is 'Rajiv' and predicate is 'author'.

Sentences involving the predicates that describe the property of objects are denoted by *P* (*x*) where

P — The predicate,

x — is a variable denoting any object.

Here, *P* (*x*) is not a proposition. This is because *P* (*x*) involves a variable *x*, we cannot assign a truth value to *P* (*x*). But if we replace *x* by an individual object, we get a proposition, like if we replace *x* by "Rajiv" in *P* (*x*) we get a proposition.

Characteristics of predicate logic

1. Logical inferencing is allowed.
2. More accurate *KR* of facts of real world.
3. Program designing is its application area.
4. Better theoretical foundation.
5. A predicate with no variable is called as a **ground atom.**

Syntax of FOPL

A complete description of syntax from the grammar of FOPL is as follows:

Sentence → Atomic Sentence

| (Sentence Connective Sentence)

| (Quantifier variable … Sentence)

| (¬sentence)

Atomic Sentence → Predicate (Term…) | Term = Term

Term → Function (Term…)

| Constant

| Variable

Connective → ⇒ | ∧ | ∨ | ⇒

Quantifier → ∀ | ∃

Constant → a | X_1 | John | …

Variable → a | x | s |

Predicate → Before | HasColour | Raining | …

Function → Mother | LeftLeg

NOTE: Predicate calculus symbols are irreducible syntactic elements just as we have tokens in programming language.

Rules for predicate calculus symbols —

1. Set of letters (uppercase or lowercase) is allowed.
2. Set of digits (0 to 9) is allowed.
3. Underscore (_) is allowed.

But,

1. Blanks and non-alphanumeric characters cannot be used.
2. Special characters like $, *, #, /, are not allowed.

For example.

Valid symbols	Invalid symbols
white	2black
son-of	Ab % b
father-of	**3
Rajiv	— parrot

> **NOTE:** Parentheses, commas and periods are used to construct well formed structure but do not denote objects or relations in the world. These are known as **improper symbols.**

Symbols used

1. **Predicate symbols:** They denote relations or functional mapping from the elements of a domain to the values true or false

   For example.

   Brother, king, LOVE, GREATER, EQUAL, MARRIES etc.

2. **Function symbols:** They denote relations defined on a domain. **For example.** Father of, Age of, plus etc.

3. **Variable symbols:** Lowercase unsubscripted or subscripted letters like *x, y, z, t, u, v* etc.

   They can assume different values over a given domain.

4. **Constants:** They are fixed value terms. They are individual symbols which are names of objects like john, rajiv, 1, 2, 3, *a*, *b*, *c* etc.

5. **Quantifiers:** They are of two types —

   (*a*) ∃ **(or existential quantifier)** where (∃*x*) means for some *x* or there is no *x*

   (*b*) ∀ **(or universal quantifier)** where (∀*x*) means for all *x*.

   We will discuss about it a bit later.

6. **Logical Operators / Connectives:** FOPL uses the same five connectives of PL i.e.

   ~ (not), ∧ (and), ∨ (or), → (implication) and ↔ (equivalence).

   Please note that function and predicate symbols take a specified number of arguments. If they take n arguments then it is called as n-place function and predicate respectively. Also note that constants, variables and functions are referred to as terms.

   Predicates are referred to as atomic formulas or atoms.

Precedence of operators & quantifiers

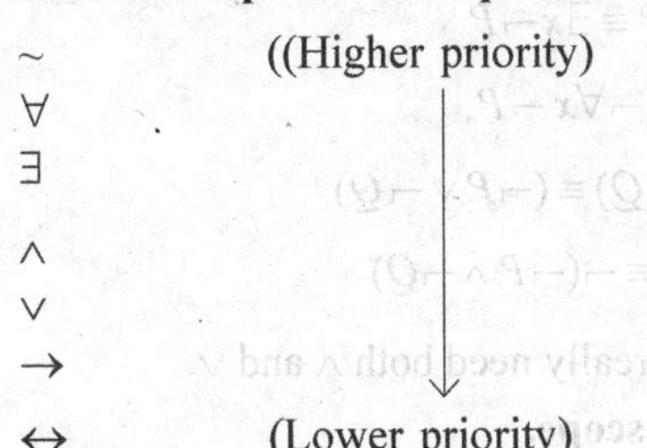

Quantifiers {∀, ∃} have same priorities as ~ and parentheses have highest priorities.

Using quantifiers

(*a*) **Universal quantifier (∀)**

It is used to represent the phrase **'for all'**. It says that something is true for all possible values of a variable.

For example. (*a*) John loves everyone

In predicate calculus, we write it as

$(\forall x)$ *LOVE* (john, x)

(*b*) for all $n, x^n = x \cdot x \cdot x \ldots x$-times is written as $\forall x\ \forall n\ Q(x, n)$ where

(*b*) **Existential quantifier ($\exists x$):**

It is used to represent the Phrase '**there exist.**' It indicates that the variable is time for at least one interpretation.

For example. (*a*) "There exists x such that $x^3 = 8$." is written as —

$\exists x$: R(x). Where R(x) is $x^3 = 8$.

(*b*) Lord Ram has a crown on his head.

$\exists$x Crown (x) $\wedge$ On head (x, Ram)

NOTE: ($\forall$) uses $\rightarrow$ connective whereas $\exists$ uses $\wedge$ connective

(*c*) **Nested quantifiers:**

We can use both $\forall$ and $\exists$ quantifiers separately.

For example. 'Brothers are siblings' can be written as —

$\forall x\ \forall y$ Brother (x, y) $\rightarrow$ Sibling (x, y)

or $\forall x, y$ sibling (x, y) $\leftrightarrow$ sibling (y, x)

Example 2: 'Everybody loves somebody' can be written as —

$\forall x\ fy$ loves (x, y)

or $Q(x, n) = x^n$.

Connection between $\forall$ and $\exists$

The two quantifiers are actually intimately connected to each other, through negation. Saying that everyone dislikes garlic is the same as saying that there does not exist someone who likes the garlic:

$\forall x \neg$ likes (x Garlic) $= \neg \exists x$ likes (x, Garlic)

We can go one step further: "Everyone likes ice cream" means that there is no one who does not like ice cream:

$\forall x$ likes (x, Ice Cream) $= \neg \neg \exists x$ likes (x, Ice Cream)

Because $\forall$ is really a conjunction over the universe of objects and $\exists$ is a disjunction, it should not be surprising that they obey de Morgan's rules. The de Morgan rules for quantified and unquantified sentences are:

1. $\forall x \neg P \equiv \neg \exists x P$
2. $\neg \forall x P \equiv \exists x \neg P$
3. $\forall x P \equiv \neg \exists x \neg P$
4. $\exists x P \equiv \neg \forall x \neg P$
5. $\neg P \wedge \neg Q \equiv \neg (P \vee Q)$
6. $\neg (P \wedge Q) \equiv (\neg P \vee \neg Q)$
7. $P \wedge Q \equiv \neg(\neg P \vee \neg Q)$
8. $P \vee Q \equiv \neg(\neg P \wedge \neg Q)$

Thus, we do not really need both $\forall$ and $\exists$ as we do not really need both $\wedge$ and $\vee$.

The range over which a variable is valid is called its scope.

For example. $(\forall x)$ (MAN (x) $\rightarrow$ Mortal (x))

Here, scope of $(\forall\ x)$ is (MAN (x) $\rightarrow$ Mortal (x))

An occurrence of a variable x in a formula is said to be **bound** if and only if the occurrence is within the scope of a quantifier employing the variable x, else a variable is said to be **free.**

For example. In $(\forall x)\ P(x, y)$

x is bound

and y is free

Example 2: In $(\exists x)(\forall y)\ P(x, y) \wedge Q(x)$

x and y are bound in $P(x, y)$ x is free in $Q(x)$ *as* $Q(x)$ is outside the scope of $(\exists x)$ and $(\forall y)$.

A formula is said to be **closed** if there are no free occurrence of any variable in it.

For example. $(\exists x)(\forall y)(P(x, y) \wedge Q(x))$ is a closed formula

whereas $(\forall y)\ P(x, y)$ is not.

We are in a position to solve some problems now.

EXAMPLE 1: Represent the following facts in predicate logic —

(*a*) **Snow is white.**

(*b*) **Marcus was a man.**

(*c*) **Marcus was a Pompeian.**

(*d*) **All Pompeians were Romans.**

(*e*) **Caesar was a ruler.**

(*f*) **All Romans were either loyal to Caesar or hated him.**

(*g*) **Everyone is legal to someone.**

(*h*) **Marcus tried to assassinate Caesar.**

(*i*) **If it rains then sky will be cloudy.**

(*j*) **If you will not work hard, you will fail.**

SOLUTION: (*a*) Snow (white).

(*b*) Man (Marcus).

(*c*) Pompeian (Marcus)

(*d*) $\forall x$: Pompeian $(x) \rightarrow$ Roman (x)

(*e*) Ruler (Caesar)

(*f*) $\forall x$: Roman $(x) \rightarrow$ loyal to $(x$, Caesar$) \vee$ hate x, (Caesar)

(*g*) $\forall x\ \exists y$ loyalto (x, y)

(*h*) tryassassinate (Marcus, Caesar).

(*i*) raining $\rightarrow$ cloudy (sky)

(*j*) $\neg$ Workhard $\rightarrow$ fail

EXAMPLE 2: Write the predicate forms of the following —

(*a*) **All indoor games are easy.**

(*b*) **Rajiv only likes cricket game.**

(*c*) **All dogs are mammals.**

(*d*) **Roses are red.**

(*e*) **John is father of Bob.**

SOLUTION: (*a*) $\forall x$ indoor game $(x) \rightarrow$ easy (x)

(*b*) likes (rajiv, cricket)

(*c*) $\forall x$ dog $(x) \rightarrow$ Mammal (x)

(*d*) red (roses)

(*e*) father (john, bob).

EXAMPLE 3: Given formulas S_1 and S_2 below. Show that Q (*a*) is a logical consequence of the two –

$S_1 : (\forall x) (P(x) \rightarrow Q(x))$

$S_2 : P(a)$

SOLUTION: As $(\forall x) (P(x \rightarrow Q(x))$

Now, $x = a$ in S_2

i.e., $Q(a)$ is a logical consequence of the two statements S_1 and S_2.

EXAMPLE 4: Translate the following statements in FOPL—

(*i*) All empolyees earning more than Rs. 60,000 per year pay income tax.

(*ii*) No employee of University earns more than the VC.

(*iii*) Only old people get sick.

(*iv*) All men are people.

(*v*) All Pompeians were Romans.

(*vi*) All Romans were either loyal to Caesar or hated him.

(*vii*) People only try to assassinate rulers they are not loyal to.

(*viii*) Everyone is loyal to someone.

(*ix*) It is now 2013.

(*x*) Mohan has exactly two friends.

(*xi*) American vegetarians do not take milk but Indian vegetarians do.

(*xii*) For every natural number, there is a natural number greater than it.

(*xiii*) Nothing beautiful is evil.

(*xiv*) Some highly qualified scientists are unemployed in Russia but in America all qualified scientists are employed.

SOLUTION: (*a*) For all *x*, if *x* is an employee and *x* earns more than 60,000, *x* pay tax.

Let employee be EMPLOYEE and pay tax be TAX.

Then, we get—

$\forall x$: ((EMPLOYEE (x) & GE ($i(x)$, 60,000) $\rightarrow$ TAX(x)).

(*b*) Let employees $= x$

and $VC = y$

For all *x* and for all *y*, if *x* is employee and *y* is *VC* then *x* cannot earn more than *y*.

$\therefore \quad \forall xy\, ((E(x)\ \&\ P(y) \rightarrow \sim GE(i(x), i(y)).$

(*c*) There exists some *x*, if *x* is people and *x* is old,

Let people be $P(x)$,

Old be $O(x)$,

Sick be $S(x)$

$\therefore$ We get—

$\exists x: (P(x)\ \&\ O(x) \rightarrow S(x))$

(*d*) For all x, if x is men, x is people.

Let Men $\rightarrow$ MEN

People $\rightarrow$ PEOPLE

$\therefore \quad \forall x$: MEN $(x) \rightarrow$ PEOPLE(x)

(*e*) For all x, if x is Pompeians, x were Romans.

$\forall x$: Pompeian $(x) \rightarrow$ Roman (x)

(*f*) For all x, if x were Romans, x were loyal to Caesar or x hated him.

$\therefore \quad \forall x$: Roman $(x) \rightarrow$ LOYAL $(x$, Caesar$) \vee$ HATE $(x$, Caesar$)$

(*g*) $\forall xy$: PEOPLE$(x) \wedge$ RULER$(y) \wedge$ ASSASSINATE $(x, y) \rightarrow \sim$ LOYAL, To (x, y)

(*h*) For all x, x is loyal to y.

$\forall x : \exists y$: Loyal (x, y)

(*i*) now = 2013

(*j*) Let $E(x)$ where x is a person,

$M(x)$ where x is a Mohan.

$F(x)$ x has friend.

a for 2 as constant

$\therefore \quad \forall x\ (M(x) \rightarrow F(a, x))$

(*k*) Let $E(x) - x$ is vegetarian.

$A(x) - x$ is American.

$I(x) - x$ is Indian.

$M(x) - x$ takes milk.

$\sim M(x) - x$ do not take milk.

$\therefore \quad \exists x\ (E(x)\ \&\ A(x) \rightarrow \sim M(x))$

$\exists x\ (E(x)\ \&\ I(x) \rightarrow M(x))$

(*l*) For all x and y, if x is natural number and y is natural number, y is greater than x.

Let $N(x)$ be x as natural number,

$N(y)$, y is a natural number.

$G(x, y)$, x is greater than y.

$\forall x, y\ (N(x)\ \&\ N(y) \rightarrow a\ (y, x))$

(*m*) For every x, if x is nothing beautiful, x is evil.

$\forall x\ (\sim B(x) \rightarrow E(x))$.

This can also be written as—

For every x, if x is nothing and x is not beautiful, x is evil.

$\forall x : (\sim B(x) \rightarrow N(x) \rightarrow E(x))$

where $B(x)$, x is beautiful. $N(x)$, x is nothing.

$E(x)$, x is evil.

(*n*) Let us denote the following—

$S(x) : x$ is highly qualified scientist

$A(x) : x$ is American (scientist in America)

$R(x) : x$ is Russian (scientist in Russia)

$E(x) : x$ is employed.

$\sim E(x) : x$ is not employed

$\therefore \quad \forall x : (S(x) \;\&\; A(x) \rightarrow E(x))$

$\exists x\, (S(x) \;\&\; R(x) \rightarrow E(x))$

EXAMPLE 5: Convert into FOPL statements:

(*i*) If x is connected to y by z, y is connected to x by z.

(*ii*) If you can get to y from z and you can get to z from y, you can get to z from x.

(*iii*) If x is connected to town y by highway z and bicycles are allowed on z, you can get to y by bike from x.

(*iv*) Town A is connected to Town B by Road 1.

(*v*) Apples are food.

(*vi*) Bill eats peanuts and is still alive.

(*vii*) Bill is brother of SUE.

(*viii*) All Pompeians died when volcano erupted in 79 A.D.

(*ix*) All men are mortal.

(*x*) Town–A and Town–E are not connected by Road 3.

(*xi*) Bikes are allowed on road-3, road-4 and road-5.

SOLUTION: (*i*) $\forall x, y, z : (\text{CONNECTED}\ (x, y, z) \rightarrow \text{CONNECTED}\ (y, x, z))$

(*ii*) $\forall x, y, z : (\text{GETTO}\ (z, y) \text{ and } \text{GETTO}\ (y, z) \rightarrow \text{GETTO}\ (x, z))$

(*iii*) $\forall x, y, z\ (\text{CONNECTED}\ (x, y, z) \text{ and } \text{BIKE}\ (z) \rightarrow \text{GETTO}\ (x, y))$

(*iv*) $\forall a, b$ road-1 CONNECTED (a, b, road 1)

(*v*) For all x, if x is apple, x is food.

$A(x) : x$ is apple.

$F(x) : x$ is food.

$\therefore\ \forall x : (A(x) \rightarrow F(x))$

(*vi*) $B(x) : x$ is bill.

$P(x) : x$ eats peanuts.

$A(x) : x$ is alive.

$\therefore\ \forall x : (B(x) \rightarrow P(x) \;\&\; A(x))$

(*vii*) Brother (Bill, Sue)

(*viii*) Erupted (volcano, 79) $\wedge\ \forall x$ [Pompeian (x) $\rightarrow$ died (x, 79)]

(*ix*) For all x if x is men, x is mortal.

(*x*) If x is town A and y is town B, x and y are not connected by road-3.

$\therefore\ \forall x, y, z : \sim \text{CONNECTED}\ (x, y, z)$ or

$\forall x, y, z : (\text{Town}\ (x) \;\&\; \text{Town}\ (y) \rightarrow \sim \text{CONNECTED}\ (x, y, z)$

(*xi*) $\forall x : \text{BIKE}\ (x)$

$\forall y : \text{BIKE}\ (y)$

$\forall z : \text{BIKE}\ (z)$.

Inferencing in predicate logic

The rules of inference for the propositional formulas are applicable to predicate calculus. So propositional formulas are also predicate formulas. We have to just replace propositional variables by predicate variables.

For example.

1. $\exists x(P(x) \vee Q(x)) \equiv \exists x\, P(x) \vee \exists x\, Q(x)$
2. $\exists x(P \vee Q(x)) \equiv P \vee (\exists x\, Q(x))$
3. $\forall x(P(x) \wedge Q(x)) \equiv \forall x\, P(x) \wedge \forall x\, Q(x)$
4. $\forall x\,(P \wedge Q(x)) \equiv P \wedge (\forall x\, Q\,(x))$
5. $\neg(\exists x\, P(x)) \equiv \forall x \neg\,(p\,(x))$
6. $\forall x\, P(x) \Rightarrow \exists x\, P(x)$
7. $\neg(\exists\, x\, P(x)) \equiv \exists x \neg\, P(x))$

We are in a position to solve some problems now.

Q. 1. Represent the following in symbol logic:

(*a*) All that glitters is not gold.

(*b*) Any person who is respected by every person is a king.

(*c*) God helps those who help themselves.

(*d*) Jack and Jill went up the hill.

(*e*) Ram likes Sita.

Ans. (*a*) $\neg\forall x$ Glitters $(x) \rightarrow$ Gold

(*b*) $\exists x \forall y$ King (x)

(*c*) $\forall x$ helps (God, helps (x, x))

(*d*) together (went up (jack), went up (jill) $\rightarrow$ hill

(*e*) likes (Ram, Sita)

Resolution in Predicate Logic

In predicate logic, we need to compare the arguments of the literals also. In predicate logic, the existential and universal quantifiers are used. We do **skolemisation for that skolemisation is removing existential quantifiers and replacing the corresponding variable by a constant or a function.** A constant or a function is called as **skolem constant or function** respectively.

Reşolution Steps

It requires that all statements be converted into a nonmalized clausal form. Its procedure is given below:

Step 1: Eliminate all implication and equivalency connectives (use $\sim P \vee Q$ in place of $P \rightarrow Q$ and $(\sim P \vee Q)$ and $(\sim Q \vee P)$ in place of $(P \leftrightarrow Q)$

Step 2: Move all negations in, to the immediately preceding atom. Use P in place of $\sim(\sim P)$ and De Morgans's Law, $\exists x \sim F[x]$ in place of $\sim(\forall x) F(x)$ and $\forall x \sim F[x]$ in place of $\sim(\exists x)(F[x])$.

Step 3: Rename Variables, if necessary, so that all quantifiers have different variable assignments, i.e., rename variables so that variables bound by one quantifier are not the same as variables bound by a different quantifier.

For example.: In the expression $\forall x(P(x)) \rightarrow (\exists x(Q(x)))$

rename the second "**dummy**" variable x which is bound by the existential quantifier to be a different variable, say y, to give $\forall x (P(x) \rightarrow (\exists y\, Q(y)))$.

Step 4: **The process of eliminating the existential quantifiers through a substitution process requires that all such variables be replaced by something called "Skolem functions" which are the arbitrary functions which can always assume a correct value required for an existentially quantified variable. In this 4th step we skolemize by replacing all existentially quantified variables with skolem functions.**

Step 5: Move all universal quantifiers to the left of the expression and put the expression on the right into CNF.

Step 6: Eliminate all universal quantifiers and conjunctions since they are retained implicitly. The resulting expressions are 'clauses' and the set of such expressions is said to be in clausal form.

EXAMPLE. Convert the expression: $\exists x\, \forall y\, (\forall z\, P(f(x), y, z)$

into clausal form: $\rightarrow (\exists u\, Q(x, u)$ **and** $\exists v\, R(y, v)))$

SOLUTION.

Step 1: Applying step (1):

$\exists x\, \forall y\, (\sim (\forall z)\, P(f(x), y, z) \vee (\exists u\, Q(x, u) \text{ and } (\exists v)\, R(y, v)))) \; (\exists v)\, R(y, v))))$

$[\because F \rightarrow G = \sim F \vee G]$

Step 2: Applying step (2) we get —

$\exists x \forall y\, (\exists z \sim P(f(x), y, z) \vee (\exists u\, Q(x, u) \text{ and } (\exists v)\, R(y, v))) \; (\exists v)\, R(y, v)))$

Step 3: Step (3) is not required.

Step 4: $\forall y\, (\sim P(f(a), y, g(y)) \vee (Q(a, h(y)) \text{ and } R(y, I(y)))$

[$\because$ u exists as an existential quantifier, x **exists as an existential quantifier and so does v.** So, in this step, we need to remove them and this can be done by replacing x with a, u with $h(y)$ and v with $I(x)$.]

Step 5: After applying step 5, the result is

$\underbrace{\forall y\, ((\sim P(f(a), y, g(y)) \vee Q(a, h(y))}_{F_1} \text{ and } (\sim P(f(a), y\, g(y)) \vee R(y, I(y)))$

Step 6: After application of step 6 we obtain:

$\sim P(f(a), y, g(y)) \vee Q(a, h(y))$

$\sim P(f(a), y, g(y) \vee R(y, I(y))$

Thus, given FOPL sentence has been converted into clausal form.

Inference Rules in FOPL

Like *PL*, a key inference rule in FOPL is modus porens. *For example*.:

Assertion: *LION* (*leo*)

Implication: $\forall x$ *LION* $(x) \rightarrow$ *FE ROCIOUS* (x)

Conclusion: *Ferocious* (*leo*)

Representation using rules

Rules can be considered as a subset of predicate logic. They have become a popular representation scheme for expert systems (also called as rule-based systems). They were first used in general problem solver (GPS) system in early (1970s). **Rules have two component parts: a LHS referred**

to as the antecedent, premise, condition or situation and a RHS known as the consequent conclusion, action or response. LHS is also known as the if part and the RHS as the then part of the rule. Some rules also include an also part. Examples of such rules are:

IF : The temperature is greater than 95°C.

THEN: Open the relief valve.

These rules are stored in KB. The interpreter or inference engine inspects the LHS of each rule in KB and replaces the contents of working memory by the RHS of the rule. **We are in a position to solve some examples now.**

Q. 1. Resolve the following example wff into its clausal form.

$$(\forall x)\{P(x) \rightarrow \{(\forall y)[P(y) \rightarrow P(f(x,y))] \wedge \sim (\forall y)[Q(x,y) \rightarrow p(y)]\}\}$$

Ans. S1: Eliminate implication symbols — all occurrences of the → symbol in a wff are eliminated by making the substitution $\sim X1 \vee X2$ for $X1 \rightarrow X2$ throughout the wff. So, this substitution yields:

$$(\forall x)\{\sim P(x) \vee \{(\forall y)[\sim P(y) \vee P(f(x,y))] \wedge \sim (\forall y)[\sim Q(x,y) \vee p(y)]\}\}$$

S2: Reduce Scopes of negation symbols — We want each negation symbol, ~, to apply to at most one atomic formula. By making use of de Morgan's laws we get:

$$(\forall x)\{\sim P(x) \vee \{(\forall y)[\sim P(y) \vee P(f(x,y))] \wedge (\forall y)[Q(x,y) \wedge \sim p(y)]\}\}$$

S3: Standardize variables — Instead of writing, $(\forall x)[P(x) \rightarrow (\exists x)\, Q(x)]$, we write

$$(\forall x)[P(x) \rightarrow (\exists y)\, Q(y)]$$

i.e., one type of dummy variable should be used with each type of quantifier. So in our wff, x-variable (dummy viz.) is used with universal (∀) quantifier whereas y is used with Existential quantifier (∃). Standardizing our example wff yields:

$$(\forall x)\left\{\sim P(x) \vee \left\{(\forall y)[\sim P(y) \vee P(f(x,y))] \wedge (\exists w)[Q(x,w) \wedge \sim P(w)]\right\}\right\}$$

S4: Eliminate existential quantifiers — Consider the wff : $(\forall y)[(\exists x)\, P(x,y)]$ which might be read as "for all y, there exists an x (possibly depending on y) such that $P(x,y)$." Note that because existential quantifier is within the scope of a universal quantifier, we allow the possiblity that value x that exists might depend on the value of y. Let this dependence be explicitly defined by some function $P(x,y)$. which maps each value of y into x that "exists". Such a function is called a **skolem function**. If we use the skolem function in place of the x that exists, we can eliminate the existential quantifier 'all' together and write $(\forall y)\, P[g(y), y]$.

NOTE. If the existential quantifier being eliminated is not within the scope of any universal quantifiers, we use a skolem function of no arguments, which is just a constant. Thus, $(\exists x)\, P(x)$ becomes $P(A)$ where the constant symbol A is used to refer to the entity that we know exists.

Eliminating all existentially quantified variables from given (there is just one) in our wff yields:

$$(\forall x)\{\sim P(x) \vee \{\forall y)[\sim P(y) \vee P(f(x,y))] \vee [Q(x, g(x)) \wedge \sim P(g(x))]\}\}$$

where $\boxed{w = g(x)}$; $g(x)$ is a skolem function.

S5: Convert to prenex form — We may now move all of the universal quantifiers to the front of the wff. The resulting wff is said to be in **prenex form**. So we get:

$$(\forall x)(\forall y)\{\sim P(x) \vee \{[\sim P(y) \vee P(f(x,y))] \wedge [Q(x, g(a)) \wedge \sim P(g(x))]\}$$

S6: Put the matrix in CNF—We may put any matrix into CNF by repeatedly using one of the distributive rules, i.e.,

$$\times 1 \vee (\times 2 \wedge \times 3) \text{ by } (\times 1 \vee \times 2) \wedge (\times 1 \vee \times 3).$$

So, our equation wff becomes:

$$(\forall x)(\forall y)\{[\sim P(x) \vee \sim P(y) \vee P(f(x, y))] \wedge [\sim P(x) \vee Q(x, g(x))] \wedge [\sim P(x) \vee p(g(x))]\}$$

S7: Eliminate universal quantifiers—We get:

$$\sim P(x) \vee \sim P(y) \vee P(f(x, y)) \wedge [\sim p(x) \vee Q(x, g(x))] \wedge [\sim P(x) \vee \sim P(g(x))]$$

S8: Eliminate $\wedge$ symbols—We get

$$\left.\begin{array}{l} \sim P(x) \vee \sim P(y) \vee P[f(x, y)], \\ \sim P(x) \vee Q[x, g(x)], \\ \sim P(x) \vee \sim P[g(x)] \end{array}\right\} \text{is required clausal form}$$

Q. 2. Show the validity of the following sentences."All men are mortal. John is a man. Therefore John is mortal."

$$(\forall x)\{P(x) \rightarrow \{(\forall y)[P(y) \rightarrow P(f(x, y))] \wedge \sim (\forall y)[Q(x, y) \rightarrow p(y)]\}\}$$

Ans. Say,

MAN (x)— x is a man.

MORTAL (x)— x is mortal.

In *FOPL*, we have

$$((\forall x)(\text{MAN}(x) \rightarrow \text{MORTAL}(x)) \wedge \text{MAN(John)}) \rightarrow \text{MORTAL(John)}$$

Convert it to Skolem form —

$$\propto : \sim ((\text{MAN}(x) \vee \text{MORTAL}(x)) \wedge \text{MAN(John)}) \vee \text{MORTAL(John)}$$

If we show that $\sim\propto$ is unsatisfiable then $\propto$ is valid.

$$\sim \propto : (\sim \text{MAN}(x) \vee \text{MORTAL}(x)) \wedge \text{MAN(John)} \wedge \sim \text{MORTAL(John)}$$

$\therefore$ A set of clauses, S, that can be obtained from $\sim\propto$ is —

$$S = \{\sim \text{MAN}(x) \vee \text{MORTAL}(x), \text{MAN(John)}, \sim \text{MORTAL(John)}\}$$

If we show that S is unsatisfiable then $\sim\propto$ is also unsatisfiable and hence $\propto$ is valid. In tree form,

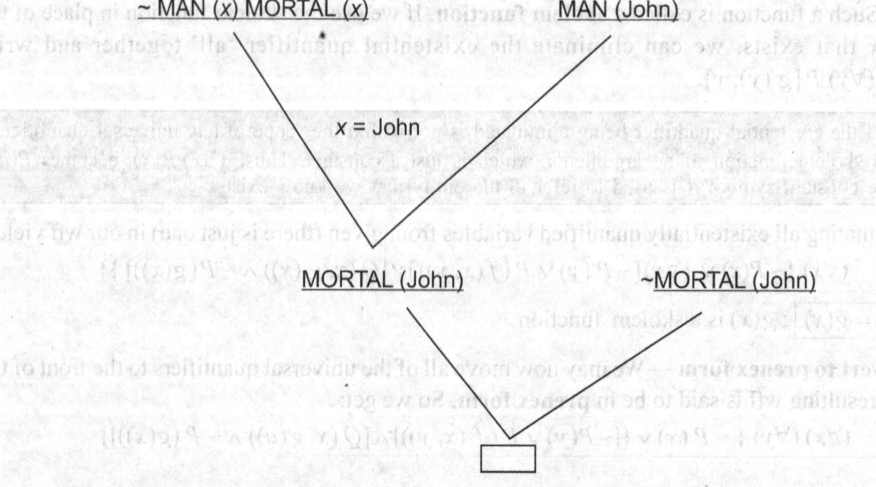

Q. 3. Given the following predicates, show how resolution process can be applied to resolve —

$T: P \vee Q \vee R \quad U: \sim P \vee R \quad V: \sim Q \quad W: \sim R$

Ans. The resolution tree is —

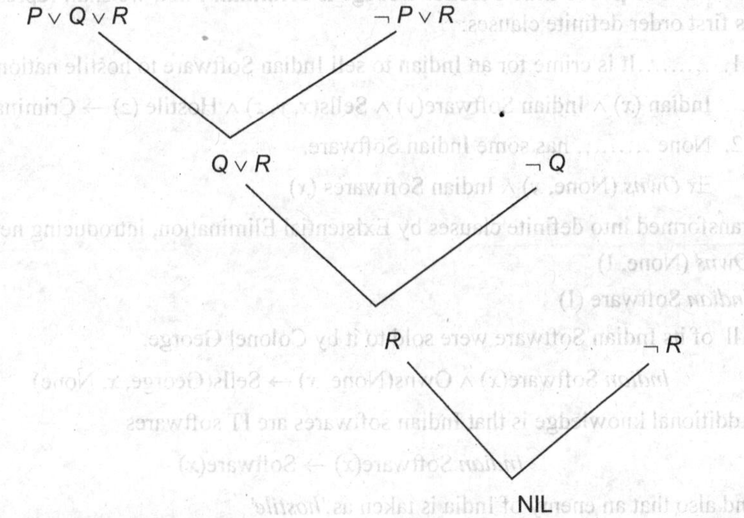

Q. 4. Consider the following axioms —

$P, (P \wedge Q) \rightarrow R, (S \vee T) \rightarrow Q, T$

Prove that *R* is true by resolution.

Ans. We negate the goal, i.e., we negate *R*, i.e, $\neg R$. We apply resolution now —

We convert the given axioms into clausal form —

1. P 2. $\neg P \vee \neg Q \vee R$ 3. $\neg S \vee Q$ 4. $\neg T \vee Q$ 5. T

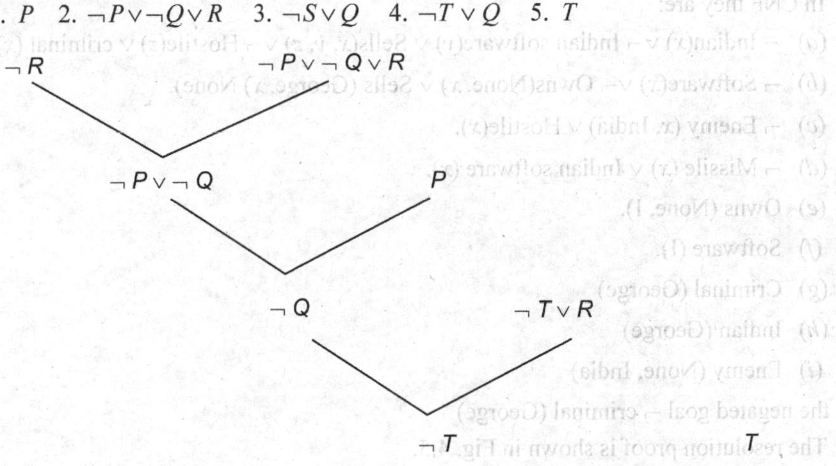

Q. 5. Consider the following problem:

The law says that it is crime for an Indian to sell Indian Software to hostile nations. The country, named None, an enemy of India has some Indian software and all its software were sold to it by Colonel George who is an Indian. Give its resolution proof.

Ans. We want to prove that Colonel George is criminal. First, we shall represent these facts as first order definite clauses:

1. ....It is crime for an Indian to sell Indian Software to hostile nations.

   Indian $(x) \wedge$ Indian Software$(y) \wedge$ Sells$(x, y, z) \wedge$ Hostile $(z) \rightarrow$ Criminal (x)

2. None .... has some Indian Software.

   $\exists x$ *Owns* (None, x) $\wedge$ Indian Softwares (x)

which is transformed into definite clauses by Existential Elimination, introducing new constant I

Owns (None, I)

Indian Software (I)

3. All of its Indian Software were sold to it by Colonel George.

   Indian Software$(x) \wedge$ Owns(None, x) $\rightarrow$ Sells(George, x, None)

   Additional knowledge is that Indian softwares are IT softwares

   Indian Software$(x) \rightarrow$ Software(x)

   and also that an enemy of India is taken as '*hostile*'

   Enemy(x, India) $\rightarrow$ Hostile(x)

4. *George who is an Indian ....*

   Indian (George)

5. The country None, an enemy of India ....

   Enemy (None, India)

In CNF they are:

(*a*) $\neg$ Indian$(x) \vee \neg$ Indian software$(y) \vee$ Sells$(x, y, z) \vee \neg$ Hostile$(z) \vee$ criminal (x).

(*b*) $\neg$ Software$(x) \vee \neg$ Owns(None, x) $\vee$ Sells (George, x) None).

(*c*) $\neg$ Enemy (x, India) $\vee$ Hostile(x).

(*d*) $\neg$ Missile $(x) \vee$ Indian software (x).

(*e*) Owns (None, I).

(*f*) Software (I).

(*g*) Criminal (George)

(*h*) Indian (George)

(*i*) Enemy (None, India)

and the negated goal $\neg$ criminal (George)

The resolution proof is shown in Fig. 4.5.

This knowledge base is simple and contains no function symbols and is an example of Datalog knowledge base.

Resolution proves that KB $\models P$ by proving KB $\vee \neg P$ is unsatisfiable that is by deriving empty clause. Resolution proof is given in Fig. 4.5.

We may notice the "single spine" beginning with the goal clause, resolving against clauses from the knowledge base until the empty clause is generated. This is characteristic of resolution on Horn clause knowledge bases.

This example makes use of Skolemisation and involves clauses which are not definite clauses. This results in a somewhat complex structure. The problem in English is as follows:

To prove Vibhuti Killed Lucy

1. Everyone who loves all animals is loved by someone.
2. Everyone who kills an animal is loved by no one.
3. Gaurav loves all animals.
4. Either Gaurav or Vibhuti killed the cat who is named Lucy.
5. Did Vibhuti kill the cat?

Goal, G to prove that Vibhuti killed Lucy.

Conversion is First-order Logic and the negated goal.

(*a*) $\forall x\ [\forall y\ \text{Animal}(y) \rightarrow \text{Loves}\ (x,y)] \rightarrow [\exists y\ \text{Loves}\ (y, x)]$.

(*b*) $\forall x\ [\exists y\ \text{Animal}\ (y) \wedge \text{Kills}\ (x, y)] \rightarrow [\forall z \neg \text{Loves}\ (z, x)]$.

(*c*) $\forall x\ \text{Animal}\ (y) \rightarrow \text{Loves}\ (\text{Gaurav}, x)$.

(*d*) Kills (Gaurav, Lucy) $\vee$ Kills (Vibhuti, Lucy)

(*e*) Cat(Lucy)

(*f*) $\forall x\ \text{Cat}(x) \rightarrow \text{Animal}\ (x)$.

(*g*) Kills (Vibhuti, Lucy)

and conversion to CNF to each sentence gives

(*a*) Animal $(F(x)) \vee$ Loves $(G(x), x)$

(*b*) $\neg$ Loves $(x, F(x)) \vee$ Loves $(G(x), x)$

(*c*) $\neg$ Animal $(y) \vee \neg$ Kills$(x, y) \vee \neg$ Loves(z, x)

(*d*) $\neg$ Animal $(x) \vee \neg$ Loves (Gaurav, x)

(*e*) Kills(Gaurav, Lucy) $\vee$ Kills (Vibhuti, Lucy)

(*f*) Cat (Lucy)

(*g*) $\neg$ Cat(x) $\vee$ Animal(x)

(*h*) $\neg$ Kills (Vibhuti, Lucy)

After conversion the first sentence from order conversion gives two sentences.

The proof can be paraphrased in English as:

Suppose Vibhuti did not kill Lucy. We know that either Gaurav or Vibhuti did; thus Gaurav must have. Now Lucy is a cat and cats are animals, so Lucy is an animal. Because anyone who kills an animal is loved by no one, so no one loves Gaurav. But in the knowledge base it is given that Gaurav loves all animals, so someone loves him, so we have a contradiction. Therefore, Vibhuti killed the cat, Lucy.

The Resolution is given in Fig. 4.6.

The proof answers the question "Did Vibhuti kill the cat?"

But often we ask more general question, such as "who killed the cat?"

Resolution can do this by doing a little more work. The goal is $\exists$w kills (w, Lucy) which when negated becomes $\neg$ kills (w, Lucy) in CNF. Repeating the proof in the above Fig., with the new negated goal, we obtain a similar proof tree, the substitution then becomes $w/_{\text{vibhuti}}$ in one of the

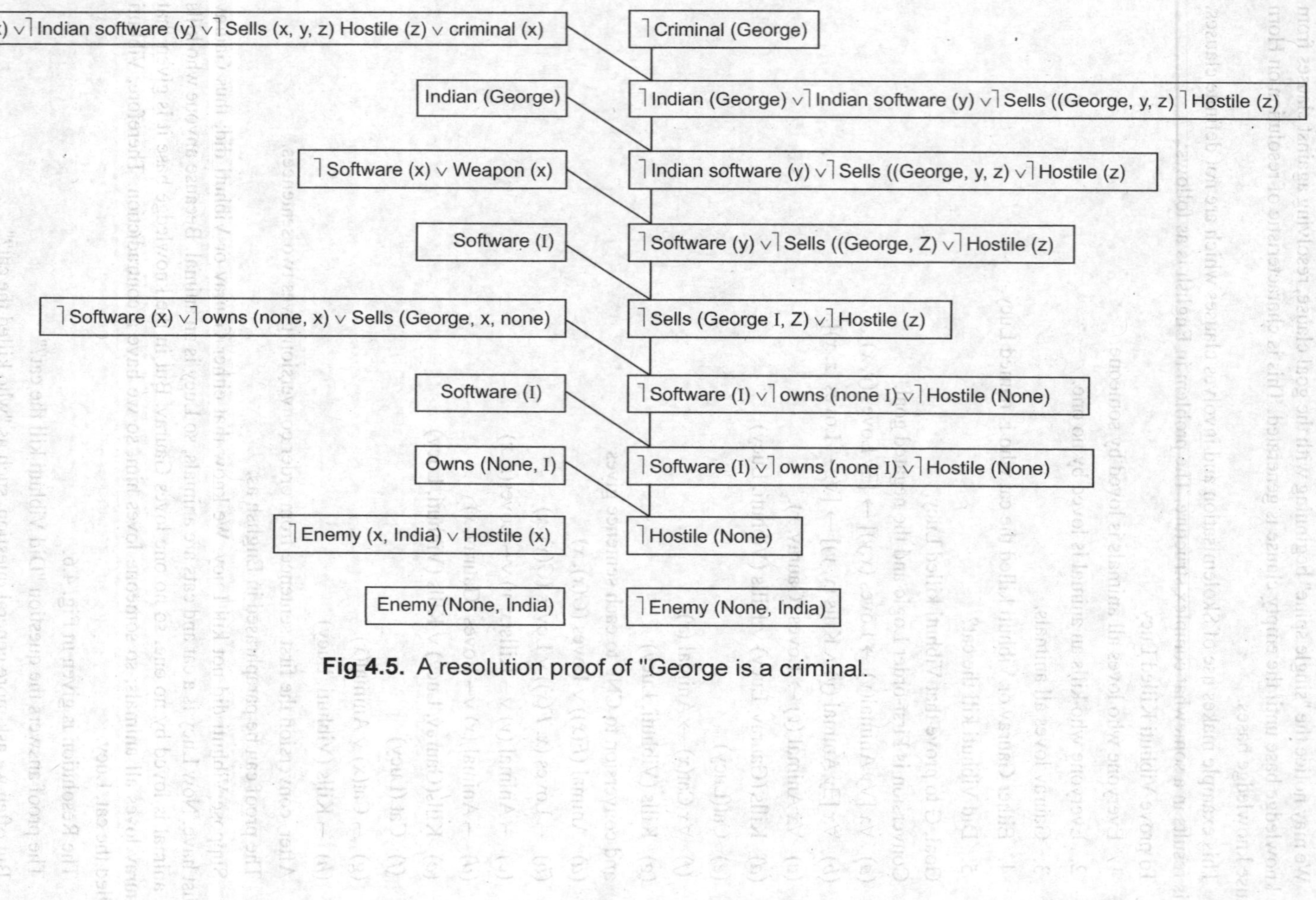

Fig 4.5. A resolution proof of "George is a criminal.

steps. (The reader should repeat the above proof with the new unification), concluding that Vibhuti is killer of cat Lucy.

Unfortunately resolution can produce non-constructive proofs for existential goals. *For example* ¬ Kills (w, Lucy) resolves with Kills (Gaurav, Lucy) ∨ Kills (Vibhuti, Lucy) to give Kills (Gaurav, Lucy), which resolves again with ¬ Kills(w, Lucy) to yield the empty clause. Here, w has two different bindings in this proof – Vibhuti or Gaurav. This is surprising, the procedure of resolution tells that someone, either Vibhuti or Gaurav, killed Lucy. **This type of double bindings is not quite common**, and can be avoided by

(*i*) Either restricting the allowed resolution steps so that w (query variable) is bound once in a given proof. Then we need to be able to backtrack over the possible bindings.

(*ii*) Or be adding a special **answer literal** to the negated goal. This then becomes

¬ Kills (w, Vibhuti) ∨ Answer(w).

At present the resolution process generates an answer only when a clause is generated containing just a *single* answer literal (answer(Vibhuti) in the Fig. 4.6. The non-constrictive proof would produce the clause

Answer (Vibhuti) ∨ Answer(Gaurav)

which is, in fact, the no answer.

Thus, we have seen how the process of deduction can derive new facts (answer) from the given facts (knowledge base). Further, resolution theorem can be used to answer yes-no questions such as Did Vibhuti kill the cat?

Resolution can also be used to answer fill-in-the-blanks type of questions, such as "Was the cat killed?" or " Who killed the cat?" Even "When was the cat killed" can be answered by adding new facts in the knowledge base. But yes-no and fill-in-the-blank questions are not the only kinds of questions which can ever be asked.

This must be mentioned here that the technique of deduction does not contain the answer to all conceivable questions. In general, it is necessary to decide on the kinds of questions which will be asked and to decide a *knowledge representation* method appropriate for those questions. *For example,* even we might ask "How was the cat killed?" or "Why was the cat killed?" So method of **resolution** is not yet complete and needs further research.

4.3 UNIFICATION ALGORITHM

Unification is the recursive process of merging two or more predicates with constants or with some variables. We check whether by performing some substitution for variables, the predicates can be made identical.

For example. Small town (x)¬ Small town (Delhi)

Cannot be merged (or resolved) because there may be various values for x.

Similarly, predicate lady and lady (Ajay) cannot be resolved as the first predicate doesn't have any variable and second predicate has some variable / constant.

Unification is used for unifying the axioms in inferencing mechanism. It is a recursive process. The substitutions for the variables are tried to generate identical and opposite predicate sets such that they can be combined. Unification tries to find out the complementary literals in two clauses and deletes them, thereby forming a new literal. **Please understand that whenever two identical and opposite literals are obtained, they are merged (or resolved).** This is true for clauses having no variables. When the literals have variables, the process becomes complicated. Thus, we use **substitutions** here. Substitution may be of a variable by a constant, of a variable by another variable or of a variable by a function that doesn't contain the same variable.

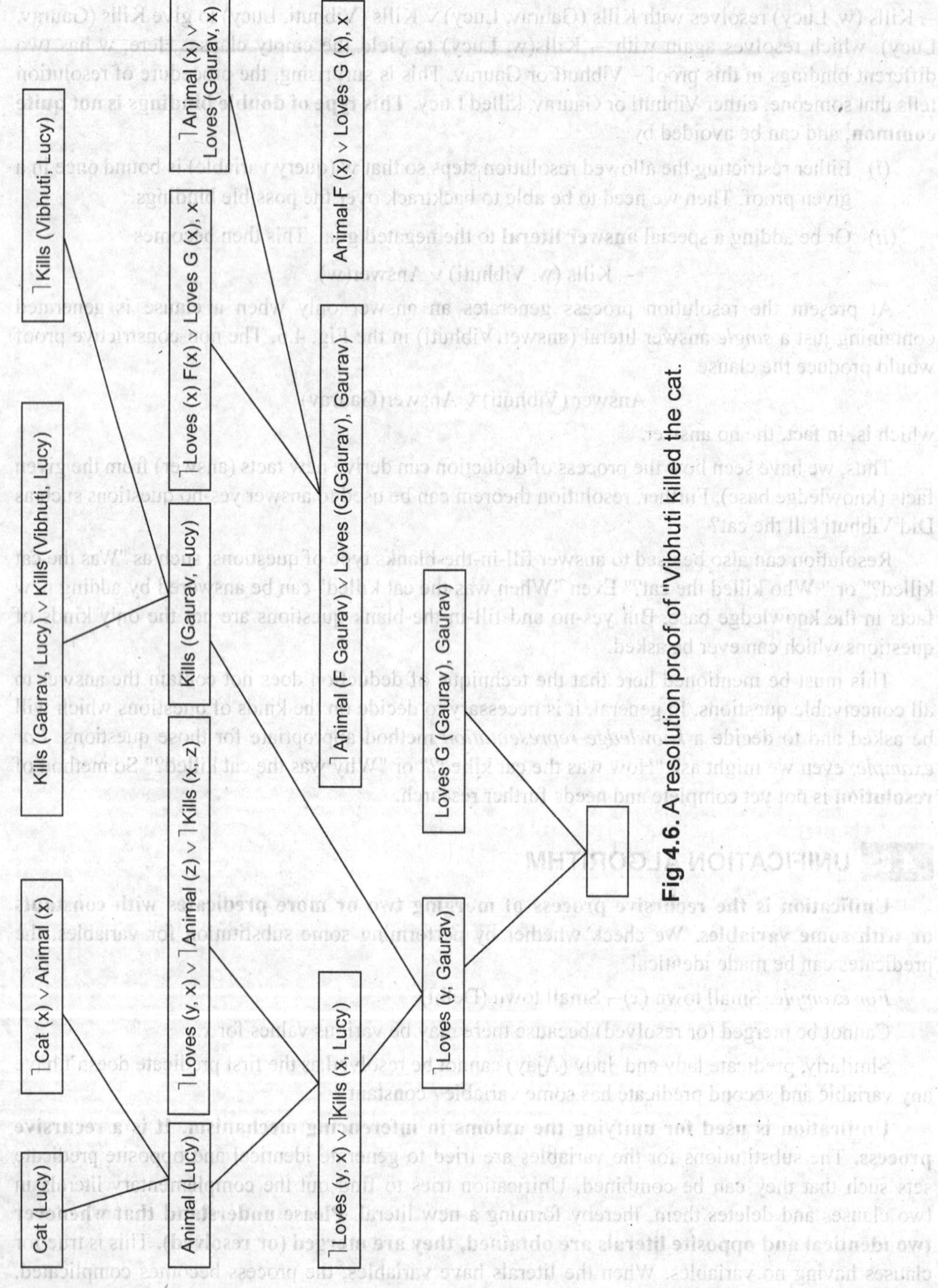

Fig 4.6. A resolution proof of Vibhuti killed the cat.

Let us write the unification algorithm first.

Algorithm: Verify: (U, V)

1. If *U* and *V* are both variables or constants then
   (*a*) If *U* and *V* are identical, then return null.
   (*b*) If *U* is a variable then if *U* occurs in *V*, then return {*FAIL*} else return {*U*/*V*}.
   (*c*) If *V* is a variable, then if *V* occurs in *U*, return {FAIL} else return {*U*/*V*}.
   (*d*) Return {FAIL}
2. If the initial predicate symbols in *U* and *V* are not identical, return {FAIL}.
3. If *U* and *V* have a different number of arguments, then return {FAIL}.
4. Set SUBSET to NULL.
5. For $i \leftarrow l$ to the number of arguments of *U*.
   (*a*) Call unify with the ith argument of *U* and the ith argument of *V* putting the result in *S*.
   (*b*) If *S* contain {FAIL}, return {FAIL}?
   (*c*) If *S* is not equal to NULL
      (*i*) Apply 5 to be the remainder of both *U* and *V*.
      (*ii*) Set subset equal to APPENDS (S, SUBSET).
6. Return SUBSET.

Working: We try to unify, say, the following predicates —

$P(x, x)$

and $\neg P(y, z)$

Firstly, we check the predicates. Here these are same and opposite. Next, we check their arguments. Now, *P* has its 1st argument as '*x*' whereas $\neg$ *P* has '*y*' as its 1st argument./ These can be made similar if we substitute *x* in place of *y* in both predicates. **Please note here that since x and y are variables so these substitutions are possible.** Many a time, the situation is that one predicate has variable and another predicate has constant, then only variable can be replaced by the constant. the constant cannot be replaced by variable. **Also note that the replacement of one variable by another should be done throughout all occurrence of that variable in all predicates.** The replacement of *y* by *x* is denoted by *x*/*y*. So, now the predicates are —

$P(x, x)$

and $P(x, z)$

Now, we come to the 2nd argument of both the predicates. To match, *x* should be replaced by *z*. But this cannot be done as the substitution of *x* by *y* and *z* both is not possible in one set of problem. Hence, the two literals cannot be unified.

On the other hand, if predicates are —

$P(x, x)$

and $\neg P(y, y)$

And if we substitute *x*/*y* (i.e., *x* for *y*) then they become

$\neg P(x, x)$

and $\neg P(x, x)$ and these can be **unified**.

We are in a position to solve some examples now.

Q.1. Unify the following clauses —

$P(x, f(z), \text{mary})$

$\neg P(x, y, z)$.

Ans. We substitute z/mary in both the clauses —

$P(x, f(\text{mary}), \text{mary})$

$\neg P(x, y, \text{mary})$. Now, these two clauses

differ in their 2nd argument only, so we replace $y/f(\text{mary})$ and we get —

$\neg p(x, f(\text{mary}), \text{mary})$.

∴ Finally, the two clauses are —

$P(x, f(\text{mary}), \text{mary})$

and $\neg p(x, f(\text{mary}), \text{mary})$

∴ Now, they can be unified (or merged) together.

Q. 2. Suppose we have the following query — Whom does Ravana know? And that there are four sentences in the KB.

Knows (Ranana, Sita).

Knows (*y*, Rama)

Knows(*y*, Mother (*y*))

Knows (*x*, Radha)

Unify given sentence with the above four sentences.

Ans. Given: Sentence is.

Knows (Ravana, *x*) ...(1)

∴ Following results are obtained by unifying (1) with given sentences

1. UNIFY (Knows (Ravana, *x*), Knows (Ravana, Sita)

   = (*x*/Sita)

2. UNIFY (Knows (Ravana, *x*), knows(y, Ram)

   = (*x*/Ram, *y*/Ravana)

3. UNIFY (Knows (Ravana, *x*), knows (*y*, Mother(*y*))

   = (*y*/Ravana, *x*/mother(Ravana))

4. UNIFY (Knows (Ravana, *x*), knows (*x*, Radha) = fail

In this last unification, the two constants cannot be instantiated to the same variable '*x*' at the same time. This problem can be solved by assigning **different variables** to two sentences. '*x*' in the knows (*x*, Radha) can be changed to '*y*'. Now, the unification will work by standardising one of the two sentences being unified which means renaming its variables to avoid name clashes.

For example, renaming '*x*' in knows (*x*, Radha) to a new variable '*y*' without changing its meaning is as follows.

UNIFY (knows (Ravana, *x*), knows (*y*, Ravana)

= [*x*/Radha, *y*/Ravana]

NOTE. 1. Say, we are attempting to unify the expression

$$F(x, x)$$
$$f(g(x), g(x))$$

That is, if we accept $g(x)$ as a substitution for 'x' then we would have to substitute it for 'x' in the remainder of the expressions. But this leads to **infinite recursions** since it is not possible to eliminate x.

2 Unification works well for two arguments. But there could be more than one such **Unifier**.

For example Consider again,

UNIFY knows (Ravana, x), knows (y, z)

∴ Substitutions could be

(y/Ravana, x/z)

or (y/Ravana, x/Ravana, z/Ravana)

First substitution gives, knows (Ravana, z) and **Second substitution** gives knows (Ravana, Ravana).

The second result can be obtained from the first (y/Ravana, x/z) by an additional substitution (z/Ravana). **Please note that the first unifier is more general than the second because the second can be derived from the first.** Also we conclude that for every unifiable pair of expressions there is a single **most-general-unifier** (MGU). In this example, it is (y/Ravana, x/z).

4.4 FORWARD CHAINING, BACKWARD CHAINING, AND CONFLICT RESOLUTION

A.I. solves our problems by searching a solution search-tree (called as search space) from the initial state to the goal state. We have rule-based system architecture that has a set of rules, a set of facts and an inference engine. Given a set of rules, the new knowledge can be inferred using two rules —

(*a*) Forward chaining / Forward reasoning.

(*b*) Backward chaining / Backward reasoning.

Forward chaining (or reasoning) starts from the start state and proceeds towards the goal state. On the other hand backward chaining starts from the goal state and proceeds towards the start state.

For example. : Turbo Prolog (an A.I. language, 5 G), uses backward chaining (or reasoning).

Forward reasoning / data-driven inferencing

As we have already studied that rules are stored in KB in form of atomic formula in some form like propositional or predicate logic. **The process of instantiating the left side of rules, executing them from left to right, matching the left part of the sentence with the existing expression and if the match occurs then replacing it by the right part of the rule is called as Forward reasoning or Forward chaining or Data-driven search.** In next step, this right hand side of the previous rule is considered as left side of present rule to find applicability of a rule. So the finding of the rule becomes *Subgoals* to be fulfilled. These subgoals may in turn cause new subgoals to be established and so on, until the facts are found to match the lowest subgoals conditions. **Whenever the goal is achieved, the search process stops.**

For example. Say, we have a database with the following elements —

A	G	E
A	C	B

(database having facts)

& the set of rules as —

$F \,\&\, B \rightarrow Z$

$C \,\&\, D \rightarrow F$ (Rules in a *KB*)

$A \rightarrow D$

We assume that each time the set of rules is tested against the database, only the first (topmost) rule that matches is executed. So the rule $A \rightarrow D$ is executed only once although it matches the database every time. **This database is also known as a working memory (WM).**

How it works? The first rule which fires is $A \rightarrow D$ because A is already in the database. So, this rule shows the existence of D (i.e., inferring) and D is placed in the database. So, our database now is —

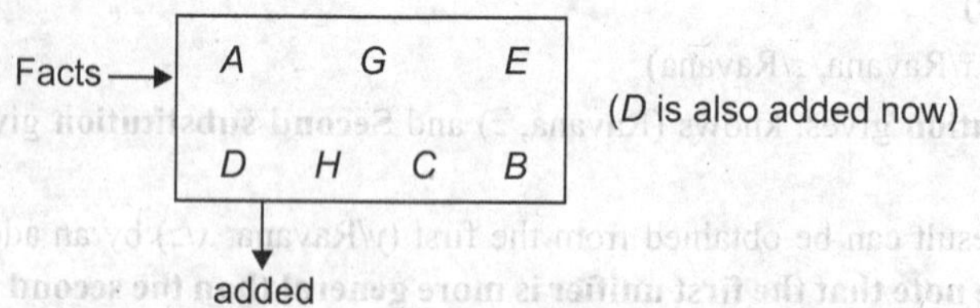

This causes the second rule C and $D \rightarrow F$ to fire and as a consequence F is inferred and placed in the database. This in turn causes the tired rule F and $B \rightarrow Z$ to fire placing Z in the database i.e.

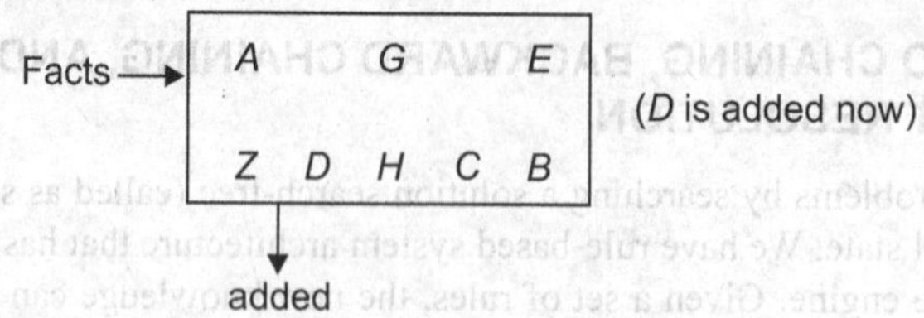

∴ The inference chain so formed is—

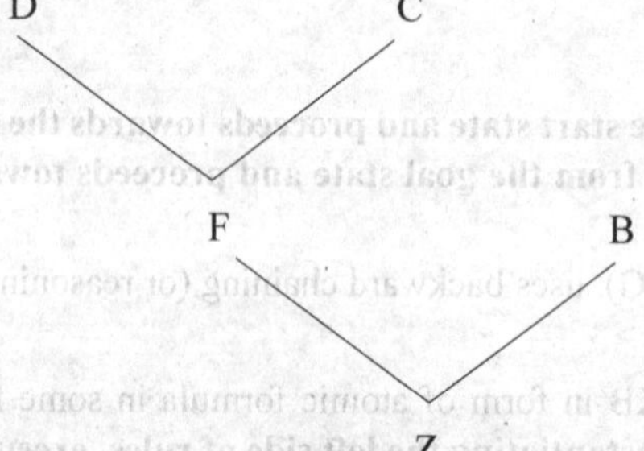

This is known as forward chaining. It is also called as a data-driven search as the input data is used to guide the direction of inference process.

Let us write its algorithm now.

Algorithm: Forward chaining

Repeat: Collect the rule whose condition matches a fact in database (or WM).
Do actions indicated by the rule — added facts to WM 'or delete facts from *working memory*).
Until: Problem is solved or no condition matches.

Alternative Algorithm: Forward Chaining

Repeat
Collect the rules whose conditions match facts in database (or WM)
If more than one rule matches then use conflict resolution strategy to eliminate all but one.
else
do actions indicated by the rules i.e., add facts to the database/ or delete facts from WM, until a problem is solved or no condition matches.

Backward chaining/Backward reasoning/Goal-driven inference

It is a process of reasoning in which within a rule it matches the existing state with the right hand part of the rule and if the match occurs, it is replaced by left hand side of the rule. Actually, backward chaining means reasoning from goals back to facts. The focus is on the search. The rules and facts are processed using backward chaining interpreter.

Let us write its algorithm now.

Algorithm: Backward chaining

Prove goal G:

If G is in the initial facts, it is proven. Please find a rule which can be used to conclude G and try to prove each of that rules conditions.

Which one to select?

If we apply both forward and backward algorithms then our searching becomes a bidirectional search. This results in a hybrid reasoning. Which reasoning to select depends on the nature of the problem. It depends on the following factors:

(*a*) **Number of starts and goal states.**

We proceed from a smaller set of states to a larger set of states.

(*b*) **Direction of branching factor (b)**

Branching factor is defined as the average number of nodes that are generated from a single node. **Please remember that the reasoning is performed in the direction of lower branching factor (b).**

(*c*) **Problem's requirement**

Certain applications like medical diagnosis need backward chaining as they need the justification of the solution too. **Note that it is important to choose the reasoning in the direction that corresponds to the way in which the user thinks.** Actually, we can use hybrid reasoning for such systems. Programming languages, like PROLOG, support backward chaining.

We need to check the rule form. If both left and right hand side contain assertion, then forward chaining can match assertions on the left side of a rule and add to the state description of assertion on RHS. **Please understand here that if arbitrary procedures are allowed at right in the rule then a rule will not be reversible.**

Some production languages allow only reversible rules and some do not. **Also note that when irreversible rules are used then a commitment to the direction of search must be made at the time the rules are written.**

Conflict Resolution

The set of rules that have their conditions stratified by working memory elements forms a *conflict set.* **A conflict is said to occur if more than one rules are found to fire in one cycle.** In such a scenario, the control structure must determine which rule to fire from this conflict set of active rules. This process of selection is called as **"conflict resolution". So, conflict resolution normally selects a single rule to fire.** There are 3 conflict resoltuion mechanisms:

(*a*) Refractory (*b*) Receiving (*c*) Specificity

Refractory: In this mechanism, a rule should not be allowed to fire more than once on the same data. This prevents undesired loops.

Recency: Here we rank instantiation in terms of recency of elements in the premise of the rule. **The rule which has highest priority is fired first.**

Specificity: More specific rules are better because they take more of data into account. It is also known as a strict condition as it injects more know ledge in the KB, when it is fired.

Other mechanisms are also used like—

(*a*) Most recently used: It chooses the most recently used rule from the conflict set for firing. It represents a dfs.

(*b*) Most recently added: It selects the rule which is most recently added in the set of rules. It is a dynamic policy as in this policy new production rules are added, deleted or modified automatically in dynamic KB during execution.

We are in a position to solve an example now.

EXAMPLE 1. Consider the following database and the set of rules given below:

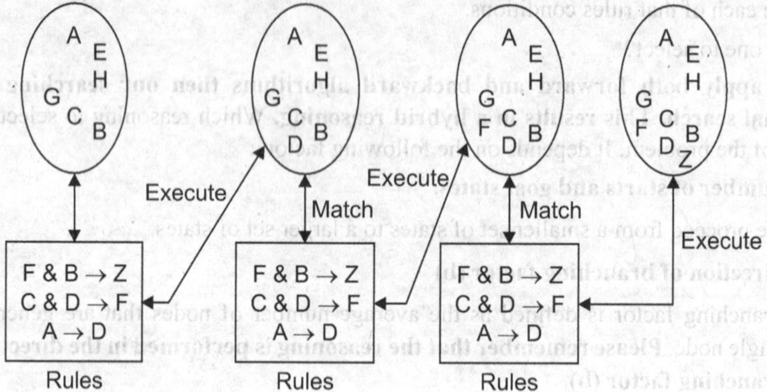

Explain how forward chaining works in this example. Also show backward chaining. Which is more cost-effective?

SOLUTION. The rules in this example, use letters as facts in the database to explain the situations or concepts.

For examples., F and $B \rightarrow Z$

means

It situation F exists

and situation B exists

THEN : situation Z also exists.

Let us see now how these rules work.

Assume that each time the set of rules is tested against the database, only the first (topmost rule which matches is executed. That is why, in the figure given, the rule ($A \rightarrow D$) is executed only once even though it matches the database every time.

The **first rule** that fires is $A \rightarrow D$ because A is already in the database. As consequence of this rule, the existence of D is inferred and D is placed in the database. This causes the second rule, C and $D \rightarrow F$ to fire, as a consequence F is inferred and placed in the database. This in turn causes the 3rd rule F and $B \rightarrow Z$ to fire placing Z in the database. **Please understand that this technique is called as forward chaining because the search for new information seams to be proceeding in the direction of the arrow separating the left and right hand sides of the rules.** The system which uses information on the left hand side to derive information on the right is shown in Fig 4.7(a).

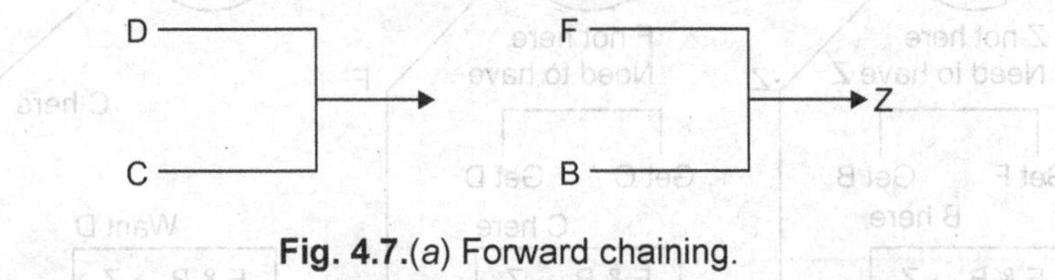

Fig. 4.7.(*a*) Forward chaining.

Say, we use this system with the goal of determining whether or not situation Z existed. We might think that it worked quite well, finding quickly the fact that Z did exist. Unfortunately, this is just over simplification. Practically speaking, the process of drawing inference is not simple. This is so because a **real expert system** will not have just three rules but will have hundreds or even thousands of them. If we use a system that is very large just to find out about Z many rules would be fired which had nothing to do with Z, then a large number of inference chains and situations could be derived in the process which were valid but unrelated to Z. **Please note that if our goal is to infer one particular fact Z, forward chaining could waste both time and money.** In such a case, **backward chaining** might be more cost-effective. With this inference technique, the system starts with what it wants to prove. Like, to find if the situation Z exists and as such executes those rules which are relevant to its establishment.

The Fig. 4.7(b) shows how backward chaining would work using rules given above.

Step 1: The system is told to establish (if possible) that situation Z exists. It first checks the database for Z and when that fails, searches for rules which conclude Z, i.e. have Z on the right side of the arrow. It finds the rule F and $B \rightarrow Z$ and decides that it must establish F and B in order to conclude Z.

Step 2: The system tries to establish F, first checking the database and then finding a rule which concludes F. From the rule, C and $D \rightarrow F$, the system decides that C and D must be established to conclude F.

Steps 3 to 5: In these steps, the system finds C in the database but decides it must establish A before it can conclude D. It then finds A in the database.

Steps 6 to 8: In these steps, the system executes the 3rd rule to establish D, then executes the second rule to establish F and finally executes the first rule to establish the original goal, Z. The inference chain created here is identical to the one created by forward chaining. (This is left as an exercise for the students). **But one point to remember is that the two approaches depend on the method in which data and rules are searched.**

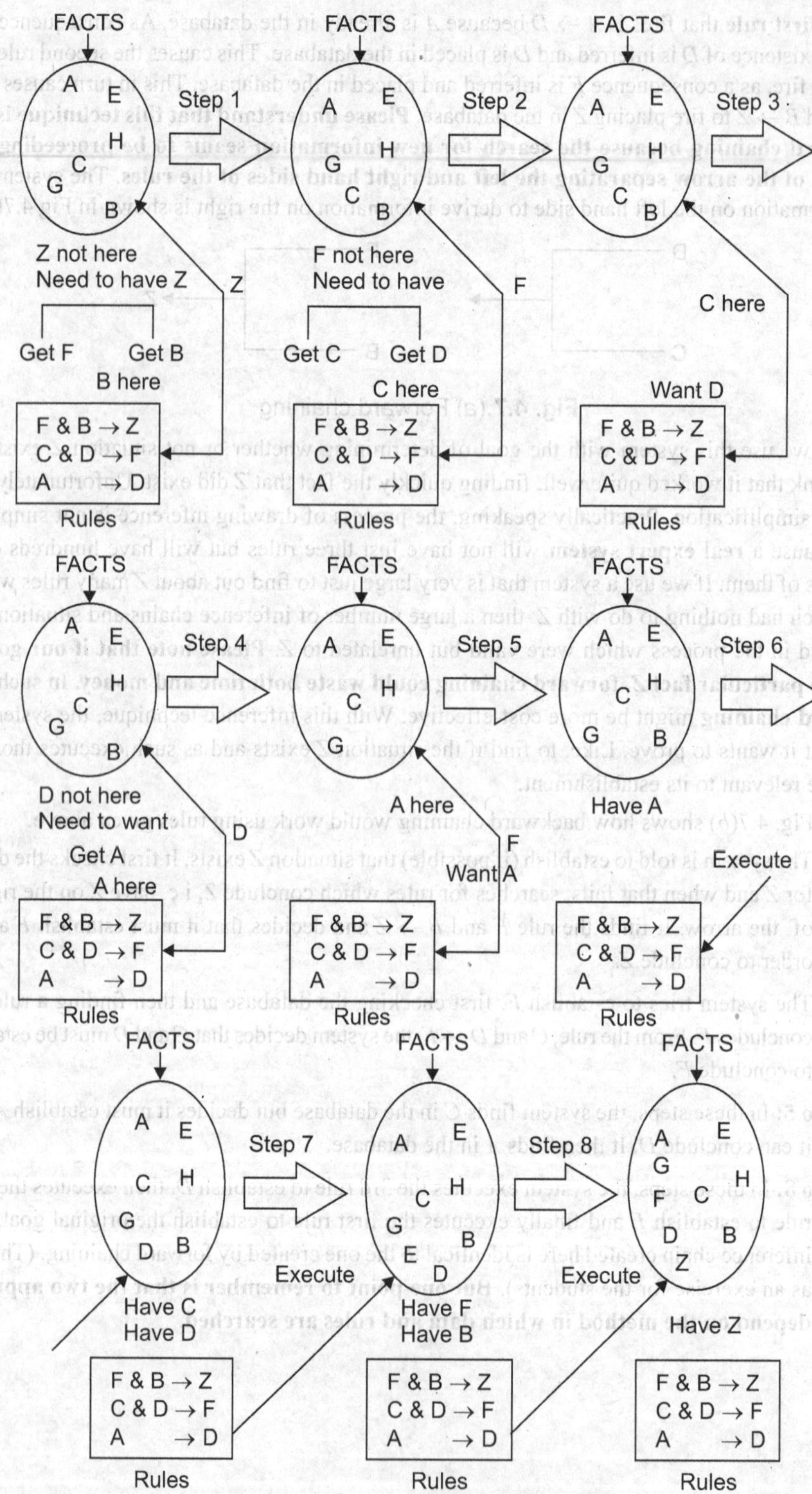

Fig. 4.7(*b*) Forward and Backward chaining.

4.5 STRUCTURED KNOWLEDGE REPRESENTATION

We have some more advanced KR techniques that focus on the structure of knowledge like semantic networks, conceptual graphs, conceptual dependencies and scripts, cyc and object oriented representation. We discuss these one by one now.

4.5.1 Slots and semantic nets/semantic network/associated networks

A slot is a subclass of intangible and is of many types. Defining slots refers not to the properties of the frame but to the properties of the object represented by the frame. **A slot is an attribute value pair in the simplest form. A filler is a value that a slot can take. For example.** it can be a numeric, string value or a pointer to another slot. A **weak slot** and filler structure does not consider the constant of the representation. They are of two types —

(*a*) Semantic networks (nets) or associated networks.

(*b*) Frames.

Let us discuss semantic networks first. They are an alternative to predicate logic as a form of knowledge representation. **The idea is that we can store our knowledge in form of a graph.** A semantic network consists of nodes connected by arcs.

Nodes represent objects in the real world.

Arcs represent relationships between those objects.

For example.

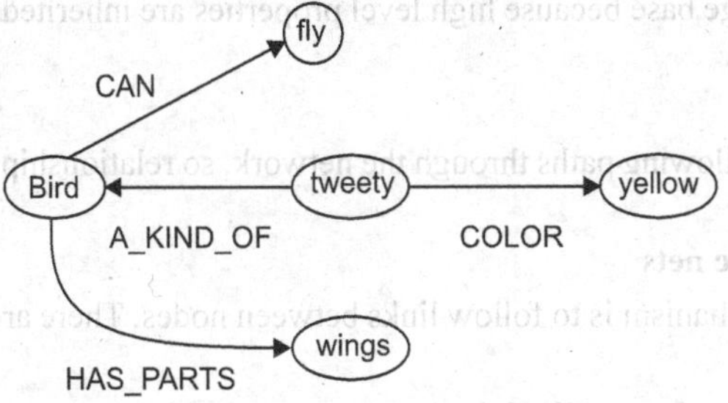

Fig. 4.8 Semantic network (net) example

Fig. 4.8 shows that tweety is a kind of bird who can fly. It is yellow in colour and has wings.

These networks permit **property inheritance also. It means that nodes which are members or subsets of other nodes may inherit properties from their higher level ancestor nodes.**

For example.

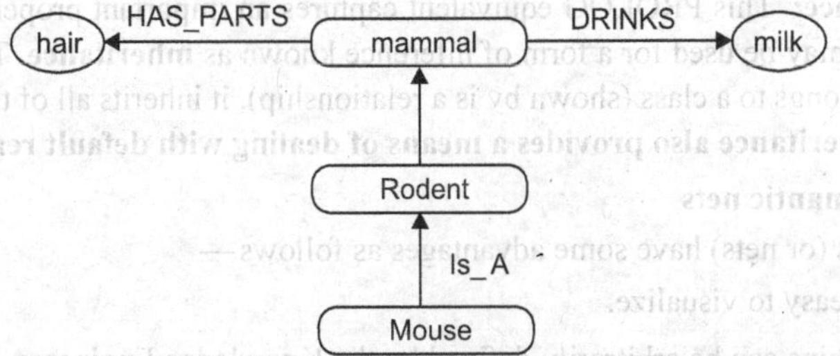

Fig. 4.9 Property inheritance in a hierarchical network

So, it is possible to infer from above net that a mouse has hair and drinks milk.

This concept of inheriting a property is called as property inheritance. The properties of a subclass can be modified and can be given different values. Each subclass will thus have its own defined values. **Please understand that the semantic network based knowledge representation mechanism is useful where an object or concept is associated with many attributes and where relationships between objects are important.**

Applications: Semantic nets have been used in natural language research to represented complex sentences expressed in English.

Properties of semantic nets

Semantic nets exhibit following properties knowledge representation scheme:

1. Expressiveness

Semantic nets allow representation of facts and relationship between facts. The levels of hierarchy provide a mechanism for representing general and specific knowledge. This representation is a model of human memory and it is therefore relatively understandable.

2. Effectiveness

They support inference through property inheritance. They can also be easily represented by *PROLOG, LISP* and *other A.I.* languages making them amenable to computation, as shown by "is-a" arc in LISP given by $\forall x$ [Great-Dane $(x) \rightarrow$ Dog (x)].

3. Efficiency

They reduce the size of the knowledge base. Knowledge is stored only at its highest level of abstraction rather than for every instance or example of a class. Further they help maintain the consistency in knowledge base because high level properties are inherited by subclasses and are not added for each subclass.

4. Explicitness

Reasoning equates to following paths through the network, so relationship and inference are explicit in the network lines.

Inferencing in semantic nets

The basic inference mechanism is to follow links between nodes. There are two ways of inferencing used here—

(*a*) Intersection Search. (*b*) Inheritance.

(*a*) **Intersection search: It is the process of finding the relationship among objects by spreading activation out from each of the two nodes and seeing where the activation met.** This is achieved by assigning a **special tag** to each visited node. There are many advantages including entity-based organization and fast parallel implementation. However, every structured question needs highly structured networks.

(*b*) **Inheritance:** This PROLOG equivalent captures an important property of semantic nets that they may be used for a form of inference known as **inheritance.** The idea is that if an object belongs to a class (shown by is a relationship), it inherits all of the properties of that class. **Inheritance also provides a means of dealing with default reasoning.**

Advantages of semantic nets

Semantic networks (or nets) have some advantages as follows—

1. They are easy to visualize.
2. Relationships can be arbitrarily defined by the Knowledge Engineers.
3. Formal definitions of semantic networks have been developed.
4. Related knowledge is easily clustered.

5. Are efficient in space requirements.
6. Projects are represented only once.

Disadvantages of Semantic Nets

1. Inheritance from multiple sources can cause problems.
2. Facts placed inappropriately cause problems.
3. There are no standards about node and arc value.

Types of Semantic Net

A semantic network or net is a graphic notation for representing knowledge in pattern interconnected nodes and arcs. Common to all these nets is a declarative graphic representation that can be used either to represent knowledge or to support automated systems for reasoning about knowledge. Some versions are highly informal while other versions are formally defined systems of logic. Following are the 6 most common kinds of semantic nets—

1. **Definitional networks** emphasize the subtype or is-α **relation between a concept type and a newly defined subtype.** The resulting network, also called a **generalization or subsumption hierarchy,** supports the rule of inheritance for copying properties defined for a super type to all of its subtypes. Since definitions are true by definition, the information in these networks is often assumed to be necessarily true.
2. **Assertional networks are designed to assert propositions. Unlike definitional networks the information in an assertional network is assumed to be contingently true, unless it is explicitly marked with a modal operator.** Some assertional networks have been proposed as models of the **conceptual structures** underlying natural language semantics.
3. **Implication networks use implication as the primary relation for connecting nodes.** They may be used to represent patterns of beliefs causality, or inferences.
4. **Executable networks include some mechanism, such as marker passing or attached procedures, which can perform inferences, pass messages, or search for patterns and associations.**
5. **Learning networks** build or extend their representation by acquiring knowledge from examples. The new knowledge may change the old network by adding and deleting nodes and arcs or by modifying numerical values, called **weights,** associated with the nodes and arcs.
6. **Hybrid networks:** They combine two or more of the previous techniques, either in a single network or in separate but closely interacting networks.

We are in a position to solve some examples on nets now.

Q. 1 Construct a semantic net representation for the following—

(*a*) Pompian (Marcus), Blacksmith (Marcus).

(*b*) Raj gives Lucy a gift.

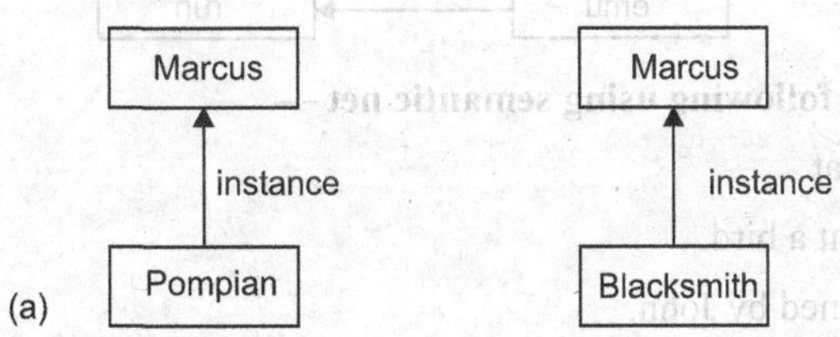

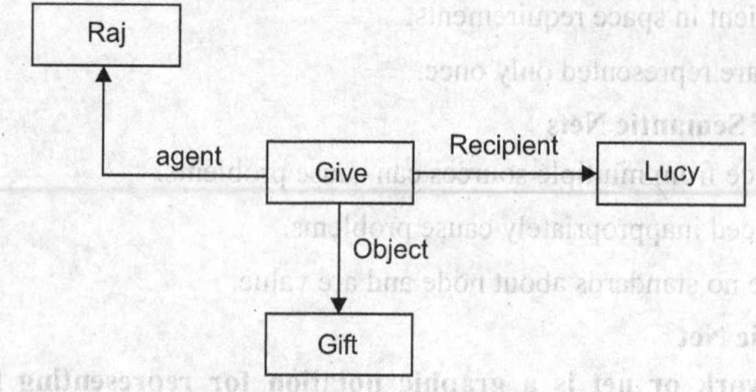

(b)

Q. 2 Construct a semantic net representation for the following —

(*a*) Every dog has bitten a mail carrier.

(*b*) Every batter hit a ball. **[MDU, BE (CSE) 8th sem. Dec. 2004]**

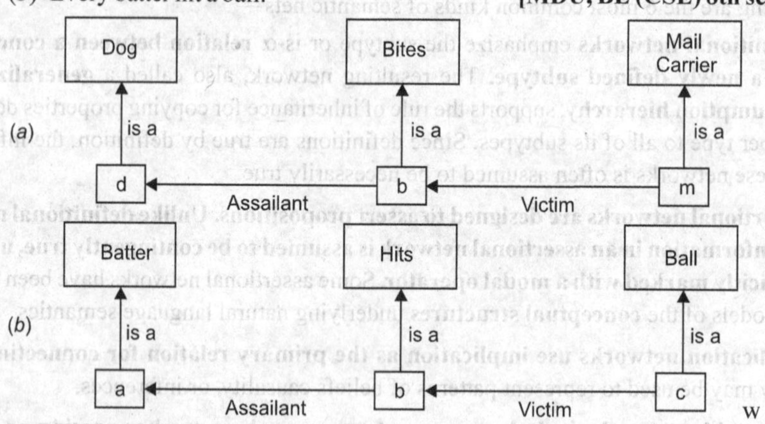

Q. 3 Represent the following using nets —

(*a*) Emus are birds.

(*b*) Typical birds fly and have wings.

(*c*) Emus run.

Ans. Its Semantic net is as follows

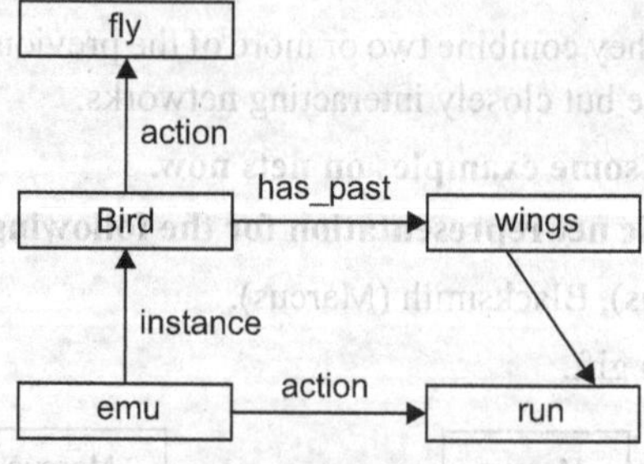

Q. 4. Represent the following using semantic net —

(*a*) Tom is a cat.

(*b*) Tom caught a bird.

(*c*) Tom is owned by John.

(*d*) Tom is ginger in color

(*e*) Cats like cream.

(*f*) The cat sat on the mat.

(*g*) A cat is a mammal.

(*h*) A bird is an animal.

(*i*) All mammals are animals.

(*j*) Mammals have fur.

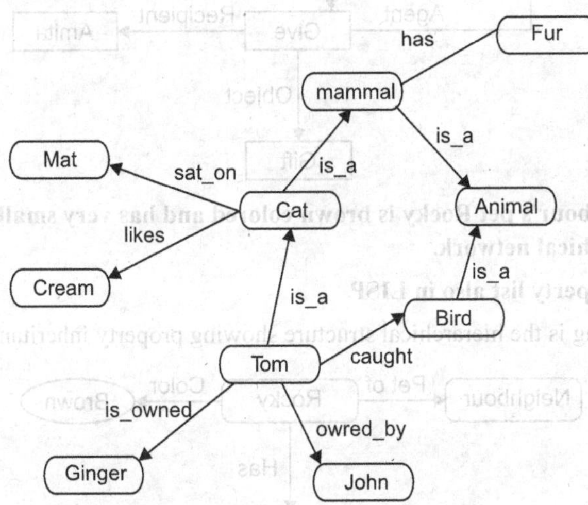

Q. 5. Represent the following in net form —

'Asif is taller than Rashmi'

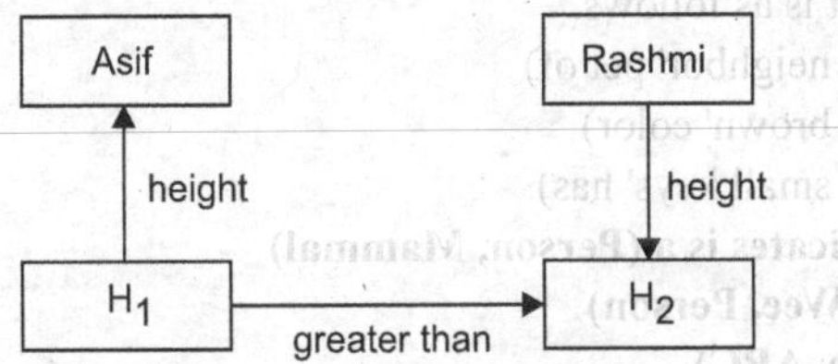

Q. 6. Draw the semantics network of the following sentences

(*a*) Bobby gives Amita a gift.

(*b*) Bobby told Krishana that he gave Amita a gift.

Ans. (*a*) Its semantic representation is as follows

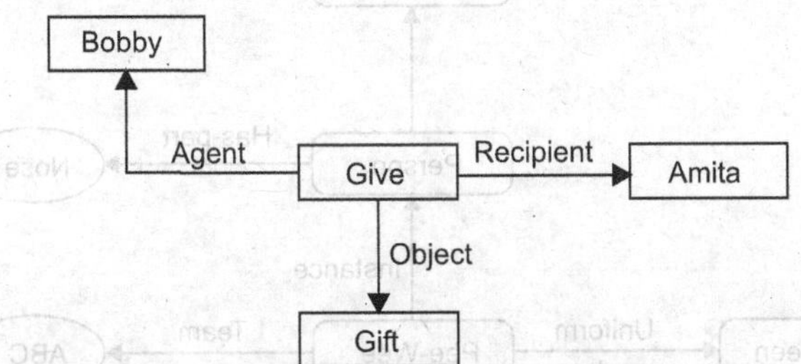

NOTE: The arcs define the relationships between the predicate (GIVE) and the concepts like AMITA and GIFT, associated with that predicate.

(*b*) Its semantic representation is as follows

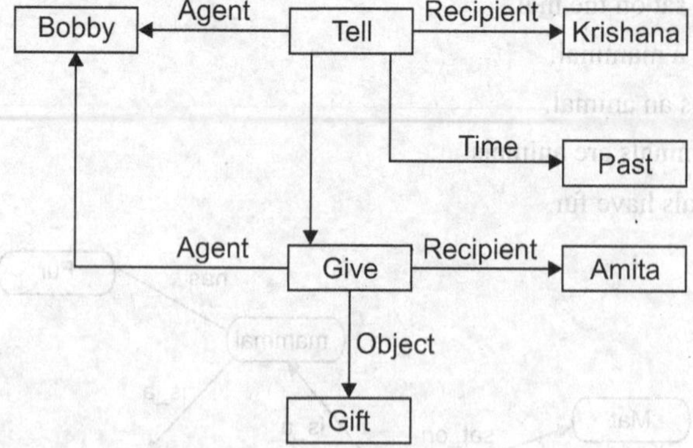

Q. 7. "Our neighbour's pet Rocky is brown colored and has very small legs". Represent it as a hierarchical network.

Give its property list also in LISP.

Ans. The following is the hierarchical structure showing property inheritance.

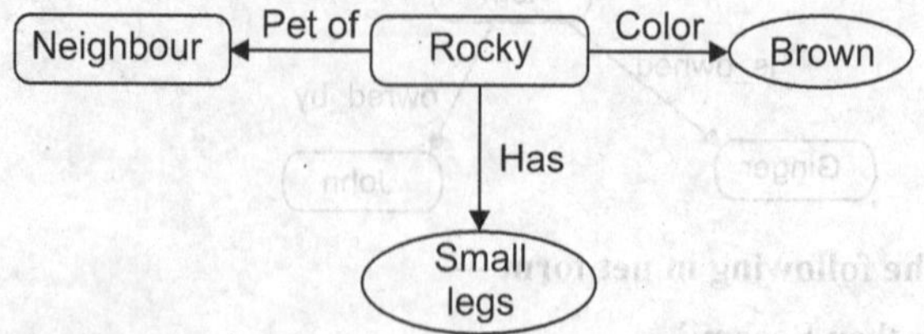

The property list is as follows.
(putprop 'rocky' neighbor' pet of)
(putprop 'rocky' brown' color)
(putprop 'rocky' small keys' has)

Q. 8. Given the predicates is a (Person, Mammal)
(instance (Pee-Wee, Person)
(team (Pee-Wee, ABC)
uniform color (Pee-Wee, Green)
Express the above in the form of semantic or associative network.

Ans.

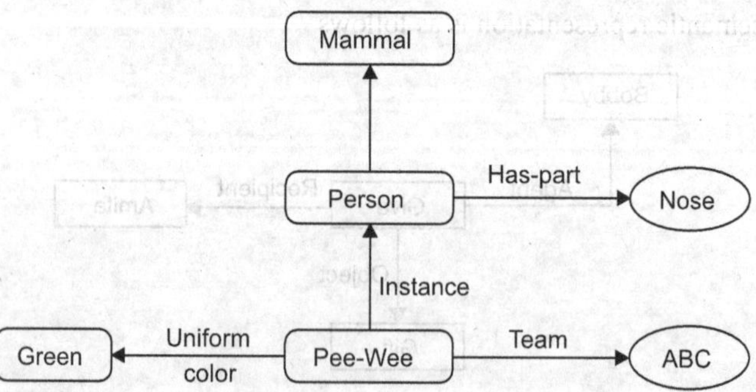

Q. 9. Represent the following as a semantic network.

(a) Amit gave the book to Mersa.

(b) Prem is 6 feet tall and he is taller than Amit.

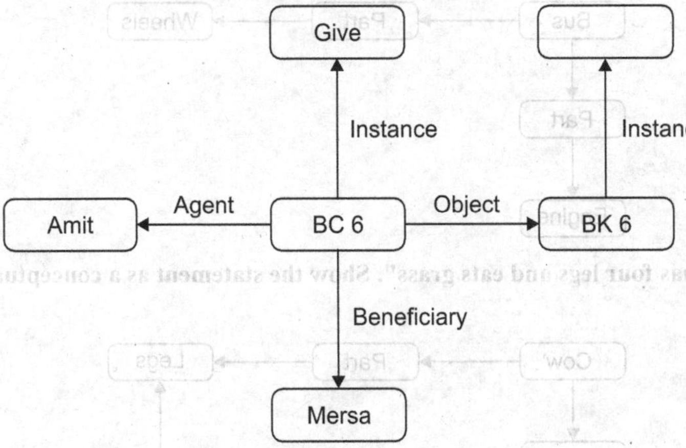

Give

Instance

Instance

Ans. (*a*) Amit ← Agent — BC 6 — Object → BK 6

Beneficiary

Mersa

Prem

Amit

Height

(*b*) H 1 — Taller-than → H 2

Value

6-Feet

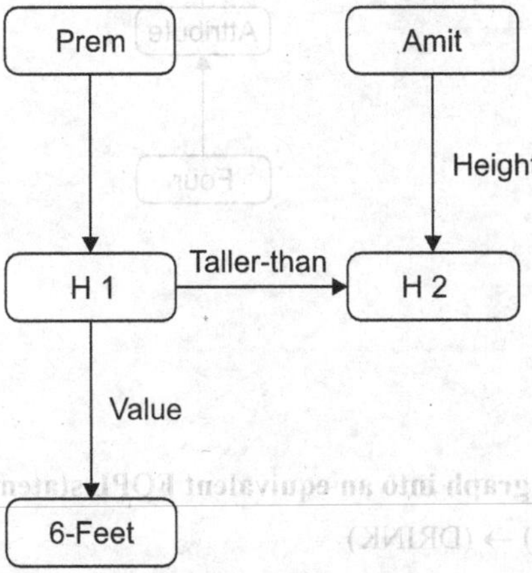

Q. 10. Construct a conceptual representation for the sentence, "Every car has an engine"

Ans. The conceptual graph representation is

[CAR : ∀] → (PART) → (ENGINE)

Q. 11. Transform the FOPL statement equivalent conceptual graph.

$\forall x$ Normal (x) and Grown (x) → Walk (x).

Ans. The conceptual graph is as follows.

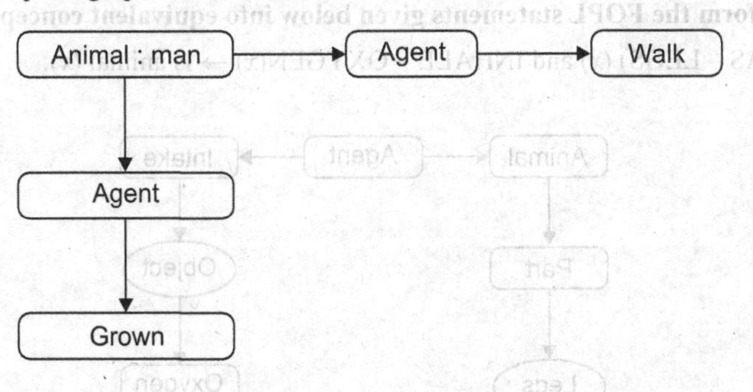

Q. 12. Give conceptual graph for the statement.—"Every bus has wheels and engine".

Ans.

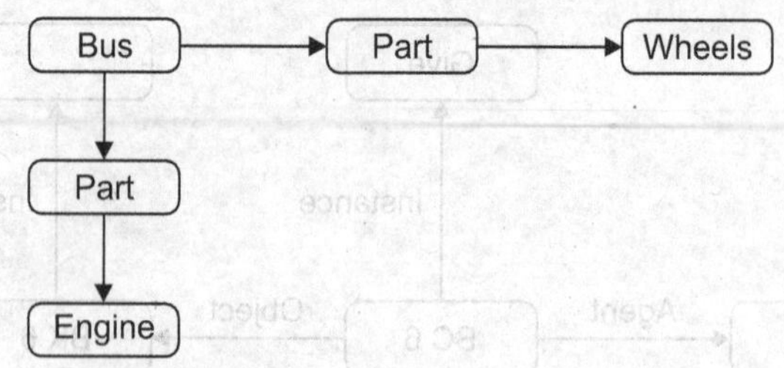

Q. 13. "A cow has four legs and eats grass". Show the statement as a conceptual graph.

Ans.

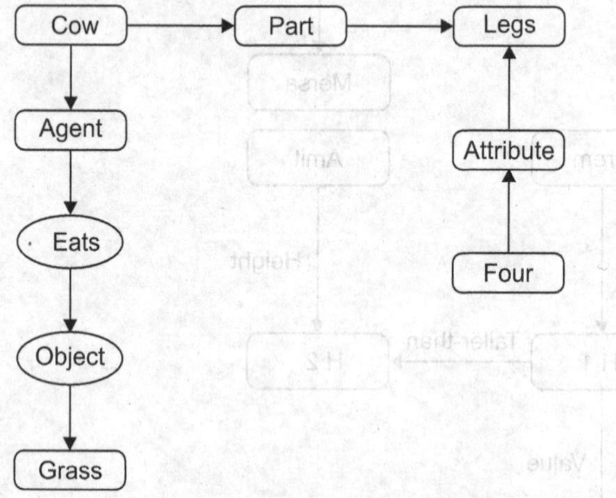

Q. 14. Convert the following conceptual graph into an equivalent FOPL statement.

[CAMEL : clyde] → (Agent) → (DRINK)

→ [(OBJECT) → (WATER) → (ATTRIBUTE)

→ [50 – GALLONS].

Ans. E(x) for x is a camel.

D(x) for x is drinks water.

G(x) for drinks 50 gallons of water.

$\therefore$ $\exists x\ (E(x)$: clyde) & $D(x) \to G(x))$

Q. 15. Transform the FOPL statements given below into equivalent conceptual graph.

$\forall x$(HAS – LEGS) (x) and INHALE – OXYGEN(x) → is animal (x).

Ans.

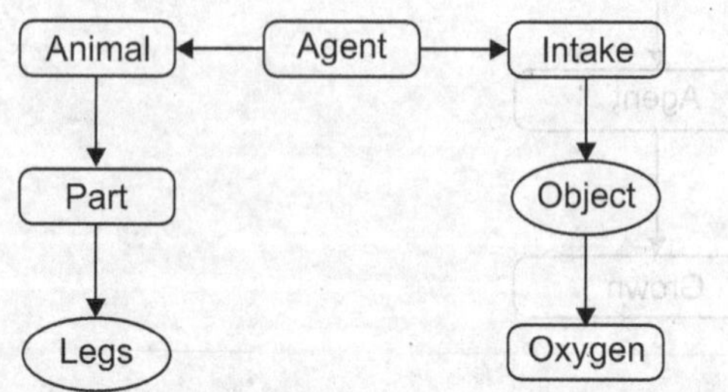

Q. 16. Draw conceptual graph of the statement—"Sparrow ate a fat insect".

Ans. The conceptual graph for the statement is as follows.

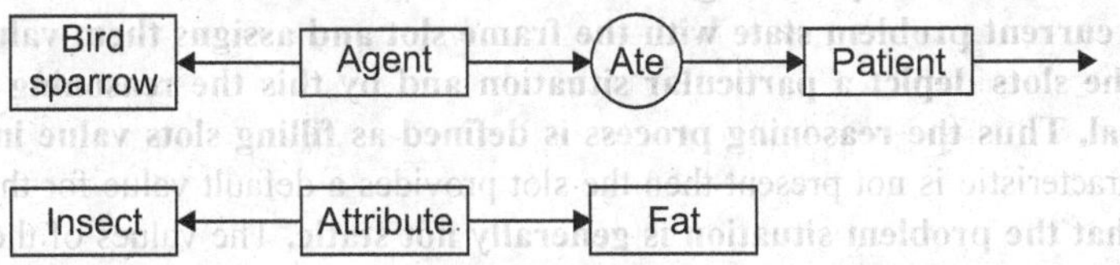

Q. 17. "Joe is eating food with a spoon." Draw conceptual graph of the statement.

Ans. The statement can be shown in two ways.

1. **Linear form of conceptual graph**

   [PERSON : joe] → (Agent) → [EAT] → (OBJECT) → [FOOD : soup] – (INSTRUMENT) → [SPOON]

2. **Conceptual graph representation**

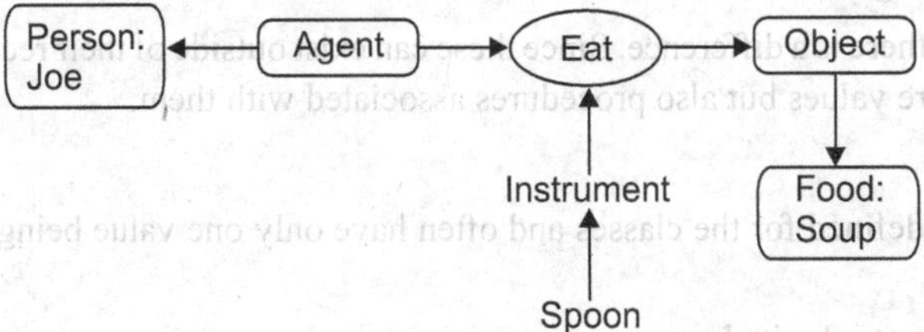

4.5.2 Frames

In 1975, Marvin Minsky coined the term frame. It is a method used to represent conceptual and Commonsense knowledge. Minsky proposed the organisation of knowledge in form of small packets called as **frames**. It is used to represent activities associated with conceptual events taking place, in say, a supermarket, theatre, college, university etc. This knowledge in form of frame is stored in the KB. The contents of the frames are slots which have certain values. The slots may be of any type and of any size slots have names and values (or subfields) called as **facets**. Facets may also have names and any number of values. An appropriate frame is selected from the memory for reasoning. Frames are of 2 types —

(*a*) **Declarative frames:** Frames consisting of only descriptive type of knowledge.

(*b*) **Procedural frames:** A frame having knowledge about the action or procedures.

So, a frame is a collection of attributes or slots and associated values that describe some real world entity.

NOTE: Frames → have slots for various objects → slots have values

A **frame-system** is a collection of objects. Each object contains a number of slots. A slot represents an attribute. Each slot has a value. The value of an attribute can be another object.

A general frame structure is shown below:

(< frame name >

(< slots 1 > (facet 1 < value l > … value k >)

(facet 2 < value 1 > … value k >)

:

(facet n <value n > … <value k>)

The frames can be attached with another frame to create **network of frames. Reasoning, using frames is done by instantiation process. The process in which the given situation is matched with frames that are already existing is known as instantiation. The reasoning process tries to match the current problem state with the frame slot and assigns them values. The values assigned to the slots depict a particular situation and by this the reasoning process moves towards a goal. Thus the reasoning process is defined as filling slots value in frames.** If the given slot characteristic is not present then the slot provides a default value for the characteristic. **Please note that the problem situation is generally not static.** The values of the corresponding slots are updated if there is any deviation in the characteristic.

Types of Slots

Slots are of three types as follows:

I. Inherent slots

(*a*) These slots are specified by the use for each class and the values are given during the instantiating of this class to obtain an object.

(*b*) These are comparable with the recording field of data and hence are the characteristic of the knowledge under consideration.

(*c*) However, there is a difference. Since these can exist outside of their recording they can have one or more values but also procedures associated with them.

II. Meta slots

(*a*) These are defined for the classes and often have only one value being related to the given class.

(*b*) These are **not** inherited.

(*c*) Such an attribute is the **ako** (a – kind– of) link mentioned in the semantic networks which relates one class to a more general class.

(*d*) Each class is related by **ako** to at least one other class. There exists exactly one class **linked** to itself, which is the vertex of the graph of **ako** links.

(*e*) The slot **ako** determines one of the fundamental interests of the object representation — INHERITANCE.

(*f*) At the level of instanced frames, it allows (by default) a frame to inherit certain values of the classes to which it is bound (related) by **ako**. If this frame is bound to several others, there can be **multiple** inheritance. The value of **ako** is a set of frames.

III. Instantiated slots

(*a*) Are defined for objects which are instances of classes.

(*b*) As priori, their creation is automatic during instantiating since they are ascribed to the instantiated class.

(*c*) This type of attribute is the **isa link** mentioned for semantic networks.

Please note that each slot possesses an arbitrary number of facets. These are the declarations or procedures associated to the attributes.

Many languages like LISP (i.e. List Processing) has in-build procedures to create, access, modify, update and display frames.

We must keep the following points in mind—

1. Instances of SLOT are slots.
2. Associated with SLOT are attributes that each instance will inherit.
3. Each slot has a domain and a range.

4. Since slot is a set of all slots, so can be represented by metaclass called slot.
5. To compute attribute involves a procedure to compute its value.

Advantages of Frames

1. Are very flexible.
2. Are similar to human knowledge organization, easier to understand logic or rules.

Disadvantages of Frames

1. No standards.
2. Very generalized approach
3. No associated reasoning mechanism.

Problems with both semantic nets and frames

1. Both net and frames are weak slot and filler structures. Both are arbitrary.
2. Both are useful for representing certain sorts of knowledge.
3. Both lack semantics i.e., precise meaning.
4. Logic generalizes these schemes.
5. Syntax of KR scheme is irrelevant.

4.5.3 Conceptual Dependencies (CDs)

In 1977, Roger *C* Schank developed CD structures. CD is used to represent knowledge again. This representation should be powerful enough to represent these concept of sentences of natural language. **CD theory states that different sentences which have same meaning should have some unique CD representation.** In CD theory, 5 different types of ontological (state of being) building blocks are distinguished —

(*a*) Entities.
(*b*) Actions.
(*c*) Conceptual cases.
(*d*) Conceptual Dependencies.
(*e*) Conceptual tenses.

Entities

(*a*) Picture Producer (PP) are actors that perform different acts.
(*b*) Picture Aiders (PA) are supporting properties or attributes of producers.
(*c*) ACT: Actions done by an actor to an object.
(*d*) LOCs: Shows the location of action,

Actions

(*a*) Primitive actions (ACTs).
(*b*) **Action Aiders** *(AA)* are properties or attributes of primitive action.

For **primitive actions,** a typical CD set is —

ATRANS	Transfer (example., 'give')
INGEST	Ingest into the body (example. 'eat')
EXPEL	Expel from body (example. 'cry')
ATTRANS	Abstract transfer (example. 'owner ship')

MORE	Move a body part (example. 'kick')
GRASP	Grasp an object (example. 'clutch')
PROPEL	Throw an object (example. 'push')
PTRANS	Physical transfer (example. 'go')
MTRANS	Mental transfer (example. 'tell')
CONC	Conceptualize (i.e., think about something).
ATTEND	Direct sensory orange to observe (example. listen).

The main goals of this theory are —

1. To capture the implicit concept of a sentence and make it *explicit*.
2. To help in drawing inferences from sentences.
3. For any 2 or more sentences that are identical in meaning, there should be only one representation of meaning.
4. To develop language conversion packages.
5. To provide a means of representation which are language independent.

In addition to the actors and objects other concept of time, location, source and destination are also used in *CD* representation—

(*i*)	O	:	Object case relationship
(*ii*)	r/R	:	Recipient case relationship
(*iii*)	p	:	Part
(*iv*)	f	:	future
(*v*)	t	:	transition
(*vi*)	Is	:	Start transition
(*vii*)	Tf	:	finish transition
(*viii*)	k	:	continuing
(*ix*)	?	:	interrogative
(*x*)	/	:	negative
(*xi*)	nil	:	present
(*xii*)	delta	:	timeless:
(xiii)	C	:	Conditional.

For example 1: Ram gives Anjali a book.

Its *CD* structure is as follows—

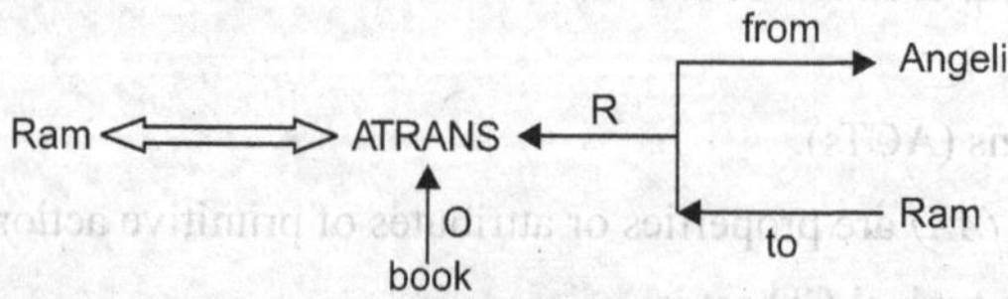

where the symbols used are —

(*a*) **Arrow:** indicates the direction of dependency.

(*b*) **Double arrow** indicates two-way link between actor and actions.

(*c*) **ATRANS** is a primitive to describe this event.

(*d*) *O* represents object case relationship.

(*e*) *R* indicates recipient case relationship.

Example 2: The man took a watch

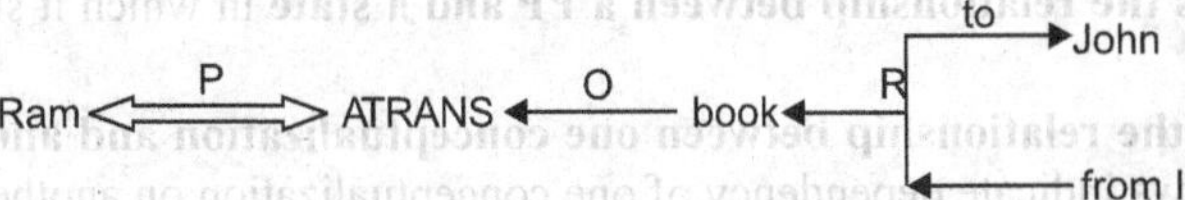

Here, 'men' is an actor and 'watch' is the object of the action 'took'.

Example 3: I gave John a book

Many a times, actors are missing from a sentence. This is a challenge. *For example.* 'Rajiv fell', sentence has a missing actor as another force "gravity" was acting. In such cases, we need additional optional notations:

R = reason
r = results
i = intends
d = direction
I = Instrument
R = recipient, state change.

So, the sentence '*Rajiv fell*' in CD is as follows—

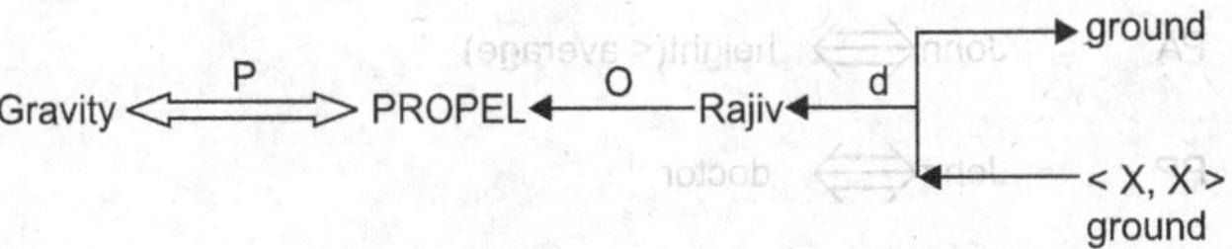

Parsing a sentence into CD representation is analogous to the process of parsing using a case grammar. The basic algorithm for building CD structure is as follows—

S1 : Obtain the root lexical item.

S2 : Access the lexical entry for the item and obtain the association tests and actions.

S3 : Perform the specified actions given with the entry.

We must study some rules for CD representation.

Rules of CD

Rule 1 describes the relationship between an actor and the event he or she causes. This is a two-way dependency since neither actor nor event can be considered primary. The letter above the dependency link indicates past tense.

Rule 2 describes the relationship between PP and PA that is being asserted to describe it. Many state descriptions, such as height, are represented in CD as numeric scales.

Rule 3 describes the relationship between two PPs, one of which belongs to the set defined by the other.

Rule 4 describes the relationship between a PP and an attribute that has already been predicated of it. The direction of the arrow is towards the PP being described.

Rule 5 describes the relationship between two PPs one of which provides a particular kind of information about the other. The three most common types of information to be provided in this way are procession (shown as POSS-BY), location (shown as LOC), and physical containment (shown as CONT). The direction of the arrow is again toward the concept being described.

Rule 6 describes the relationship between an ACT and the PP that is the object of that ACT. The direction of the arrow is toward the ACT since the context of the – specific ACT determines the meaning of the object relation.

Rule 7 describes the relationship between an ACT and the source and the recipient of the ACT.

Rule 8 describes the relationship between an ACT and the instrument with which it is performed. The instrument must always be a full conceptualization (i.e., it must contain an ACT), not just a single physical object.

Rule 9 describes the relationship between an ACT and its physical source and destination.

Rule 10 represents the relationship between a PP and a state in which it started and another in which it ended.

Rule 11 describes the relationship between one conceptualization and another that causes it. Notice that the arrows indicate dependency of one conceptualization on another and so point in the opposite direction of the implication arrows. The two forms of the rule describe the cause of an action and the cause of a state change.

Rule 12 describes the relationship between a conceptualization and the time at which the event occurred is described.

Rule 13 describes the relationship between one conceptualization and another, that is, the time of the first. The example for this rule also shows how CD exploits a model of the human information processing system; see is represented as the transfer of information between the eyes and the conscious processor.

Rule 14 describes the relationship between a conceptualization and the place at which it occurred.

	Rule	Example	
1.	PP ⇔ ACT	John ⇔(p) PTRANS	John run.
2.	PP ⇔ PA	John ⇔ height(< average)	John is tall.
3.	PP ⇔ PP	John ⇔ doctor	John is a doctor.
4.	PP ⇑ PA	boy ⇑ nice	A nice boy.
5	PP ⇑ PP	dog ⇑ Poss-by John p	John's dog.
6.	ACT ← pp	John ⇔ PROPEL ←(o) cart	John pushed the cart.
7.	ACT ←(R) → PP, < PP	John ⇔(p) ATRANS ←(R) to → John, from < Mary; ↑(o) book	John took the book from Mary.
8.	ACT ←(I) ⇕	John ⇔(p) INGEST ←(I) John ⇑ do; ↑(o) ice-cream; do ↑(o) spoon	John ate ice cream with a spoon.
9.	ACT ←(D) → PP, < PP	John ⇔(p) PTRANS ←(D) field, bag; ↑(o) fertilizer	John fertilized the field.
10.	PP ⇔ → PA, < PA	Plants ⇔ → size >, < size	The plants grew.

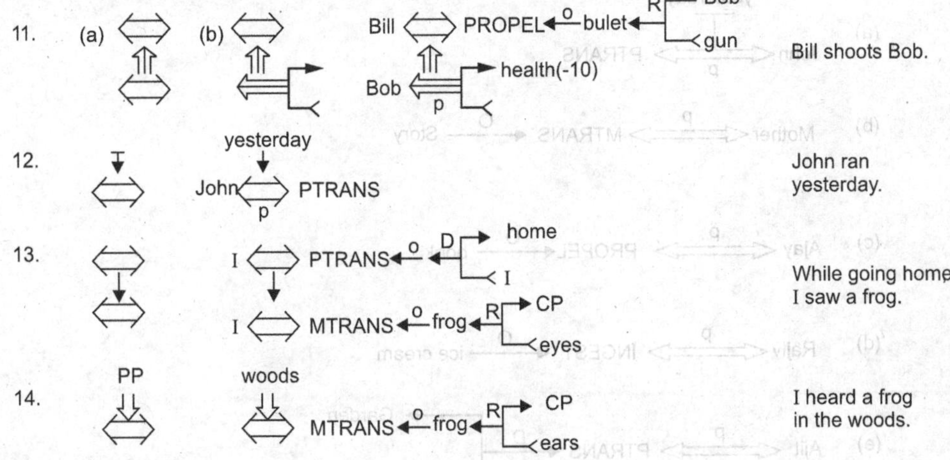

Fig. 4.10. Rules of CD

Advantages of CD

1. Lesser number of inference rules are required if we use CD primitives.
2. Many inference rules are already shown in CD structure.
3. The holes in the initial structure help to focus on the points which still is to be established.
4. Smaller number of primitive ACTs (i.e. 14).
5. Language free representation.

Disadvantages of CD

1. Knowledge must be decomposed into low level primitives.
2. A lot of inference is still needed.
3. Complex representations for simple actions also.
4. Lot of memory is required for storing complex representations.
5. It is not easy to find correct set of primitives.
6. Graph matching is NP – hard.

Applications of CDs

1. SAM (Script Applier Mechanism) — Script to understand stories.
2. PAM (Plan Applier Mechanism) — Scripts to understand stories.
3. MARGIE (Meaning, Analysis, Response Generation and Inference on English)
   It is a model of natural language understanding.

We are in the position to solve some problems now.

Q. 1. Represent the following in CD —

(*a*) John ran yesterday.
(*b*) My mother told me a story.
(*c*) Ajay pushed the book.
(*d*) Rajiv eats ice cream.
(*e*) Ajit fertilized the garden.

(a) John ⟺ PTRANS (p; yesterday)

(b) Mother ⟺ MTRANS ← Story (p; O)

(c) Ajay ⟺ PROPEL ← book (p; O)

(d) Rajiv ⟺ INGEST ← ice cream (p; O)

(e) Ajit ⟺ PTRANS (p); D: → Garden, ← boy; O: fertilizer

Q. 2. Give the CD representation of the following sentences.

(*i*) Joe gave Sue a flower.

(*ii*) Mohan will eat pizza with fork.

(*iii*) Charlie drove the car.

(*iv*) Since smoking can kill you, I stopped.

(*v*) Bill is a programmer.

(*vi*) Mary goes.

(*vii*) Mary will go.

(*viii*) Neeraj cried.

(*ix*) Bill threatened John with a broken nose.

(*x*) Anil punched Ram.

(*xi*) Ram lied.

(*xii*) Joe told Lucy he would not go to movies with her. Her feelings were hurt.

(*xiii*) Prem went to the park with peacocks.

(*xiv*) John will eat noodles with fork and knife.

(*xv*) Mohan is a sales manager.

(*xvi*) Kapil ate some soup.

(*xvii*) Mohan gave some books to Reeta.

(*xviii*) He will speak.

(*xix*) Anil will go tomorrow.

(*xx*) While going home, he saw a peacock.

(*xxi*) Ram heard noises in the kitchen.

(*xxii*) Hair is short.

(*xxiii*) Hari is a nice boy.

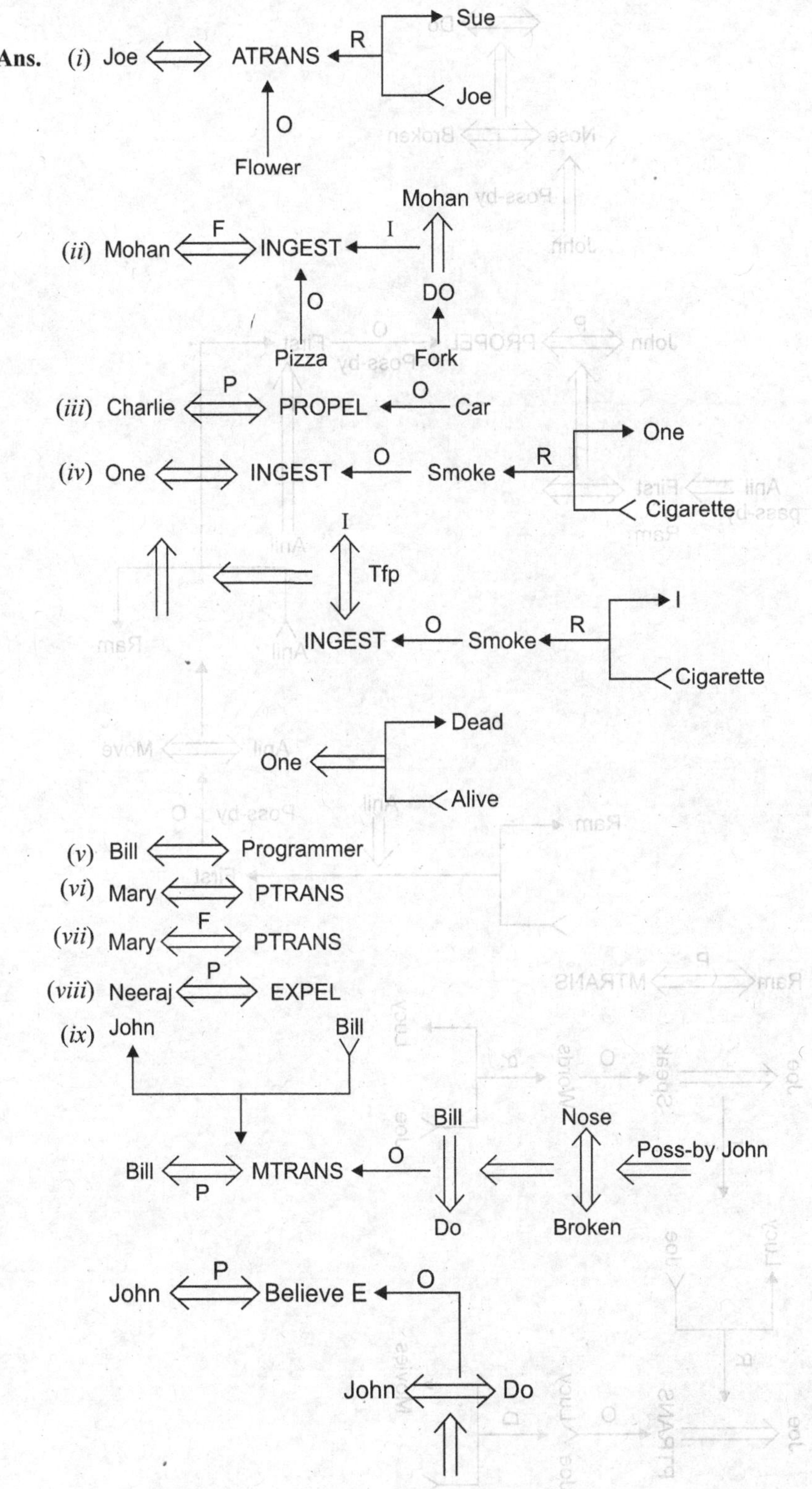
Ans. (i) Joe
ATRANS
R
Sue
Joe
O
Flower
(ii) Mohan
F
INGEST
I
Mohan
DO
O
Pizza
Fork
(iii) Charlie
P
PROPEL
O
Car
(iv) One
INGEST
O
Smoke
R
One
Cigarette
I
Tfp
INGEST
O
Smoke
R
I
Cigarette
One
Dead
Alive
(v) Bill
Programmer
(vi) Mary
PTRANS
(vii) Mary
F
PTRANS
(viii) Neeraj
P
EXPEL
(ix) John
Bill
Bill
P
MTRANS
O
Bill
Do
Nose
Broken
Poss-by John
John
P
Believe E
O
John
Do

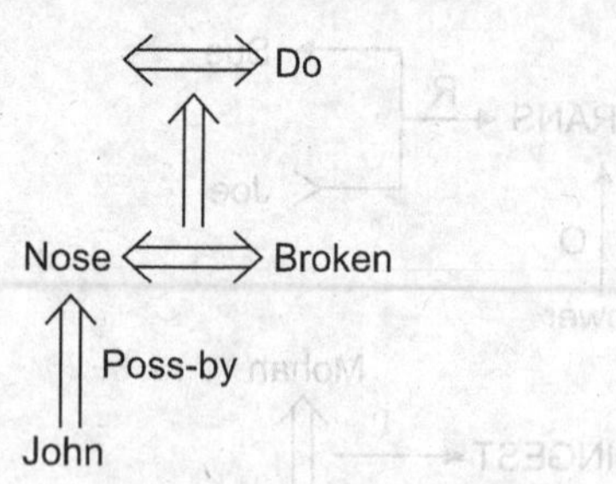

(x)

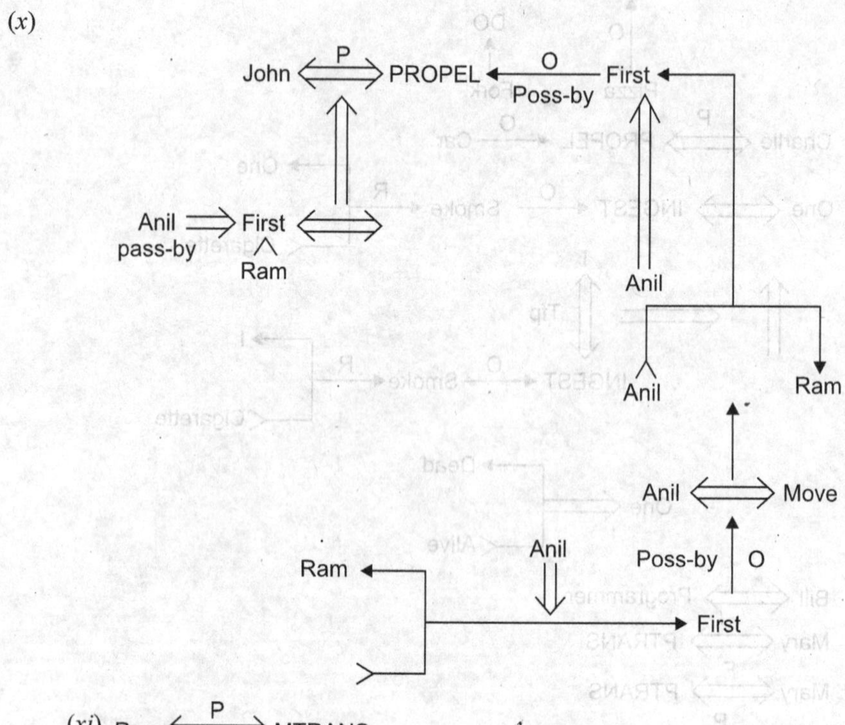

(xi) Ram $\overset{P}{\Longleftrightarrow}$ MTRANS

(xii)

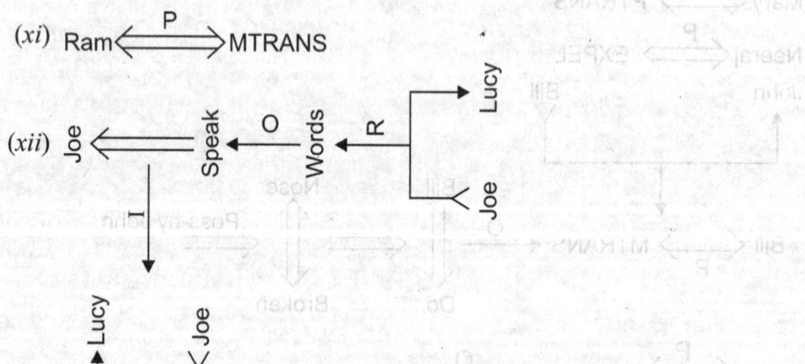

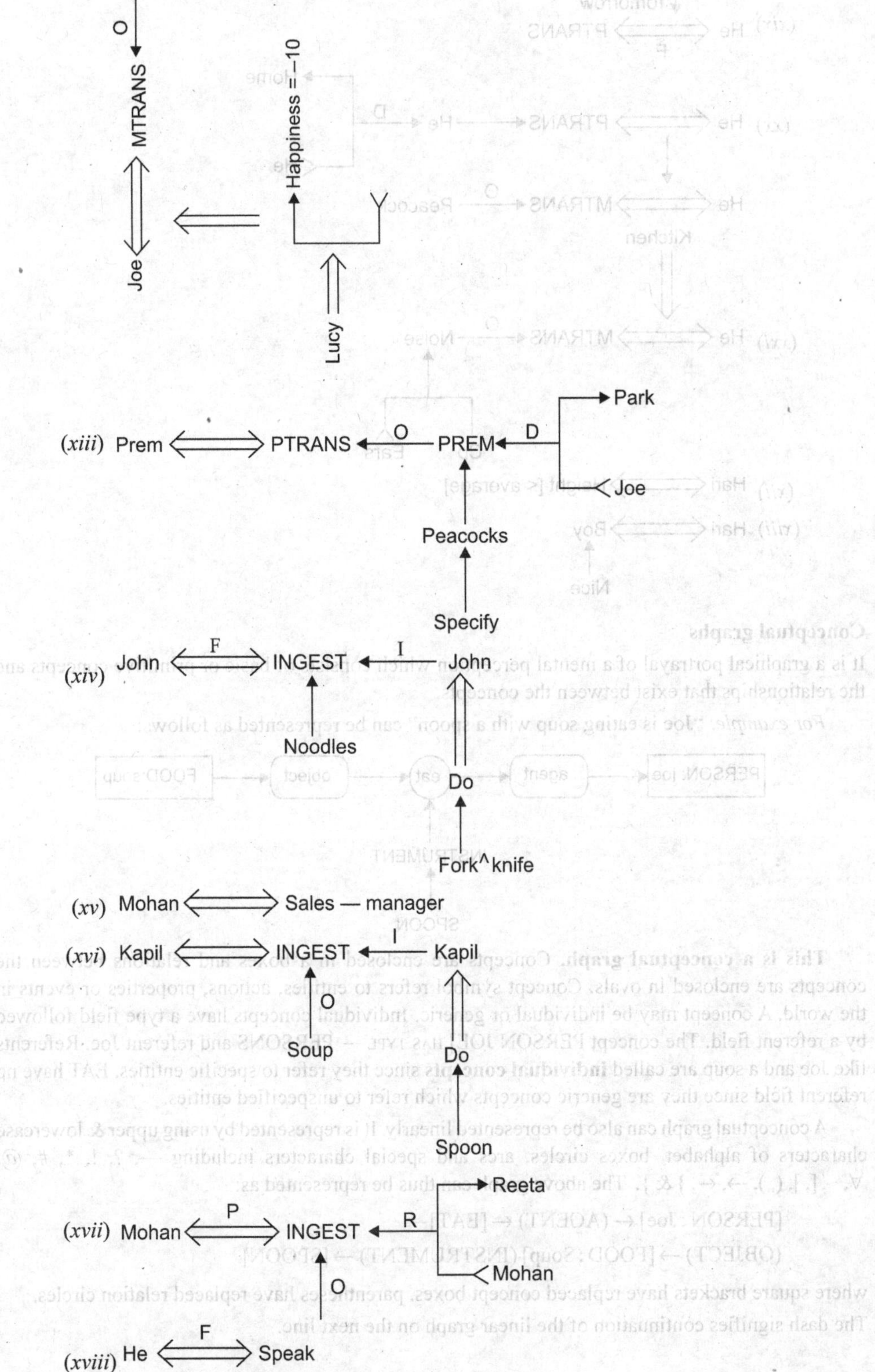

O
MTRANS
Joe
Happiness = –10
Lucy
(xiii) Prem
PTRANS
O
PREM
D
Park
Joe
Peacocks
Specify
(xiv) John
F
INGEST
I
John
Noodles
Do
Fork^knife
(xv) Mohan
Sales — manager
(xvi) Kapil
INGEST
I
Kapil
O
Soup
Do
Spoon
Reeta
(xvii) Mohan
P
INGEST
R
Mohan
O
(xviii) He
F
Speak

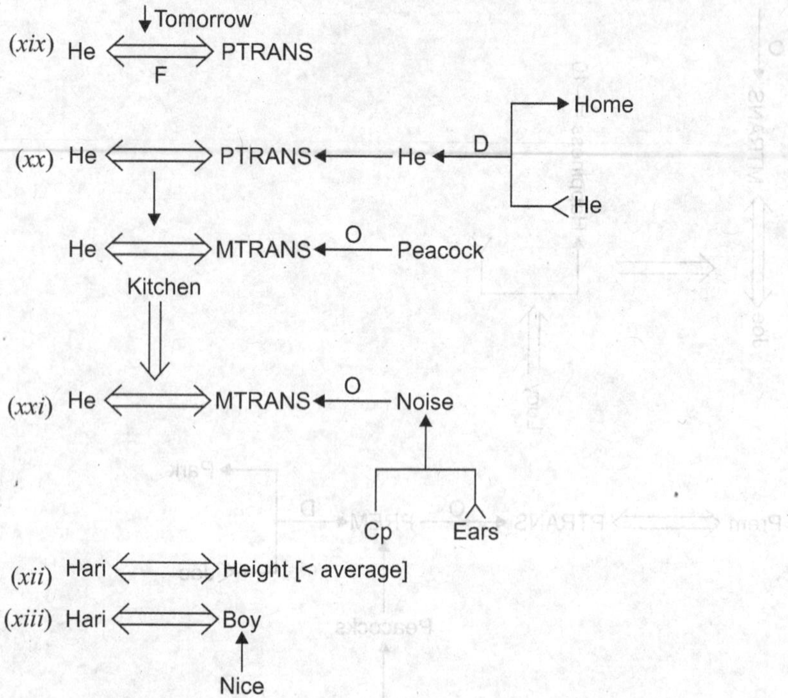

Conceptual graphs

It is a graphical portrayal of a mental perception which consists of basic or primitive concepts and the relationships that exist between the concepts.

For example: "Joe is eating soup with a spoon" can be represented as follows:

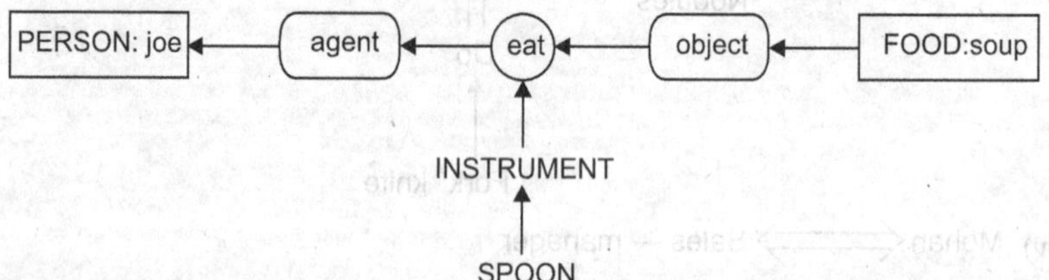

This is a conceptual graph. Concepts are enclosed in a boxes and relations between the concepts are enclosed in ovals. Concept symbol refers to entities, actions, properties or events in the world. A concept may be individual or generic. Individual concepts have a type field followed by a referent field. The concept PERSON JOE] HAS TYPE — PERSONS and referent Joe. Referents like Joe and a soup are called **individual concepts** since they refer to specific entities. EAT have no referent field since they are generic concepts which refer to unspecified entities.

A conceptual graph can also be represented linearly. It is represented by using upper & lowercase characters of alphabet, boxes circles, arcs and special characters including —, ?, !, *, #, @, ∀, ~, [,], (,), →, ←, } & }. The above graph can thus be represented as:

$$[\text{PERSON} : \text{Joe}] \leftarrow (\text{AGENT}) \leftarrow [\text{EAT}] -$$

$$(\text{OBJECT}) \rightarrow [\text{FOOD} : \text{Soup}]\ (\text{INSTRUMENT}) \rightarrow [\text{SPOON}]$$

where square brackets have replaced concept boxes, parentheses have replaced relation circles. The dash signifies continuation of the linear graph on the next line.

Example. 2. The sentence "Every car has an engine" can be represented as a conceptual graph —

$$[CAR : \forall] \rightarrow (PART) \rightarrow [ENGINE]$$

This conceptual graph can be converted into its FOPL as follows:

$$\forall x \, \exists y \, (CAR\,(x) \rightarrow (ENGINE\,(y) \,\&\, PART\,(x, y)))$$

We are in a position to solve examples now.

Q. 1. Express the following concepts as an associative network structure —

Company *ABC* is a software development company. Three departments within the company are Sales, Administration & Programming. Joe is the manager of Programming. Bill and Sue are programmers. Sue is married to Sam. Sam is an editor for Prentice Hall. They have 3 children and they live on Elm Street. He wears glasses and is 5 feet 4 inches tall.

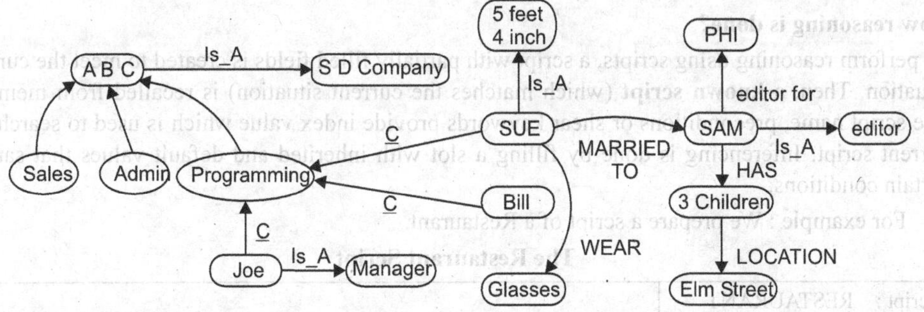

Q. 2. Represent the following as an associative network.

"GGSIPU is a State University established by the Act of Parliament. It has 9 schools of studies and 12 divisions to support the academic activities at the headquarters. It has 44 regional centres spread over the whole country. Each school and division is headed by a Director and each regional centre is headed by a Regional Director".

Ans.

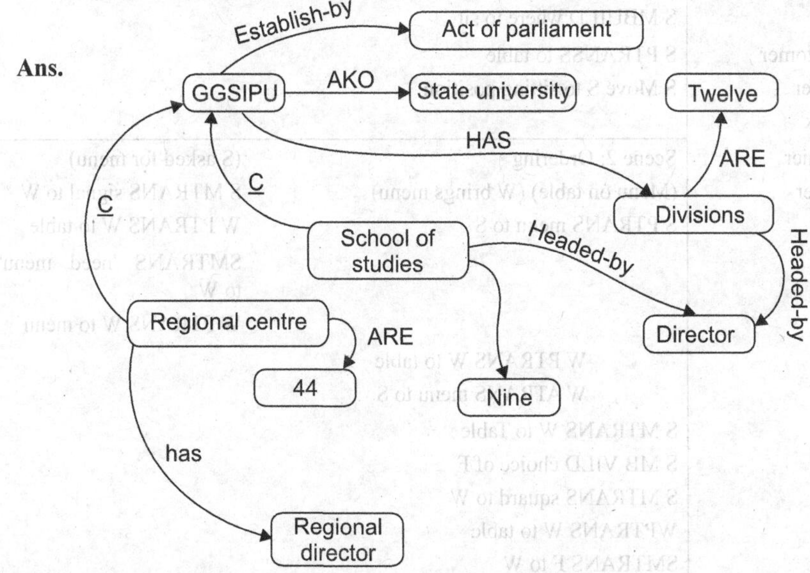

4.8.4 Scripts

A script is a structure that prescribes a set of circumstances which could be expected to follow on from one another. It is similar to a chain of situations which could be anticipated. Like a script for a play, the script's structure is defined in terms of —

(*a*) Actors (*b*) Roles (*c*) Props and (*d*) Scenes.

Please note that the slots in a script correspond to the parts of the event which are filled with CD primitives. It could be considered to consist of a number of slots or frames but with more specified robes. Scripts are frame-like structures to represent knowledge grouped from our common experiences like going to a movie, eating in a bar, visiting a doctor or shopping in a MALL etc.

Scripts are useful because —

(*a*) Events tend to occur in known runs or patterns.

(*b*) Entry conditions exist which allow an event to take place.

(*c*) Casual relationships between events exist.

(*d*) Prerequisites exist.

How reasoning is done?

To perform reasoning using scripts, a script with partially filled fields is created to meet the current situation. Then, a **known script** (which matches the current situation) is recalled from memory. The script name, preconditions or shear keywords provide index value which is used to search the current script. Inferencing is done by filling a slot with inherited and default values that satisfy certain conditions.

For example : We prepare a script of a Restaurant.

The Restaurant Script

Script : RESTAURANT		
Track : Coffee shop		
Propos : Tables		
Menu	Scene 1: Entering	
F = Food	S PTRANSS into restaurant	
Check	S ATTEND eyes to tables	
Money	S MBUILD where to sit	
Roles: S = Customer	S PTRANSS to table	
W = Waiter	S Move S to sitting position	
C = Cook		
M = Cashier	Scene 2: Ordering	(S asked for menu)
O = Owner	(Menu on table) (W brings menu)	S MTRANS signal to W
	S PTRANS menu to S	W PTRANS W to table
		SMTRANS 'need menu' to W
		W PTRANS W to menu
	W PTRANS W to table	
	W ATRANS menu to S	
	S MTRANS W to Table	
	S MB VILD choice of F	
	S MTRANS squard to W	
	WPTRANS W to table	
	SMTRANS F to W	
	W PTRANS W to C	
	W MTRANS (ATRANS F) to C	

Entry conditions: S is hungry. S has money. Results: S has less money O has more money. S is not hungry. S is pleased (optional).	CMTRANS no F to W WPTRRANS W to S W MTRANS no F to S (go back to*) or (go to Scene 4 at no pay path)	CDO (prepare F script) to Scence 3
	Scene 3 : Eating CATRANS F to ww ATRANS F to S S INGEST F Option: REturm to Scene 2 to order more; otherwise, go to scene 4	
	Scene 4: Exiting	
	S MTRANS to W (W ATRANS check to S W MOVE (write check) W PTRANS W to S W ATRANS check to S S ATRANS tip to W S PTRANS S to M S PTRANS S to out of restaurant (No pay path)	

Let us write an other script now.

Script Name: Interaction with car salesperson

PROPS	**Scenes**
Car showroom Car Feature Booklet Money Time	**Scene 1** • Customer enters the showroom • Search for a particular brand. • Salesperson attends customer and welcomes him
ROLES Customer Salesperson Owner Cashier	**Scene 2** • Sales person shows various cars • Customer selects particular car • Salesperson describes its features
INITIAL • Customer needs a car • Customer has more money • Salesperson has details about car • Availability of car in showroom • Owner has less money	**Scene 3** • Customer asks for a test drive • Salesperson takes him on a drive **Scene 4** • Customs is ready to buy • Customser asks for bill and warranty • Salesperson gets him warranty book and bill

RESULTS	Scene 5
• Customer bought a car • Salesperson got commission • Customer has less money • Owner has more money • Particular car count decreases	• Customer pays the money • Salesperson deposits it with cashier • Customer to gives commission to salesperson • Drives car back home

TRACKS none

Please note the following points about scripts:

1. If a particular script is to be applied then it must be activated and this activation depends on its significance.
2. If a topic is mentioned in passing then a pointer to that script could be held. Else if the topic is important then the script should be opened.
3. Having too many scripts is dangerous.
4. If events follow a known trail, then we can use scripts to represent the action involved and use them to answer detailed questions.
5. Different trails may be allowed for different outcomes of scripts.

Advantages of scripts

(*a*) They have ability to predict events.

(*b*) A single coherent interpretation may be built up from a collection of observations.

Disadvantages of scripts

(*a*) They are less general than framer.

(*b*) They are not suitable to represent all kinds of knowledge.

Applications of scripts

Shank and his team at YALE University used scripts in one system named as SAM — Script applier mechanism. SAM reads and reasons with text to demostrate an understanding of stories that were script based.

SUMMARY

This chapter discusses about advanced knowledge representation techniques like frames, nets, CG, CD and scripts. KR is one of the critical aspects to make our computer behave intelligently.

MULTIPLE CHOICE QUESTIONS [MCQs]

1. Data when processed gives information and Information when processed gives —

(*a*) Knowledge (*b*) Domain (*c*) Wisdom (*d*) None of these.

2. The knowledge about what we know is —

(*a*) Meta knowledge (*b*) Mini knowledge

(*c*) Micro knowledge (*d*) None of the above.

3. Concepts, objects, nets, logic etc are the examples of

(*a*) Tacit knowledge (*b*) Explicit knowledge

(*c*) Knowledge base (*d*) None of the above.

4. According to Robert Kowalski
   (*a*) Logic = Algorithm + Control (*b*) Algorithm = Logic + Control
   (*c*) Algorithm = Logic – Control (*d*) None of the above
5. The process of producing proofs by refutation or contradiction is known as —
   (*a*) Resolution (*b*) Proposition (*c*) Unification (*d*) None of these.
6. The universal quantifier is —
   (*a*) $\exists$ (*b*) $\wedge$ (*c*) $\forall$ (*d*) =
7. The process of eliminating existential quantifiers is known as
   (*a*) Resolution (*b*) Skolemisatio (*c*) Unification (*d*) None of these.
8. The Recursive process of merging two or more predicates with constants or with some variables is known as —
   (*a*) Resolution (*b*) Proposition (*c*) Unification (*d*) Proposition
9. Forward chaining is a —
   (*a*) Data-driven search (*b*) Goal-driven search
   (*c*) Heuristic search (*d*) None of the above.
10. A CD primitive that is used to do mental transfer is –
   (*a*) ATRANS (*b*) ATTRANS (*c*) PTRANS (*d*) MTRANS

ANSWERS

1. (*a*)	2. (*a*)	3. (*b*)	4. (*b*)	5. (*a*)
6. (*c*)	7. (*c*)	8. (*c*)	9. (*a*)	10. (*d*)

CONCEPTUAL SHORT QUESTIONS WITH ANSWERS

Q. 1. What is chaining?

Ans. In inferencing process, the rules are applied in succession till a situation arrives that there is no rule which is applicable. It is called as **chaining.**

Q. 2. What do you mean by a Universe of Discourse?

Ans. The universe of discourse or domain of discourse indicates the following —

(*a*) A set of entities that quantifiers deal with.

(*b*) Entities can be a set of integers, a set of real numbers, a set of students etc.

Universe is the domain of individual variables. Even propositions in logic are statement of an object of a universe.

Q. 3. What is matching? Name some matching techniques.

Ans. In matching process, the LHS of rule is compared with the input and all rules that match are extracted. Actually, both the current state of the problem and its preconditions are matched with the LHS of the rule. This is known as **matching**. Some matching techniques are as follows —

(*a*) Indexing

(*b*) Matching with variable

(*c*) Complex matching variable.

Q. 4. What is a Horn clause?

Ans. In a logic, a **Horn clause** is a clause (a disjunction of literals) with at most one positive literal. A Horn clause with exactly one positive literal is a ***definite clause;*** a Horn clause with no positive literals is sometimes called a ***goal clause,*** especially in logic programming. A ***Horn formula*** *is a* **conjunctive normal form formula whose clauses are all Horn;** in other words, it is a conjunction of Horn clauses. A ***dual-Horn*** clause is a clause with at most one **negative** literal. Horn clauses play a basic role in logic programming and are important for constructive logic.

The following is an example of a definite Horn clause:

$$\neg P \vee \neg q \vee \ldots \vee \neg t \vee u$$

Such a formula can be rewritten in the following form, which is more common in logic programming and similar fields:

$$(p \wedge q \wedge \ldots \wedge t) \rightarrow u$$

The relevance of Horn clauses to theorem proving by first-order resolution is that the resolution of two Horn clauses is a **Horn clause**. Moreover, the resolution of a goal clause and a definite clause is again a goal clause. In automated theorem proving, this can lead to greater efficiencies in proving a theorem represented as a goal clause. In fact, Prolog is a programming language based on Horn clauses.

Horn clauses are also of interest in computational complexity, where the problem of finding a set of a variable assignments to make a conjunction of Horn clauses true is a P-complete problem, *sometimes called HORNSAT*. This is P's version of a boolean satisfiability problem, a central NP-complete problem.

NOTE: The name "Horn clause" comes from the logician Alfred Horn who first pointed out the significance of such clauses.

Q. 5 Represent the following in FOPL—

1. Lipton is a tea.
2. Lata is a child who drinks tea.
3. Ruma dislikes children who drink tea.
4. Ruma disliked Lata. **[UPTU, B.Tech (CSE) – 6th Sem., 2004-05]**

Ans. (*i*) Tea (Lipton)

(*ii*) $\exists x$ [child (x) $\wedge$ drinks (x, tea)]

$\exists x$ [child (Lata) $\wedge$ drinks (Lata, tea)]

(*iii*) $\forall x$ [drinks (x, tea) $\Rightarrow$ dislikes (Ruma, x)]

(*iv*) Dislikes (Ruma, Lata).

Q. 6. Express following knowledge as a semantic network with nodes and labeled arcs. "Sam is Vice-President in ABC Corp. He is married to Kay and has a male child named Joe. Joe goes to school. Sam plays golf and owns a silver colored German-made car Mercedes Benz." [UPTU, B.Tech (CSE) 6th Sem., 2004-5]

Ans. Semantic net diagram:

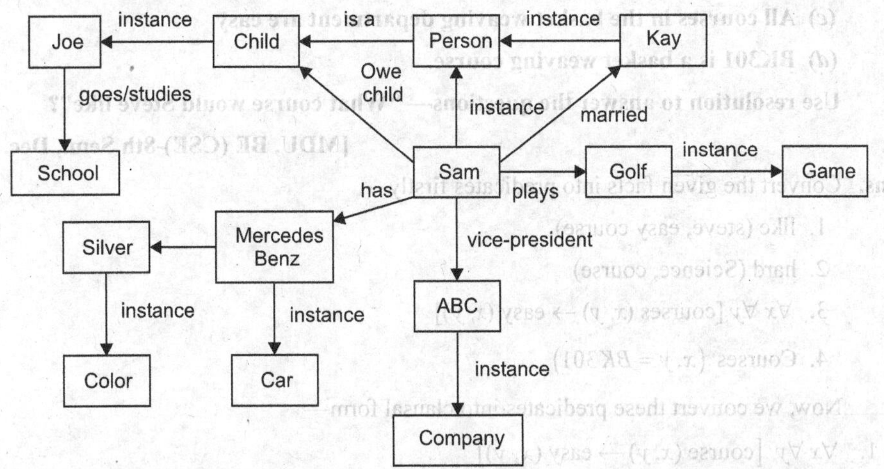

Q. 7. Sam, Clyde and Oscar are elephants. We know the following facts about them —

(*a*) Sam is pink.

(*b*) Clyde is gray and likes Oscar.

(*c*) Oscar is either pink or gray (but not both) and likes Sam.

[MDU, BE (CSE) — 8th Sem., May 2007]

Use resolution to prove that gray elephants like pink elephant, i.e., prove that

$$[\exists x, y][\text{grey } (x) \wedge \text{pink } (x) \wedge \text{likes } (x, y)]$$

Ans. 'SAM is pink' can be represented as—

pink (Sam) ...(1)

Similarly, other two facts can be represented as—

grey (clyde) ∧ likes (clyde, oscar) ...(2)

and (pink (oscar) ∨ grey (oscar) ∧ likes (oscar, sam) ...(3)

Given:

$$[\exists x, y][\text{grey } (x) \wedge \text{pink } (x) \wedge \text{likes } (x, y)]$$

Grey [x] from 2 it implies—

Grey [Clyde] but does not fulfil the criteria of pink.

∴ from (3) we get—

Grey (Oscar), Pink (Oscar)

and also likes (Oscar, Sam)

∴ $x \Rightarrow$ Oscar

$y \Rightarrow$ Sam

It means that Oscar likes Sam.

Q. 8. Assume the following facts —

(*a*) Steve only likes easy courses.

(*b*) Science courses are hard.

(*c*) All courses in the basket weaving department are easy

(*d*) BK301 is a basket weaving course.

Use resolution to answer the questions— "What course would Steve like"?

[MDU, BE (CSE)-8th Sem., Dec. 2005]

Ans. Convert the given facts into predicates firstly –

1. like (steve, easy course) ...(1)
2. hard (Science, course) ...(2)
3. $\forall x\, \forall y$ [courses (x, y) → easy (x, y)]
4. Courses $(x, y = BK301)$

Now, we convert these predicates into clausal form—

1. $\forall x\, \forall y\ [\text{course}\ (x, y) \rightarrow \text{easy}\ (x, y)]$

$\forall x\, \forall y\ [\neg \text{course}\ (x, y) \vee \text{easy}\ (x, y)]$

$$\left[\begin{array}{l} \because \neg(\neg P) = P \\ \& \neg(a \wedge b) = \neg a \vee \neg b \\ \& \neg(a \vee b) = \neg a \wedge \neg b \end{array}\right]$$

2. Course (x, y = BK 301)

$[\forall x \forall y (\neg \text{ course } (x, y) \vee \text{easy } (x, y)] \wedge \text{course } (x, y = \text{BK } 301)$

$\Rightarrow \text{easy } (x, \text{BK } 301)$ ...(3)

This implies that BK301 is an easy course.

Now, consider equation (1) and equation (3):

Like (steve, easy course) ∧ easy (x, BK301)

∴ Steve likes BK301

Now, consider (1) and (2)

Like (steve, easy course) ∧ hard (Science, courses)

⇒ steve doesn't like science

What course would Steve like?

It is clearly proved by equation (3) that Steve likes BK301.

Q.9 Given two clauses— Loves (Father (a), a) and loves (y, x). What must be generated as a result of resolving these two clauses? [MDU, BE (CSE)-8th Sem., Dec 2005]

Ans. Given:

loves (Father (a), a) and loves (y, x)

a = x

Father (a) = y

Father (x) = y

This means that Father of x is y.

Now, love (Father (a), a)

loves (y, x) ∨ loves (x, y)	
loves (Father (a), a)	loves (Father (a), a)
loves (y, x)	loves (x,y)
∴ Father (a) = y	∴ Father (a) = x
and a = x	and a = y

Which is NOT possible.

Thus, these two clauses cannot be unified.

Q. 10. The following statements are given —

(*i*) Rishi likes to eat peanut.

(*ii*) Rishi eats whatever John eats.

(*iii*) John eats only eatables.

(*iv*) Anybody who eats eatables is a human being.

(*v*) Peanut is an eatable.

(*a*) Convert these into wff and clausal form.

(*b*) Is John a human being? Answer this using back tracking and resolution.

[MDU. BE (CSE)-8th Sem., May 2005]

Ans. (*a*) The WFF notations are—

1. Likes (Rishi, Peanut)
2. ∀xy eats (Rishi, y) → eats (John, y)
3. ∀y eats (John, y)
4. ∀x ∀y eats (x, y) → human being (x)
5. eatable (y = peanut)

Its clausal form is as follows —

1. Likes (Rishi, y1) ...(1)
2. ∀y eats (Rishi, y) → eats (John, y)

   ∀x ¬ eats (Rishi, y) ∨ eats (John, y)

∴ ¬ eats (Rishi, y2) ∨ eats (John, y2) ...(2)

3. ∀y eats (John, y) is

   eats (John, y3) ...(3)

4. ∀x ∀y eats (x, y) → human being (x)

   ∀x ∀y ¬ eats (x, y) ∨ human being (x)

∴ ¬ eats (x1, y4) ∨ human being (y4) ...(4)

5. eatable (y = peanut) is

   eatable (y5) ...(5)

6. Is John a human being?

   i.e. human being (John)

We start with opposite of this (i.e. negation)

¬ human being (John)

∴ Using back tracking and Resolutions we get —

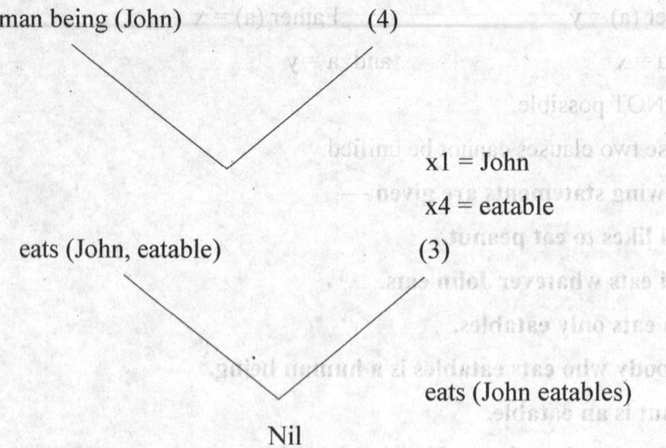

∴ It is proved that John is a human being.

Q. 11. Assume the following facts —

(*a*) Ram likes only easy courses.

(*b*) Engg. courses are hard.

(*c*) All courses in Arts are easy.

(*d*) AR04 is an Arts course.

Use resolution to answer the question, "What course would Ram like?"

[MDU, BE (CSE)-8th Sem., Dec. 2004]

Ans. Let us find its Predicate clause firstly,

$\exists y$ easy (y) $\rightarrow$ likes (Ram, y)

$\exists y$ easy course (x) $\rightarrow$ hard (x)

$\forall x$ art course (x) $\rightarrow$ easy (x)

art course(AR04)

∴ Its clausal form is—

like (Ram, easy courses)

hard course (Engineering)

easy (art courses)

AR04 (art course). Now, we use resolution to prove our query.

like (Ram, easy courses) ¬ hard courses (Engineering)

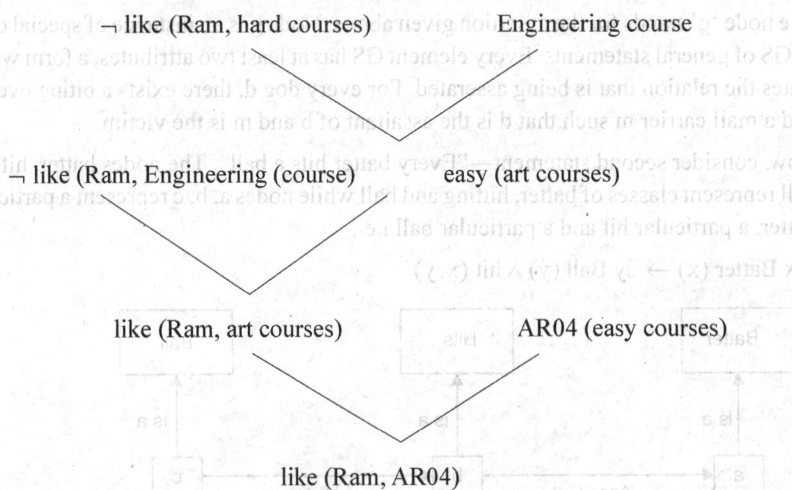

∴ Answer is: Ram likes AR04.

Q. 12. Describe the term 'Partitioned Semantic Net'. Also construct a Partitioned semantic Net representation for the following:

(*a*) Every dog has bitten a mail carrier.

(*b*) Every batter hits a ball. **[MDU, BE (CSE)-8th Sem., Dec. 2004]**

Ans. It is a representation for simple quantified expressions in a semantic net in which semantic net is partitioned into a hierarchical set of spaces each of which corresponds to the scope of one or more variable.

(*a*) Consider a simple net corresponding to statement—"The dog bit the mail carrier", given below—

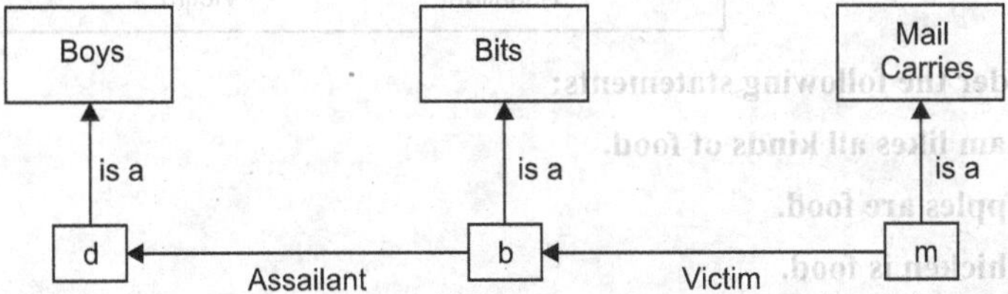

The nodes–Dogs, Bite and bitings and Mail carriers. Nodes d, b and m represent a particular dog, a particular biting and a particular Mail carrier. This fact can easily be represented by a single net with no partitioning. If we represent the fact "Every dog has bitten a mail carrier" or the logic.

$\forall x \text{ Dog}(x) \rightarrow \exists y \text{ Mail} - \text{carrier}(y) \wedge \text{Bite}(x, y)$

Example,

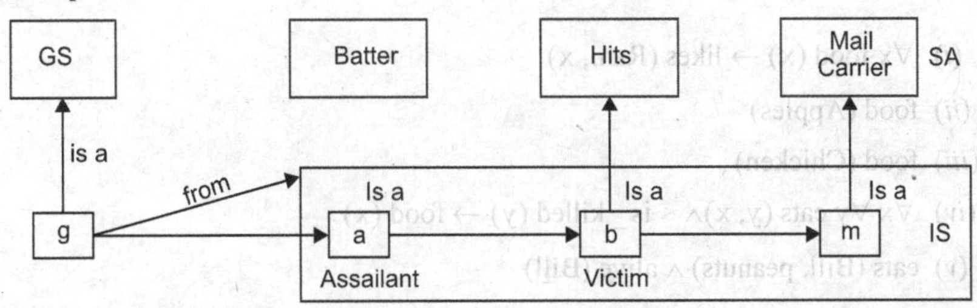

The node 'g' stands for the assertion given above. Node g is an instance of special class of GS of general statements. Every element GS has at least two attributes, a form which states the relation that is being asserated. For every dog d, there exists a biting event b and a mail carrier m such that d is the assaitant of b and m is the victim.

(*b*) Now, consider second statement—"Every batter hits a ball". The nodes batter, hit and ball represent classes of batter, hitting and ball while nodes a, b, c represent a particular batter, a particular hit and a particular ball i.e.,

$\forall x$ Batter (x) $\rightarrow \exists y$ Ball (y) $\wedge$ hit (x, y)

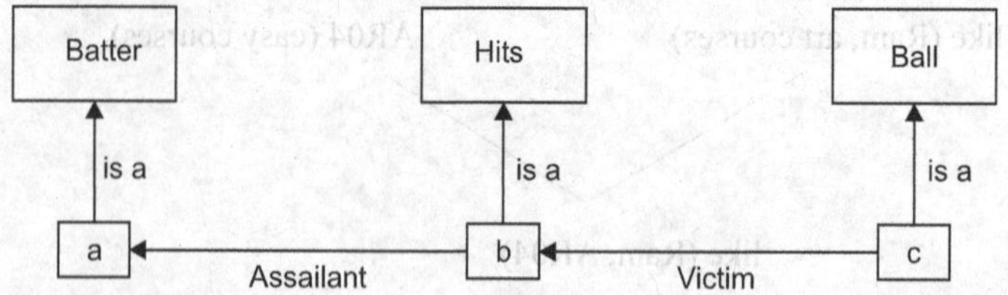

To represent this face, we take node g which stands for assertion given above. Node g is an instance of the special class GS of general statements. Every element of GS has at least two attributes, a form which states the relation that is being asserted and one or more $\forall$ connections.

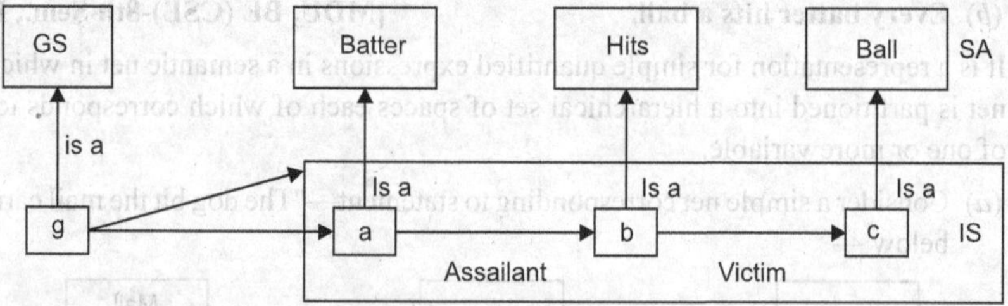

Q. 13. Consider the following statements:

(*i*) Ram likes all kinds of food.

(*ii*) Apples are food.

(*iii*) Chicken is food.

(*iv*) Anything anyone eats and isn't killed by is food.

(*v*) Bill eats peanuts and is still alive.

(*vi*) Rita eats everything Bill eats.

Translate these sentences into formulas in predicate logic.

[MDU, BE (CSE)-8th Sem., & RTM, Nagpur Univ. BE (IT), Winter 2007 & 2008]

Ans.

(*i*) $\forall x$ food (x) $\rightarrow$ likes (Ram, x)

(*ii*) food (Apples)

(*iii*) food (Chicken)

(*iv*) $\forall x \forall y$ eats (y, x) $\wedge$ ~ is_killed (y) $\rightarrow$ food (x)

(*v*) eats (Bill, peanuts) $\wedge$ alive (Bill)

(*vi*) $\forall x$ eats (Bill, x) $\rightarrow$ eats (Rita, x)

Q. 14. Say, whether or not the following pairs of expressions are unifiable and show the most general unifier for each unifiable pair —

(*a*) P(x,B,B) and P(A,y,z)

(*b*) P (g (f(v)), g(u)) and P(x, x).

(*c*) P (x, f(x0) and P (y, y)

(*d*) P (y, y, B) and P (z, x, z)

(*e*) 2 + 3 = x and x = 3 + 3

Ans. (*a*) Yes, is unifiable. The most general unifier is —

A / x, B / y, B / z

(*b*) Yes". Unifier is g(u)/x, f(v)/u

(*c*) No. It doesn't unify.

(*d*) Yes. B/z, B/y, B/x

(*e*) Yes. First replace x by y in 2nd expression (standardizing variables) then (2 +3)/y and (3 + 3)/x.

Q. 15. Explain why P (f (x, x), A) does not unify with P (f (y, f (y, A)), A).

Ans. The problem involves an attempt to unify f (x, x) with f (y, f (y, A)). In these expressions, the outer f's match and y can be substituted for x leaving the problem of unifying y with f (y, A). Here, since y occurs in f (y, A), these two expressions cannot be unified.

Q. 16. Convert the following to clause form:

1. $((\exists x)[P(x)] \vee ((\exists x)[Q(x)]) \supset (\exists x)[P(x) \vee Q(x)]$
2. $(\forall x)[P(x) \supset (\forall y)[(\forall z)[Q(x,y)] \supset \neg(\forall z)[R(y,x)]]]$
3. $(\forall x)[P(x) \supset (\exists x)[(\forall z)[Q(x,y)] \vee (\forall z)[R(x, y, z)]]$
4. $(\forall x)[P(x) \supset Q(x,y)] \supset ((x\ y)[P(y)] \wedge (\exists z)[Q(y,z)])$

Ans.

1. $((\exists x)[P(x)] \vee ((\exists x)[Q(x)]) \supset (\exists x)[P(x) \vee Q(x)]$

$(\neg((\exists x)[P(x)] \vee (\exists x)(Q(x)) \vee (\exists x)[P(x) \vee Q(x)]$

$(\neg((\exists x)[P(x)] \wedge \neg(\exists x)(Q(x)) \vee (\exists x)[P(x) \vee Q(x)]$

$((\forall x)[\neg P(x)] \wedge (\forall x)!\neg Q(x) \vee (\exists x)[P(x) \vee Q(x)]$

$((\forall x)[\neg P(x)] \wedge (\forall x)!\neg Q(y) \vee (\exists x)[P(z) \vee Q(z)]$

$((\forall x)[\neg P(x)] \wedge (\forall y)[\neg Q(y)] \vee [P(Sk) \vee Q(Sk)]$

$(\forall x)(\forall z)[[\neg P(x)] \wedge Q(y)] \vee [P(Sk) \vee Q(Sk)]]$

$[\neg P(x) \wedge Q(y)] \vee [P(Sk) \vee Q(sk)]$

$[\neg P(x) \wedge P(Sk) \vee Q(Sk)] \wedge [\neg Q(y) \vee P(Sk) \vee Q(Sk)]]$

$[\neg P(x) \wedge P(Sk), Q(Sk)] [\neg Q(z) \vee P(Sk) \vee Q(Sk)]$

2. $(\forall x)[P(x) \supset (\forall y)[(\forall z)[Q(x,y)] \supset \neg(\forall z)[R(y,x)]]]$

$(\forall x)[\neg P(x) \vee (\forall y)[(\forall z)Q(x,y)] \supset \neg(\forall z)[R(y,x)]]]$

$(\forall x)[\neg P(x) \vee (\forall y)]\neg(\forall z)[Q(x,y)] \vee \neg(\forall z)[R(y,x)]]]$

$(\forall x)[\neg P(x) \vee (\forall y)][(\exists z)]\neg Q(x,y) \vee (\exists z)[\neg R(y,x)]]]$

$(\forall x)[\neg P(x) \vee (\forall y)](\exists z)[\neg Q(x,y)] \vee (\exists z)[\neg R(y,x)]]]$

$(\forall x)[\neg P(x) \vee (\forall y)[\neg Q(x,y) \vee \neg R(y,x)]]]$

$(\forall x(\forall y)\neg P(x) \vee \neg Q(x,y) \vee \neg R(y,x)]$

$\neg P(x) \vee \neg Q(x,y) \vee \neg R(y,x)$

$\}\neg P(x), \neg Q(x,y), \neg R(y,x)\}$

3. $(\forall x)[P(x) \supset (\exists x)[(\forall z)[Q(x,y)] \vee (\forall z)[R(x,y,z)]]$

$(\forall x)[\neg(\forall x)[P(x)] \vee (\exists x)[(\forall z)[Q(x,z)] \wedge (\forall z)[R(x,y,z)]]$

$(\forall y)[(\exists x)[\neg P(x)] \vee (\exists x)[(\forall z)[Q(x,z)] \vee (\forall z)[R(x,y,z)]]]$

$(\forall y)[(\exists x)[\neg P(x)] \vee (\exists x)[(\forall z)[Q(t,z)] \vee (\forall u)[R(t,y,u)]]]$

$(\forall y)[\neg P(f_1(y)) \vee (\forall z)[Q(f_2(y),z)] \vee (\forall u)[R(f_2(y),y,u)]]]$

$(\forall y)(\forall z)(\forall u)[\neg P(f_1(y)) \vee Q(f_2(y),z)] \vee R(f_2(y),y,u)]$

$\neg P(f_1(y) \vee Q(f_2(y),z) \vee R(f_2(y),y,u)$

$\{\neg P(f_1(y)), Q(f_2(y)),z), R(f_2(y),y,u)\}$

4. $(\forall y)[(\forall x)[P(x) \supset Q(x,y)] \supset ((\exists y)[P(y)] \wedge (\exists z)[Q(y,z)]]]$

$(\forall y)[\neg(\forall x)P(x) \supset Q(x,y)] \vee (\exists y)[P(y)] \wedge (\exists z)[Q(y,z))]]$

$(\forall y)[\neg(\forall x)[\neg P(x) \vee Q(x,y)] \vee ((\exists y)[P(y)] \wedge (\exists z)[Q(y,z))]]$

$(\forall y)[(\exists x)[P(x) \wedge \neg Q(y,z))] \vee ((\exists y)[P(y)] \wedge (\exists z)[Q(y,z)]]]$

$(\forall y)[(\exists x)[P(x) \wedge \neg Q(y,z))] \vee ((\exists u)[P(u)] \wedge (\exists z)[Q(y,z)]]]$

$(\forall y)[[P(f_1(y)) \wedge \neg Q(f_1(y),y)] \vee [P(f_2(y)) \wedge Q(z,f_2(y))]]]$

$(\forall y)[[P(f_1(y)) \vee P(f_2(y))] \wedge [P(f_2(y)) \vee Q(y,f_2(y))]]] \wedge [\neg Q(f_1(y),y) \vee P(f_2(y))]$
$\wedge [\neg Q(f_1(y),y) \vee Q(y,f_2(y))]]]$

$[P(f_1(y)) \vee P(f_1(y))] \wedge [P(f_1(y_1) \vee Q(y,f_3(y)] \wedge [\neg Q(f_1(y_1,y) \vee P(f_2(y)]$
$\wedge [\neg Q(f_2(y_1,y), Q(y,f_2(y))]]]$

$[(\exists x)P(x)] \supset Q(A)$

$[\neg(\exists x)P(x)] \vee Q(A)$

$[(\forall x)\neg P(x)] \vee Q(A)$

$[(\forall x)[\neg P(x)] \vee Q(A)]$

$[(\forall x)][P(x)] \supset Q(A)]$

After this transformation, we recognize that any formula of the form $\gamma \supset \gamma$ is valid.

Analogous operations on the second formula show that it too is valid.

The third formula is an instance of the well-known invalid formula $(\exists x)\gamma(x) \supset (\forall x)\gamma(x)$.

A counter example is P(a) is False. P(B) is True, and Q(A) is False (for A being some element of the domain).

Q. 17. Convert the following formula into one that has neither an existential quantifier nor a Skolem function.

$(\forall x, y)\{\exists z)[0n(x,z) \wedge \text{Above }(z,y)] \supset \text{Above }(x,y)\}$?

Ans. We use the following steps:

$(\forall x, y)\{\exists z)[0n(x,z) \wedge \text{Above }(z,y)] \supset \text{Above }(x,y)\}$

$(\forall x, y)\{\neg\exists z)[0n(x,z) \wedge \text{Above }(z,y)] \vee \text{Above }(x,y)\}$

$(\forall x, y)\{(\forall z)\neg\{0n(x,z) \wedge \text{Above }(z,y)\} \vee \text{Above }(x,y)\}$

$(\forall x, y)\{(\forall z)\{\neg 0n(x,z) \vee \neg\text{Above }(z,y)\} \vee \text{Above }(x,y)\}$

$(\forall x, y, z)[\neg 0n(x,z) \vee \neg\text{Above }(z,y) \vee \text{Above }(x,y)]$

An equivalent form is:

$(\forall x, y, z)\{[0n(x,z) \wedge \text{Above}(z,y)] \supset \text{Above}(x,y)]$

Q. 18. Use resolution refutation on a set of clauses to prove that there is a green object if we are given:

- **If pushable objects are blue, then nonpushable ones are green.**
- **All objects are either blue or green but not both.**
- **If there is a nonpushable object then all pushable ones are blue.**
- **Object 01 is pushable.**
- **Object 02 is not pushable.**

1. **Convert these statements to expressions in first-order predicate calculus.**
2. **Convert the preceding predicate-calculus expressions to clause form.**
3. **Combine the preceding clause form expressions with the clause form of the negation of the statement to be proved and then show the steps used in obtaining a resolution refutation.**

Ans.

1. 1. $(\forall x)[P(x) \supset B(x)] \supset (\forall x)[\neg P(x) \supset G(x)]$

2 *a.* $(\forall x)[B(x) \supset \neg G(x)]$

2 *b.* $(\forall x)[G(x) \vee B(x)]$

3. $(\exists x)\neg P(x) \supset (\forall x)[P(x) \supset B(x)]$

4. P(01)

5. $\neg$P(02)

2. 1 *a.* $P(SK) \vee P(x) \vee G(x)$

1 *b.* $\neg B(SK) \vee P(x) \vee G(x)$

2 *a.* $\neg B(x) \vee \neg G(x)$

2 *b.* $B(x) \vee G(x)$

3. P(x) ∨ ¬P(y) ∨ B(y)
4. P(01)
5. ¬P(02)

3. 6. (negation of theorem): ¬G(x)
7. (resolving 6 and 2b yields) B(x)
8. (resolving 7 and 1b yields) P(x) ∨ G(x)
9. (resolving 8 and 5 yields) G(02)
10. (resolving 9 and 6 yields) contradiction.

Q. 19. The function cons(x,y) denotes the list formed by inserting the element x at the made of the list y. We denote the empty list by Nil; the list (2) by cons (2, Nil); the list (1, 2) by cons (1, cons (2, Nil)); and so on. The formula Last (1, e) is intended to mean that i.e. the last element of the list 1. We have the following axioms:

- (∀u) [Last(cons(u, Nil), u)]
- (∀x y z) [Last(y, z) ⊃ Last(cons(x, y), z)]

1. Prove the following theorem from these axioms by the method of resoltion refutation: (∃v)[Last(cons(2, cons(1, Nil)), v)]
2. Use answer extraction of find v, the last element of the list (2, 1).

Ans. 1. We first write the axioms in clause form:

(*a*) Last(cons(u, Nil), u)

(*b*) ¬Last(y, z) ∨ Last(cons(x, y), z)

We then negate the goal to get:

(*c*) ¬Last(cons(2, cons(1, Nil)), v)

Resolving (b) and (c), with m.g.u. {2/x cons(1, Nil/y, v/z), we get

(*d*) ¬Last(cons(1, Nil), v)

We can now resolve (a) and (b) with m.g.u. {1/e, 1/v} to get the empty clause.

2. The axioms (*a*) and (*b*) are the same as in part (1). In order to do answer extraction a predicate Ans (*v*) is appended to the clause containing the negated goal:

(*e*) ¬Last(cons(2, cons(1, Nil)), v) ∨ Ans(v)

Resolving (b) and (e), with m.g.u {2/x, con(1, Nil)/y, v/z}, we get:

(*f*) ¬Last(cons(1, Nil), v) ∨ Ans(v)

We can now resolve (a) and (f) with m.g.u. {1/u, 1/v} to get:

(g) Ans (1)

Therefore the last element of the list (2, 1) is 1.

Q. 20. A logic circuit has four wires W1, W2, W3 and W4. It has an "and gate". A, and an "inverter", B. The input wires, W1 and W2, can be either "on" or not. If the and gate, A, is functioning properly (OK), wire W3 is "on" if and only if wires W1 and W2 both are "on". If the inverter, B, is functioning properly (OK), wire W4 is "on" if and only if wire W3 is not "on". Translate it into a set of WFFs.

Ans. $\{P(f_1(y)), P(f_2(y))\}, \{P(f_1(y)), Q(y, f_3(y))\}$

$\{\neg Q(f_1(y), y), P(f_2(y))\}, \{\neg Q(f_1(y), y), Q(y, f_3(y))\}$

$\{P(f_1(y)), P(f_2(y_1))\}, \{P(f_1(y_2)), Q(y, f_3(y_2))\}$

$\{\neg Q(f_1(y_3), y_3), P(f_2(y_3))\}, \{\neg Q(f_1(y_4), y_4), Q(y_4, f_3(y_4))\}$

Q. 21. We are given following paragraph

Tony, Mike and John belong to the Alpine Club. Every member of the Alpine Club is either a skier or a mountain climber or both. No mountain climber likes rain, and all skiers like snow. Mike dislikes whatever Tony likes and likes whatever Tony dislikes. Tony likes rain and snow.

Represent this information by predicate-calculus sentences in such a way that you can represent the question "Who is a member of the Alpine Club who is a mountain climber but not a skier?" as a predicate-calculus expression. Use resolution refutation with answer extraction to answer it.

Ans. One translation is the set of formulas

Member(Tony, Alpineclub)

Member(Mike, Alpineclub)

Member(John, Alpneclub)

$(\forall x)[\text{Member}(x\text{Alpineclub}) \supset (\text{Skier}(x) \vee \text{MC}(x))]\neg(\exists x)[\text{MC}(x) \wedge \text{Likes}(x, \text{Rain})]$

$(\forall x)[\text{Skier}(x) \supset \text{Likes}(x, \text{Snow})\}$

$(\forall x)[\text{Skier}(\text{Tony}, x) \wedge \neg\text{Likes}(\text{Mike}, x)\}$

Likes(Tony, Rain) $\wedge$ Likes(Tony,Snow)

The question is:

$(\exists x)\,[\text{Member}(x, \text{Alpineclub}) \wedge \text{MC}(x) \wedge \text{Skier}(x)]$

The clause forms of these sentences are:

1. Member(Tony, Alpineclub)
2. Member(Mike, Alpineclub)
3. Member(John, Alpineclub)
4. $\neg\text{Member}(x, \text{Alpineclub}) \vee \text{Skier}(x), \text{MC}(x)$
5. $\neg\text{MC}(x) \vee \neg\text{Likes}(x, \text{Rain})$
6. $\neg\text{Skier}(x) \vee \text{Likes}(x, \text{Snow})$

7 *a*. $\neg\text{Likes}(\text{Tony}, x) \vee \neg\text{Likes}(\text{Mike}, x)$

7 *b*. $\text{Likes}(\text{Tony}, x) \vee \text{Likes}(\text{Mike}, x)$

8 *a*. $\text{Likes}(\text{Tony}, \text{Rain})$

8 *b*. LIkes(Tony, Snow)

The clause form of the negation of the theorem to be proved (with Ans literal) is:

9. $\neg\text{Member}(x, \text{Alpineclub}) \vee \neg\text{MC}(x) \vee \text{Skier}(x) \vee \text{Ans}(x)$

The refutation is:

10. $\neg$Member(x, Alpineclub), (Skier(x) $\vee$ Ans(x) resolving 9 with 4
11. Skier(Mike)/Ans(Mike) resolving 11 and 2
12. Likes(Mike, skier) $\vee$ ans (Mike) resolving 12 with 8
13. $\neg$Likes(Tony, Skiew) $\vee$ Ans(Mike) resolving 12 with 7a
14. Ans(Mike) resolving 13 with 8b.

Q. 22. Sam, Clyde and Oscar are elephants. We know the following facts about them:

1. Sam is pink.
2. Clyde is gray and likes Oscar.
3. Oscar is either pink or gray (but not both) and likes Sam.

Use resolution refutation to prove that a gray elephant likes pink elephant; that is, prove $(\exists x, y)[Gray(x) \wedge Pink(y) \wedge Likes(x, y)]$

Ans. The clauses and negation of the theorem to be proved are:

1. P(Sam)
2. G(Clyde)
3. L(Clyde, Oscar)
4. P(Oscar) $\vee$ G(Oscar)
5. L(Oscar, Sam)
6. $\neg G(x) \vee \neg P(y) \vee \neg L(x, y)$

The resolution refutation is:

7. $\neg$G(Clyde) $\vee$ $\neg$P(Oscar) from 3 and 6
8. $\neg$P(Oscar) from 2 and 7
9. $\neg$G(Oscar) $\vee$ $\neg$P(Sam) from 5 and 6
10. $\neg$G(Oscar) from 1 and 9
11. P(Oscar) from 10 and 4
12. Nil from 11 and 8.

Q. 23. Consider the following circuit diagram —

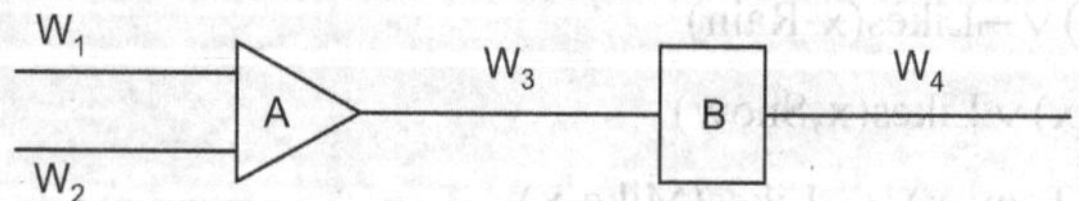

1. Use expression like ON(A), ON(W1) and so on to describe the funtioning of the circuit as defined.
2. Using the formulas describing the functioning of the circuit and assuming that all components are functioning properly and that wires W1 and W2 are "on" use resolution to show that wire W4 is not "on".
3. Again, using the formulas describing the functioning of the circuit and given that wires W1 and W2 are "on" but that wire W4 is also "on", use resolution to show that either the and gate or the inverter is not functioning properly.

Ans. 1. (*a*) $OK(A) \supset [0n(W1) \wedge 0n(W)] \equiv 0n(W3)]$

(*b*) $OK(B) \supset [0n(W3) \equiv \neg 0n(W4)]$

2. The clause forms of the above formulas are:

(a1)$\neg OK(A) \vee \neg 0n(W2) \vee 0n(W3)$

(a2)$\neg OK(A) \vee \neg 0n(W3) \vee 0n(W1)$

(a3)$\neg OK(A) \vee \neg 0n(W3) \vee 0n(W2)$

(bl)$\neg OK(B) \vee \neg 0n(W3) \vee \neg 0n(W4)$

(b2)$\neg OK(B) \vee \neg 0n(W4) \vee \neg 0n(W3)$

Here is a resolution refutation showing that W4 is not "on"

1. 0n(W4) negation of theorem
2. $\neg OK(B) \vee \neg 0n(W3)$ resolving 1 with b1
3. $\neg 0n(W3)$ resolving 2 with hypothesis, OK(B)
4. $\neg OK(A) \vee \neg 0n(W1) \vee \neg 0n(W2)$ resolving 3 with a1
5. Nil successively resolving 4 with hypotheses, OK(A), 0n(W1), 0n(W2)

3. (1a) OK(A) negation of theorem

(1b) OK(B) negation of theorem

2. $\neg 0n(W1) \vee \neg 0n(W2) \vee 0n(W3)$ resolving 1a with a1

3. 0n(W3) successively resolving 2 with hypotheses, 0n(W1) and 0n(W2)

4. $\neg OK(B) \vee \neg 0n(W4)$ resolving 3 with b1

5. $\neg OK(B)$ resolving 4 with hypothesis, 0n(W4)

6. Nil resolving 5 with lb.

Q. 24. 1. Express as predicate-calculus wffs the information in the semantic network shown here. Take care that the wffs are written in such a way that they explicitly state the inheritance cancellation information that is implicit in the inheritance hierarchy.

2. Can you prove that Fido has four legs from your predicate-calculus wffs? If not, what information would you need to add in order to complete the proof?

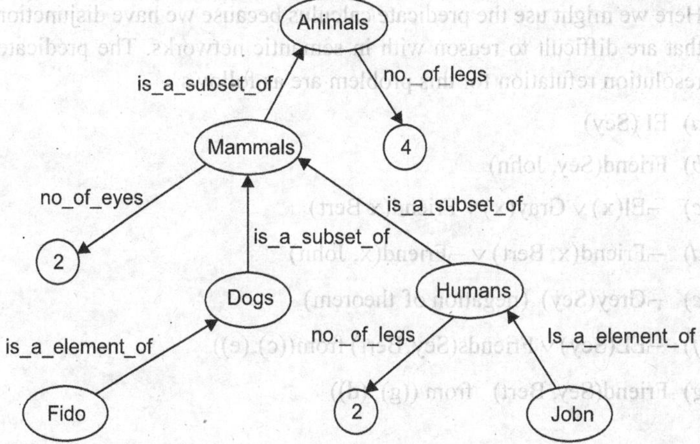

Ans. 1. The equivalent wffs are:

Def(Fido)

Human(John)

$(\forall x)[Dog(x) \supset Mammal(x)]$

$(\forall x)[Mammal(x) \supset Anjaml(x)]$

$(\forall x)[Human(x) \supset Mammal(x)]$

$(\forall x)[[Mammal(x) \wedge \neg Human(x)] \supset Haslegs(x,4)]$

$(\forall x)[Human(x) \supset Haslegs(x,2)]$

$(\forall x)[Mammal(x) \supset Haslegs(x,2)]$

2. We cannot prove Haslegs(Fido, 4) from these wffs. We would have to add ¬ Human(Fido). Or we could add something more general, such as $(\forall x)[Dog(x) \supset \neg Human(x)]$.

Q. 25. For the two examples shown here, pick the most appropriate knowledge representation system and encode the statements of the examples in the selected representation. Use your representation and a reasoning system appropriate to it to answer the question in each example. Example in some detail how the reasoning system arrives at the answer-showing resolution refutations, for example, if a reasoning system based on resolution is used. Use diagrams if they are helpful in your explanations.

1. Typically, birds fly. Ostriches are birds. Oliver is an ostrich. Ostriches do not fly. Q. Does Oliver fly?
2. Seymore is an elephant and John's friend. All elephants are gray or a friend of Bert. No friend of Bert is a friend of John. Q. Is Seymore gray?

Ans. 1. Here because of the nonmonotonic character of the statements, we might use a semantic network with property inheritance and cancellation of inheritance. In this case, we would have the fact the birds fly associated with the BIRDS node and the fact that ostriches do not fly associated with the OSTRICHES node. The OSTRICHES node is a descendant of the BIRDS node, and therefore, the fact that ostriches do not fly cancels the fact the birds do. Since Oliver is an ostrich, we conclude from the net that Oliver does not fly. (Note that the net formalism would allow us to say, in addition, that Oliver does fly, which we might do it we had some special information that Oliver was some sort of mutant flying ostrich).

2. Here we might use the predicate calculus because we have disjunction and statements that are difficult to reason with in semantic networks. The predicated encoding and resolution refutation for this problem are as follows

(*a*) EI (Sey)

(*b*) Friend(Sey, John)

(*c*) $\neg El(x) \vee Gray(x) \vee Friend(x\ Bert)$

(*d*) $\neg Friend(x, Bert) \vee \neg Friend(x, John)$

(*e*) $\neg Grey(Sey)$ (negation of theorem)

(*f*) $\neg EL(Sey) \vee Friends(Sey, Bert)$ from((c),(e))

(*g*) Friend(Sey, Bert) from ((g), (d))

(*h*) ¬Friend(Sey, John) from ((g), (d))

(*i*) Nil from ((*h*), (*b*))

So, we have proved that Seymore is gray.

Q. 26. What is a stereotypical knowledge?

Ans. A type of knowledge that scripts attempt to capture with the aim of allowing a computer to make similar inferences about incomplete stories (Schank and Abelson, 1977).

Q. 27. What are demons in AI? Name some demons used in conventional programming too.

Ans. Demons are the procedures which are activated at anytime during a program execution depending on the conditions evaluated in demon itself. For example. –If–added procedure (executed when new information is placed in the slot), **If-removed procedure** (executed when information is deleted from the slot) and **If-needed procedure** (executed when information is needed from the slot but the slot is empty.

Examples of demons used in the conventional programming are—

(*a*) Error detection

(*b*) Default commands.

(*c*) End-of-File detection (EOF).

Q. 28. Given are the axioms in clause form:

1. Man (Marcus)

2. Pompeian (Marcus)

3. ~Pompeian (a_1) v Roman (a_1)

4. Ruler (Caesear)

5. ~Roman (a_2) v loyal (a_2 Caesar) v hate (a_2, Caesar)

6. Loyal (a_3, f1(a_3))

7. ~Main (a_4) v ~ ruler (b_1) v ~ assassin (a_4, b_1) v loyal (a_4, b_1)

8. assassin (Marcus, Caesar)

Give resolution proof of hate(Marcus, Caesar).

Ans. To prove :-

Did Marcus hate Caesar?

We negate this statement as

~hate (Marcus, Caesar)

There is no axiom in clausal form starting with literal ~ hate.

Prove ~ hate (Marcus, Caesar)

Clause ~ hate (Marcus, Caesar)

Clause 5 has hate

~Roman (a_2) v loyal (a_2 Caesar) v hate (a_2 Caesar)

a_2 is Marcus we have clause as

~Roman (Marcus) v Loyal (Marcus, Caesar) v hate (Marcus Caesar)

Resolving both we get :-

~Roman (Marcus) v loyal (Marcus, Caesar)

Now select 3 clausal form.

~ Pompeian (a_1) v Roman (a_1) where a_1 is Marcus.

Statement will be

~ Pompeian (Marcus) V Roman (Marcus)

We get new clause after resolving.

C1: ~Roman (Marcus) v loyal (Marcus, Caesar)

C2: ~ Pompeian (Marcus) v Roman (Marcus)

Resolvent is ~ Pompeian (Marcus) v loyal (Marcus, Caesar)

Now take clause 2 which is

Pompeian (Marcus)

Resolvent is loyal (Marcus, Caesar)

Now C1 is loyal (Marcus, Caesar)

Select 7th axiom as:

~man (a_4) v ~ ruler (b1) v ~ assassin (a_4, b1) V loyal (a_4, b_1)

where a_4 = Marcus

b_1 = Caesar

Statement will be

C2 ~ man (Marcus) v ~ ruler(Caesar) v ~assassin (Marcus, Caesar) v loyal (Marcus, Caesar)

Negate C1 as ~ loyal (Marcus, Caesar).

Resolvent will be:

~ man (Marcus) v ~ ruler (Caesar) v ~ assassin (Marcus, Caesar) V loyal (Marcus, Caesar)

Now clause is 1

man (Marcus)

Then new resolvent

~ ruler (Caesar) v ~ assassin (Marcus, Caesar) v loyal (Marcus, Caesar)

Clause 4 is ~ ruler (Caesar) v ~ assassin (Marcus, Caesar) v loyal (Marcus, Caesar) Resolvent is

~ assassin (Marcus, Caesar)

Clause 8 is assassin (Marcus, Caesar)

Resolvent is empty

Diagramatically, it is shown as follows

–hate (Marcus, Caesar) 5

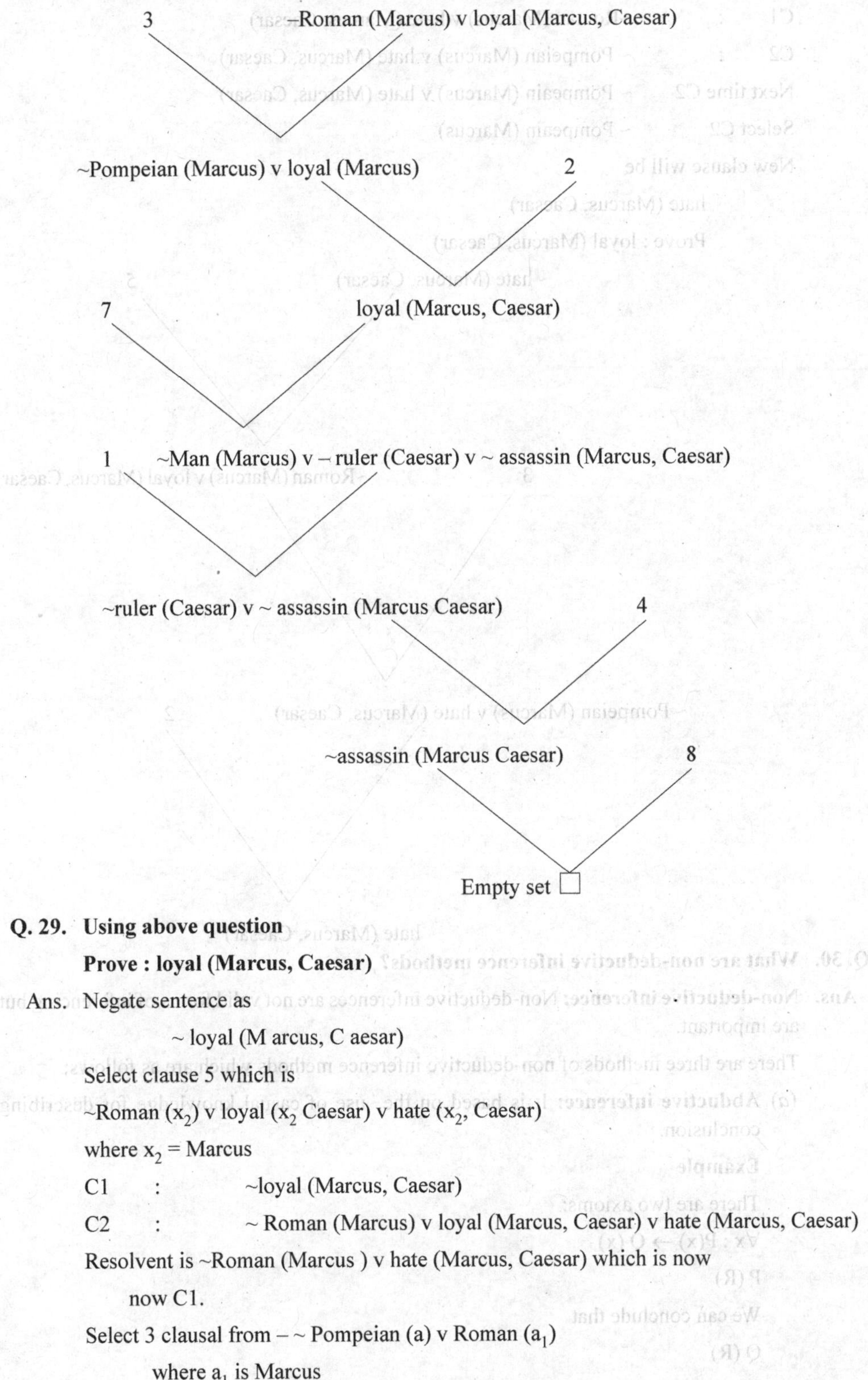

Q. 29. Using above question

Prove : loyal (Marcus, Caesar)

Ans. Negate sentence as

~ loyal (M arcus, C aesar)

Select clause 5 which is

~Roman (x_2) v loyal (x_2 Caesar) v hate (x_2, Caesar)

where x_2 = Marcus

C1 : ~loyal (Marcus, Caesar)

C2 : ~ Roman (Marcus) v loyal (Marcus, Caesar) v hate (Marcus, Caesar)

Resolvent is ~Roman (Marcus) v hate (Marcus, Caesar) which is now now C1.

Select 3 clausal from – ~ Pompeian (a) v Roman (a_1)

where a_1 is Marcus

C1 : ~Roman (Marcus) v hate (Marcus, Caesar)

C2 : ~ Pompeian (Marcus) v hate (Marcus, Caesar)

Next time C2 ~ Pompeain (Marcus) v hate (Marcus, Caesar)

Select C2 ~ Pompeain (Marcus)

New clause will be

hate (Marcus, Caesar)

Prove : loyal (Marcus, Caesar)

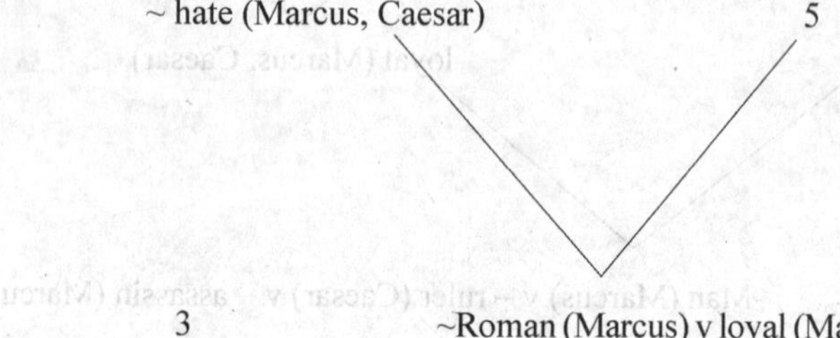

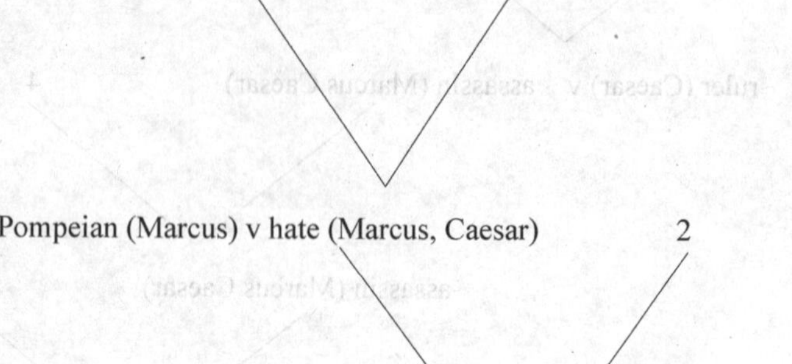

hate (Marcus, Caesar)

Q. 30. What are non-deductive inference methods?

Ans. Non-deductive inference: Non-deductive inferences are not valid forms of inferencing but are important.

There are three methods of non-deductive inference methods which are as follows:

(*a*) **Abductive inference:** It is based on the use of casual knowledge for describing conclusion.

Example

There are two axioms:

$\forall x : P(x) \rightarrow Q(x)$

P (R)

We can conclude that

Q (R)

Another example is

Measles (x) → Spots

This means people having measles get spots. If we notice the spots, we may conclude, person has measles. This may be a wrong conclusion. Deriving conclusions in such a manner is default reasoning. Abductive reasoning is useful if some measure of certainty is attached to it.

(*b*) **Inductive inference:**

Inductive inference is recurring inference. It means if there is some event, it will be true for all the events or entities in the class.

For example: We see that some dogs have tails by which we conclude that all dogs have tails but in real a breed of dogs do not have tail.

Inductive inference can be given as

$$P(a_1), P(a_2) \ldots\ldots, P(a_n)$$

$$\forall x : P(x)$$

(*c*) **Analogical Inference:**

Analogical inference is based on experiences. When there are certain similar situations as we experience in the past, we relate the situations or events. For example : If there is an event P related to Q, then we conclude that P^1 is related to Q^1 in the same manner. Analogical inference is the combination of all other inferences such as deductive, abductive and inductive inference.

Q. 31. Give five methods of representation of knowledge.

Ans. The methods of representation of knowledge are as follows

(*i*) FOPL

First order predicate logic.

(*ii*) Associative networks.

(*iii*) Conceptual graph.

(*iv*) Fuzzy logic.

(*v*) Frames.

EXERCISE QUESTIONS

Q. 1. (*a*) Represent the following sentences in predicate logic—

1. Marcus was a man.
2. Marcus was a Pompeian.
3. All Pompeians were Romans.
4. Caesar was the ruler.
5. All Romans were either loyal to Caesar or hated him.
6. Everyone is loyal to someone.
7. People only try to assassinate rulers they are not loyal to.
8. Marcus tried to assassinate Caeser.

From these, answer the question "Was Marcus loyal to Caesar"?

(*b*) What are semantic networks? How can semantic networks be converted to frames?

(*c*) Write a script for "Eating in a restaurant". **[RTM Nagpur BE (IT) Summer 2009]**

Q. 2. (*a*) Explain difference between procedural and declarative knowledge.

(*b*) Assume the following facts —

1. Steve only likes easy courses.
2. Science courses are hard.
3. All courses in commerce department are easy.
4. COM302 is a commerce course.

(*c*) Convert the following into clausal form —

1. Everyone is loyal to someone.
2. John likes all kinds of food.

(*d*) Write short notes on —

1. Forward v/s Backward Reasoning.
2. Control knowledge.
3. CD
4. Scripts. **[RTM Nagpur, BE (IT) 7th Sem., Winter 2009]**

Q. 3. (*a*) Explain the difference between predicate logic and propositional logic.

(*b*) Represent the following using predicate calculus notation —

1. There is a red part in bin that has a circular shape.
2. Raghav is computer science student but not a pilot or a football player.
3. The owner of car also owns the boat.
4. All people need air. **[RTM Nagpur, BE (CSE)-7th Sem., Summer 1996]**

Q. 4. Assume the following facts —

1. Prasad only likes easy courses.
2. AI courses are hard.
3. All courses in Data Mining department are easy.
4. DM108 is a Data Mining Course.

(*a*) Use Resolution to answer the question- "Which course would Prasad like?"

(*b*) Also design clausal form for above sentences in FOPL using proper Axioms, Functions, Predicates, Variables and Constants.

(*c*) Hence with respect to resolution, explain. "What is proof by refutation"?

[RTM Nagpur University, BE (CSE)- 7th Sem., Summer 2004]

Q. 5. Express the following things in predicate calculus—

(*a*) All p's are q's.

(*b*) Some p's are q's.

(*c*) John hit everyone who was near him.

(*d*) Nobody does anything without a reason. **[PTU, MCA 4th Sem., 2009]**

Q. 6. (*a*) What do you mean by semantic nets?

(*b*) Define frames. **[PTU B. Tech. (CSE)-7th/8th Sem., 2009]**

Q. 7. (a) Give the CD structure to parse the following sentence —

"John wanted Mary to go to the store".

(*b*) Represent the following sentences using symbolic logic:

1. A drunker is enemy of himself.
2. Father of John loves the mother of mary.
3. All students like a good teacher.
4. Fruits and vegetables are nutritions.
5. God helps those who help themselves.

(*c*) "Some medicines are dangerous only if taken in excessive amount". Translate the above sentence into formulas in predicate logic and then to clausal form.

(*d*) Describe semantic net and frames with suitable examples.

[UPTU., B. Tech. (CS)- 7th Sem., 2007]

Q. 8. (*a*) Explain the difference between the following — Semantic Nets and Frames.

(*b*) Represent the following sentence in FOPL, convert it into clausal form explaning each step —

"All engineering students who know programming will either get good placement or admission in some university for higher studies".

(*c*) Using the following problem, illustrate how resolution is used to derive new facts from already existing facts —

Given facts

(*i*) Steve likes computer courses.

(*ii*) Computer software can be software or Hardware courses.

Derive: Steve likes AI.

(*d*) Write short notes on — Unification procedure.

[DTU (DCE)-ME (CS) 5th Sem., 2005]

Q. 9. Draw the semantic network and write atomic formulae for the English sentence given below:

"Manju playing with a red ball".

[Cochin University of Science & Technology B. Tech (CSE)-7th Sem., Oct. 1999]

Q. 10. (*a*) Construct a semantic net representations of the following —

(*i*) Rajesh is Indian, Rajesh is a lecturer.

(*ii*) Vikram but his new video CD to his brother-in-law.

(*b*) Explain-Conceptual dependency.

[GGSIPU, B.Tech. (CSE)-8th Sem., May 2008]

Q. 11. (*a*) Explain why these two sentences cannot be unified—

1. $p(x) \vee (q(f(x)) \wedge r(y))$

2. $p(x) \vee (q(f(r)) \wedge r(s))$

(b) Construct a semantic net representation of the following:

"Gopal is Indian, Gopal is lecturer".

[GGSIPU, B.Tech (CSE)-8th Sem., May-June 2009]

Q. 12. (*a*) Create a script about shopping in a super market.

(*b*) Write down a substitution which unifies the following sentences:

1. $\text{likes(homer, dineer}(x)) \wedge (\text{today}(A) \rightarrow \text{dineer}(x))$

2. $\text{likes(homer, dineer(cooked\_by}(y)) \wedge (\text{today}(Z) \rightarrow \text{dineerCcooked} - \text{by(magie))))}$

(c) What is a slot in a frame? **[GGSIPU, B.Tech (CSE)-8th Sem., May-June 2009]**

Q. 13. What are the merits/demerits of semantic net over semantic frames?

[GGSIPU, B.Tech (CSE)-8th Sem., May 2010]

Q. 14. (a) Explain the rules to unify two predicates.

(b) Represent the following facts as predicates and convert them to clausal form, explaining the steps of conversion:

1. Any student who is intelligent or hardworking will pass the exam in good marks.

2. Anyone who is passed with good marks gets a job.

(*c*) Assume that "Shiva is neither hardworking nor intelligent". Using resolution prove that Shiva does not get a job. **[GGSIPU, B. Tech. (CSE) 8th Sem., May 2010]**

Q. 15. What kind of knowledge is represented by the semantic nets? Give an example of KB represented by semantic nets and explain how inferences are done in Semantic Nets?

[GGSIPU, B. Tech. (CSE) 8th Sem., May 2010]

Q. 16. (*a*) Create a script for "appearing for an examination."

(*b*) A new operator $\oplus$, or exclusive-or may be defined by the following truth table—

P	Q	$P \oplus Q$
T	T	F
T	F	T
F	T	T
F	F	F

Create a propositional calculus expression using $\wedge, \vee$ and $>$ that is equivalent to $P \oplus Q$.

(*c*) Explain CD using an example. **[GGSIPU, B. Tech. (CSE) 8th Sem., 2011]**

5 CHAPTER REASONING UNCERTAINTY

5.0 INTRODUCTION

Reasoning means deriving conclusions from the available set of data and information. We deal with many types of situations in this real world that are full of uncertainties. Our AI systems should be such that they should be able to handle these uncertainties. These uncertainties occur because the knowledge that we acquire is from beliefs and hypotheses. When we get some new information or when our beliefs change, we face uncertainty. Experimental errors, Randomness, lack of evidences are all the causes of uncertainties. **The knowledge stored in KB is incomplete. So, an intelligent AI system should be able to handle these uncertainties. Note that the normal logical problem solving techniques-propositional and predicate logic cannot handle such uncertain situations.** To handle uncertain situations, the uncertain knowledge needs to be represented and thus reasoned.

5.1 UNCERTAIN KR METHOD

Certain events are "**certain events**" like "New Delhi is the Capital of India" but some events like "It may rain today" are "**uncertain events**" These uncertain events need to be stored in KB now. To achieve this, the uncertain situation is represented by attaching a **degree of belief factor**. It is related to the probability theory. So, representation of uncertain events uses the following terminology—

(*a*) **Belief:** It is any meaningful and coherent expression that can be represented. It may be true or false.

(*b*) **Belief factor:** It indicates the correctness of knowledge. The value of this factor is between 0 and 1.

(*c*) **Evidence:** It is the observation (s) obtained in the real world.

(*d*) **Hypothesis:** It is a justified belief that is supported by some evidence. It is not known to be true.

(*e*) **Knowledge:** It is a true justified belief.

(*f*) **Meta knowledge:** It is the knowledge about the knowledge.

How to reason this uncertain knowledge?

AI aims at building intelligent systems to solve those real world problems that involve uncertainties. Reasoning is done on uncertain information contained in the KB. **Please understand that without this ability an AI system is just like other programming languages or like a search table doing sequential search.** So, we can say,

AI $\longrightarrow$ used to build intelligent systems $\longrightarrow$ Use facts and rules stored in KB

Three types of reasoning are used here—

1. Inductive Reasoning

It is based on the generalizations of the previous experiences about the problem. For e.g. Consider the situation—

(*a*) Rajiv is an Associate Professor.

(*b*) He teaches in a college.

Now, if some one asks you to guess about college environment then from your experience, you can infer that college has — Professors, Lecture Rooms, Conference Rooms, Labs, play grounds etc.

This is known as inductive **reasoning.** In AI field, this method is used in **machine learning.**

2. Abductive Reasoning

It is an unsound rule of inferencing meaning that the conclusion is not necessarily true for every interpretation made out of the environment. It is not very reliable reasoning method and is preferred in cases where knowledge is incomplete. It looks back through the chain of events to do reasoning.

For e.g. If a student fails in his/her exam although the paper is easy. To find the reason as to why he/she failed, we need to look back in the chain of events that paper is easy, student studied, student failed, teacher is not strict. This type of reasoning is **abductive reasoning.**

3. Deductive Reasoning

It is a kind of explicit, non-reversible reasoning that works on standard logic.

For e.g., "If mobile is OFF", it is certain that no calls can be made. This is deductive reasoning. But the reverse is NOT true.

5.1.1 Monotonic versus Non-Monotonic Reasoning

Monotonic Reasoning	Non-Monotonic Reasoning
1. All new knowledge that is added to the KB must be consistent with the previous knowledge.	1. In uncertain situations addition of new axioms may contradict with earlier and might be required to be removed from the KB.
2. The size of the KB always increases monotonically.	2. The size of the KB increases-non monotonically.
3. No retractions of rules (removals) are allowed.	3. Allow retractions also i.e., removal of contradictory facts.
4. Inference methods available are insufficient.	4. Inference methods are complete and justified.
5. Traditional KR techniques like PL, FOPL, Propositional logic cannot accommodate the real world's changing situations. **For e.g.:** PL, FOPL, Propositional logic, Theorem Proving etc.	5. These systems like TMS allows the revision in belief and accommodate the real world changing situations. **For e.g.:** Truth Maintenance Systems (TMS).

5.1.2 TMS-Truth Maintenance Systems (or Belief or Revision Maintenance Systems)

1. TMS are "truth-maintenance systems" which have been implemented to permit a form of non monotonic reasoning by permitting the addition of changing (even contradictory) statements to a knowledge base.

2. Also known as "belief-revision" and "revision-maintenance-systems" are companion-components to inference system, (of our basic KBS).

3. Main job– of TMS is to maintain "**consistency of knowledge**" being used by the problem solver and not to perform any inference functions.

   As such, it **frees** the problem solver from any concerns of consistency and allows it to concentrate on the problem solution aspects.

4. TMS also gives the inference–component, the latitude to perform non-monotonic inferences.

5. When new discoveries are made, this more recent information can displace previous conclusions that are no longer valid. In this way, set of beliefs available to the problem solver will continue to be current and consistent.

   For e.g., Shows role of TMS

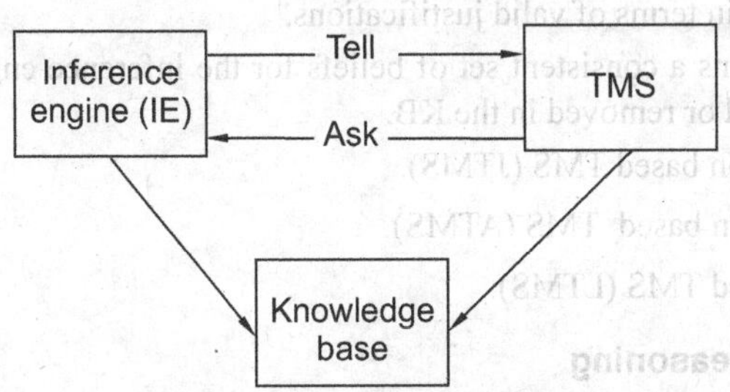

Fig. 5.1 Architecture of the problem solver with a TMS.

Working: The inference engine (IE) solves domain problems based on its current belief set, while the TMS maintains the currently active belief set. The updating process is incremental. After each inference, information is exchanged between the two components. The IE tells the TMS what deductions it has made. The TMS, in turn, **asks** question about current beliefs and reasons for failure. If maintains a consistent set of beliefs for the IE to work with even if now knowledge is added and removed.

For e.g., S1: Say, KB contained the propositions P, P → Q and modus ponens.

S2: From this, the IE would right fully conclude Q and add this conclusion to the KB.

S3: Later, if it was learned that ~P was appropriate, if would be added to the KB resulting in a contradiction.

S4: Consequently, it would be necessary to remove P to eliminate the inconsistency. But, with P now removed, Q is no longer a justified belief. It too should be removed.

This type of belief revision is the job of the TMS.

7. Actually, the TMS does not discard conclusions like Q as suggested. That could be wasteful, since P may again become valid, which would require that Q and facts justified by Q be received. Instead, the TMS maintains **dependency records** for all such conclusion. These records determine which set of beliefs are current (which are to be used by the IE). Thus, Q would be removed from the current belief set by making appropriate updates to the records and not by erasing Q. Since Q would not be lost, its rederivation would not be necessary if P became valid once again.

8. TMS maintains complete records of reasons of justifications for beliefs. Each proposition or statement having at least one valid justification is made a part of the current belief set. Statements lacking acceptable justifications are excluded from this set. When a contradiction is discovered, the statements responsible for the contradiction are identified and an

appropriate one is retracted. This in turn may result in other retractions and additions. The procedure used to perform this process is called "**dependency-directed back tracking**".

9. TMS maintains records to reflect retractions and additions so that the IE will always known its current belief set. The records are maintained in the form of a "dependency- –network".
   (*a*) The **nodes** in the network represent KB entries such as premises, conclusions, inference rules and the like.
   (*b*) **Attached** to the nodes are justifications which represent the inference steps from which the node was derived.

Nodes in the belief set must have valid justifications.

A premise (or a node with no justification) is a fundamental belief which is assumed to be always true. Premises need no justifications. They form a base from which all other currently active nodes can be explained in terms of valid justifications.

Thus, TMS maintains a consistent set of beliefs for the inference engine to rely upon even if new knowledge is added or removed in the KB.

For e.g., (*a*) Justification based TMS (JTMS).

(*b*) Assumption based TMS (ATMS).

(*c*) Logic based TMS (LTMS).

5.1.3 Probabilistic Reasoning

It is a statistical method of reasoning based on some numeric value assigned to them. It involves 4 methods—

(*a*) Bayesian belief networks.

(*b*) Dempster Shaffer theory.

(*c*) Reasoning with certainty factors.

(*d*) Fuzzy reasoning.

Let us discuss these reasoning one by one.

5.1.3.1 Bayesian belief networks

Bayesian networks are the graphical representation of dependent events. These networks are an easy graphical representation of real world dependent events. These are directed acyclic graphs in which **nodes represent the events** or evidence **and the arcs represent their dependence.**

Basic Properties of Bayesian networks

1. They have a set of random, discrete or continuous variables generating the nodes of the network.
2. They have directed links or arrows connecting a pair of nodes.

   For e.g. (a) ⟶ (b)

   Here, 'a' is parent of 'b'.
3. Each nodes (n_i) has a conditional probability distribution i.e.,

   P (n_i|parent (n_i))

This quantifies the effect of parent on the node.

4. **The graph has no directed cycles** i.e., these networks are directed acyclic graphs (DAG).
5. **The topology of graph** indicates that node specifies the conditional independence relationships of the problem.

6. Once belief network is constructed, an inference engine of an intelligent system can use it to maintain and propagate beliefs. If some new information is received, the effects of same can be propagated throughout the network until **equilibrium probabilities are reached.**

7. **At equilibrium all propositions will have consistent probabilities.**

For example : Medical diagnosis systems like CASNET uses this reasoning.

5.1.3.2 Dempster Shafer Theory

There are various theories available for example Bayesian networks that consider or find out the belief from some premises from a single permit of observation.

Dempster Shafer theory considers the fact that the observations or correct belief can be made out by not one degree of final belief but it actually considers an interval defined as,

(Belief, Plausibility)

1. The degree of correct observation lies between 0 to 1 according to the range of above interval.
2. Belief is made on certain facts that are considered to be true and plausibility is based on the value of belief.

$$\boxed{\text{Plausibility} = 1 - \text{Belief}\ (\neg S)}$$

3. The value of the interval defined by the Dempster shafer ranges from 0 (uncertainty) to 1 (certain).
4. When the value of belief on the some observation is, 's 'that belief ($\neg S$) is 1, the plausibility is 0 and its 1 otherwise.

EXAMPLE:

Let us consider a set that considers a diagnosis problem from bacterial in infection. It is {All, Flu, Cold, Pneu}, where

All : Allergy

Flu : Flu

Cold : Cold

Pneu : Pneumonia

5. The Dempster Shafer theory applies not only to the members of sets but also to its subsets including the Singleton set.

We will call the set as θ.

θ: {All, Flu, Cold, Pneu}

If there are n members of the set, then total no. of subsets that are there can be 2^n.

6. The degree of functionality, 'm' can then be found out from the set θ.
7. The degree of functionality 'm' can apply not to all members of sets.

For example, consider that a value fever that may not happen in the case of allergy.

Therefore, only following members of set are

θ': = { Flu, Cold Pneu}

8. Giving values to these subsets, the value of m i.e. degree of functionality can be found out.

5.1.3.3 Reasoning with Certainty Factors (CF)

The certainty factors are human estimates of symton/cause relationship and their probability measures. In this type of reasoning, we need to combine the effects of all of the facts and assign a single value to the rule known as CF i.e., here the problem is represented as a simple rule as follows—

IF p and q and r THEN S(CF).

Please note that CF-certainty factor will hold good if we are certain about facts. Also note that a new CF would be calculated whenever there is any change in the measure of belief of any or all of the facts.

Certainty theory does not produce an algebra for correct reasoning. It **is adhoc** meaning that the confidence of human expert in his result is approximate, heuristic and informal.

For e.g.: MYCIN expert system uses this type of reasoning.

The certainty theory makes simple assumption for creating and assigning confidence measures 'for' and 'against' any given situation.

5.1.3.4 Fuzzy Logic Reasoning

According to George Boole, human thinking and decision are based on Yes or No reasoning or logic 1 and logic 0. Accordingly, Boolean algebra was developed. Even expert systems founded this logic. But it has been argued that **human thinking does not always follows crisp** YES or NO logic rather it is quite **vague, uncertain, imprecise or fuzzy in nature**. Based on the nature of fuzzy human thinking, **Lofti Zadeh**, a computer scientist at the University of California, Berkeley, originated the fuzzy logic or fuzzy set theory in 1965. Classical set theory/crisp set theory (given by George Cantor) is fundamental to the study of fuzzy sets. **Please understand that as Boolean logic had its roots in the theory of crisp sets, fuzzy logic has its roots in the theory of fuzzy sets.**

Also note that this process of making a crisp quantity fuzzy is known as fuzzification. We do this by recognizing that many of the quantities we consider to be crisp and deterministic are actually non-deterministic. They carry considerable uncertainty. If the form of uncertainty happens to arise because of imprecision, ambiguity or vagueness then the variable is probable fuzzy and can be represented by a membership function.

> **NOTE:** Reasoning about imprecise propositions is an ultimate goal of fuzzy logic and is referred to as approximate reasoning.

Features of membership characteristics functions

1. It describes vague natural real world concepts.
2. A fuzzy set admits the possibility of partial members with associated membership characteristic function value.
3. The degree of an object belonging to a fuzzy set is denoted by membership value between 0 and 1.
4. A membership function associated with given fuzzy set maps input value to its appropriate membership value.
5. Uncertainties are represented with membership functions and then this function is manipulated in a method defined in fuzzy theory.

Laws of operations on fuzzy sets

1. **Law of Equality:** "If A and B are two fuzzy sets such that A, B $\subseteq$ U then A = B iff mA(x) = mB(x) for all x $\in$ U".
2. **Law of containment:** "A $\subseteq$ B iff mA(x) $\leq$ mB(x) for all x $\in$ U.
3. **Union law:** " A $\cup$ B is the smallest fuzzy subset of which both A and B are subsets."
4. **Intersection law:** " A $\cap$ B is the largest fuzzy subset which is a subset of both A and B".
5. **Distributive law**

   (*a*) $A \cup (B \cap C) = (A \cup B) \cap (A \cup C)$

   (*b*) $A \cap (B \cup C) = (A \cap B) \cup (A \cap C)$

6. **Associative law**

   (*a*) $(A \cup B) \cup C = A \cup (B \cup C)$

   (*b*) $(A \cap B) \cap C = A \cap (B \cap C)$

7. **Commutative law**

   (*a*) $A \cup B = B \cup A$

   (*b*) $A \cap B = B \cap A$

8. **Idempotency law**

   (*a*) $A \cup A = A$

   (*b*) $A \cap A = A$

Certain other laws used on membership characteristics functions are as follows–

(*a*) **Union law**

m(A(x) ∪ B(x)) or mA(x) or B(x)

= MAX{mA(x), mB(x)}

(*b*) **Intersection law**

m(A(x) ∩ B(x)) or mA(x) or B(x)

= MIN{mA(x), mB(x)}

(c) **Negation law**

Negation of mA(x) = 1 – mA(x)

(*d*) **Dilation**

If A is a fuzzy set such that $A \subseteq U$, for all $x \in A$, the dilation of A is defined as–

$DIL(A) = [mA(x)]^{1/2}$ for $x \in U$

(*e*) **Concentration**

The concentration of A is defined as–

$CON(A) = [mA(x)]^2$ for all $x \in U$

(*f*) **Normalization**

The normalization of A is defined as–

NORM (A) = mA(x)/MAX {mA(x)}

NOTE: Concentration is opposite of dilation.

Normalization is the process of normalizing all characteristic functions to the same base. These operations are used to manipulate the membership characteristic function according to the variation in fuzziness of a function.

To summarize, we can say in nutshell that because real world situations are very vague and cannot be crisply defined, so they are modeled using fuzzy theory only in AI.

SUMMARY

We encounter various situations in our real life where the outcome is uncertain. This chapter focuses on how this type of knowledge is represented and reasoned. Various theories have been given to accomplish the same.

MULTIPLE CHOICE QUESTIONS [MCQS]

1. The knowledge about the knowledge is known as

(*a*) knowledge (*b*) Meta knowledge

(*c*) Knowledge base (d) None of the above.

2. A type of reasoning which is based on generalizations of previous experience about the problem is known as

(*a*) Inductive reasoning (*b*) Aductive reasoning

(*c*) Deductive reasoning (*d*) None of the above.

3. PL and FOPL are examples of

(*a*) Monotonic reasoning (*b*) Non-monotonic reasoning

(*c*) TMS (*d*) None of the above.

4. TMS stands for

(*a*) True management system (*b*) Teller management system

(*c*) Truth maintenance system (*d*) None of the above.

5. Which unit makes inferences based on current set of beliefs

(*a*) Inference engine (*b*) TMS

(*c*) KB (*d*) None of the above.

6. CASNET uses

(*a*) Fuzzy logic reasoning (*b*) Bayesian belief networks

(*c*) Dempster shaffer theory (*d*) None of the above.

7. MYCIN uses

(*a*) Reasoning with certainity factor (*b*) Fuzzy logic

(*c*) Bayesian networks (*d*) None of the above.

8. Fuzzy logic has its roots in the theory of

(*a*) Crisp sets (*b*) Fuzzy sets

(*c*) Boolean algebra (*d*) None of the above.

9. The process of making a crisp quantity fuzzy is known as

(*a*) fuzzification (*b*) de-fuzzification

(*c*) assumption (*d*) None of the above.

10. Concentration is opposite of

(*a*) Fuzzification (*b*) Dilation

(*c*) Normalization (*d*) None of the above.

ANSWERS

1. (*b*) **2.** (*a*) **3.** (*a*) **4.** (*c*) **5.** (*a*)

6. (*b*) **7.** (*a*) **8.** (*b*) **9.** (*a*) **10.** (*b*)

CONCEPTUAL SHORT QUESTIONS WITH ANSWERS

Q. 1. In a database, a rule is defined as (P1 and P2) or P3? R1 (0.8) and R2 (0.3) where P1, P2, P3 are premises and R1, R2 are the conclusions of the rule with CFs 0.8, 0.3 respectively. If any running program has produced P1, P2 and P3 with CFs as 0.5, 0.8, 0.2 respectively. Find CF of results on the basis of premises.

Ans. The CF of R1 is 0.8 (given)

∴ CF of R1 based on premises will be

$$= 0.8 * 0.5$$

$$= 0.40.$$

Similarly, CF of R2 based on premises will be (0.3 * 0.5) = 0.15.

Q. 2. An admissions committee for a college is trying to determine the probability that an admitted candidate is really qualified. The relevant probabilities are given in the Bayes network shown here. Calculate P(A/D).

Ans. 1.

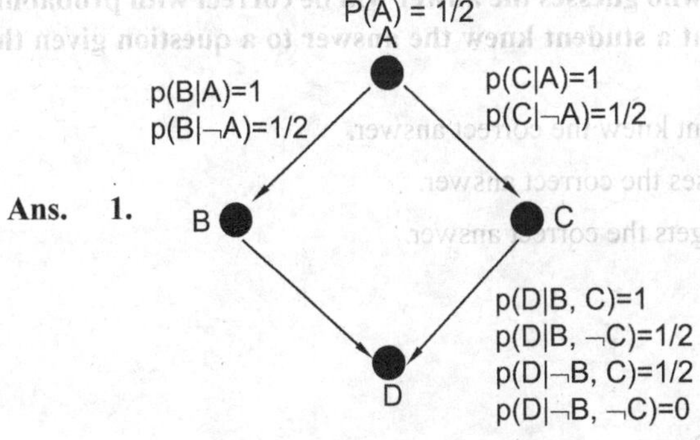

A = application is qualified

B = applicant has high grade point average

C = applicant has excellent recommendations

D = applicant is admitted.

Find p(A/D) = ?

Ans. 2. $p(A|D) = p(A, D)/p(D)$

$$\begin{aligned} p(A,D) = {} & p(D|B, C)p(B|A)p(C|A)p(A) \\ & + p(D|B, \neg C)p(B|A)p(\neg C|A)p(A) \\ & + p(D|\neg B, C)p(\neg B|A)p(C|A)p(A) \\ & + p(D|\neg B, \neg C)p(\neg B|A)p(\neg C|A)p(A) \\ = {} & 1/2 \end{aligned}$$

$$\begin{aligned} p(D) = {} & p(D/B, C)p(B/A)p(C/A)p(A) \\ & + p(D|B, \neg C)p(B|A)p(\neg C|A)p(A) \\ & + p(D|\neg B, C)p(\neg B|A)p(C|A)p(A) \\ & + p(D|\neg B, \neg C)p(\neg B/A)p(\neg C|A)p(A) \\ & + p(D|B,C)p(B|\neg A)p(C|\neg A)p(\neg A) \\ & + p(D|B, \neg C)p(B|\neg A)p(\neg C|\neg A)p(\neg A) \end{aligned}$$

$$+ p(D|\neg B,C)p(\neg B|\neg A)p(C|\neg A)p(\neg A)$$

$$+ p(D|\neg B,C)p(\neg B|\neg A)p(\neg C|\neg A)p(\neg A)$$

$$= 3/4$$

Therefore, $p(A|D) = 2/3$.

Q. 3. What is defuzzification?

Ans. It is the process of **Rounding fuzzy set off** from its location in the unit hypercube to the nearest vertex in a geometric sense. If a fuzzy set is a collection of membership values or a vector of values on the unit interval then defuzzification reduces this vector to a single scalar quantity. Aggregating two or more fuzzy output sets yields a new fuzzy set in the fuzzy inference algorithm. A result in form of a fuzzy set is converted into a crisp result by this process of defuzzification.

Q. 4. In answering a question in TNPCE, a student either knows the answer or guesses. Let p be the probability that he knows the answer and $(1 - p)$ be the probability that he guesses. Assume that a student who guesses the anwer will be correct with probability 1/5. What is the probability that a student knew the answer to a question given that he answered it correctly?

Ans. Let E_1 be the event that the student knew the correct answer.

E_2 be the event that student guesses the correct answer.

A be the student that the student gets the correct answer.

We need to find $P(E_1|A)$.

From the data,

$$P(E_1) = p$$

and $$P(E_2) = 1 - p$$

and $$P(A|F_2) = \frac{1}{5}$$

$P(A|E_1)$ = P(the student gets the correct answer given that he knew the correct answer) = 1

$$\therefore \quad P(E_1|A) = \frac{P(E_1)\,P(A \mid E_1)}{P(E_1)\cdot P(A \mid E_1) + P(E_2)\cdot P(A \mid E_2)}$$

$$= \frac{p(1)}{p(1) + (1-p)\frac{1}{5}}$$

$$= \frac{5p}{4p+1}.$$

Q. 5. Compare JTMS and LTMS in a tabular form.

[GGIPU, B. Tech (CS)-8th Sem., 2nd Internal Test]

Ans.

JTMS (by Jon Doyle)	LTMS (by Mc Allester)
1. It is a justified TMS.	1. It is a logic based TMS.
2. It is used for Non-monotonic reasoning where information is incomplete.	2. It uses default logic and non-monotonic reasoning, abductions and inheritance.

JTMS (by Jon Doyle)	LTMS (by Mc Allester)
3. Representation is in a manner where rules are used.	3. Representation is in a manner where logic is used.
4. Both logic and its contradiction are not asserted.	4. Both logic and contradictions are asserted.

EXERCISE QUESTIONS

Q. 1. (*a*) What are the different types of fuzzy membership function? What is the criteria to define a fuzzy membership function?

(b) How uncertainty is captured using probabilistic reasoning? How is it different from handling uncertainty using fuzzy logic?

[GGIPU, B. Tech (CSE)-8th Sem., May 2011]

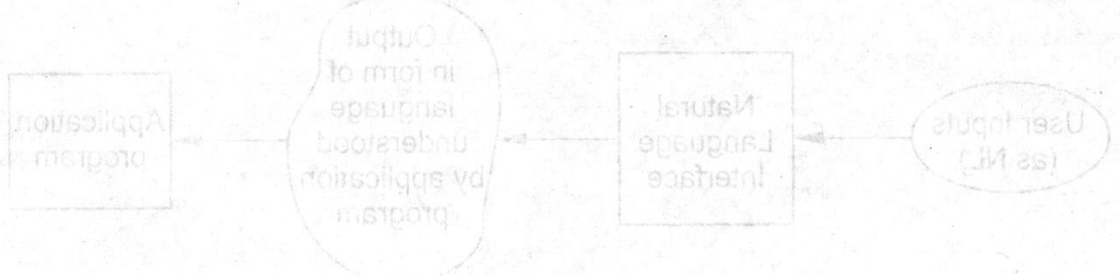

6 CHAPTER

NATURAL LANGUAGE PROCESSING

6.0 INTRODUCTION

A **natural language** is any of the languages naturally used by humans that is not artificial or man-made language. Natural Language Processing (NLP) is a subfield of AI and linguistics. NLP provides methods for performing useful tasks with natural languages. To give a feel of a human expert, computer is needed to interact with the user in natural languages. **What is done in NLP?** The answer is here.

S1 : User inputs in form of a natural language.

S2 : It goes to the Natural Language Interface (NLI).

S3 : Output is obtained in a language form that is understood by the application program.

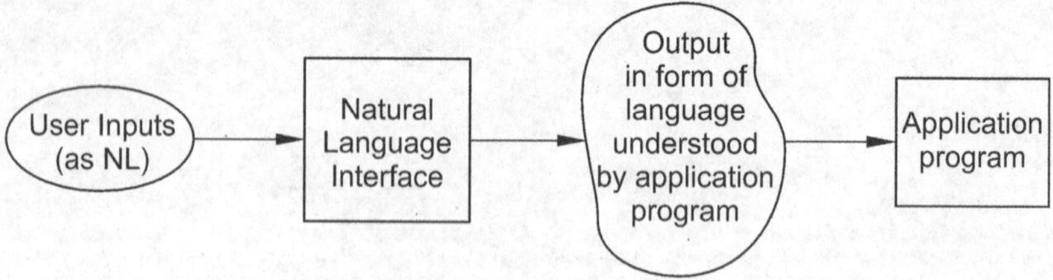

Fig. 6.1 NLP system.

KBS need query languages for information retrieval. A good system should interact with database in natural language. To interact with the database in natural languages, computer is required to have basic knowledge of alphabets, lexicon, grammar, words formation, sentence formation rules of that language. Also required are general knowledge, commonsense knowledge, domain specific knowledge etc for sentence interpretation in a proper way—

NLP includes—

(*a*) Speech Synthesis.

(*b*) Speech Recognition.

(*c*) Natural language understanding.

(*d*) Natural language generation.

(*e*) Machine Translation.

Speech synthesis: Synthesis of natural sounding speech is complex as it needs some understanding of what is being spoken to ensure for correct information.

Speech recognition: Basically, the reduction of continuous sound waves to discrete words.

Natural language understanding

It involves moving isolated words to meaning.

Natural language generation

It involves generating appropriate NL responses to unpredictable inputs.

Machine Translation (MT): Translation of one NL into another.

Please note that natural language understanding is sometimes referred to as an AI-complete problem because natural language recognition seems to require extensive knowledge about the outside world and the ability to manipulate it.

6.1 NLP

6.1.1 Levels of Knowledge Used in Language Understanding

Language understanding needs—

(*a*) **Phonological knowldge**

A phoneme is the smallest unit of sound and relates to the sound of word.

(*b*) **Syntactic knowledge**

It relates to how words are put together to form grammatically correct sentence.

(*c*) **Semantic knowledge**

It relates to the meaning of words and phrases and how they combine to form a meaningful sentence.

(*d*) **Morphological knowledge**

It relates to word construction from basic units called **morphemes.**

(*e*) **Pragmatic knowledge**

It relates to the use of sentence in different contexts and how the contexts affect the meaning of sentences.

(*f*) **Word knowledge**

It relates to the language a user must have in order to understand and carry on a conversation.

6.1.2 Phases of Natural Language Understanding

1. **Morphological analysis:** Individual words are analyzed into their components, and nonword tokens, such as punctuation, are separated from the words.
2. **Syntactic analysis:** Linear sequences of words are transformed into structures that show how the words relate to each other. Some word sequences may be rejected if they violate the language's rules for how words may be combined. For example, an English syntactic analyzer would reject the sentence "Boy the go the to store".

Syntactic analysis determines: Whether the sentence is a legal sentence of the language or generates legal sentences using a grammar and lexicon and if so returns a fare tree for the sentence representing its structure. It is the process of parsing that is computers, equivalent of diagramming a sentence.

3. **Semantic analysis:** The structures created by the syntactic analyzer are assigned **meanings.** In other words, a mapping is made between the syntactic structures and objects in the task domain. Structures for which no such mapping is possible may be rejected. **For example,** in most universes, the sentence "Colorless green ideas sleep furiously" would be rejected as **semantically anomalous.**

Thus, it is the process of extracting the meaning of an utterance as interpreted by a speaker. It takes the parse tree for the sentence and interprets it according to the possible meanings of its constituent parts. A representation of semantics may include information about different meanings of words and their characteristics.

4. **Discourse integration:** The meaning of an individual sentence may depend on the sentences that precede it and may influence the meanings of the sentences that follow it. **For example**, the word "it" in the sentence, "John wanted it" depends on the prior discourse context while the word "John" may influence the meaning of later sentences (such as, "He always had".)

A discourse is any string of language usually which is more that one sentence long. For eg., Textbooks novel, weather reports and conversations are all discourses. The meaning of an individual sentence may depend on the sentences which precede it and may also influence the meaning of the sentences which follow it.

For eg. the word 'it' in the sentence, "**Mayur wanted it**" depends on the prior **discourse**, it may refer to a bike, ,Mayur is interested in purchasing and he purchased it. While the word, 'Mayur' may influence the meaning of later sentences such as "He purchased the bike" This type of interpretation is of a pronoun or a definite noun phrase which refers to an object in a world. The resolution is based on knowledge of the world and of the previous parts of the discourse. Usually, resolution is just a matter of selecting a referent from a list of candidates but sometimes it involves the creation of new candidates.

Please understand that choosing the best referent is a process of disambiguation which relies on combining. a variety of semantic, syntactic and pragmatic information. But some clues in form of constraints are required.

The rhythm and intonation of a language refers to **Prosody**. Rhythm is often used in the babbling of infants and children's wordplay.

5. **Pragmatic analysis:** The structure representing what was said is reinterpreted to determine what was actually meant. **For example**, the sentence "Do you know what time it is?" should be interpreted as a request to be told the time.

The boundaries between these five phases are often very fuzzy. The phases are sometimes performed in sequence, and they are sometimes performed all at once. If they are performed in sequence, one may need to appeal for assistance to another. **For example**, part of the process of performing the syntactic analysis of the sentence "Is the glass jar peanut butter?" is deciding how to form two noun phrases out of the four nouns at the end of the sentence (giving a sentence of the form "Is the x >>?"). All of the following constituents are syntactically possible: glas, glass jar, glass jar peanut, jar peanut better, peanut butter, and butter. A syntactic process or on its own has no way to choose among these, and so any decision must be made by appealing to some model of the world in which some of these phrases make sense and others do not. If we do this, then we get a syntactic structure in which the constituents "glass jar" and "peanut butter" appear. Thus although it is often useful to separate these five processing phases to some extent, they can all interact in a variety of ways, making a complete separation impossible.

6.1.3 Parsing and Its Types

The process of converting a sentence into a tree that represents a sentences syntactic structure is known as parsing. It tell us whether it is a valid sentence as defined by our grammar. If a sentence is not a valid sentence then it can't be parsed.

For example : Consider the following sentence

"The white dog crossed the road". Its parse tree is as shown in Fig. 6.2.

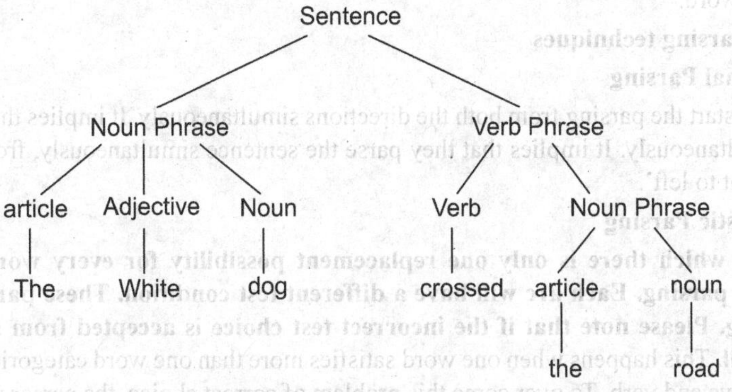

Fig. 6.2 A parsed sentence.

It is clear from the above Fig. 6.2 that how a sentence is made up of a **noun phrase** and a **verb phrase**. The noun phrase consists of an article, an adjective and a noun. The verb phrase consist of a verb and a noun phrase, in turn, consists of an article and a noun. Parsing is, thus, a typical **AI search problem** in which—

(*a*) **The initial state** is input sequence of words.

(*b*) **The goal state** is a complete tree representing the whole sentence structure.

(*c*) **The production rules** are grammar rules.

(*d*) **The parser** can be viewed as searching through the space of all possible parse trees to find the correct parse tree for the sentence in consideration.

Parsing is of two types—

(*a*) **Top-down parsing.**

(*b*) **Bottom-up parsing.**

Parse trees can be built in a top-down fashion or in a bottom-up fashion. Let us understand this now.

(*a*) **Top-down Parsing**

Building a parse tree from the top-down involves starting from a sentence and determining which of the possible rewriters for a sentence can be applied to the sentence that is being parsed. Hence, in this passing the sentence would be rewritten using the following rule:

Sentence ⟶ Noun phrase, Verb phrase

Then the verb phrase and the noun phrase would be broken down **recursively** in the same way, until only terminal symbols are left.

(*b*) **Bottom-up parsing**

To build a parse tree from the bottom-up, the terminal symbol of the sentence are first replaced by their corresponding non-terminals (e.g. dog is replaced by noun) and then these non-terminals are combined to match the right-hand sides of rewrite rules.

Fog example: 'the' and 'road' (see Fig. 6.2) will be combined using the following rewrite rule:

NounPhrase ⟶ Article, Noun

But neither of these techniques adequately exploits the constraints presented by the grammar and the input word.

Some other Parsing techniques

1. Bidirectional Parsing

These parsers start the parsing from both the directions simultaneously. It implies that they parse the sentence simultaneously. It implies that they parse the sentence simultaneously, from 'left to right' and from 'right to left'.

2. Deterministic Parsing

A parsing in which there is only one replacement possibility for every word is known as deterministic parsing. Each arc will have a different test condition. These parsers cannot do back tracking. Please note that if the incorrect test choice is accepted from some state, the parser will fail. This happens when one word satisfies more than one word categories like noun and verb or adjective and verb. To over come this problem of correct choice, the parser uses **look ahead mechanism**. But even then designing such parsers is not difficult.

3. Non-Deterministic Parsing

A parsing that allows different arcs to be labeled with the same test is known as Non-Deterministic parsing. The next test from any state may not be uniquely determined by the state and the current input word. The parser guesses at the proper constituents and then do backtrack if guess is proven to be wrong.

6.1.4 Transition Networks and Its Types

A transition network is a finite state automaton that is used to represent a part of a grammar. A transition network parser uses a number of these transition network to represent its entire grammar. Each network represents one non-terminal symbol in the grammar.

Actually, **transition network is a method of parsing which represents the grammar as a set of finite state machines (FSM).** A FSM is a model of computational behaviour where each node represents an internal state of the system and the **arcs** are the means of moving between the states. They are used in automata theory to represent grammar. In case of parsing of natural language, the arcs in the networks represent either a terminal or a non-terminal symbol. Rules in the grammar correspond to a path through a network. Each non-terminal is represented by a different network.

When moving from one state to the next through the network, the parser tests the **label** on the **arc**.

Case 1. If it is a terminal symbol, the parser will check whether it matches the next word in the input sentence.

Case 2. If it is a non-terminal symbol, the parser moves to the network for that symbol and attempts to find a path through that.

Case 3. If it finds a path through that network it returns to the higher-level network and continues. If the parser fails to find a path through that network, it backtracks and attempts another path. If it succeeds in finding a path, the sentence is a **valid one**.

Please understand that the parsing of the sentence continues in this fashion until the top-level sentence network is successfully traversed. Also note that the transition network allows each non-terminal to be represented in a single network rather than by numerous rules. This makes this approach more concise than grammars. But there is a disadvantage too. These transition network does not produce a parse tree for sentences. Also tracing the path through the network can be unclear for complex sentences.

How do we represent transition networks?

Transition networks are based on application of directed graphs (or digraphs) and finite state automata. This graph is now used to represent the syntactic structure of the sentence.

Nodes—Represent various states.

Arcs—Represent transition from certain states to final state.

We start at a given node, transverse an arc if the current word in the sentence is in the category on the arc. **Please note that if an arc is followed, the current word is updated to the next word. Also note that a sentence is accepted by transition network, if there is a path from the start node to a final node with arc accounting for every word in a sentence.**

How it works?

In each transition network, S_1 is the start state. When a phrase is applied to a transition network, the first word is compared against one of the arcs leading from the first state. If this word matches one of those arcs then the network moves to the next state.

For e.g.: Consider the following transition network—

When this network is presented with a noun phrase, it will move from state S_1 to State S_2.

Please understand that if a phrase is presented to a transition network and no match is found from the current state then that network cannot be used and another network must be tried. Also remember that transition networks can be used to determine whether a sentence is grammatically correct, at least as per the rules of the grammar the networks represent. And parsing using transition involves exploring a search space of possible parses in a depth-first fasion. Let us consider an example to understand this **"A dog sat"**.

We begin in state S1 in the sentence transition networks. To proceed, we must follow the arc that is labeled as Noun phrase. Thus, we move out from the sentence network into the Noun phrase network. The first arc of the Noun phrase network is labeled as **Noun**. So, we move into the Noun networks. We now follow each of the arc in the Noun network and discover that our first word, 'A', does not match any of them. Hence, we **backtrack** to the next arc in the Noun phrase network. This arc is labeled as Article, so we move onto the Article transition network. Here, on examining the second label we find that the first word i.e. matched by the terminal symbol on this arc. Therefore, we consume the word, "A", and move on to the state S_2 in the **Article network**. Because this is a success node, we are able to return to the **Noun phrase network** and move on to the state S_2 in this network. We now have an arc labeled Noun. As before, we move into the Noun network and find that our next word, "dog" matches. So, we move to state S_4 in the Noun phrase network. This is a success node and so we move back to the sentence network and repeat the process for the verb phrase arc. **Please note that it is possible for a system to use transition networks to generate a derivation tree for a sentence and also to determine whether the sentence is grammatically valid, it parses it fully to obtain further information by semantic analysis from the sentence.** This can be done by simply having the system build up the tree by noting which arc it successfully followed—

For e.g.: When it successfully follows the Noun phrase arc in the sentence network, the system generates a root node labeled sentence and an arc leading from that node to an new node labeled Noun phrases when the system follows the Noun Phrase network and identifies an article and a noun, these are similarly added to the tree. In this way, a full parse tree for a given sentence can be generated using transition networks.

As explained earlier that the starting point in studying ATN'S is the finite–state transition diagram (FSTS) as shown below.

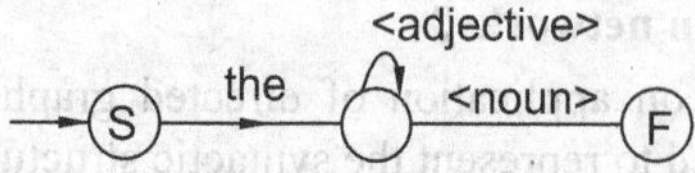

Fig. The FSTD that can process any noun phrase starting with "the".

FSTD diagrams consist of a set of **nodes** and **arcs** connecting the node. The rules followed are:-

1. All terminal symbols (words of the sentence) are represented as **arcs.**
2. One state (or node) is defined as 'S' the START state and one subset of states as the FINAL state 'F'.
3. A FSTD specifies a (dynamic) **process** for operating on arbitrary sentences instead of a static relationship between words as in a semantic network. **That is why an ATN is sometimes called as a finite state machine.**

The FSTD processes the input sentence, one word at a time, checking to see if the word matches the prescribed structure . **If it matches**, the word is placed on the appropriate arc and removed from the input sentence. When the final state is reached with no words in the sentence left over, we say the FSTD has accepted the sentence i.e., we **know that the sentence matches the syntactic structure specified by the FSTD**. The FSTD in figure will accept any sentence segment beginning with the, ending with a noun' and containing an arbitrary number of adjectives inbetween. Like, the big, white, dog would be accepted by this FSTD.

The main problem with FSTD is that it can recognize only sentences written as a regular language (type 3) which is the most restrictive of chomsky's four categories of language. It cannot handle sentences from the more general context-free (type -2) grammar.

Merits and demerits of parsing using transition networks

This type of parsing is simple but not very efficient. No attention is given to potential ambiguities or the need of words to agree with each other.

Other variants (types) of transition networks

Augmented Transition Networks (ATNs)

ATN or augmented transition network was given by William Woods in 1970. The ATN method of parsing sentences integrates many concepts from Chomsky's (1957) formal grammar theory with a matching process resembling a dynamic semantic network. Such parsing schemes may be considered as recursive pattern matching in which the string of words of the sentence are mapped onto a meaningful syntactic pattern. **Please note that the characteristics of an ATN can be understood by studying the progression from finite-state transition diagrams through recursive transition network to augmented transition networks. Also note that each level of this progression represents increased levels of incorporating options for semantic input into the formal syntactic structure of the parsing program.** The objective is to take an arbitrary input sentence and assign each word of the sentence its proper part of speech.

1. It is a modified form of transition networks.
2. It uses top down parsing procedure to gather various types of information to be later used for understanding system.
3. ATNs have the ability to apply tests to arcs.
4. ATN for a sentence will be

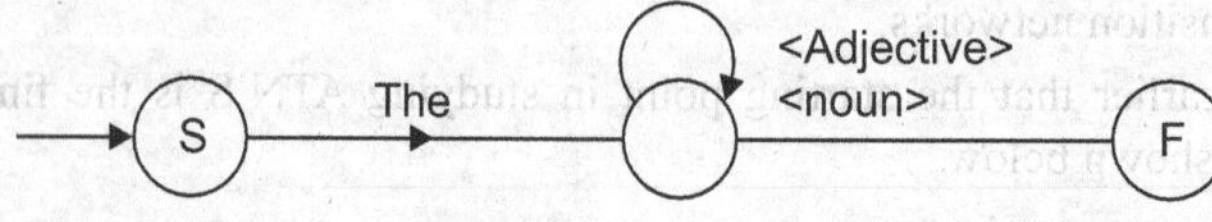

But, here, the arc from node S_2 to S_3 would be **conditional. The condition here, will be that the number of verbs should be same as the number of nouns, only then S_2 to S_3 transition is possible**. The conditions on the arc are calculated by the procedures that are attached to the arcs. The procedure attached to an arc is called when the network reaches that arc. These procedures, as well as, carrying out checks on agreement, are able to form parse tree from the sentence that is being analyzed.

5. ATNs not only do parsing but also collects the sentence features for further analysis.
6. ATNs represent sentence structure using a slot filler representation which reflects more of the functional role of phrases in a sentence.

Recursive Transition Networks (RTNs)

RTN is a recursive transition network which permits arc labels to refer to other networks (including the networks own name) and they in turn may refer back to the referring network rather than just permitting word categories used previously.

For e.g., Consider the RTN shows in Fig. 6.5 where the main network calls two sub networks—a NP and a PP network.

The top network in the figure is the top level (sentence) network and the lower level networks are for NP and PP arc states. The arcs corresponding to these states will be transversed only if the corresponding sub networks (b) or (c) are successfully transversed. Note that the arc named POP is used as a dummy arc to signal the successful completion of the sub network and a return to the node following the arc from which it was called.

The capability for recursion gives the RTN a considerable advantage over its predecessor, the FSTD. There is no restriction on the level of hierarch or **recursion with RTNs**. That is, a **sub-network may call another sub-network which may, in turn, call another and so on. Recursion is supported by allowing a sub-network to call itself.**

There is also no restriction on the number of sub-networks which may be called from a certain arc. Several sub-structures may be investigated simultaneously, and thus RTNs have the capability of parallel processing. Often, of course, many of the parallel sub-networks will fail to parse the phrase they are examining because it may not fit the structure specified by the RTN.
However, even context-free grammars cannot handle all English sentence structure. To extend the capabilities of syntactic parsers, the augmented transition network (ATN) was invented.

To further extend the capacity of finite state transition diagrams to handle more general context-free language, a recursion mechanism was added to the FSTD and it became a **recursive transition network** (RTN). This extension is like adding a subroutine capability at each arc. Now, in addition to containing a terminal (word), an are may contain the name of a sub-network to which the control may be transferred to parse like a prepositional phrase. When the sub-network is finished, control returns to the subsequent node and the processing continues.

Advantages of RTN

1. No restriction on the level of hierarchy or **recursion** with RTNS. **It means that a sub-network may call another sub-network which may call another and so on. This process is known as recursion.** Recursion is supported by allowing a sub-network to call itself.
2. No restriction on the number of sub-networks which may be called from a certain arc. Several sub-structures may be investigated simultaneously. **Thus, RTNs have the capability of parallel processing too.**

Many parallel sub-networks will fail to parse the phrase they are examining because it may not fit the structure specified by the RTN.

NOTE: Even context free grammars cannot handle all English sentence structures. To further extend the capabilities of syntactic parsers, ATNS were invented.

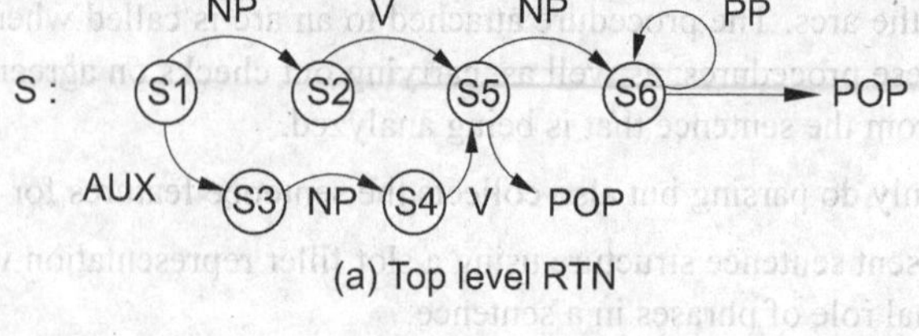

(a) Top level RTN

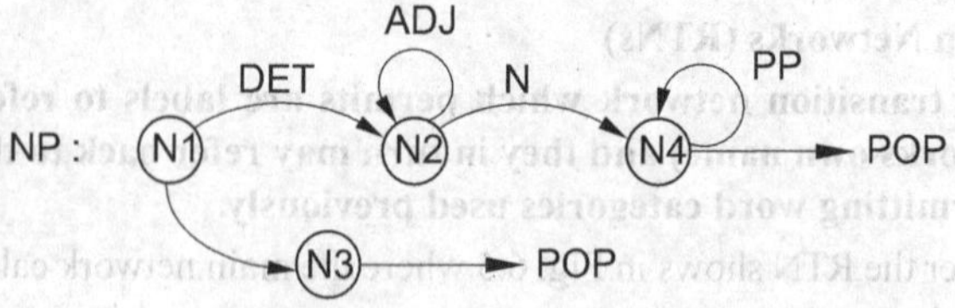

(b) Noun phrase subnetwork

PREP NP

PP : P1 P2 P3 POP

(C) Prepositional phrase subnetwork

Fig. 6.5 Recursive transition network (RTN).

6.1.5 Chart Parsing

The chart is a record of all the substructures build during parsing. It is also known as a **well-formed substring table**. Chart parsing works on the **principle of dynamic pgoramming** i.e., it uses and stores solutions of smaller part of a sentence to solve larger problems. Chart parsing works **incrementally** i.e., word by word. **In worst case,** chart parsing will parse a sentence of n words in $O(n^3)$ time. In many cases, it will perform better than this and will parse most of the sentences in $O(n^2)$ or even $O(n)$ time.

For example, say the sentence is —

"The cat eats a big rat"

It's initial chart is as follows—

(0) The (1) cat (2) eats (3) a (4) big (5) rat (6)

Fig. 6.6 Initial chart for given example.

How its chart parsing is done?

The chart of Fig. 6.6 show seven verticals which will become connected to each other by edges. The edges will show how the constituents of the sentence combine together.

The chart parser starts by adding the following edge to the chart—

$$\left[0, 0, \text{Target} \longrightarrow \bullet\ \text{Sentence}\right]$$

This notation means that the edge connects vertex 0 to itself. The first two numbers in the square brackets show which vertical the edge connects. Target is the target that we want to find which is really just a place holder to enable us to have an edge that requires us to find a whole sentence. The **arrow** indicates that in order to make what is on its LHS (target) we need to find what is on its RHS (sentence). The **dot** shows what has been found already on its LHS, and what is yet to be found on its RHS.

Now, consider the following edge, show in chart of Fig. 6.7.

(0) The (1) cat (2) eats (3) a (4) big (5) rat (6)

Fig. 6.7 Partial chart for the given sentence.

Now, the chart parser adds the following edge—

$$[0, 2, \text{Sentence} \longrightarrow \text{Nounphrase} \bullet \text{Verphrase}]$$

This means that an edge exists connecting nodes 0 and 2. The dot shows us that we have already found a Noun phrase (the cat) and that we are looking for a verb phrase. Once we have found that verb phrase, we will get what is on the LHS of the arrow i.e., a sentence.

The chart parser can add edges to the chart using the following three rules:

Rule 1: If we have an edge [x, y, A → B · C], which needs to find a C, then an edge can be added that supplied that C i.e., the edge [*x*, *y*,(*c*) → E], where E is some sequence of terminals or non-terminals which can be replaced by C.

Rule 2: If we have two edges [x, y, A → B · CD] and [*y*, *x*, *C* → E] then these two edges can be combined together to form a new edge i.e. [x, z, A→ BC · D].

Rule 3: If we have an edge [x, y, A → B · C] and the word at vertex y is of type C, then we have found a suitable word for this edge and so we extend the edge along to the next vertex by adding the following edge

$$[y, y+1, A \rightarrow BC \bullet]$$

Let us apply these three rules to our example now.

We start with the edge [0, 0, Target . sentence] which means that to find our target, we must first find a sentence.

Use rule-1, so we can add the following edge to chart:–

$$[0, 0, \text{sentence} \rightarrow \text{Noun phrase Verb phrase}]$$

This means that we must now find a Noun phrase and a Verb phrase. We now apply rule-1 again, to try to find a suitable Noun phrase, which involves adding the following edge:

$$[0, 0, \text{Noun phrase} \rightarrow \cdot \text{ Article Noun phrase}]$$

Now, we can apply rule-3 because the word at the end of this edge (form vertex 0 to vertex 0) is "The", which is an article. This would be determined by looking the word up in a lexicon. Hence, we can now add the following edge:

$$[0, 1, \text{Noun phrase} \rightarrow \text{Article} \cdot \text{Noun phrase}]$$

Now, we are looking for another Noun phrase, so we use rule-1 again to add the following edge:

$$[0, 1, \text{Noun phrase} \rightarrow \cdot \text{ Noun}]$$

We can now use rule-3 again because the next word is indeed a Noun, to add the following edge to the chart:

$$[0, 2, \text{Noun phrase} \rightarrow \text{Noun} \bullet]$$

This process continues, until we have reached an edge in which we have found everything we need. So, the **final edge** will be –

$$[0, 6, \text{Sentence} \rightarrow \text{Noun phrase Verbphrase} \bullet]$$

To build a parse tree from the chart, we modify rule-2 so that when it combines two edges together, it stores in the new edge information about the two edges that were combined to form the children edges. Then, when the parse has completed, we can obtain the parse tree directly from the edges of the tree by starting from the first edge and **recursively** examining the children edges of each node.

SUMMARY

English, Hindi, French etc are all natural languages but computers cannot understand them. NLP or computational Linguistics is the scientific study of languages from a computational perspective. A computer is said to be intelligent only if it can understand the commands given in natural languages.

MULTIPLE CHOICE QUESTIONS [MCQS]

1. KBS stands for
   (*a*) Knowledge based software (*b*) Knowledge basis system
   (*c*) Knowledge based system (*d*) None of the above.
2. The process of converting a sentence into a tree that represents a sentence's syntatic structure is known as
   (*a*) Parsing (*b*) Grammar
   (*c*) Discourse integration (*d*) None of the above.
3. ATN stands for
   (*a*) Automated Teller Network (*b*) Automatic Truth Network
   (*c*) Augmented Transition Network (*d*) None of the above.
4. Which is the following is NOT Transition Network—
   (*a*) ATN (*b*) RTN (*c*) ATM (*d*) None of the above.
5. Chart parsing works on the principle of
   (*a*) Dynamic programming (*b*) Backtracking
   (*c*) Greedy method (*d*) None of the above.
6. In worst case, the time complexity of chart parsing is
   (*a*) O(n) (*b*) $O(n^2)$ (*c*) $O(n^3)$ (*d*) All of the above.

ANSWERS

1. (*c*) **2.** (*a*) **3.** (*c*) **4.** (*c*) **5.** (*a*)
6. (*c*)

CONCEPTUAL SHORT QUESTIONS WITH ANSWERS

Q. 1. What are the various passes in natural language processing system? Explain the problem (syntactic, semantic or pragmatic), if any, with the following sentences—

(*a*) Mohan a letter Mary sent to. (*b*) He takes a tea with milk.
(*c*) Rice flies like an apple. (*d*) A boy study in a college.

[MDU, BE (CSE)-6th Sem., Dec. 2007, 2008 and GGSIPU, B. Tech (CS)-8th Sem., May 2010]

Ans. NLP phases are as follows—

1. Speech segmentation

In most spoken languages, the sounds representing successive letters blend into each other, so the conversion of the ana log signal to discrete characters can be a very difficult process. Also in natural speech, there are hardly any pauses between successive words; the location of those boundaries usually must take into account grammatical and semantic constraints, as well as the context.

2. Text segmentation

Some written languages like Chinese, Japanese and Thai do not have single - word boundaries either, so any significant text parsing usually requires the identificaiton of work boundaries, which is often a non-trivial task.

3. Part-of-speech tagging

Many words have more than one meaning; we have to select the meaning which makes the most sense in context.

4. Syntactic ambiguity

The grammar for natural languages is ambigous i.e., there are often multiple possible parse trees for a given sentence. Choosing the most appropriate one usually requires semantic and contextual information. Specific problem components of syntactic ambiguity include sentence boundary disambiguation.

5. Imperfect or irregular input

Foreign or regional accents and vocal impediments in speech, typing or grammatical errors, OCR errors in texts.

6. Speech acts and plans

A sentence can often be considered as an action by the speaker. The sentence structure alone may not contain enough information to define this action.

Let us answer for the given sentences now—

(*a*) **Mohan a letter Mary sent to**

This sentence is **syntactically** and **semantically** wrong but **pragmatically** correct.

(*b*) **He take a tea with milk**

This sentence is **syntactically** wrong.

(*c*) **Rice flies like an apple**

This sentence is **pragmatically** and **syntactically** wrong.

(*d*) **A boy study in a college**

This sentence is semantically incorrect.

Q. 2. Name some NLP systems along with their year of development.

Ans. (*a*) ELIZA System (1966-67)—By Weizenbaun at MIT.

(*b*) LUNAR System (1970)

(*c*) SHRDLU System (1970).

LUNAR is a question–answering system in AI. SHRDLU was a dialogue system which could converse with a human user.

Q. 3. Draw a parse tree for the sentence—"Viru hits the ball".

[UPTU, B. Tech (CSE) 6th Sem., 2004-05]

Ans.

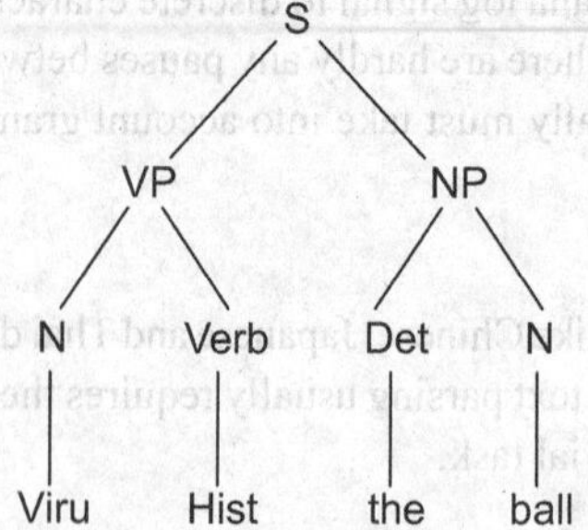

This is a CFG i.e., context-free grammar which is a collection of productions of the form S → NP VP i.e., a constituent S can consist of sub-constituents NP and VP.

Q4. Explain top-down and bottom-up parsing for the following grammar—

S → NP VP

NP → ART N

VP → V NP

N → boy/frog

V → ate/kissed

ART → the/a

where S is initial symbol for sentences

NP is a Noun phrase

VP is Verb phrase

N is Noun

V is Verb

and ART is article

Apply this grammar on the following sentence— "A boy ate the frog" and write top-down and bottom-up parsing. [UPTU, B. Tech (CSE)-6th Sem., 2004-05]

Top-down parsing	Bottom-up parsing
S → NP VP	→ the/a boy/frog ate/kissed the/a boy/frog
→ ART N VP	→ the/a boy/frog ate/kissed the/a N
→ the/a N VP	→ the/a boy/frog ate/kissed NP
→ the/a boy/frog VP	→ the/a boy/frog V NP
→ the/a boy/frog V NP	→ the/a boy/frog VP
→ the/a boy/frog ate/kissed NP	→ the/a N VP
→ the/a boy/frog ate/kissed ART N	→ ART N VP
→ the/a boy/frog ate/kissed the/a N	→ NP VP
→ the/a boy/frog ate/kissed the/a boy/frog	→ NP VP → S

Applying the grammar to given sentence gives—

Top-down parsing		Bottom-up parsing
S → NP VP	→	A boy ate the frog
→ ART N VP	→	A boy ate the N
→ A N VP	→	A boy ate ART N
→ A boy VP	→	A boy ate NP
→ A boy V NP	→	A boy V NP
→ A boy ate NP	→	A boy VP
→ A boy ate ART N	→	A N VP
→ A boy ate the N	→	ART N VP
→ A boy ate the frog	→	NP VP
	→	S

Q5. What is Fillmore's grammar? Give an example.

[Coachin University of Science & Technology, B. Tech. (CSE)-8th Sem., Oct 2000]

Ans.

1. Fillmore grammar is also called as **case grammar**. Case grammar provides a different approach to the problem of how syntactic and semantic interpretation can be combined. Grammar rules are written to describe syntactic rather than semantic regularities. But the structures, rules are produced correspond to semantic relations rather than to strictily syntactic ones. As an example, consider the two sentences and the simplified forms of their conventional parse trees shown in Fig. 6.9.
2. Case grammar describes the relationship between verbs and their arguments parsing using a case grammar is usually expectation-driven. Once verb of the sentence is located, it can be used to predict the noun phrases that will occur and to determine the relationship of those phrases to the rest of the sentences.

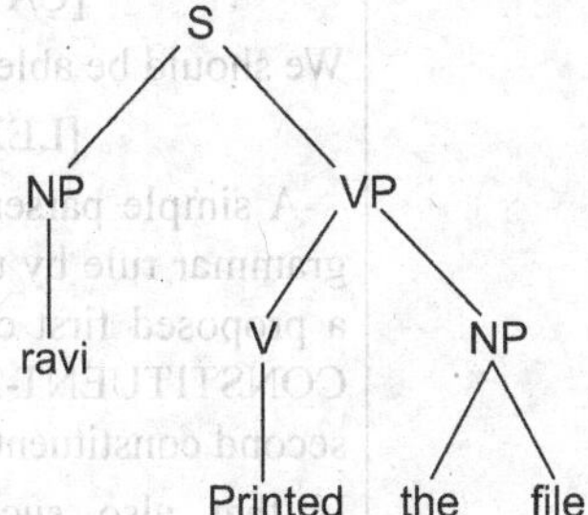

Fig. 6.9 Parsing

3. A case grammar describes the correct set of deep cases. Some of the cases are given as follows:
   - Agent – Investigator of the action.
   - Instrument – cause of the event.
   - Dative – entity affected by the action.
   - Factitive – object.
   - Locative – place of the event.
   - Source – place from which something moves.

Q.6. NLP is a classical AI problem. Explain how.

Ans. **1. Minimal input data**

The natural language statement does not contain the message but is a minimal specification to allow an intelligent reader to construct the message.

2. Knowledge based

The interpretation of the message is based on the large part of the knowledge that the reader already has.

3. Local ambiguity

Many wrong interpretations are superficially consistent with the input.

4. Global constraints

There are many different kinds of constraints on the interpretation of the input.

5. Capturing the infinite

A language understanding system must capture inifinite form — rules sufficient to understand a potentially infinite set of statements.

Q. 7 What is the difference between logical unification and graphical unification?

Ans.

Logical Unification	Graphical Unification
1. The inputs to the logical unifications are treated as logical formulas.	1. The inputs to the graph unification must be treated as sets.
2. Order in which attribute-value pairs are stated matters.	2. Order does not matter.
For eg f(g(a), h(b)) is different than f(h(b), g(a))	**For eg** if a rule is described as a constituent as follows [CAT : DET LEX : {1}] We should be able to match this constituent as [LEX : the CAT : DET] A simple parser can use the method to apply a grammar rule by unifying CONSTITUENT-1 with a proposed first constituent. If that succeeds then CONSTITUENT-2 is **unified** with a proposed second constituent. If that also succeeds then a new constituent corresponding to the value of BUILD IS PRODUCED. If there are variables on the value variables in the value of BUILD which were bound during the matching of constituents then those binding will be used to build the new constituent.

Q. 8. Derive the parse tree for the sentence "Bill loves the frog where the following rules are used.

S → NP VP

NP → N

NP → DET N

CP → V NP

DET → the

V → loves

N → bill frog

Ans.

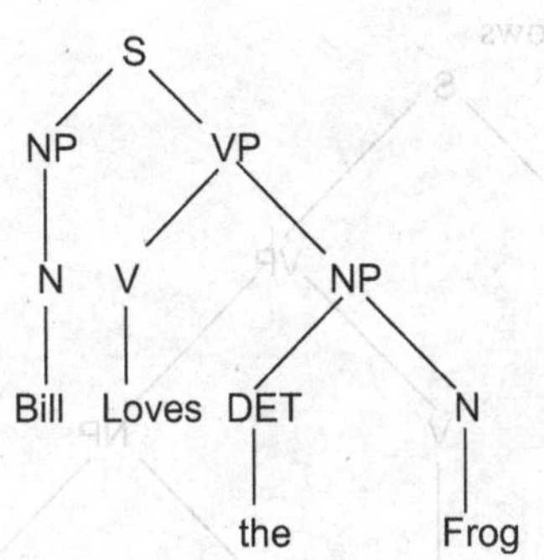

Q. 9. Develop a parse tree for the sentence "Shyam slept on the platform" using following rewrite rules.

S → NP VP

NP → N

NP → DET N

VP → V PP

PP → PREP NP

N → Shyam | platform

DET → the

PREP → on

Ans.

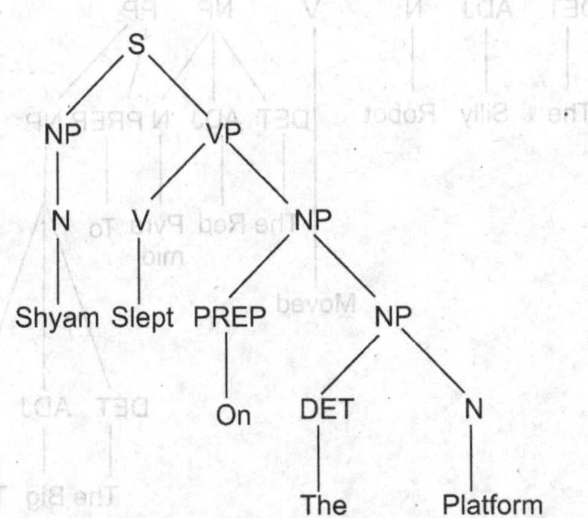

Q. 10. Draw the parse tree for sentence "Mary likes a chocolate" where rewrite rules are given as below:

S → NP VP

NP → N

NP → DET N

VP → V PP

DET → a

V → likes

N → Mary/chocolates.

Ans. The pares tree is as follows

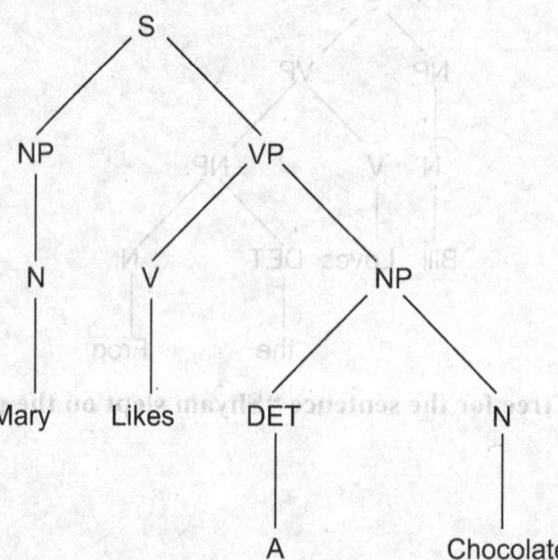

Q. 11. Given the following parse tree for the sentence— "The silly robot moved the red pyramid to the big table." Write down the context free grammar.

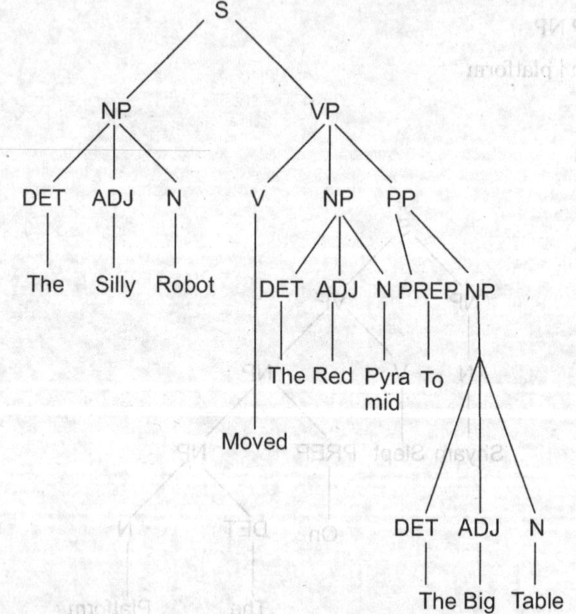

Ans. Its context free grammar is

S → NP VP

NP → DET ADT N

VP → V NP PP

NP → V PP

NP → DET ADJ N

PP → PREP NP

NP → DET ADJ N

DET → the

ADJ → silly/red/big

N → robot/pyramid/table

V → moved

PREP → to

Q. 12. Given are the rewrite rules, draw a parse tree for the sentence — "Remove the pump with the wrench in the box."

S → V NP VP

NP → DET N

PP → PREP NP

NP → DET N PP

PP → PREP NP

NP → DET N

DET → the

V → remove

N → pump/box

PREP → with/in

Ans. The parse tree is a follows.

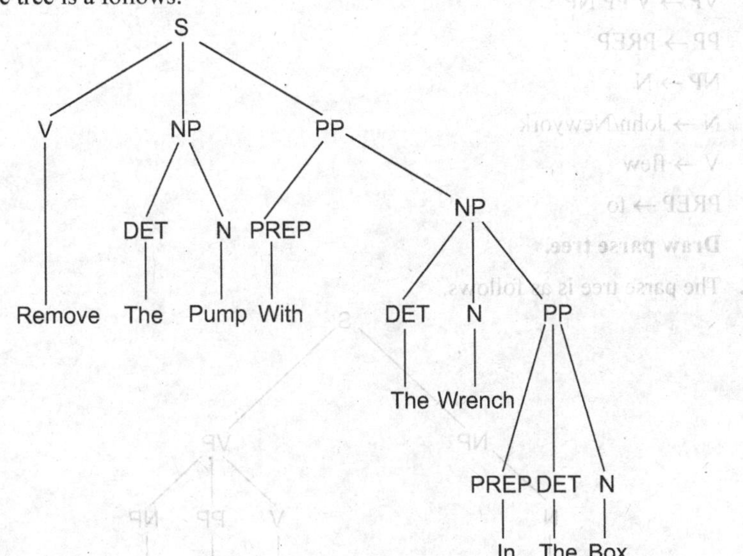

Q. 13. Given the rewrite rules for the sentence — "The boy kissed a rabbit". Draw the parse tree.

S → NP VP

NP → ART N

VP → V NP

NP → ART N

V → kissed

ART → the/a

N → boy/rabbit.

Ans. The parse tree is as follows.

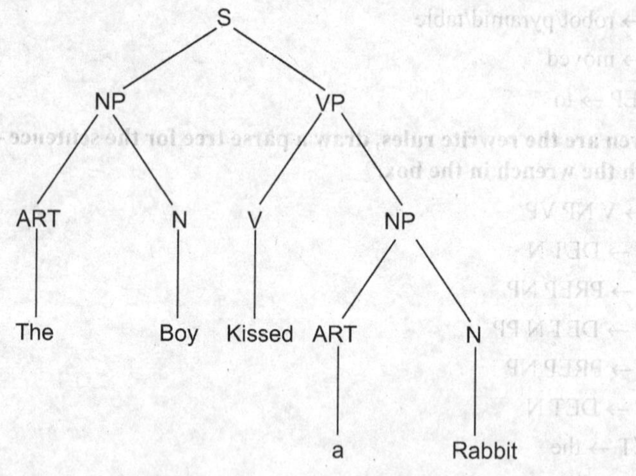

Q. 14. Given is a sentence "John flew to Newyork" Rewrite rules are given as:-

S → NP VP

NP → N

VP → V PP NP

PP → PREP

NP → N

N → John/Newyork

V → flew

PREP → to

Draw parse tree.

Ans. The parse tree is as follows.

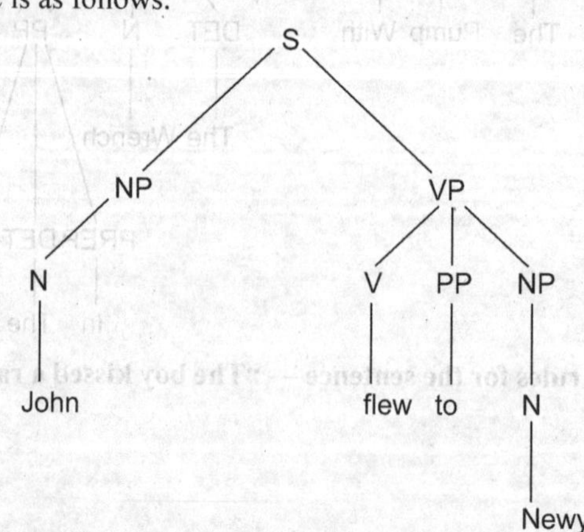

Q. 15. Draw the syntax (parse tree) when rewrite rules are given for the sentence "John saw Mary and the boy with a telescope".

S → NP VP

NP → N

VP → V NP PP

NP → N

PP → PREP NP

NP → DET N PP

NP → DET N

PP → PREP NP

N → John/Mary/boy/telescope

V → Saw

PREP → and/With

DET → a/the.

Ans. The parse tree is.

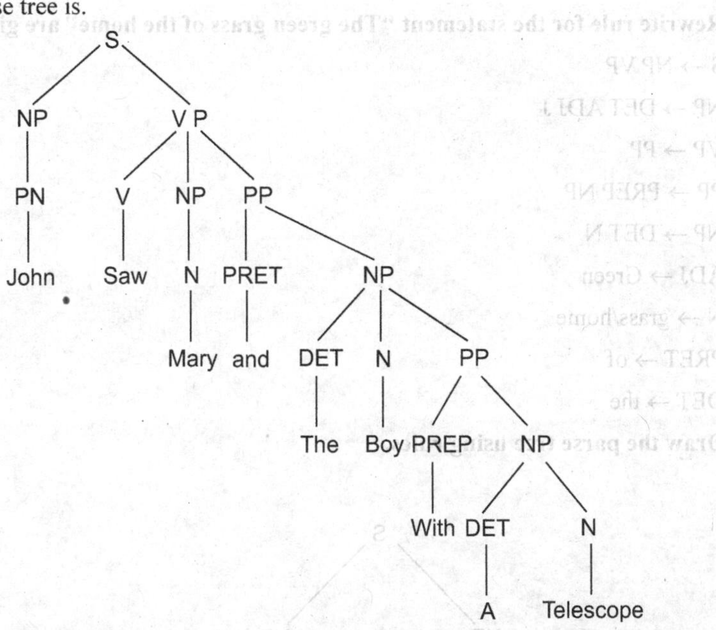

Q. 16. Draw the parse tree for the sentence— "A student deleted the file". The rewrite rules are as given below:-

S → NP VP

NP → DET N

VP → V PP

PP → NP

NP → DET N

DET → a/the

N → student/file

V → deleted.

Ans.

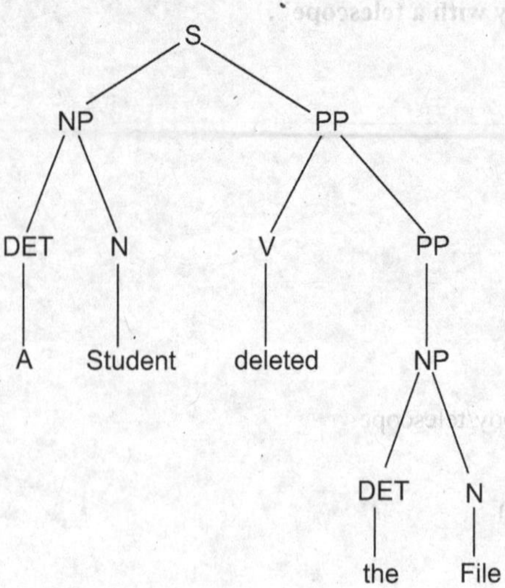

Q. 17. Rewrite rule for the statement "The green grass of the home" are given as follows.

S → NP VP

NP → DET ADJ J

VP → PP

PP → PREP NP

NP → DET N

ADJ → Green

N → grass/home

PRET → of

DET → the

Draw the parse tree using rules.

Ans.

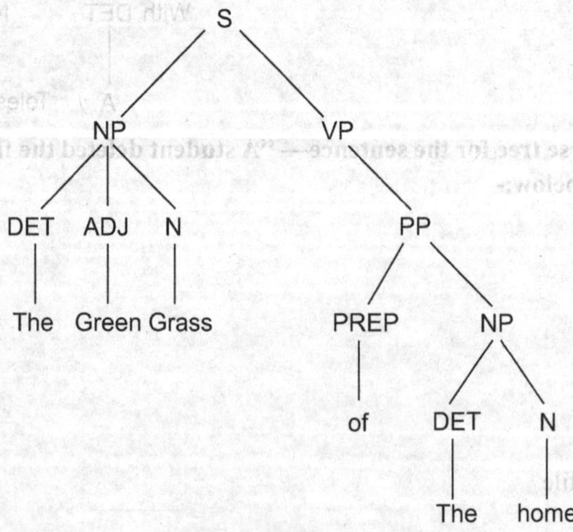

Q. 18. Given is the parse tree for the sentence as— "The plane flew above the Clouds."

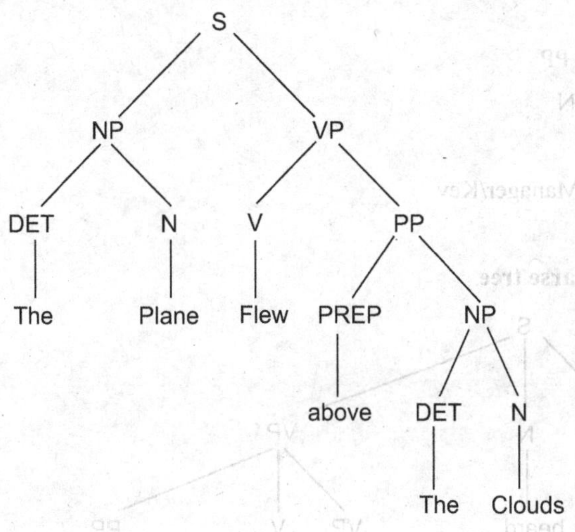

Write the rewrite rules or

Context free grammar for this tree.

Ans. S → NP VP

NP → DET N

VP → V PP

PP → PREP NP

NP → DET N

DET → the

PREP → above

N → plane/clouds

V → flew.

Q. 19. Given is the parse tree for the sentence as— "Nidhi gave the manager the key."

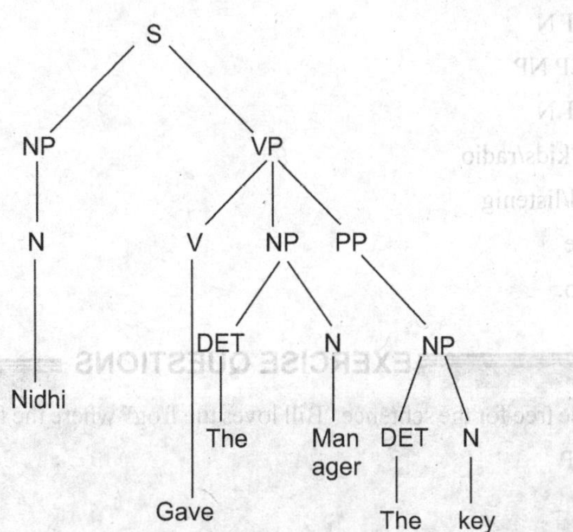

Ans. S → NP VP

NP → N

VP → V NP PP

NP → DET N

DET → the

N → Nidhi/Manager/Key

V → gave

Q. 20. Given the parse tree

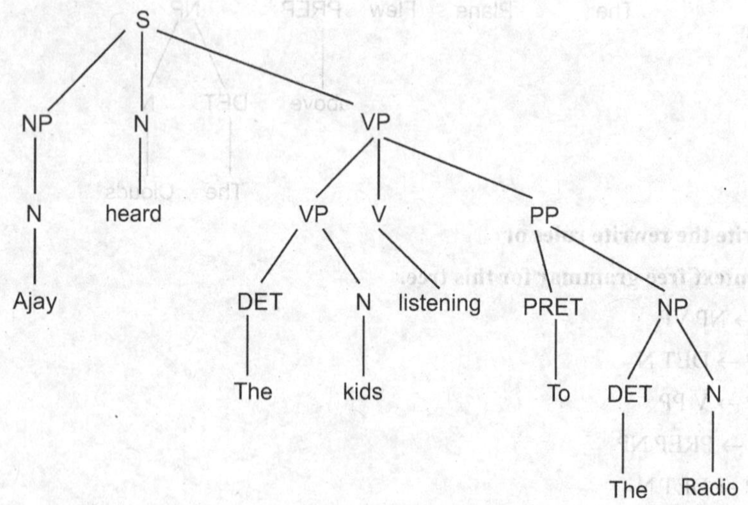

Write its context free Grammar.

Ans. S → NP VP

NP → N

VP → NP V PP

NP → DET N

PP → PREP NP

NP → DET N

N → Ajay/kids/radio

V → heard/listenig

DET → the

PREP → to.

EXERCISE QUESTIONS

Q. 1. Give a parse tree for the sentence "Bill loves the frog" where the following rules are used—

S → NP VP

NP → N

NP → DET N

VP → V NP

DET → the

V → loves

N → bill/frog

[GGSIPU, B. Tech (CSE)-8th Sem., May 2008 & PTU, MCA-4th Sem., 2009]

Q. 2. Describe ATN. **[GGIPU, B. Tech (CSE) 8th Sem., May 2009]**

Q. 3. (*a*) What are important challenges in Natural Language Understanding?

(*b*) What are the various applications of NLP?

(*c*) Explain the various activities which are performed during Morphological Analysis and Syntactic processing with the help of following sentence: I want to see Raju's photo.

[GGSIPU, B. Tech (CSE)-8th Sem., May 2010]

Q. 4. What are the different ways in which ambiguity results in natural langauge statements? Give an example of each type. **[RTM, Nagpur University BE (IT)-7th Sem., Summer 2003]**

Q. 5. Develop a parse tree for the sentence- "Jack slept on the table" using the following rules—

S → NP VP

NP → DET N

PP → PEP NP

V → Slept

PRBP → on

NP → N

VP → VPP

N → Jack/table **[RTM, Nagpur University, BE (IT)-7th Sem.,**

DET → the **Summer 2008 & Winter 2008]**

Q. 6. (*a*) Explain types of a grammars used in NLP.

(*b*) What are the levels of knowledge used in Natural Language Understanding.

[RTM Nagpur University, BE (IT)-7th Sem., Summar 2009]

Q. 7. (*a*) Explain the problems you may face in parsing Indian Languages?

(*b*) Design an ATN for recognizing the language { $a^n b^{2n} c^{3n}$, for n > 0}.

[Cochin University, B. Tech (CSE)-8th Sem., May 2004]

Q. 8. (*a*) Explain how lexical, semantic and Syntactic analysis are carried out in NLP.

(*b*) Briefly explain different parsing techniques.

[CUSAT, B. Tech (CSE)-8th Sem., Oct. 2004]

Q. 9. (*a*) Using CFG, draw and explain a parse tree for the English Sentence—"The man bites the dog".

(*b*) Explain how can we combine syntac and semantic knowledge. Use sentence, if required.

[CUSAT, B. Tech (CSE)-8th Sem., Oct 2004]

Q. 10. What are the various phases of NLP? **[MDU, BE (CSE)-6th Sem., Dec. 2008]**

Q. 11. (*a*) Describe chowsky hierarchy of languages.

(*b*) Differentiate between syntactic and Semantic processing.

[GGSIPU, B. Tech (CSE)-8th Sem., May 2011]

7 CHAPTER

LEARNING

7.0 INTRODUCTION

Learning is done by viewing, listening, interactions, studying and by experience. Learning provides us the power to reason, ability to handle new situations and enables us to act in an intelligent way. Human beings are intelligent as they possess knowledge of world. Similarly, making a machine intelligent means it should have the power of learning. So, **Machine learning** is a challenge now. An **intelligent machine** should be able to learn new things and to adapt to new situations rather than simply doing steps as they are made to do. **Please understand that a machine cannot be called intelligent, if it does not have power of learning.** In literature, many definitions of learning have been given. Let us give some here too—

1. Herbert Simon (1983)

"Learning denotes changes in the system that are adaptive in the sense that they enable the system to do the same task or tasks more efficiently and more effectively the next time."

2. Marvin Minsky (1986)

"Learning is making useful changes in the working of our mind."

3. Ryszard Michalski (1986)

"Learning is constructing or modifying representations of what is being experienced."

4. Mitchell (1997)

"A computer program is said to learn from experience (E) w.r.t. some class of tasks (T) and performance measure (P), if its performance at tasks in T, as measured by P, improves with experience E".

The learning problem is divided into three types—

(*a*) Unsupervised learning

It finds a model that matches a stream of input experiences and is able to predict what new experience to expect.

(*b*) Supervised learning

It **classifies** (be able to determine) what category something belongs to after seeing a number of examples of things from each category or regression (given a set of numerical input/output examples, discover a continuous function that would generate the outputs from the inputs).

(*c*) Reinforcement learning

The agent is rewarded for good responses and punished for bad ones. They can be analyzed in terms of decision theory, using concepts like utility. The mathematical analysis of machine learning algorithms and their performance is a branch of theoretical computer science known as computational learning theory.

7.1 CONCEPT OF LEARNING

The major paradigms of machine learning are as follows—

(*a*) **Rote learning** by memorization (saving knowledge so that it can be used again).

(*b*) **Induction** involves the process of learning by example where a system tries to induce a general rule from a set of observed instances.

(*c*) **Analogy.** It can recognize similarities in information already stored. It can determine correspondence between two different representations.

(*d*) **Genetic Algorithms (GA)** are a part of evolutionary computing, a way of solving problems by mimicking processes. Nature uses selection, crosses over, mutation and accepting to evolve a solution to a problem.

(*e*) **Reinforcement.** It assigns rewards, positive or negative, act end of a sequence of steps, it learns which actions are good or bad.

Let us now discuss the general block diagram model of learning.

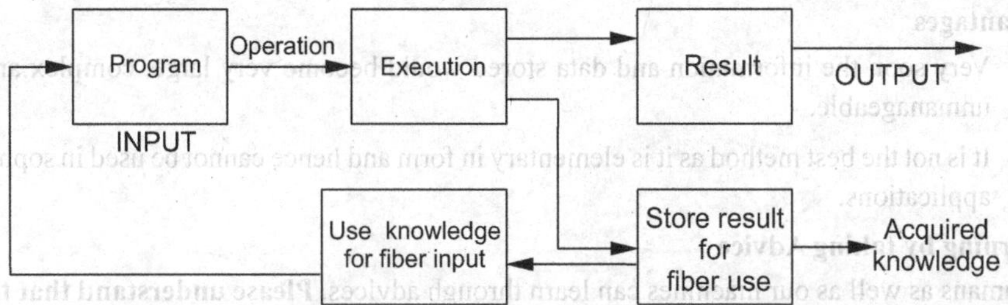

Fig. 7.1 General block diagram of a learning system.

As shown in Fig. 7.1, the input program is any general program executed for solution of a problem. The results are reported as output. These results are also stored back to acquire knowledge for future use. This simply means that, if a similar problem is required to be solved next time, the results can automatically be taken from previously acquired knowledge. **Please note that learning involves generalization from experience.** A system is said to be learning if it not only does the repetition of same task more effectively but also the similar tasks of the related domain. It covers a wide range of phenomenon:

(*a*) Knowledge acquisition.

(*b*) Skill refinement.

Knowledge acquisition refers to a situation in which computer executes one program and remembers the process for future use.

Skill refinement means the ability because of which, by doing some task repeatedly people tend to solve the task in lesser time. By practice skill tends to get refined.

Same capabilities are expected out of machines also.

7.2 FIVE TYPES OF LEARNING

There are five main methods of learning in context of machines. They are as follows—

(*a*) Rote learning

(*b*) Learning by taking advice

(*c*) Learning by induction

(*d*) Learning by deduction (or Relevance-based Learning).

(*e*) Learning by analogy

I. Rote Learning/Learning through memorization

Rote learning is based on the principle of **caching**. Caching means to store data of a particular task.

For example, if say, a chess is played then the winning sequence of moves will simply be remembered by the players involved. Next time, instead of arbitrarily selecting from all possible moves, they will select a move from among the winning moves. **Please note that by repeatedly remembering the winning situation, the choice of move becomes improved.** This is what humans can do and hence we expect this much from our machines also. If our machine uses this technique of data caching then a significant amount of time can be saved as our intermediate results are already stored and are being only reused here.

Advantages

1. It enables machine to store organized information.
2. It is faster to reuse information stored than to collect it.
3. We get generalized information stored in the database using Rote learning.

Disadvantages

1. Very soon the information and data stored would become very large, complex and hence unmanageable.
2. It is not the best method as it is elementary in form and hence cannot be used in sophisticated applications.

II. Learning by taking Advice

Both humans as well as our machines can learn through advices. **Please understand that this kind of learning takes place when a computer runs a particular program by taking advice from its programmer (or creator of that program).**

Here the knowledge provided by the teacher is at a level more general than that usable by the performance element. The system has to particularize this general advice to specific situations.

For example: The advice often given to novices trying to learn card games.

Also note that much of our education involves this type of learning. The main problem to be tackled by the learning element here is transforming the general purposes knowledge into specific rules and heuristics which can be used by the performance element. This process is called as **operationalisation**. For a realistic model we have to assume that the advice is given in natural language which further complicates the problem. This is a difficult learning problem and there are a few interesting models proposed.

III. Learning by Induction

Induction involves drawing general conclusions from specific observations. Learning from examples and **learning by discovery** are instances of inductive learning. Most of the knowledge that the human race has acquired about its environment is through the process of induction.

For example: Observing the specific facts that the sun has risen in the east on day 1, day 2 etc., we infer a general statement, namely, sun always rises in the east.

IV. Learning by Deduction/Relevance-based Learning

Another method of inferring some conclusions from a given set of statements is deduction. Here, we start with a set of so called **axioms** and using rules of logic, derive conclusion. Provided that the logic we use is consistent, all the derived statements are true if the original axioms are true. **Please note**

here that the deduction is a truth preserving process whereas induction is not. This is because from a given set of observations there are infinitely many inductive conclusions possible. Hence, while learning from examples, we have to pay special attention to the problem of how far should the observations be generalized. Presence of counter examples helps us from **overgeneralization**. But even then there may be many possible generalizations and hence the learning system should be provided with enough background knowledge for it to prefer **good** generalizations.

For example: Starting with the statements—

S1: All people attending workshops on expert systems are computer scientists.

S2: Mr. X attended a workshop on expert systems.

We can derive conclusion—

Mr. X is a Computer Scientist.

If the first two statements are true then so is the derived conclusion. **This is because in deduction we go from the general to the specific.** On the other hand, in induction we go from the **specific to general** and hence it is not possible to guarantee, in general, the correctness of the conclusions.

For example, observing that Mr. X, Mr. Y and so on, all of whom are Computer Scientists, attend workshops on expert systems, we can inductively conclude that all people attending workshops on expert systems are Computer Scientists. **But please note that the truthness of the starting premises does not guarantee truthness of the conclusion.** But if we can find one person attending workshop on expert systems who is not a Computer Scientist, we can immediately prove the inductive conclusion to be false. **Thus, we can think of induction as falsity preserving.** Incidentally, this is the reason why counter examples play a crucial role in development of scientific theories.

V. Learning by Analogy

Here, the knowledge provided by the teacher is useful for solving an analogous though not identical problem. Hence, the learning element needs to make some inferences to decide how this knowledge needs to be transformed so that it is useful for the problem at hand. There is not much work done in this area.

7.3 OTHER TYPES OF LEARNING

There are various other types of learning as follows—

(*a*) Concept Learning (CL).

(*b*) Explanation Based Learning (EBL).

(*c*) Symbol Based Learning (SBL).

(*d*) Relevance Based Learning (RBL)/Deductive Learning.

Let us discuss them now.

I. Concept Learning

The problem of learning a single concept from examples and counter examples is called as **concept learning.**

Associated with each concept learning problem is a domain of objects which is characterized by a set of attributes. Each object in the domain is described by a tuple of values – one for each attribute. A subset of the domain is the concept. The learning system is provided (by the teacher) with some objects from the domain and is also told whether each object belongs to the concept or not. All objects belonging to the concept are called **positive examples** and all other objects from the domain are called **negative examples**. The system is expected to learn a representation of the concept which can be used by it for deciding whether a given object belongs to the concept.

Concept learning is the simplest case of learning from examples. To understand its relevance let us consider an example. Suppose we need an expert system for diagnosing some diseases. The data needed for diagnosis will be some symptoms of the patient (e.g., temperature, whether he has headache etc.) and results of clinical tests (e.g., presence of pus cells in urine etc.). Suppose the system should be rule-based and for simplicity we assume that each rule has a condition part that is a Boolean function of the data and an action part that gives the diagnosis. We want the system to acquire the rules by interacting with an expert. The expert will show the system various cases and his diagnosis. If we restrict our attention to learning rules for diagnosing a single disease, what we have is a concept learning problem. Here the attributes are the symptoms and clinical tests. Positive and negative examples are cases provided by the expert. **The objective is to learn a decision procedure for diagnosing the diseases. This type of learning is useful even if the initial knowledge base is hand coded. The system can periodically interact with expert to check correctness of its diagnosis.** In areas where the system is making mistakes, the expert can supply the system with some typical cases and the system will automatically update its knowledge base. Since the expert is generally not a computer scientist, it is easier for him to discuss typical cases than to examine and modify the knowledge base of the system. **It may be noted that for the system to learn it must possess some minimal knowledge regarding the various attributes etc.**

The first issue to be addressed while developing algorithms for concept learning is the choice of representation for the concept. The representation should be usable by the decision procedure and it should be suitable for the learning algorithm. We will be considering two representations – **decision trees and logic expressions.**

In a **decision tree** all nodes except the leaf nodes are labeled by a question (involving, generally the value of one attribute). All the edges from an node are labeled by possible answers for the question. The leaf nodes are labeled by decisions or the class labels. Suppose we have a concept represented as a decision tree and we have to use this for deciding whether a given object belongs to the concept. We start at the root node. At each node we answer the question at that node for the current object and thus take the appropriate edge from the node. Finally when we come to a leaf node its label will be the decision.

A **logic expression** is directly usable as the condition in an if-then rule for making decision. By using simple structures for the logic expression it is possible to learn the concept as a logic expression. Consider a concept learning problem with N attributes Y_i, taking values in sets v_i, $1 \le i \le N$. We distinguish between two logic expressions for representing a concept.

Defintion 2.1 A logic expression of the form

$$[Y_1 \in v_1] /\backslash \ldots /\backslash [Y_N \in v_N],\ v_i \subseteq v_i,\ v\ i,$$

is said to be in Conjunctive Normal Form (CNF).

Here each expression of the form $[Y_i \in v_i]$ is called a **selector.** It is true if the value of the attribute is in the corresponding set. Since this can be viewed as a disjunction of equality predicates each of which tests if Y_i is equal to some element of v_i, a selector is said to have internal disjunctions.

Defintion 2.1 A logic expression of the form

$$C_1 \backslash/ C_2 \backslash/ \ldots \backslash/ Cm,\ m \ge 1,$$

where each C_i is a CNF expression, is said to be in Disjunctive Normal Form (DNF).

In the next section we will consider algorithms for learning concepts as CNF or DNF expressions and also as decision trees.

The representation chosen for the concept determines the set of all possible concepts, the so called concept space. For example, for CNF concepts the concept space will be the set of all possible tuples of the form $(A_1,\ldots, A_N)$, where A_i V_i. The set of all possible examples will be called the instance space. The input to the learning system will be points in the instance space using which the system searches over the concept space to find best concept. If we use logic expressions for concepts then all examples (which are N-tuples of values for all attributes) are CNF concepts. Hence all examples will be points in the concept space. This is referred to as single representation trick which is useful because the examples can serve as starting points for the search over the concept space. To define the goal of this search process we need to decide what is the 'best' concept. A concept is said to be consistent if it explains all the examples. That is, if it satisfies all positive examples and none of the negative examples. But consistency by itself is not sufficient; the disjunction of all +ve examples is a consistent concept though it has no generalisation capability. If our concept space contains only CNF concepts, then we cannot any way converge to disjunction of all examples. Then the way we define the notation of generalization determines the type of concepts that the learning system converges to. **In general if we use DNF concepts then we need to employ some heuristic evaluation function to make the system prefer 'good' generalizations.**

Another feature that affects the search process is whether we are required to process one example at a time or we are allowed to store all the examples and process them together. In the former case we say that the learning is incremental. While incremental learning is very much desired, often it is difficult to learn incrementally, especially while learning DNF concepts or decision trees.

Before we complete this section it may be remarked that the concept learning problem we have discussed here is very similar to the problem of learning discriminant functions in pattern recognition. The main difference is that here the attributes may not be numerical values and there may not be any algebraic structure on the sets where the attributes take values. Hence the traditional pattern recognition algorithms that assume real valued features, are not very useful for concept learning. Also since the subjective is knowledge acquisition for expert systems, we want the learnt concepts to be represented in a form easily comprehensible to humans. That is why we use logic expressions and decision trees rather than discriminant functions to represent the learnt knowledge.

II. Explanation Based Learning (EBL)

Learning is of 2 types—

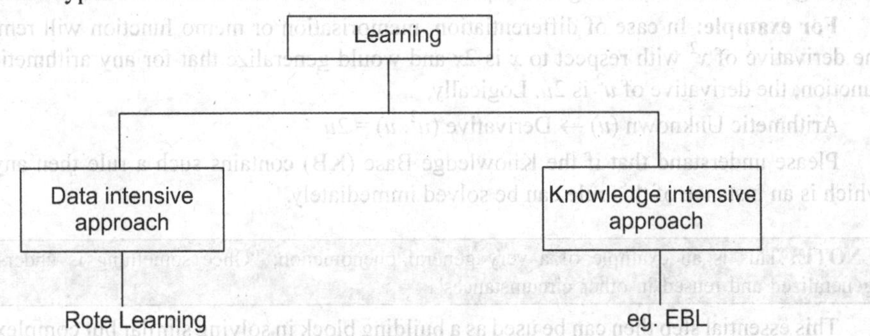

Fig. 7.2 EBL

In **data intensive** approach, the main focus is on given **data**. Large number of positive and negative examples are given to the machine and based on the outcomes of these examples, the machine learns. **For example:** Rote learning.

In **knowledge intensive** approach, the main focus is on **knowledge.** It is a kind of **analogical learning**. It is also called as **situation based learning.**

For example: EBL uses this approach.

In games like chess, medical diagnosis etc., knowledge plays a vital role. In these systems, a critical situation is handled and the machine is given the example to handle this situation This is

EBL. So, here one example in form of a knowledge solution or past experience is sufficient for learning a new solution. **In general, in EBL, the emphasis is given to learn more by taking the critical examples rather than by having more examples.** In EBL, one positive training example is given to machine in order to perform the learning. **Please note that in EBL, the learned knowledge is valid knowledge.** It is obtained by performing a **deductive reasoning process** on a set of facts. In EBL, while problem solving, its salient features are abstracted. These features are as follows—

(*a*) Formal statement about goal.

(*b*) Minimum one training example.

(*c*) Domain theory that relates to the concept and training example.

(*d*) Criteria for applying an operator.

This information is stored in the KB. When a new problem is to be solved using EBL, a matching is performed between the new problem and existing problem details. If partial matching occurs, that solution is taken from the KB and modified according to new problem. Thus, we can conclude that EBL program attempts to learn from a single example by explaining why it is an example of target concept. When program formalizes the explanation, it generalizes this explanation and stores for further use. The system learns this way and its performance improves.

EBL is a form of deductive learning where the learner develops a logical explanation of how the positive training example defines a concept. In EBL, first of all, the concept is formulated using training example and domain theory and then it is generalized by regression formulae.

EBL

An EBL system attempts to learn from a single example *x* by explaining why *x* is an example of the target concept (predicate) instead of learning through a large number of examples. The explanation is then generalized and the system's performance is improved through the availability of background knowledge. The process is known as **memorisation** (or memo function). **It is defined as the phenomenon to accumulate a database of input/output pairs in which when a function is called, it first checks the database to see whether it can avoid solving the problem.** EBL further creates general rules depending on the problem to be solved which cover an entire class of cases.

For example: In case of differentiation, memorisation or memo function will remember that the derivative of x^2 with respect to x is $2x$ and would generalize that for any arithmetic unknown function; the derivative of u^2 is $2u$. Logically,

Arithmetic Unknown (u) $\rightarrow$ Derivative (u^2, u) = $2u$

Please understand that if the Knowledge Base (KB) contains such a rule then any new case which is an instance of this rule can be solved immediately.

NOTE: This is an example of a very general phenomenon: "Once something is understood, it is generalized and reused in other circumstances".

This essential step then can be used as a building block in solving similar but complex problems.

EBL Algorithm

EBL follows the following algorithm:

Step 1: Given an example (say of fork or of differentiation), construct a proof such that the goal predicate applies to the example using the available background knowledge.

Step 2: In parallel, construct a generalized proof tree for the variablised goal using the same inference steps as in the original proof.

Step 3: Construct a new rule whose left side consists of the leaves of the proof tree and whose right hand side is the variablised goal.

Step 4: Drop any condition(s) which are true regardless of the values of the variables in the goal.

Efficiency

EBL basically works in two steps: **explain** and **generalize.** Sometimes a rule can be generalized in a number of ways, which reflects the efficiency of the algorithm. Three factors contribute to its efficiency:

1. Adding large number of rules can slow down the reasoning process because the inference mechanism must still check those rules even in cases where they do not yield a solution. **Please note that it increases the branching factor in the search space.**
2. To compensate for the slowdown in reasoning process, the derived rules must offer significant increase in speed for the cases which they cover. This increase arises mainly because the derived rules avoid dead ends which would otherwise be taken.
3. Derived rules should be as general as possible so that they apply to the largest possible set of cases.

A common approach to ensure that derived rules are efficient is to insist on the **operationality of each subgoal** in the rule. **Also note that a subgoal is operational if it is easy to solve.** Unfortunately, there is unusually a trade–off between operationality and generality. **More specific subgoals are easier to solve but cover fewer cases only.** Also operationality is a matter of degree, one or 2 steps is definitely operational but may not hold good for 10 or 100 steps. Finally, the cost of solving a given subgoal depends on what other rules are available in the knowledge base. It can expand (up or down) as more and more rules are added. So, EBL systems face a really complex optimization problem in trying to maximize the efficiency of the given initial KB. It is also possible to derive a mathematical model of the effect on overall efficiency of adding a given rule and to use this model to select the best rule to add.

Please understand that when the recursive rules are involved, the analysis can become very complicated. One approach that is promising can be to address the problem of efficiency empirically, simply by adding several rules and then identifying which are useful and actually would speed up the process.

Conclusions

By generalizing from the past examples, EBL makes the KB more efficient for the kind of problems to which it can be applied. Hence, if this EBL system is carefully designed then it is possible to obtain better speed-ups.

NOTE: In 1991, Samuelson and Rayner showed that a reasonably large PROLOG-based natural language system designed for speech-to-speech translation between Swedish and English was able to achieve real-time performance only by the application of EBL to the parsing processes.

Advantages

1. EBL allows learning from a single training instance.
2. EBL forms generalizations that are relevant to specific goals.
3. Learner can select relevant aspects of training examples.

III. Symbol Based Learning (SBL)

SBL involves 3 tasks mainly—

1. **Specification of goal** and data.
2. **Representation of learned knowledge.** In learning problems, the concepts are represented as conjunctive sentences containing variables.
3. **Set of operations.** Once the training session is over, the learner should generate a heuristic rule or plan objecting its goal. This requires the ability to manipulate representations. The operations, here, include—

- Generalizing symbolic expressions.
- Specializing symbolic expressions.
- Adjusting weights in Neural Network (NN)
- Or Modifying the program's representation.

We create **generalizations** by replacing the constants with variables and **specializations** by replacing variables with constants.

IV. RBL/Deductive Learning

An American agent comes to India as a visitor. He/she firstly meets an Indian named Rajiv. On hearing his speech in Hindi, he concludes that all Indians speak Hindi. Note that this agent doesn't conclude that all Indian men are called as Rajiv. Hence, we can generalize this observation—

All Indians speak Hindi: Herein, the visitor-agent has some background knowledge like people in a given country, usually, speak the same language. In First-Order logic, this can be represented as–

Nationality $(x, n) \wedge$ Nationality $(y, n) \wedge$ Language $(x, l) \rightarrow$ language (y, L) ...(1)

i.e., if 'x', and 'y' have the same nationality 'n' and 'x' speaks language l, then y also speaks 'l'. But the observation, Nationality (Rajiv, Indian) $\wedge$ Language (Rajiv, Hindi) along with the given knowledge shown in sentence 1, the following implication holds:

Nationality $(x, \text{Indian}) \rightarrow$ Language (x, Hindi)

Please understand that the sentences (as in equation (1)) **express a strict form of relevance that nationality of a person determines his/her language** or we can say that the language is a function of nationality. These sentences are called as **functional dependencies** (or FDs): In a syntax (given by Davis in 1985), it can be rewritten as—

Nationality $(x, n) >$— Language (x, l) ...(2)

NOTE: In English, it means that nationality determines language

Equation (2) shows that the FD (or determination) is really a relationship between the **predicates—Nationality** and **Language.**

From equations (1) and (2) it is crystal clear that it becomes rudimentary that the prior, background knowledge concerns the relevance of a set of features to the goal predicate. This knowledge together with the observations, allows the agent to infer a new general rule, based on observations:

Hypothesis $\wedge$ Description $\in$ Classifications

Background $\wedge$ Descriptions $\wedge$ Classification $\in$ Hypothesis ...(3)

Please note that this type of generalization is called Relevance-based Learning (RBL). Also note that although RBL does make use of the content of the observation in creating hypothesis yet it does not generate hypotheses which go beyond the logical content of the background knowledge and the observations. This is a **deductive form of learning.** Because it cannot by itself amount for the creation of the new knowledge from a scratch, so it is also called as **relevance-based** or **deductive learning.**

FDs or determinations are very vital as they specify a sufficient basic vocabulary from which hypotheses concerning the goal predicate can be constructed. This can be proved by showing that a given FD is logically equivalent to a statement that the correct definition of the goal predicate is one of the set of definitions expressible using the predicates on the left hand side of the FD. Hence, reduction in the hypothesis space size should make it easier to learn the goal predicate. The gains can be qualified using a simple analysis—

If $|H|$ is the size of hypothesis space then for Boolean functions log ($|H|$) examples are required to arrive at a reasonable hypothesis. For a learner having n Boolean features participating in the construction of hypothesis—

$|H| = O(\log 2^{2^n})$. This means that the examples required will be $O(2^n)$. **Also note that if the determination contains d predicates in the left hand side, the learner will require only $O(2^d)$ examples.** This shows a **reduction of** $O(2^{n-d})$ as compared to learning through classification of examples.

7.4 GENETICS ALGORITHM (GA)

There is a need for a tool or a technique which reduces human dependency and decision making should be done based on same algorithm or a mathematical formula. Genetic Algorithms (GA) are **intrinsically parallel.** Most other algorithms are **serial** and can only explore the solution space to a problem in one direction at a time. GA has **multiple offspring** i.e., they can explore solution space in multiple directions at once. If one path turns out to be a dead end, they can easily eliminate it. GAs perform well in problems for which the fitness landscape is complex—ones where the fitness function is discontinuous, noisy, changes over time or has many **local optima**. Many search algorithms can become trapped by local optima if they reach the top of a hill on the fitness landscape. However, crossover is the key element that distinguishes GAs from other methods such as hill-climbers and simulated annealing . **Please note that without crossover, each individual solution is on its own, exploring the search space in its immediate vicinity without reference to what other individuals may have discovered. Also note that with crossover in place, there is a transfer of information between successful candidates.** Individuals can benefit from what others have learned and schemata can be mixed and combined with the potential to produce an offspring that has the strengths of both its parents. GAs can manipulate many parameters simultaneously. GAs use parallelism and hence can produce multiple equally good solutions to the same problems possibly with one candidate solution optimizing one parameter and another candidate optimizing a different one. A human overseer can then select one of these candidates to use.

Do you know? GAs know nothing about the problems they are deployed to solve. GAs make random changes to their candidate solutions and then use the fitness function to determine whether those changes produce an improvement.

7.5 NEURAL NETS

Neural computing is the study of networks of adaptable nodes which, through a process of learning from task examples, store experimental knowledge and make it available for use. The configurations and algorithms in neural computing are biologically inspired structures that perform useful tasks. **Please understand that the human nervous system consists of about 10^{11} neurons and 10^{15} interconnection. Also note that these numbers cannot be matched by an artificial NN, the tasks that can be performed by ANN are also severely limited.**

Fig. 7.3 shows the structure of a pair of biological neurons. **Dendrites extend from the cell body to other neurons where they receive signals at a connection point called a synapse.** On the receiving side of the synapse, these inputs are conducted to the cell body where they are summed, some inputs tending to excite the cell, others tending to inhibit its firing. When the cumulative excitation in the cell body exceeds a threshold, the cell fires, sending a signal down the axon to other neurons.

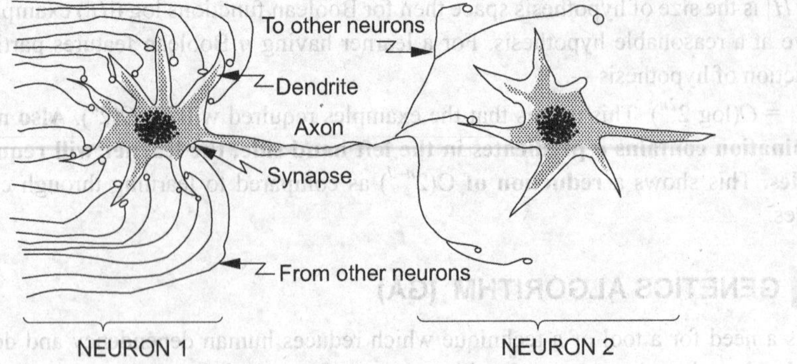

Fig. 7.3 Structure of a pair of biological neurons.

Basic computing unit

We consider a simple adaptable node (Fig. 7.4) which we will use to explain the features of ANN.

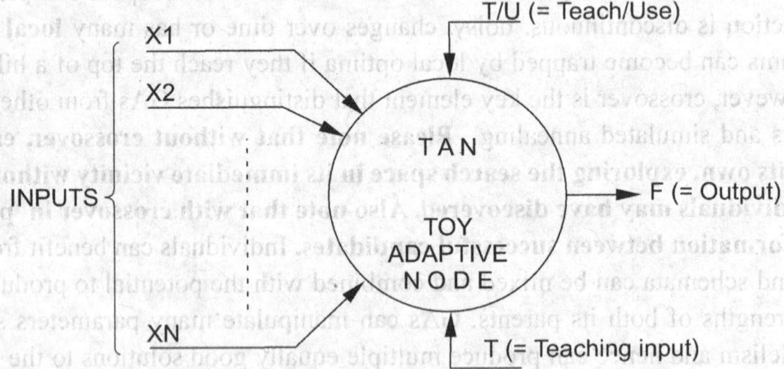

Fig. 7.4 A Toy Adaptive Node (TAN)

Network Structures

Fig. 7.5 shows some network structures using the basic computing elements (TANs). We use these structures to introduce some key ideas of NN, namely, associative nets, hidden layers, hard learning visible and hidden units. We also use them to explain the main features of NN, namely, distributed and located information, association and recall of information, and storing of knowledge.

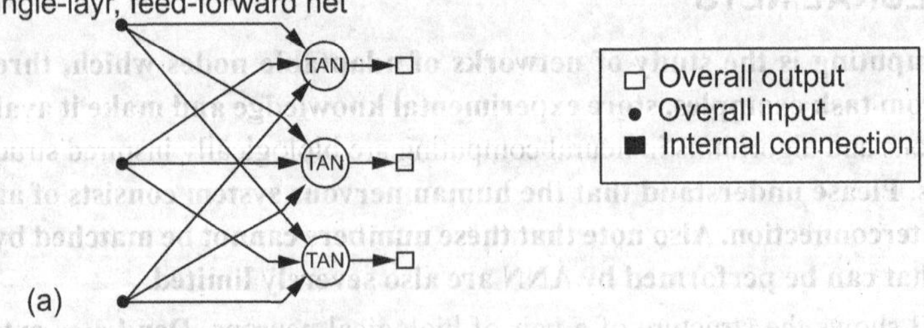

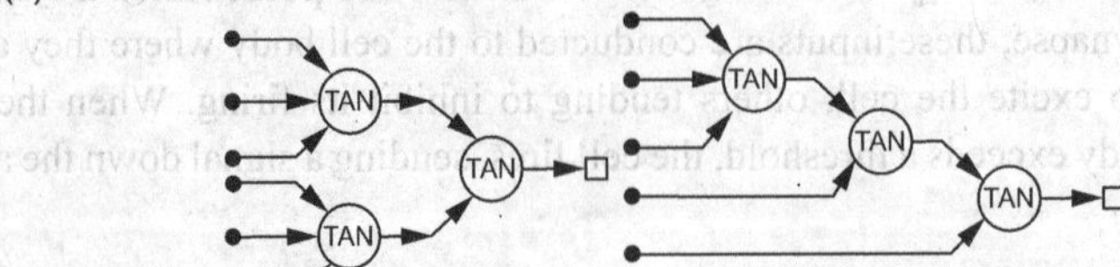

(iii) Feedback nets

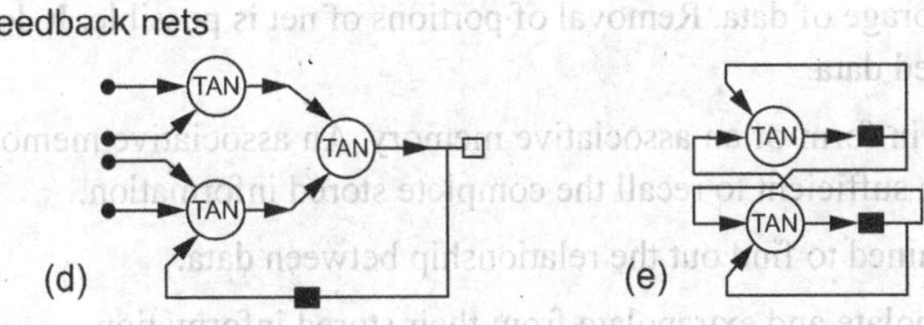

Fig. 7.5 Some network structures using the basic computing elements (TANs).

Neural net is a widely used technique for learning by charging the weights assigned to the nodes or arcs of a network. However, their name is a misnomer since they bear little resemblance to actual neural mechanisms. Fig. 7.6 shows a typical neural net—.

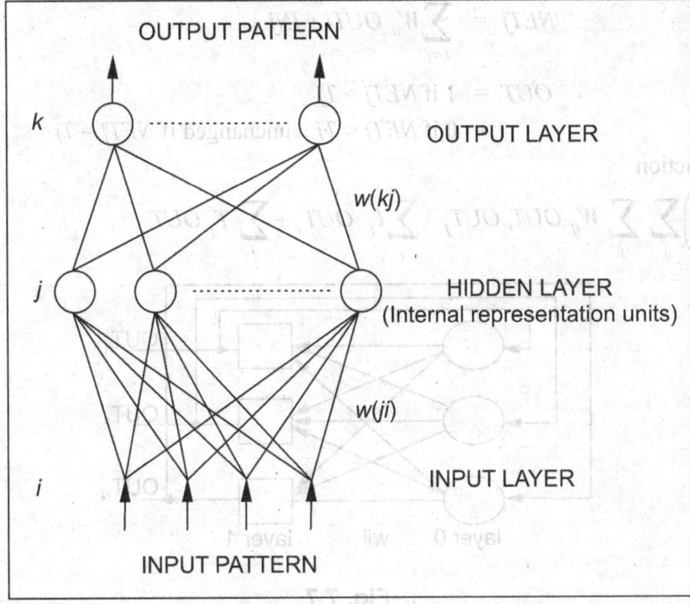

Fig. 7.6 Typical neural net.

Its input is a sequence of number that indicates the relative proposition of some selected features and whose output is another sequence of number that indicates the most likely concept characterized by that combination of features.

For example: in case of OCR-output character Recognizer, the **features** might represent lines, curves and angles and the concept might represent the letters that have those features.

> **Do you know?** In a NN, the structure of nodes and arcs is fixed and the only changes that may occur are the assignment of weights to the arcs.

When a new input is presented, the weights on the arcs are combined with the weights on the outputs. In learning stage, the system is told whether the predicted weights are correct and various methods of back propagation are used to adjust the weight on the arcs that leads to the result.

Neural networks support digital computers with the ability to make sensible decision to learn by experience.

Main features of ANNs are as follows:

1. Distributed Storage of data. Removal of portions of net is possible. It does not degrade the quality of stored data.
2. Data is stored in form of an associative memory. An associative memory is one in which partial data are sufficient to recall the complete stored information.
3. Nets can be trained to find out the relationship between data.
4. Nets can interpolate and extrapolate from their stored information.
5. Quality of stored images degrades as some portion of net is removed.

APPLICATION OF NN

Travelling Salesman Problem

Hopfield Net

$$NETj = \sum_{i=j} W_{ij}\ OUTi + INj$$

$$OUT = 1 \text{ if } NETj > Tj$$

$$= 0 \text{ if } NETj < Tj \quad \text{unchanged if } NETj = Tj$$

Energy function

$$E = \left(-\frac{1}{2}\right)\sum_i \sum_j W_{ij}\ OUT_i\ OUT_j - \sum_j l_j\ OUT_j + \sum_j T_j\ OUT_j$$

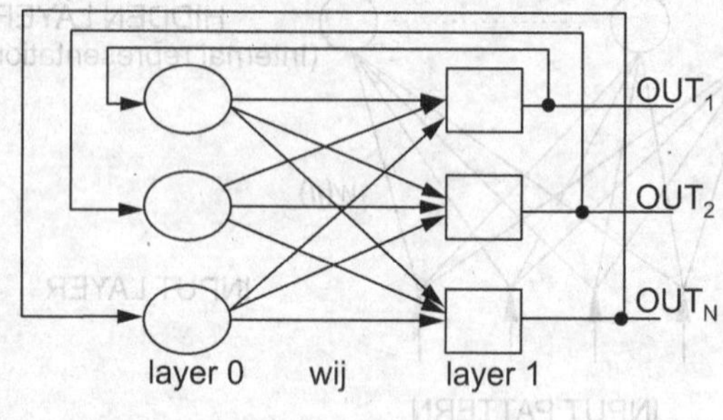

Fig. 7.7

Travelling Salesman Problem:

	Order visited			
City	1	2	3	4
A	0	1	0	0
B	0	0	0	1
C	1	0	0	0
D	0	0	1	0

E_1 –Energy fucntion must be low for only those solutions for which there is a single 1 in each column and row.

E_2 –Energy function must favour solutions having short distances.

$$E_1 = \frac{A}{2}\sum_x \sum_i \sum_{j\neq i} OUT_{xj} + \frac{B}{2}\sum_x \sum_i \sum_{y\neq x} OUT_{xi} + \frac{C}{2}\left[\left(\sum_x \sum_i OUT_{xi}\right) - r\right]$$

$$E_2 = \left(\frac{1}{2}\right) D \sum_x \sum_{y\neq x} \sum_i d_{xy}\ OUT_{xi}\left(OUT_{yi+1} + OUT_{yi-1}\right)$$

Weights:

$$W_{xi,yi} = A\,\delta_{xy}(1-\delta_{ij}) \quad \text{(Prevents more than a single 1 within a row)}$$

$$= B\delta_{ij}(1-\delta xy) \quad \text{(Prevents more than a single 1 within a column)}$$

$$= -C \quad \text{(Global inhibition)}$$

$$= D\,d_{xy}(\delta_{ji} + i + \delta_{ji-1}) \quad \text{(Distance term)}$$

Bias weight for each neuron *Cn*.

Activation function:

$$OUT = \left(\frac{1}{2}\right)\left[1+\tanh\left(\frac{NET}{U_0}\right)\right]$$

Perception

McCulloch-Pitts Model of Artificial Neuron

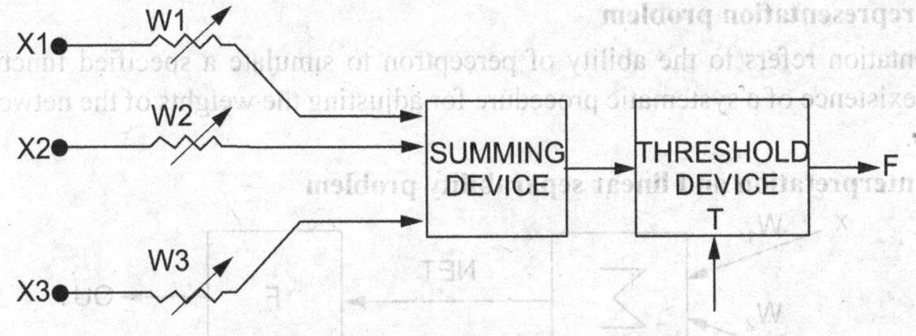

Fig. 7.8 M-P model of neuron.

Perceptron

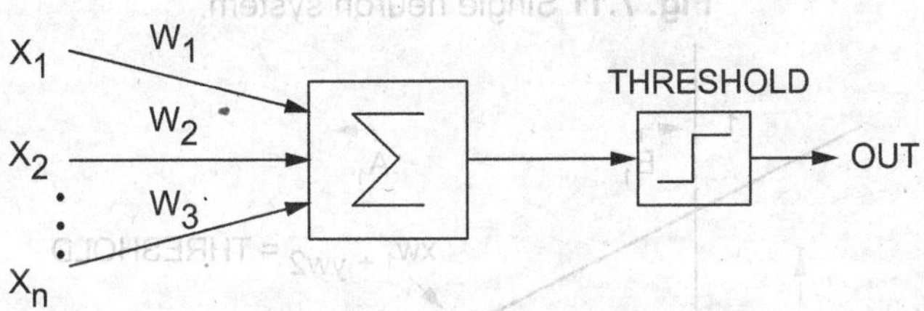

Fig. 7.9 Perceptron-M-P node with some additional, fixed preprocessing

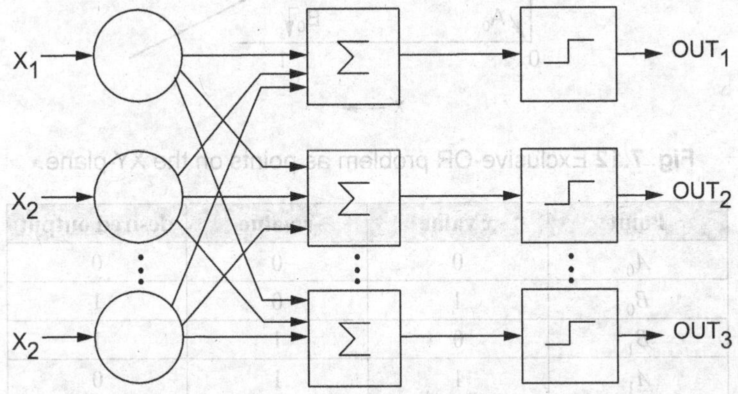

Fig. 7.10 Multioutput perceptron.

Perceptron classification problem

Given *k* vectors *vi, i = 1,...k*, each of dimension n, suppose they are partitioned into two subsets I and I_1. The perceptron classification problem is:

Build a network consisting of threshold switching elements such that output is 1 for all input vectors in l+ and 0 for all input vectors in l.

Perceptron learning (training) problem

The **perceptron learning (training) problem** is:

Change the weights and thresholds of the various neurons adaptively until classification occurs.

Hebb's rule: Change in weight connecting unit i to unit j is proportional to the product of the output of unit j and the activation value of unit i.

Delta rule: Change in weight connecting unit j to unit i is proportional to the product of the output of unit j and the difference between the desired and actual outputs of unit i.

Perceptron representation problem

Representation refers to the ability of perceptron to simulate a specified function. Learning refers to the existence of a systematic procedure for adjusting the weights of the network to produce that function.

Geometric interpretation and linear separability problem

Fig. 7.11 Single neuron system.

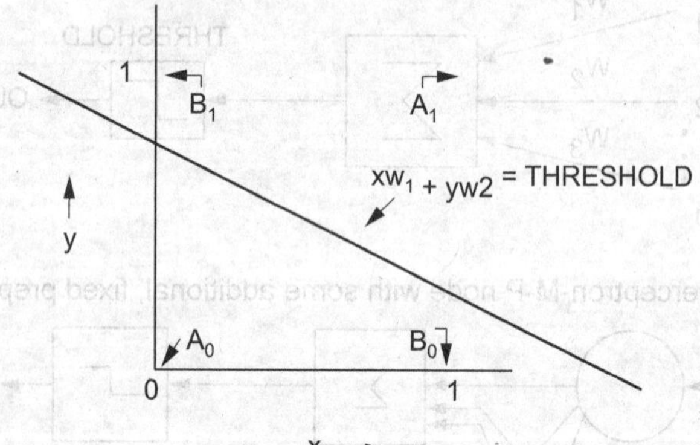

Fig. 7.12 Exclusive-OR problem as points on the XY-plane.

Point	*x* value	*y* value	desired output
A_0	0	0	0
B_0	1	0	1
B_1	0	1	1
A_1	1	1	0

Fig. 7.13 Exclusive-OR truth table.

SUMMARY

Learning is an incessant process. An intelligent machine should be able to learn new things. There are various ways of learning means change in the system or its KB brought about its interaction with a teacher or external environment so that the system improves its performance on a class of tasks.

MULTIPLE CHOICE QUESTIONS [MCQS]

1. Saving knowledge so that it can be used again is known as

(*a*) Rote learning (*b*) Induction (*c*) Deduction (*d*) None of the above.

2. Rote learning is based on the principle of

(*a*) Caching (b) Forwarding (*c*) Backtracking (*d*) None of the above.

3. EBL uses

(*a*) Data intensive approach (*b*) Knowledge intensive approach

(*c*) Divide and conquer (*d*) None of the above.

4. Human nervous system consists of

(*a*) 10^{10} neurons (*b*) 10^{11} neurons (*c*) 10^{12} neurons (*d*) 10^{14} neurons

5. The rule used to change weight is

(*a*) Kirchoff's rule (*b*) Hebb's rule (*c*) Boehm's rule (*d*) None of the above.

ANSWERS

1. (*a*) **2.** (*a*) **3.** (*b*) **4.** (*b*) **5.** (*b*)

CONCEPTUAL SHORT QUESTIONS WITH ANSWERS

Q. 1. What are identification trees?

Ans. It is a learning method that uses tree representation of any problem indicating all possibilities. It is a sort of decision tree only. For example, for medical diagnoses, surveys etc it is used.

Q. 2. Draw the block diagram of a general learning system.

[RTM Nagpur Univ. B.Tech IT-7th Sem., 2009]

Ans. Figure below shows the block diagram of a general learning system.

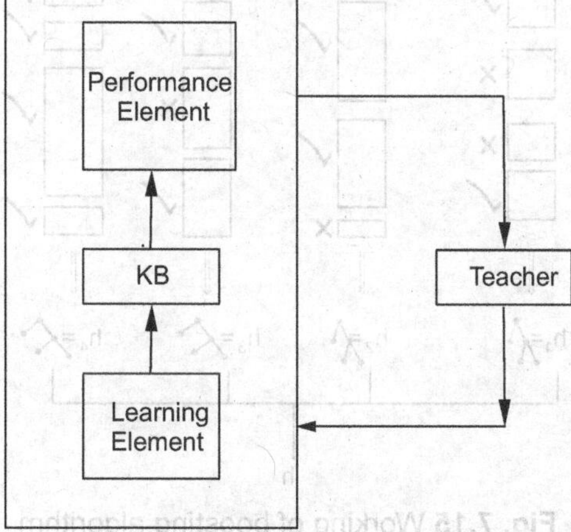

Fig. 7.14

There is some class of tasks that the system is expected to learn. The teacher watches the performance on some problem from this class and provides the system with an evaluation. Using this, the learning element modifies the current KB. Through this process of interaction, the system acquires the needed knowledge to improve its performance. **Please note that the performance element must be capable of solving the class of problems.**

Q. 3. What is learning by discovery?

Ans. A form of learning from examples where the teacher does not supply the answers. The learning system has to look for inherent regularities in the mass of data for inferring general rules.

For example: Discovery of Kepler's law. Kepler analysed the mass of data on planetary motion and came out with some 'beautiful' laws which generalise all the examples.

Q. 4. What is learning through clustering?

Ans. Clustering is the process of grouping or classifying objects on the basis of a close association or shared characteristics. It is essentially a discovery learning process in which similarities patterns are found among a group of objects.

Q. 5. What is matching?

Ans. The process of comparing two structures or patterns for equality is known as matching. It may serve to control the sequence of operations, to identify or classify objects or to retrieve items from a database.

Q. 6. Discuss Boosting Algorithm of Ensemble Learning.

Ans. The most widely used ensemble method is called **boosting.** It works on the concept of a **weighted training set.** In such a training set, each example has an associated weight, $w_i \geq 0$. **Please note that the higher is the weight of an example, the higher is the importance attached to it during the learning of a hypothesis.**

Working Boosting starts with $w_j = 1$ for all examples, i.e., training set. From this the first hypothesis, h_f, is generated. This hypothesis will classify some of the training examples correctly and some incorrectly. In order for the next hypothesis to perform better on the misclassified example, the weights of the misclassified ones are increased. From this new weighted training set, the hypothesis, h_2, is generated.

The process is continued until M hypothesis have been generated where M is the input of the boosting algorithm. **The final ensemble hypothesis** is a weighted–majority combination of M hypothesis, each weighted according to how it will perform on the training set. The process is shown below (Fig. 7.15).

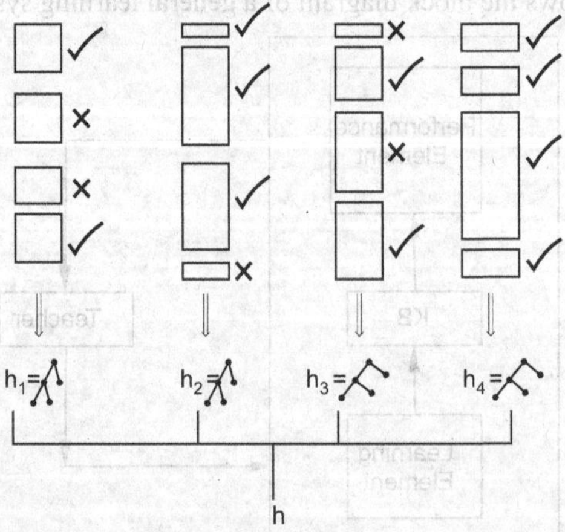

Fig. 7.15 Working of boosting algorithm.

Conventions

1. Each **rectangle** in the figure corresponds to an example.
2. The **height** of the rectangle corresponds to the **weight.**
3. The **ticks** and **crosses** indicate whether the example is classified correctly by the current hypothesis in the final ensemble.

It has been observed that the predictions improve as the ensemble hypothesis gets more complex.

Next, we review the premise with which we started, i.e., the example pair $(x, f(x))$, i.e., how do we know that the hypothesis, h, is close to the target function $f(x)$ if we do not know f. The answer to this is based on **Computational Learning Theory,** a field that includes AI, statistics and theoretical computer science.

Principle: "Any hypothesis which is seriously wrong will almost certainly be found out with high probability after a small number of examples because it will make on incorrect prediction".

Please understand that any hypothesis which is consistent with a sufficiently large set of training examples is unlikely to be seriously wrong, i.e., it must be probably approximately correct (PAC). **Any learning algorithm which returns hypotheses which are probably approximately correct is called as a PAC–learning algorithm. Also understand that this leads to one important criterion on the connection between the training and the test examples, the hypothesis is to be approximately correct on the test set, not on just training set. The basic assumption** is that the training and test sets are drawn randomly and independently from the same population of examples with the same probability distribution. **This is known as a stationary assumption.** This assumption is important **because without this assumption the ensemble learning cannot predict at all.**

EXERCISE QUESTIONS

Q. 1. (*a*) Explain artificial neurons. Use necessary diagram.

(*b*) Calculate the logic function 'AND' or "OR" using McCulloch-Pitts neurons.

(*c*) Explain the Perceptron Training algorithm.

[UPSAT, B. Tech., (CSE)-8th Sem., Oct. 2004]

Q. 2. What is learning? Explain Rote Learning and Induction Learning.

[RTM Nagpur Univ., BE (CSE)- 7th Sem., Summer 2009]

Q. 3. (*a*) What is declarative knowledge?

(*b*) What is baring by induction? **[PTU., M.C.A., 4th Sem., 2009]**

Q. 4. Design a learning automation that selects TV channels based on day of week and time of day (3 evening hours only) based on preference of your family. (Specify the preferences of your family clearly). **[GGSIPU., B.Tech. (CSE)- 8th Sem., May 2008]**

Q. 5. What are different types of learning.

[GGSIPU., B.Tech. (CSE)- 8th Sem., May-June 2009]

Q. 6. (*a*) Give a short description of process of learning using Back Propagation NN.

(*b*) Give a flow graph for developing a genetic algorithm.

[GGSIPU., B.Tech. (CSE)- 8th Sem., May 2010]

Q. 7. (*a*) Describe an Automation. Extend it to learning automation.

(*b*) Pick one problem area that you feel would justify the energy required to design an expert system solution and spell out the problem in some detail. Based on your intuition, which aspects of this solution would be most difficult to automate?

Q. 8. (*a*) What are the different types of learning? Explain with an example.

(*b*) Why is the process of knowledge acquisition so tedious?

[GGSIPU., B.Tech. (CSE)- 8th Sem., May 2011]

CHAPTER

EXPERT SYSTEMS

8.0 INTRODUCTION

Expert Systems are computer programs which store the factual and inferential knowledge of human experts in a narrow domain. They can assist and advise users, provide explanations, inform the user at any point of the solution which hypothesis they are pursuing, why they have chosen a particular strategy and what conclusion they have drawn so far. An expert system is an AI program which uses knowledge to solve problems which would normally require a human expert. It attempts to reproduce the performance of one or more human experts. Let us compare a human expert and an artificial Expert System in a tabular form—

Human Expert	Artificial Expert Systems
1. Humans are naturally perishable.	1. They are permanent.
2. They are expensive.	2. They are costly to develop but cheaper to operate.
3. They are inconsistent.	3. They are consistent.
4. They are difficult to transfer.	4. They are easy to transfer.
5. They are difficult to document.	5. They are easy to document.
6. They are adaptive.	6. They need to be told.
7. They are creative.	7. They are uninspired.
8. They possess sensory experience.	8. They need symbolic input.
9. They have broad focus.	9. They have narrow focus.
10. They can deal with common sense knowledge.	10. They need technical knowledge.

In AI literature, many definitions of expert systems have been given. Let us give some of them now:

1. **Any problem that can be solved by your in-house expert in a 10-30 minute telephone call can be developed as an expert system** (By M. Firebaugh).
2. **Expert system or a KBS includes a sizable KB consisting of facts about the domain and heuristics for applying these facts.**
3. **Expert systems use knowledge rather than data to control the solution process.**
4. **An Expert System is a program that emulates the interaction a user might have with a human expert to solve a problem.**
5. **An expert system is designed to act as an expert in a particular domain.**

But please understand here that an expert system is different from a software system. Let us see how:

Expert System	Software Systems
1. They use knowledge base.	1. They use database.
2. Lesser data is kept together.	2. Large data is kept separately.
3. They use reasoning mechanism and heuristics.	3. They use algorithms.
4. They use inference engine.	4. They use compilers.
5. They are developed by knowledge engineers.	5. They are developed by software engineers.
For example: DENDRAL, MYCIN, LITHO, TIMM, XCON, CLIPS etc.	**For example:** C/C++, JAVA 2 etc.

But we should understand the first point of the above table of difference that knowledge base is different from a database. So, we tabulate the differences in a tabular form now.

Knowledge Base	Data Base
1. It stores information at a higher level of obstraction.	1. They are a collection of data representing facts.
2. It operates on a class of objects.	2. It operates on a single object.
3. They use power of inferencing.	3. Information needs to be explicitly stated.
4. Representation is by logic or rules or frames or scripts or nets.	4. Represented by relational, hierarchical or network model.
5. It is used for data analysis and planning.	5. It is maintained for operational purpose only.

8.1 CHARACTERISTICS OF ES

The main characteristics of ES are as follows—

1. They reduce the cost of accessing information as it allows dissemination of information held by one or small group of experts to less expensive people.
2. Knowledge in an ES can be formalized, tested and validated.
3. They allow integration from different sources.
4. They use symbolic knowledge representations.
5. The response time of an ES should be adequate.
6. Increase the probability, frequency and consistency of making good decision.
7. Help distribute human expertise.
8. Permit dynamism through modularity of structure.

A program talking about 'medicine' will be a KBS whereas a system having knowledge about medicine which is able to perform medical treatment will be an expert system.

8.2 NEED OF AN ES AND ITS JUSTIFICATION

As explained earlier also, a human expert is perishable but artificial expert system is not. It is permanent. If there is one expert then the problem cannot be solved if that expert is not experienced.

So, we take group of experts as then the solution is more efficient. One expert system can be used at different places at the same time. ES are tools of mass production. Emotions also have no effect on expert systems. In nutshell, an ES is like a tutor for someone who is interested in learning. ES have variety of applications—medicine, engineering, geology, I.T., basic and applied research, training, sales and marketing.

8.3 ES ARCHITECTURE

Both factual and heuristic knowledge is required for complex decision. Knowledge engineers design various components which work together to perform different functions. Fig. 8.1 shows the architecture of an ES.

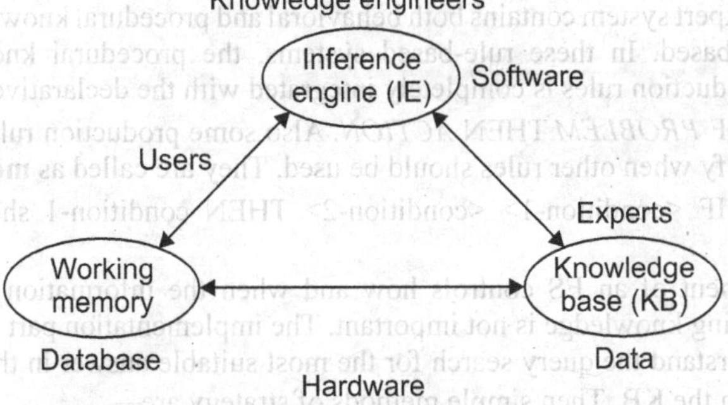

Fig. 8.1 ES architecture.

Knowledge Base (KB): It consists of problem solving rules, procedures and intrinsic data relevant to the problem domain.

Working memory: It refers to task-specific data for the problem under consideration.

Inference Engine (IE): It is a generic control mechanism that applies the axiomatic knowledge in the KB to the task-specific data to arrive at some solution or conclusion.

Do you know? IE such as VP-Expert may come from a commercial vendor.

The KB may be a specific diagnostic KB compiled by a consulting firm and the problem data may be supplied by the end user. **Please note that the KB is the central nucleus of the ES. Also note that a KB is different from a database as a traditional database environment deals with data that have a static relationship between the elements in the problem domain whereas a KB is created by knowledge engineers who translate the knowledge of real human experts into rules and strategies**. These rules can change depending on the existing problem scenario. KB provides the ES with the capability to recommend directions for user inquiry. These three components—KB, IE and working memory—make an ES, a modular design. The **KB constitutes** the problem solving rules, facts etc that a human expert might use in problem solving. The KB is usually stored in terms of if-then rules. The **working memory** represents relevant data for the current problem being solved. The IE is the control mechanism that organizes the problem data and searches through the KB for applicable rules. **A good expert system is expected to grow** as it learns from user feedback. Feedback is fed into the KB to make ES smarter. The three individual components of an ES are dynamic at various levels—

(*a*) Working Memory (Most dynamic)

The contents of the working memory (or data structure) changes with each problem. So, it is the most dynamic component of an expert system, assuming that it is kept current.

(*b*) **Knowledge Base (Moderately dynamic)**

A KB changes only if some new information arises that indicates a change in the problem solution procedure. Changes in KB should be carefully evaluated before being implemented. **Please note that the changes should not be based on just one consultation experience. Also note that a rule that is found to be irrelevant under one problem situation may turn out to be crucial in solving other problems.**

(*c*) **Inference Engine (Least dynamic)**

A change is made to the inference engine only if they are required to make inferential engines are changed only if the developer wishes so. **Please understand here that because frequent updates are costlier and disruptive to clients so most commercial software developers try to minimize frequent updations.**

The KB of an expert system contains both behavioral and procedural knowledge. The procedural knowledge is rule-based. In these rule-based systems, the procedural knowledge (in form of IF-THEN ELSE production rules is completely integrated with the declarative knowledge.

For example: IF *PROBLEM* THEN *ACTION*. Also some production rules provide guidelines for which they specify when other rules should be used. They are called as **meta-rules.**

For example: IF <condition-1> <condition-2> THEN condition-1 should be done before condition-2 is done.

The IE component of an ES controls how and when the information in the knowledge is applied. Merely having knowledge is not important. The implementation part of knowledge is most important, i.e., understand the query search for the most suitable answer in the KB and then apply the information from the KB. Then simple methods of strategy are—

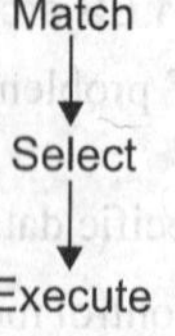

Fig. 8.2

In the process of matching, when the left side of a sequence of rules is initialized first and the rules are executed from left to right, the process is called as **forward chaining**. **When the right side of rules is instantiated first, the left-hand condition becomes subgoals.** The subgoals may in turn cause sub-subgoals to be established and so on until facts are found to match the lowest subgoals conditions.

The User Interface (UI) component enables us to communicate with an expert system. **The communication performed is bi-directional.** This is shown in Fig. 8.3.

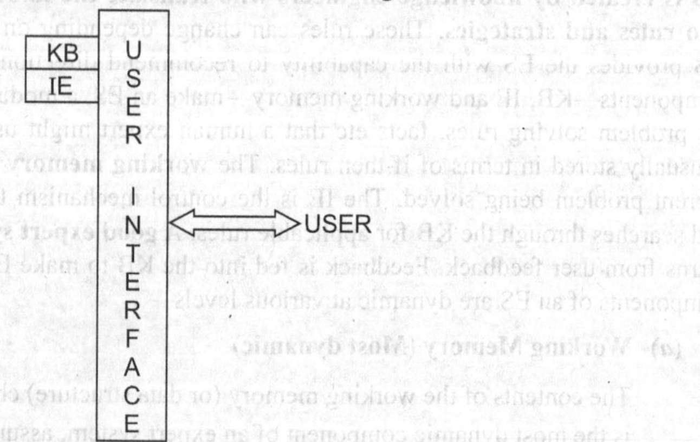

Fig. 8.3 ES components.

As the users are not as experienced as the experts, so the expert systems should be so developed that it has an easy access for the user.

8.4 STEPS TO DEVELOP AN ES

A **knowledge engineer** or an **AI specialist** or a programmer is skilled in the art of developing Expert Systems (ES).

A domain expert is an individual who has significant expertise in the domain of the ES being developed. **Please understand that it is not critical that the domain expert understand AI or expert systems that is one of the functions of the knowledge engineer. Also note that the knowledge engineer and the domain expert usually work close to each other throughout the development process.** An expert system (ES) is developed and refined over a period of several years. ES development has five stages—

*S*1: Determining the characteristics of the problem **(Identification).**

*S*2: Finding the concept to produce the solution **(Conceptualization).**

*S*3: Designing structures to organize the knowledge **(Formalization).**

*S*4: Formulating rules which embody the knowledge **(Implementation)**

*S*5: Validating the rules **(Testing).**

Development of an ES involves five steps—

Step 1: Identification.

Determining the characteristic of the problem.

Step 2: Conceptualization.

Here, the iterative process between the knowledge engineer and the domain expert continues. Diagrams are often used to clarify the problem. During this process of conceptualization it is sometimes necessary to revise the description that is generated in the stage of identification. The basic aim is to develop a clear concept of the problem.

First step of identification is shown in a flowchart form also—

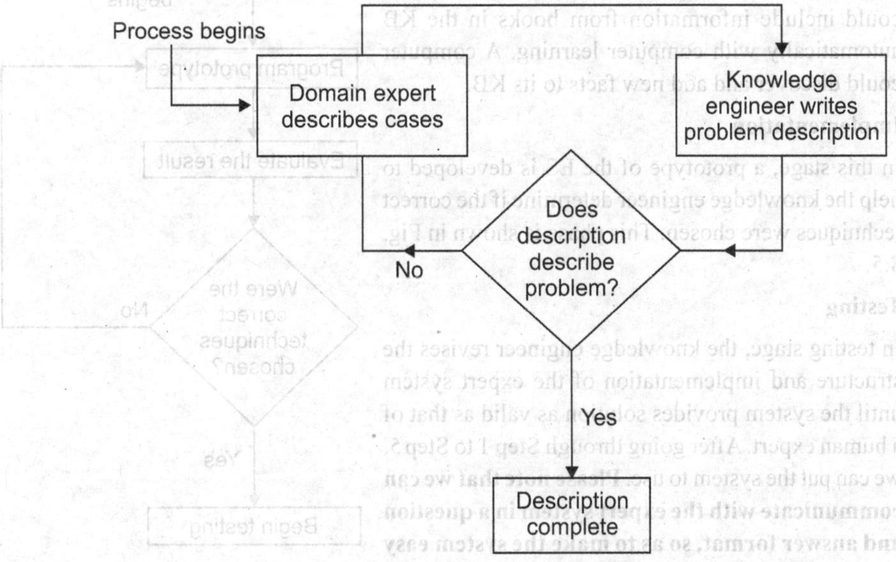

Fig. 8.3 Iterative process of identifying the problem–ES is to solve.

Next is the conceptualization phase. The iterative relationship between the identification and conceptualisations stages of ES development is shown next:

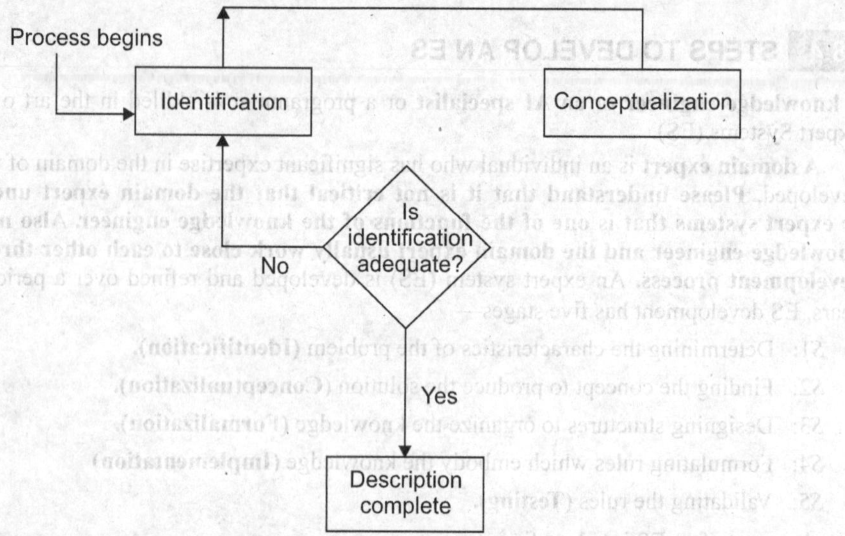

Fig. 8.4 Iterative relationship between identification and conceptualization stages.

Step 3: Formalization

In this step, the knowledge engineers select the development techniques to be used for the expert systems. If a rule-based system is developed, the knowledge engineer develops a set of rules for the domain expert to review until everyone agrees on them. To facilitate the formalization state, the AI researchers are looking for ways to reduce the amounting time required to enter the information in the KB. The goal of the simpler development tools is to enable the domain expert to create the KB. With automatic knowledge acquisition, the computer could include information from books in the KB automatically with computer learning. A computer could discover and add new facts to its KB.

Step 4: Implementation

In this stage, a prototype of the ES is developed to help the knowledge engineer determine if the correct techniques were chosen. This phase is shown in Fig. 8.5.

Step 5: Testing

In testing stage, the knowledge engineer revises the structure and implementation of the expert system until the system provides solution as valid as that of a human expert. After going through Step 1 to Step 5, we can put the system to use. **Please note that we can communicate with the expert system in a question and answer format, so as to make the system easy to use.**

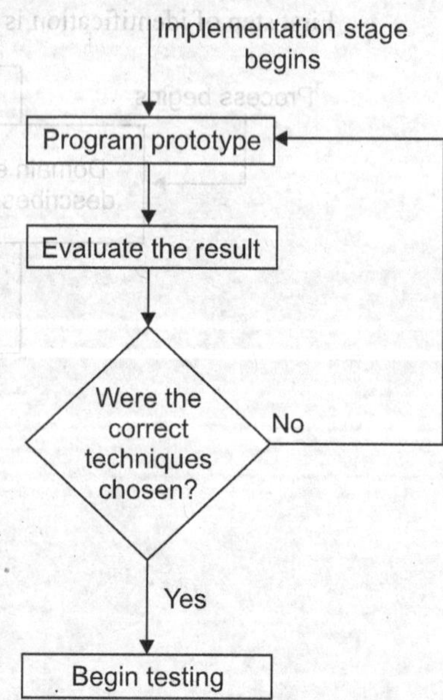

Fig. 8.5 Implementation stage.

The chances of prototype expert system executing flawless are very less initially. A **knowledge engineer** does not expect the testing process to verify that the system has been constructed entirely correctly. Testing provides an opportunity to identify the **weaknesses in the structure** and the **implementation of the system.** Testing includes—

(*a*) **System** was implemented correctly or incorrectly.

(*b*) **Rules** were implemented correctly or not.

Also understand that the results from the tests are used as feedback to return to the previous stage and adjust the performance of the system.

(*c*) System is tested for both **simple and complex problems** by the domain experts to uncover more of defects.

(*d*) An ES is finally tested to be successful only when it operates at the level of a human expert.

(*e*) The testing process is NOT complete until it indicates that the solutions suggested by the expert system are consistently valid (as valid as those provided by a human domain expert).

(*f*) The **ultimate test** of an expert system is how well it performs, not in a lab but in real-life situations. **Please understand that a completed system not only must demonstrate consistently that it can deliver the required expertise but it must also be easy to use, so that the embedded expertise can be extracted easily.** That is why, developers have gone to the extent that expert systems are among the easiest to use of all sophisticated programs.

(*g*) Expert systems are typically **interactive,** *i.e.*, they work in question and answer form. This interaction between users and ES continues until the system is able to reach a conclusion (displayed on to the screen).

8.5 CASE STUDIES: MYCIN, DENDRAL, RI AND OTHERS

Let us discuss some expert systems now.

MYCIN

MYCIN is an Expert System developed in 1970s at Stanford University. It was written in LISP language as the part of doctoral dissertation of Edward Shortliffe. Its job was to diagnose and recommend treatment for certain blood infections. It was developed to assist a physician who is not an expert in the field of antibiotics for the treatment of blood infections.

MYCIN'S KB is organized around a set of rules of the form mentioned below:

"IF condition-1 and ………condition-n are true then draw conclusion-1 and ………. conclusion n".

For example: IF

The infection is primary bacteremia.

AND the site of culture is one of the sterile sites

AND the suspected portal of entry is gastrointestinal tract

THEN

there is suggestive evidence (0.7) that infection is bacterial.

Here, the number 0.7 is called as the **Certainty Factor** (CF), which indicates how certain the conclusion is, if given conditions are satisfied.

The value of CF indicates the amount of truthness of conclusion. It states that— **"If condition-1 holds with certainty xl..........and condition-m holds with certainty-xm then draw conclusion-1 with certainty y1 and conclusion-n with certainty-yn. When we have multiple certainty factors, then their combined CF is the minimum of individual CFs AND CF (action) = CF (Premise) * CF (rule).**

How MYCIN works?

MYCIN adopts a high-level approach for the task of consultation , which is mentioned below—

If

there is a patient which requires therapy AND Consultation has been given to other organisms requiring therapy

Then

Compile a list of possible therapies and determine best one.

Herein, the symptoms of patient are matched with premise and if matching occurs, **the rule is fired.** To find out whether some rule is applicable or not, MYCIN first finds out, if there is indeed an organism present which is associated with significant disease. **Please understand that this information is obtained directly by user or via a chain of inferences. The consultation is search through a tree of goals.** The top goal is at the root of the tree and then it is divided into subgoals.

Do you know? MYCIN's control structure uses AND/OR tree.

During disease findings, sometimes multiple answers are found. To find the correct and actual output, the order in which facts and rules appears is checked. This corresponds to depth first search. MYCIN answers queries of type **"Why"** and **"how"**.

1. 'Why' questions can be asked at any time from the system. The system then responds with the action part of the rule. It displays 'how' question tells the reasoning process of how the answer was found.

Many other variants of MYCIN project are there like—

(*a*) EMYCIN: First expert shell developed from mycin'.

(*b*) PUFF: Developed using EMYCIN in the new domain of heart disorders.

(*c*) NEOMYCIN: Developed to train doctors which would take them through various example cases, checking their conclusions.

DENDRAL

The word "Dendral" is a pruned version of "Dendritic Algorithm". It was designed and developed at Stanford University in 1965. It is a collaborative work between Edward Feigenbaum, Bruce Buchanan, Joshua Lederberg and Carl Djerassi. **DENDRAL is an expert system developed for inferring process of structure elucidation of chemical compounds.** The **primary** aim was to aid organic chemists with the identification of unknown organic molecules by analyzing information from mass spectrometry graphs and the knowledge of chemistry. Dendral is not just a single program but rather a product of an interaction between two subprograms—**Heuristic-Dendral** and **Meta-Dendral,** i.e.,

DENDRAL = Heuristic-Dendral + Meta-Dendral

It is written in LISP language. Let us first of all understand these two subprograms.

Heuristic Dendral is a program that uses mass spectra or other experimental data together with knowledge base of chemistry, to produce a set of possible chemical structures that may be responsible for producing the data. A mass spectrum of a compound is produced by a mass spectrometer, and is used to determine its molecular weight, the sum of the masses of its atomic constituents. **For example**, the compound water (H_2O) has a molecular weight of 18 since hydrogen has a mass of 1.01 and oxygen 16.00, and its mass spectrum has a peak at 18 units. Heuristic Dendral would use this input mass and the knowledge of atomic mass numbers and valence rules, to determine the possible combinations of atomic constituents whose mass would add up to 18. As the weight increases and the molecules become more complex, the number of possible compounds increases drastically. Thus, a program that is able to reduce this number of candidate solutions through the process of hypothesis formation is essential.

Meta-dendral:

Meta-dendral is a knowledge acquisition system that receives the set of possible chemical structures and corresponding mass spectra as input, and proposes a set of hypotheses to explain correlation between some of the proposed structures and the mass spectrum. These hypotheses would be fed back to Heuristic dendral to test that applicability. Thus, "Heuristic dendral is a performance system and Meta-dendral is a learning system". The program is based on two important features: the plan-generate-test paradigm and knowledge engineering.

DENDRAL uses the control process of generate and test procedure (like state space search), starting with arbitrary initial state and by employing a generator, all possibilities regarding presence of compounds is generated. On these possibilities a series of tests are carried out to eliminate unwanted states.

The plan-generate-test paradigm is the basic organization of the problem-solving method, and is a common paradigm used by both **Heuristic Dendral** and **Meta-Dendral** systems. The **generator** generates potential solutions for a particular problem, which are then expressed as chemical graphs in Dendral. However, this is feasible only when the number of candidate solutions is **minimal**. When there are large numbers of possible solutions, Dendral has to find a way to put constraints that rules out large sets of candidate solutions. This is the primary aim of Dendral **planner**, which is a "hypothesis-formation" program that employs "task-specific knowledge to find constraints for the generator". Last but not least, the **tester analyzes each proposed candidate solution and discards those that fail to fulfil certain criteria. This mechanism of plan-generate-test paradigm is what holds Dendral together.**

CONGEN (CONnstraints GENerator) is a Dendral program which constructs complete chemical structures by manipulating symbols that stand for atoms and molecules. Its input is a molecular formula and a set of constraints which serve to restrict the possible inter-connections among atoms. As an output, it generates a list of all possible ways of assembling the atoms into molecular structure by imposing the given constraints.

The KB of DENDRAL basically consists of huge knowledge about organic chemistry. The entire knowledge about organic chemistry is coded in the form of production rules. One example of such a rule is—

If there are two peaks at mass units $m1$ and $m2$

AND $x1 + x2$ = molecular weight + 28

AND at least one of $x1$ or $x2$ is high

Then ketone group is present.

How DENDRAL works?

Initially, **compound testing** is planned. It is fed into program and various groups are identified. The planner's production rule MSPRUNE is used to prune the number of alternate structures in the compound. The **major task** of MSPRUNE is to generate a hypothetical spectrum for structure. To perform this task it requires knowledge about characteristics spectra of all organic groups. **This knowledge is coded in form of production rules.** Another module, MSRANK, ranks the candidates into various groups. This subsystem has the knowledge of spectrometry to rank candidate structure.

DENDRAL has the following organizational features:

1. **Knowledge Representation:** Production rules and algorithms for generating graph structures are constructed by META DENDRAL— a program which uses learning techniques to construct rules for an expert system automatically.
2. **Reasoning:** Forward chaining (data driven).
3. **Heuristics:** DENDRAL uses a variation of dfs called as generate and test. In this all hypotheses are generated and then tested against available evidence. Heuristic knowledge from the users (chemists) is also used to constrain the search.
4. **Dialogue/explanation:** The dialogue uses mixed control. The user can supply information and the system can request information as required.

Do you know? Many systems were derived from Dendral like MOLGEN, MACSYMA, PROSPECTOR, XCON and STEAMER.

R1/XCON

The R1 (later called as XCON—expert CONfigurer) program was a production-rule-based system written in OPS5 by John P. McDermott of CMU in 1978. It helped in assisting of the ordering of DEC's VAX computer systems by automatically selecting the computer system components based on the customer's requirements.

XCON interacts with the sales person, asking critical questions before printing out a coherent and workable system specification. Let us summarise R1/Xcon/features—

1. John McDemott (1982–84) of Carnegi-Mellon University, USA, wrote R1/XCON in collaboration with DEC (Digital Equipment Corporation).
2. XCON is an acronym for **expert configurer** and is used to configure VAX and PDP–11 series of computer systems sold by DEC.
3. **XCON name is used by DEC; R1 name is used by McDermott.**
4. Initially, the system contained about **300 production rules** of the standard variety for configuring the **420 possible** components of a VAX–11 system.
5. A completed system containing some 800 production rules was delivered to DEC for acceptance testing (Oct. 1979). By 1980, DEC personnel had become sufficiently familiar with the operation of XCON to assume full responsibility for its maintenance and development and they have extended it to contain over **4000 rules.**
6. XCON system was designed to replace human **"technical editors".** Such editors had been responsible for 2 operations—

   (*a*) Checking for completeness of orders,

   (*b*) Laying out the physical placement and wiring connections between component modules in the chassis.

   These tasks are fairly tedious and each of the components is specified by properties such as **voltage (*V*), frequency (*f*)**, how many **devices** it supports and how many **parts** it has. Also, the editors had information showing which components can or must be associated with other components. **This set of rules governing the relationship between components is called as constraint knowledge.**
7. XCON passed an extensive series of **performance tests.**

NOTE: To text XCON, a set of 10 configurations was submitted to the program. Results were evaluated by a team of 12 people including technical editors, technicians and engineers. Errors detected were corrected and the cycle was repeated until 50 configurations had been produced.

8. By 1986, XCON represented an investment of over 50 person-years of human effort. Since its birth, XCON has grown at a relatively uniform rate as its capabilities expanded from a single line of VAX computers to the complete VAX line and the PDP–11 line. This required an effort of about four person-years per year.
9. XCON developers found that they did not have to complete the system before putting it to use. This shows XCON's **incremental growth.**
10. XCON's developers have concluded that it will never be possible **to guarantee 100% error-free performance.** Also they observed that building an ES is an unending process.
11. Since 1980, XCON has analyzed over 100,000 unique orders and is presently operating with greater than 99% accuracy. So, it is an effective business tool today.

SUMMARY

In this chapter, we have defined what is an expert system. Why are they required? What is its architecture? How to develop an ES? Some case studies on MYCIN, DENDRAL, RI (or XCON) have been discussed.

MULTIPLE CHOICE QUESTIONS [MCQS]

Q. 1. The class of program first developed by AI researchers is

(*a*) Human expert system (*b*) Artificial expert system

(*c*) Automatic expert system (*d*) None of the above.

Q. 2. ES uses

(*a*) Knowledge (*b*) Data (*c*) Information (*d*) None of the above.

Q. 3. Data when processed becomes information and information when processed becomes

(*a*) Data (*b*) Information (*c*) Knowledge (*d*) Wisdom.

Q. 4. Which of the following is an example of an ES?

(*a*) C (*b*) C++ (*c*) JAVA 2 (*d*) MYCIN.

Q. 5. Which of the following is an exmaple of an IE?

(*a*) VP-Expert (*b*) VIP-Expert (*c*) D-Expert (*d*) C-Expert.

Q. 6. DENDRAL has two subprograms, namely

(*a*) Heuristic Dendral + KB (*b*) Heuristic Dendral—Meta Dendral

(*c*) Heuristic Dendral + Meta Dendral (*d*) None of the above.

Q. 7. DENDRAL uses

(*a*) MPRUNE (*b*) MS PRUNE (*c*) SPRUNE (*d*) None of the above.

Q. 8. XCON stands for

(*a*) Expert configurer (*b*) Extra configuration

(*c*) E-console (*d*) None of the above.

Q. 9. To train doctors, which ES was developed?

(*a*) EMYCIN (*b*) PUFF (*c*) NEDMYCIN (*d*) None of the above.

Q. 10. An example of an ES shell is

(*a*) Crystal (*b*) C (*c*) LISP (*d*) None of the above.

ANSWERS

1. (*b*)	**2.** (*a*)	**3.** (*c*)	**4.** (*d*)	**5.** (*a*)
6. (*c*)	**7.** (*b*)	**8.** (*a*)	**9.** (*c*)	**10.** (*a*)

CONCEPTUAL SHORT QUESTIONS WITH ANSWERS

Q. 1. How do we use Domain exploration, Meta knowledge and Expertise transfer in building expert system? [GGSIPU, B. Tech (CSE) 8th Sem., April 2011]

Ans. **Domain knowledge** is that knowledge that software programs encode in form of different knowledge bases. Domain knowledge is important, because it usually must be learned from software users in the domain (as domain specialists/experts), rather than from software people. Communication between end-users and software people is often difficult. They must find a common language to communicate.

Meta knowledge or **meta-knowledge** is knowledge about knowledge. More precisely speaking, meta-knowledge is systematic problem and domain-independent knowledge which performs or enables operations on another more or less specific domain-dependent knowledge in different domains/areas of human activities. Meta-knowledge can be considered as a fundamental conceptual instrument in such research and scientific domains as, knowledge engineering, knowledge management, and others dealing with study and operations on knowledge, seen as a unified object/entities, abstracted from local conceptualizations and terminologies.

Expertise transfer discusses technology and organizational behaviour issues that are barriers to the commercial success of expert systems. The issues include interfacing and integrating with existing systems, picking the correct problem, fulfilling development, goals, representing knowledge, acquiring knowledge, validating and maintaining the system, deploying and introducing expert systems in an organization, and managing organizational behaviour after development is complete. It is argued that overcoming these barriers requires technology-transfer methods that account for an expert system's size and the structure and culture of the organization involved.

Q. 2. Distinguish between DENDRAL and MYCIN in a tabular form.

Ans.

DENDRAL	MYCIN
1. It uses production rules and algorithms for generating graph structures.	1. It uses production rules implemented LISP.
2. Reasoning is done using forward chaining.	2. Reasoning is done using backward chaining.
3. It uses **data-driven** approach.	3. It uses **goal-driven** approach.
4. It uses Generate-and-test strategy.	4. It uses depth-first search.
5. It uses mixed control dialogue explanation.	5. It uses computer control for dialogue/ explanation.

Q. 3. What is the difference between an active user and a passive user?

Ans. An **active user** uses an ES directly to obtain recommendations.

A **passive user** is one who trusts the results obtained from ESs and supports the implementation of those results.

Q. 4. What is heuristic reasoning? Discuss search control methods. Distinguish between forward and backward chaining.

Ans. Human experts use a type of problem solving technique called as heuristic reasoning. Also called as the rules of thumb, it allows the expert to arrive at a good solution quickly and efficiently.

The inferencing (done by IE) is of two types—

(*a*) Forward chaining

(*b*) Backward chaining.

Forward Chaining (or data driven search)

Also called as **data driven search or antecedent search. The process of inferencing that starts with the available data and uses the inference rules to conclude more data until the desired goal is reached is called as forward chaining. An inference engine** using forward chaining searches the inference rules until it finds one in which the if-clause is known to be true. It then concludes the then-clause and adds this information to its data. It would continue to do this until a goal is reached. Because the data available determines which inference rules are used, so this method is also called as **data-driven search**.

How it is done? The given condition (fact) is matched with the left part of a rule (called as **antecedent**). When the antecedent conditions are met, **the rule is fired**. That means the rule is replaced by RHS of the rule. It now becomes the new fact to be matched with the antecedent part of another rule.

Backward Chaining (or goal-driven search)

The process of inferencing that starts with a list of goals and works backwards to see if there is data which will allow it to conclude any of these goals is called as backward chaining. An inference engine using backward chaining would search the inference rules until it finds one which has a **then-clause** that matches a desired goal. If the if-clause of that inference rule is not known to be true then it is added to the list of goals. It is a reverse process of inferencing.

How it is done?

In this, rule interpreter starts with matching "THEN" part of the rule and if match occurs, it is replaced by "IF" condition. Here, the rule interpreter starts with goal state and proceeds towards start state.

Do you know? Situations where the starting states are more than goal states, use forward inferencing.

Q. 5. Consider the set of facts F1, F2, F3.....F6 and set of consequents C1, C2, C3.....C5. The production rules are as follows—

Rule 1: IF F1 and F2 then C1

Rule 2: IF F3 and C1 then C3

Rule 3: IF F6 then C3

Rule 4: IF F2 and C3 then C4

Rule 5: IF C4 then C5

Rule 6: If C2 then C3

Rule 7: If C5 then C6

Assume that input is facts F1 and F3 that are true and the query is that whether consequent C6 is true or not. Use forward chaining and prove this query. Also use backward chaining, if user specifies that C6 has to be proved. Assume that F2 and F3 are true again. Prove that A1 is true.

Ans. (*a*) **Using forward chaining**

Rule applied	Rule States	Inferred fact
1.	applied (fired)	C1
2.	applied (fired)	C3
3.	not required	
4.	applied (fired)	C4
5.	applied (fired)	C5
6.	not required	
7.	applied (fired)	C6

Thus, rules 1, 2, 4, 5, 7 are fired. The inferred fact becomes C6 which is proved to be true.

(*b*) **Using backward chaining**

If user specifies that C6 has to be proved. Let us assume that F2 and F3 are true again. The inferencing is done as follows—

	Rule Applied	Condition matched	Inferred
C6 (given as true)	7		C5
C5	6, 5	Condition matched	C2, C4
C4	4	Condition matched	C2 and A2
C3	3	Condition matched	A3
C2	2	Condition matched	A3, C1
C1	1	Condition matched	A1, A2

With this sequence of steps, A1 is proved to be true.

Q. 6. Contrast and compare expert systems and neural nets.

Ans. The current developments in ANN technologies present new opportunities for expert system work. The following points explain this—

1. Expert system elements may be implemented with NN.
2. Areas such as speech and vision are done better with NNs.
3. ESs can be used for training NNs.
4. Knowledge acquisition and knowledge engineering problems can be addressed using NN.

5. Implicit knowledge may be provided by NNs to support explicit rule-based knowledge.

Q. 7. Write a short note on ES tools. **[GGSIPU, B. Tech. (CSE), 8th Sem., 2010]**

Ans. The commercialization of AI has been mainly in the form of expert systems and knowledge based systems. In the decade of 1980s expert systems have progressed from efforts in research laboratories aimed at building stand-alone one-of-a-kind systems, to products built and deployed in large numbers in industrial laboratory and government office settings. When early expert systems were constructed, their implementers typically began with a general purpose language such as LISP and built a number of utility data structures and programs to represent facts, rules and strategies and to perform the basic operations of the system such as rule invocation, matching, computations involving uncertainties, etc. Initially, it was often very difficult to speculate now much of that machinery was problem-specific and how much would be reusable for other fields. Once a few experimental applications had been built, the developers begin the task of abstracting out of these programs those aspects that appeared universal. Thus the well known first generation expert system MYCIN led to the development of the tool (or shell) EMYCIN (empty MYCIN). EMYCIN thus provides, based on the past experience, with diagnosis tasks associated with the diagnosis of infectious diseases, a tool with useful knowledge organization and appropriate problem solving methods for generic tasks such as medical diagnosis, pattern classification and equipment fault diagnosis.

EXPERT SYSTEM TOOLS (also called knowledge Engineering Tools) are software systems that support the development, execution and maintenance of expert systems (or knowledge based systems). As a result of widespread interest in expert system development, there has been a huge volume of activity in expert system tool development with market projections of the order of US $ 400 million by early 1990s. The tools also range for large development environments such as ART (Automated Reasoning Tool), KES (Knowledge Engineering System), CLIPS (the C Language Integrated Production System) Level 5, VAS OPS5, etc. The widely varying costs of these packages together with the often exaggerated claims in vendor literature makes selection of expert system tools a difficult task.

Table below gives a partial list of some of these tools—

Advisor	FranzLisp	Personal Consultant Plus
ART	GoldenCommonLisp	PROLOG2
ART-IM	GoldWorks	RuleMaster
Cambridge LISP68000	Insight2+	RuleMaster2
CLIPS	KEE	S.1
ExperLisp	KES	Smalltalk
Experops5	Level 15	Smalltalk
ExpertEase	MicroExpert	VAXOPS5
Expert4	NEXPERTOBJECT	ZEXPERT

Q. 8. Explain the knowledge acquisition methods adopted by expert systems.

[RTM Nagpur Univ., BE (IT)- 7th Sem., Summar 2009]

Ans. Knowledge acquisition is the process of gathering knowledge. The knowledge engineers do this by interacting and interviewing the human experts of that domain. The person interviewing the expert should also have some basic knowledge of the concerned field to find out what to ask. This collected knowledge is then encoded in a format suitable for storage in memory. This job of encoding is done by a computer specialist.

For example: COMPASS is an expert system which performs knowledge acquisition by interviewing.

The knowledge acquisition cycle performs the following steps—

(*a*) Acquires knowledge from expert.

(*b*) Documents the acquired knowledge.

(*c*) Tests the new knowledge.

Q. 9. Discuss some explanation facilities as used by ES.

Ans. Almost all expert systems can explain to users how they reach particular conclusions. The most common type of explanation mechanism deals with the following:

1. Retrospective Reasoning

It explains how the **system** reached **a particular state. For example,** the end-user may wish to know why the system needed the answer to the question it just asked or how the system arrived at a certain conclusion. Here, the system may describe the rules which led to the question or display part of the chain or sequence of rules that led to the conclusion.

2. Hypothetical Reasoning

The system explains what would have happened differently if a particular fact or rule had been different.

3. Counterfactual Reasoning

The system explains why an expected conclusion was not reached.

EXERCISE QUESTIONS

Q. 1. Explain different components of an expert system.

[RTM Nagpur Univ., BE (IT)-7th Sem., Summer 2009]

Q. 2. (*a*) Explain rule-based architecture of expert system.

(*b*) What are different applications of expert system?

(*c*) What do you mean by expert system shell?

[RTM Nagpur Univ., BE (IT)-7th Sem., Winter 2009]

Q. 3. (*a*) Draw and explain architecture of Expert System.

(*b*) What is Expert System Shell? State its advantages.

[RTM Nagpur, BE (CSE)-7th Sem., Summer 2009]

Q. 4. (*a*) What are the various methods of knowledge acquisition used in expert system? Explain with examples.

(*b*) What are various knowledge representation techniques used in expert systems? Explain with examples. **[PTU., M.C.A-4th Sem., 2009]**

Q. 5. (*a*) What do you mean by an Expert System? Why we need an Expert System? What are different kinds of problems faced during development of an Expert System?

(*b*) Identify and describe two good application areas for expert systems within a university system. **[PTU., B. Tech (CS)-7th Sem., 2009]**

Q. 6. (*a*) What is an ES? Explain its various parts.

(*b*) Explain, in short, the working of DENDRAL and MYCIN.

(*c*) Discuss the concept of uncertainty in ES.

[UPTU., B. Tech (CSE)-8th Sem., 2006-07]

Q. 7. Briefly explain any of the expert system RI (XCON) or Mycin.

[GGSIPU, B.Tech (CS)-8th Sem., May 2008]

Q. 8. Explain the architecture of an expert with a diagram.

[GGSIPU, B.Tech. (CSE)-8th Sem. May-June 2009]

Q. 9. What procedure is followed for knowledge acquisition?

[GGSIPU., B. Tech (CSE)-8th Sem., May-June 2010]

Q. 10. What are the various steps for development of Expert Systems?

[GGSIPU., B. Tech (CSE)-8th Sem., May-June 2010]

Q. 11. How is an Expert System different from other softwares like DBMS etc.

[GGSIPU., B. Tech (CSE)-8th Sem., May 2011]

CHAPTER 9 AI PROGRAMMING LANGUAGES—LISP AND PROLOG

9.0 INTRODUCTION

An AI program can be written in any programming language. But since AI programs mainly involve symbol manipulation and not numbers, so we need some representation for these symbols. We need a list data structure now and this can be easily done using LISP language. LISP stands for List Processing. It works on pattern matching rule. Now-a-days, PROLOG (Programming Logic) is also becoming very popular. Both LISP and PROLOG are common AI languages used today. There are several dialects of LISP like FRANZLISP, INTERLISP, MACLISP, QLISP, SCHEME, COMMON LISP AND XLISP.

9.1 LISP AND ITS CONSTRUCTS

List Processing or LISP, in short, was invented by John McCarthy during late 1950s. It is a language with simple syntax, with little or no datatyping and dynamic memory management. Everything in LISP is a function.

Characteristics of LISP language

1. **LISP is a functional language.** Its syntax and semantics are derived from the mathematical theory of recursive function. But it is NOT a pure functional language.
2. **Everything in LISP is a function.** A **function** is a procedure that may or may not have arguments and will always return a value.

   Do you know? Some LISP functions like SETF produce side effects also.

3. All data are in form of symbolic expression or S-expressions.
4. LISP can interpret and execute programs written in form of expressions.
5. LISP offers greatest facility to an ES builder.
6. LISP supports automatic memory management.

Basic Building Blocks of LISP

LISP has 3 basic building blocks—

(*a*) Atoms

(*b*) Lists

(*c*) Strings

Atom: An atom is a number or string of contiguous characters, including numbers and special characters.

For example : Valid atoms are —

1. this_is_a_symbolic_atom

2. Bill
3. 10007879
4. block #6
5. a1234567

And **invalid atoms** are—

1. a b c
2. 1 2 3 a b c
3. (a b)
4. (1) [∵ it is a list]

LIST: It is a sequence of atoms and/or other lists enclosed within parentheses.

For example,

Valid Lists	**Invalid Lists**
(1)	this is not a list
(this is a list)	(a, b, c d e f)
(a (a b) C def)	(abc (dc)
( )	((a b) (
(Mon Tue Wed Thu)	(1, 2
(1 2 3 4)	

String: It is a group of characters enclosed in double quotation marks.

For example,

Valid Strings	**Invalid Strings**
"this is a string"	this is not a string
"abcde #$%$\@!"	"neither is this
"please login"	nor "this"

Please remember the following points here:

1. Every expression in LISP is either an **atom** or a **list**.

   Atoms like 97, 3.1417 etc are called as NUMERIC ATOMS.

   Atoms like FIRST, FOO, + etc are called as SYMBOLIC ATOMS.
2. A list consists of a left parenthesis, followed by zero or more elements, followed by a right parenthesis i.e., ( ).
3. Since a list may contain atoms as well as other list, we will call the basic unit members as the **top elements** of the list.

   For example: 1: Top elements of the list (ab (cd) e(f)) are a, b, (c d), e and (f).

   e.g. 2: Elements c and d are top elements of sublist (c, d).
4. Elements of a list are separated by space. List themselves can be elements of another list.
5. A combination of lists within lists is called as a **nested** or **multiple** or **complex list**.
6. The number of opening and closing braces must be same. It is a very important programming rule.

How LISP programs work?

LISP programs run either on **an interpreter or a compiled code**. The interpreter examines source programs in a repeated loop called as "**read-evaluate-print**" loop. This loop **reads** the program code, **evaluates** it and **prints** the values returned by the program. The interpreter signals its readiness to accept code for execution by printing a prompt such as → symbols.

For example: To find sum of three numbers 4, 5 and 6, we type the following function call after the prompt:

→ (+ 4 5 6))

15

→

Please note that LISP uses "prefix" notation ( ) and + symbol is the function-name for the sum of arguments that follows.

The function name and its arguments are enclosed in parentheses to signify that it is to be evaluated as a function. The **read-evaluate-print** loop reads this expression, evaluates it and prints the value returned i.e. 15 in this case.

Also note that the interpreter then prints the prompt to signal its readiness to accept the next input. More complicated computations can be written as a single embedded expression.

Do you know? Comments are written after semicolon.

To exit from LISP, type Exit at the prompt (→) of LISP.

For example: (+ 3 5 8 4) gives 20.

(– 10 12) gives –2

(* 2 3 4) gives 24

(/ 25 2) gives 12.5

(/ . 2) gives $\frac{1}{0.2} = 5$

(/ 8 / 2) gives $\frac{8}{1*2} = 4$

Special cases

Three types of elements are special in that they are constant and always evaluate to themselves, returning their own value i.e., numbers and t (for logical true) and f (for logical false).

Nil is also the same as empty list( ). It is the only object in LISP that is both an atom and a list. For example,

→ 6

6 (as output)

→ t

T (as output)

→ NIL

NIL (as output)

NOTE 1: Boy or `(a b c d) has a quotation mark on top that informs the interpreter that the atom or a list should not be evaluated but should be taken literally as an atom or list. On the other hand, (a b c d) means it is a function call.

Assignments in LISP

(*a*) Setq and setf functions

Setq means set the value of atom.

Setf means set the value of function.

For example, 1: → (setq x 100) ; x ←100

100 (is output)

So, now if you type 'x' in front of LISP prompt,

→ x

100 (is output)

So, x now stores 100.

E.g.2: → (setq x (+ 3 5))

gives 8 ; x ← 8

E.g. 3: → (setq x '(+ 3 5))

(+ 3 5) is the output.

This is because quote inhibits evaluation.

E.g. 4: → y

Unbounded variable : y ; error

Similarly, for 'Setf' we take an example—

→ (setf a '(+ 1 2 3))

and if we type 'a' in front of prompt i.e.,

→ a

we get (+ 1 2 3) as output.

That is, set 'a' to (+ 1 2 3) where (+ 1 2 3) is a function.

(*b*) **Car or first top element and Cdr or rest top elements**

They are used only with lists and not with atoms. Car takes one argument, which must be a list. This function returns us the first top element of the list.

Cdr takes list as an argument and returns a list consisting of all elements except the first.

For example: → (setf a '(1 2 3 4))

→ (car a)

1 (is the output)

E.g.2 → (setf a '((/ 2) 3 4)))

→ (car a)

(1 2)

→ (cdr a)

gives (3 4) as output as it removes the first top element (i.e., (1 2)) and returns (3 4) as output.

Similarly, if we define—

(setf a '((1 2 3 4)))

→ (Cdr a)

NIL [∵ There is no 2nd top most element as '(quote) inhibits any operation]

and → (car NIL)

returns NIL

and → (cdr NIL)

returns NIL

Also, (car (cdr a))

↓

or (car (2 3 4))

gives 2 as the output.

whereas (cdr (car a))

or cdr (1) gives

Error [∵ Only '1'atom is there and car and cdr cannot operate on atoms but only on lists]

E.g. → (setf ab-list '(a b c d))

→ ab-list

(a b c d) is returned as output.

and → (car ab-list)

a (as output as (car '(a b c d)) = a)

Also, → (cdr ab-list)

→ (b c d) (as output)

And → (cadr ab-list)

→ b (as output)

And → (cdr 'ab-list)

→ error

Another exmaple,

→ (setf ab-list '((a b) a b)))

then → (car ab-list)

returns → (a b) as output.

(*c*) **Cons function**

It takes two arguments, an element and a list. It constructs a new list by making the element the first member of the list.

For example: → (cons 1 (2 3 4 5))

gives (1 2 3 4 5) as output.

E.g.:2 → (cons (* 2 3) (1))

gives ((* 2 3) 1)

(*d*) **List function**

It takes any number of arguments and makes them into a list with each argument a top member.

For example: → (list 'a '(b c))

returns (a (b c))

(*e*) **Append function**

It merges arguments of one or more lists into a single list.

For example: → (append '(a) '(b c))

returns (a b c)

E.g.2 → (append 'alist (ablist))

Error [∵ 'alist is an atom]

(*f*) **Last function**

It returns a list containing last element.

For example: → (last '(a b c d)) gives

(d) (as the output)

This is because even if we use '(quotes) then also it remains list as braces have been used.

(*g*) **Member function**

It takes two arguments, second one must be a list. If the first argument is member of 2nd one, the remainder of 2nd list is returned beginning with the member element.

For example: (member 'b '(a b d))

returns (b d) as the output.

(*h*) **Reverse function**

It takes a list as its argument and returns it in reverse order.

Fog example: → (reverse '(a (b c) d))

returns (d (b c) a)

Note here that (b c) is taken as one atom.

E.g. 2 → (reverse `(a b (c d) e))

gives (E (C D) B A) as output.

(*i*) **Quote function**

It informs interpreter that the atom or list should not be evaluated but should be taken literally as an atom or list.

For example: → (setf a `(alist))

alist

when quote is used, the content of a list is stored in variable 'a'.

Functions is LISP

The function named DEFUN is used to define functions. DEFUN means DEfine FUNction. It requires three arguments–

1. the new function name.
2. the parameters for function.
3. the function body or LISP code to do required function operations.

The **format** to define function is—

(defun function-name (<arg1>, ,arg2>…) body)

For example: → (defun avg (n1 n2 n3) (/ (+ n1 n2 n3) 3))

returns function name-avg.

To call function avg we can write—

→ (avg 1 2 3)

gives 2 as output.

Let us take another example now.

Out temperature conversion formula is

F = 1.8 C + 3 2

We write its function now—

```
→   (defun centil NIL
            (setf F (+ *1.8 (read)) 32)))
```

And now write a calling function now—

```
→   (defun centil NIL
            (print 'Enter centigrade value;)
            (centi) ; function call
            (print F))
```

Before we go further, let us write some LISP programs now.

EXAMPLE 1. Write a function to return a list in which the last element of list is removed. [Do not use the last primitive of LISP].

SOLUTION 1. (reverse (cdr (reverse '(a b c))))

EXAMPLE 2. Write a LISP function to check whether the number is divisible by 3 or NOT?

SOLUTION 2. (defun div (n)

(zerop (rem n 3)))

EXAMPLE 3. Define a function called first-element that takes list as its argument and returns the first top element of the list.

SOLUTION 3. → (defun first-element (l) (car l))

E.g. (first-element '(1 2 3 4))

gives 1 as output

EXAMPLE 4. Define a function called number-of-elements that takes a list as its only argument and returns the number of top element in it.

SOLUTION 4. → (defun number-of-elements (*l*)

(setq n length *l*)

(print n))

Some more LISP functions

(*a*) **Last function :** It returns the last element of the list.

For example: (last (1 2 3 4))

(4)

Whereas (but-last l n) trims off last n-elements.

For example: (but last '(1 2 3 4) 2)

→ (1 2)

It trims off last 2 elements as n = 2 here and returns (1 2).

(*b*) **Length function:** It returns the number of top-level elements in a list.

For example: (length (1 2 3 4))

gives 4 as output.

(*c*) **Remainder function:** It returns the remainder.

For example: → (rem 4 3)

→ 1 (as the output)

Some predicates in LISP

Predicates are the functions that test their arguments for some specific condition. It returns true (t) or false (nil) depending on the arguments. Some of them are discussed below.

1. Atom: It is a predicate that takes one argument. It returns t if the argument is an atom and nil otherwise.

For example: → (atom 'aabb)
t ; aabb is a valid
; atom

e.g.z → (atom 1)
t

2. Equal: It takes two arguments and returns 't' if they evaluate to the same value and nil otherwise.

For example: → (equal 'a (car '(a b))
t ; It means atom 'a'
; equals 'a' but
; (equal 1 1.0) returns
; NIL

3. Evenp, Numberp, oddp and zerop: Are the tests on a single numeric argument. They return t if their argument evaluates to an even number, a number, an odd number or zero respectively. Otherwise they each will return nil.

For example: → (evenp 3)
nil ; 3 is not even no.

e.g .2 (numberp 10 ab)
nil ; 10 ab is not a no.

e.g. 3 (oddp 3)
t ; 3 is an odd no.

e.g. 4 (zero .00001)
nil ; argument is not zero

e.g. 5 (zerop (– (+ 5 2) 7))
T ; as 5 + 2 = 7 and 7 – 7 = 0

4. Greaterp and lessp: Each takes one or more arguments. (*a*) **Only one argument** is used, each returns t.

(*b*) **More than one argument is used,** greaterp returns t if the arguments, from left to right, are successively larger otherwise nil is returned.

For example: → (greaterp 2 4 27)
t

Similarly, lessp requires that the arguments be successively smaller from left to right to return 't'. Otherwise it returns nil.

For example: → (lessp 5 3 1 2) returns nil.

NOTE: The predicates >= and <= have the same meaning as greaterp and lessp respectively, except they return t if successive elements are also equal.

5. Listp and null

Both take a single argument. Listp returns t if its argument evaluates to a list and nil otherwise.

For example: → (listp '(a))

t ; (a) is a valid list

Null: Returns t if its argument evaluates to nil otherwise it returns nil.

For example: → (null (nil))

t ; nil is an empty list.

Let us solve a question now.

Q. 1. Write in LISP to check whether a list is a pallindrome or NOT.

Ans. (defun pal (p)

(equal p (reverse p)))

Constructs in LISP

1. If then-else

Its syntax is—

(if <test> <then form>
<else form>)

For example: (if (plusp n) (format t "~a is positive" n))

Please note '~a' is like % d in C wherein the value of 'n' gets substituted.

2. Another form is—

(Cond (<test1> <action 1>)
(<test2> <action 2>)
⋮ ⋮
(<test n> <action n>))

Here, each <test$_i$> <action$_i$>)

where i ←1 to n, is called as a **clause**.

Let us solve some problems now.

Q. 1. Write a LISP program to find maximum of two numbers.

Ans. → (defun max2 (a b)

```
(cond ((> a b )
(format t "Max. ~a" a ))
(t (format t "Max. ~a" b))))
```

NOTE: t is for 'else'
and ~a is like % d in C-language.

∴ → (max2 '(101 400))

400 (is the output).

Q. 2. Write a LISP program to find maximum of three numbers.

Ans. → (defun max3 (a b c)

```
(cond (( > a b) (cond (( > a c)
(format t "Max ~a"
(t (format t "Max ~a"
(( > b c > (format t "Max ~a"
(t format t "Max ~a " c))))
```

So, → (max 3 '(20 30 25))

30

→

Q. 3. Write a LISP program to find maximum in a given list.

Ans. → (defun max (l)

```
        (sort (l) (>))
        (car l))
```

Q. 4. Write a LISP program to return a list without its first and last 2-elements.

Ans. → (defun rem (l)

```
   (but last (cdr l) 2))
```

Q. 5. Write a LISP program to find SUM = 1 + 2 + 3 + 4 + 5 = 15 if n = 5.

Ans. → (defun sum1 (n)

```
           (setf s 0)
           (dotimes (i n s)
           (setf s (+ s i ))))
```

Alternative solution

```
(defun sum1 (l)
    (setq sum 0)
    (loop
        (Setq p (car l)
        (setq sum (+ sum p ))
        (setq l (cdr l))
))
```

Q. 6. Write a function newlist that takes one argument and returns a list. If argument is a list then return it as a list only, else if it is an atom, then on returns it as a list.

Ans. → (defun newlist (l)

```
      (if ((listp l) l)
      (t ((atom '1) l))))
```

Q. 7. Define a LISP function that takes 2 arguments an item and a list. If the item is in the list, the function returns the list unaltered. If the item is not in the list, the function returns the list with the item entered (as the first element).

Ans. → (defun memb1 nil

```
           (print "Enter the item:")
           (setf item (read))   ; read an item
           (printf "Enter the list :")
              (Setf lt (read))      ; read a list
              (memb 2 item (t)  ; function call
        ))
```

→ (defun memb2 (item (t)

```
           (cond ((member item (t) lt)
              (t (cons items lt))
           )
           )
```

Q. 8. Write a LISP program to read nth element from a list and print it.

Ans. → (defun nth-item (m *l*)

```
                (setq n length l)  (print n)
                (setq i l)
                (dotimes (i n l)
                    (if (= i m )    (print l)
                )
                )
                )
    →           (nth-item (1 '(1 2 3 4 5 6))
                1
    →
```

DOLIST LOOP in LISP

The syntax of dolist is as follows—

```
(do list  (<elem-parameter> <list>
           <result-form>)
           <body>)
```

Let us solve some programs now.

Q. 1. **(*a*) Write a LISP program to find maximum in a LIST.**

(*b*) Write a LISP program to find maximum and minimum in a single given list.

Ans. (*a*) → (defun max1 nil

```
                print "Enter list :")
                (setf lt (read))
                (max1 lt)
        )
    →           (defun maxl (lt)
                    (setf max2 (car lt)
                          lt (cdr lt))
                    (dolist (x lt max2)
                    (cond ((> x max2)
                    (setf max2 x))
        )
        )
```

(*b*) 1. Sort the list (l).

2. (Car l) is minimum.

3. (Last l) is maximum.

```
→  (defun maxmin (lt)
   (sort lt >)
        (setq min car lt)       (print min)
        (setq max last lt)      (print max))
```

NOTE: Car and last works on list and not on arrays.

Q. 2. **Write a LISP function-intersect which takes 2 lists as arguments. It should return a list containing single occurrences of all elements which appear in both input lists.**

Ans. → (defun intersect (lt1 lt2)

```
          (setf lt3 nil)
          (dolist (x lt2 lt3)
                (cond ((member x lt1)
                (setf lt3 (cons x lt3)
          )
          )
          )
```

Arrays in LISP

Arrays are used to store items. These items may be any LISP object. Array indices in LISP start from 0.

How to create an array?

Syntax:

(Setf ar (make-array 3))

This creates an array, ar of size 3.

How to refer to array-elements?

Syntax:

(aref ar 1)

This refers to first-element in an array i.e., ar [1].

How to read an array?

Syntax:

(setf (aref ar i) (read))

e.g.1 To store item 25, one would write—

→ (setf (aref myarray 0) 25)

25

e.g.2 → (setf (aref myarray 1) 'red)

RED (is the output)

e.g.3 → (setf (aref myarray 2) '(Sam Sue Linda))

(SAM SUE LINDA) (is the output)

LOOP Construct in LISP

Syntax: (loop <body>)

Q. 1. Write a LISP program to count the number of a's in a list.

Ans. (*a*) → (defun cnt (lt)

```
          (setf n 0)
          (loop (if (endp lt)         (return n))
             (if (cond ((equal 'a (car lt)
          (setf n (+ n 1)))
          (setf lt (cdr lt))
          )
```

2D-arrays in LISP

To **define** a 2D-array, we write

→ (setf ar (make-array '(3 3)))

This will create an array of size (3 × 3).

To refer to 2D-array elements, we write—

```
→    (aref ar 2 0)
     where  ar is an array
            2 is the row-no.
            0 is the col. no.
```

∴ 3rd row and 1st column element is being referred to.

To **initialize** a 2D array, we write—

```
(setf (aref ar 2 0) 3)
```

We are in a position to write some programs now.

Q. 1. Write a LISP program to read a 2D-array and to sum its diagonal elements.

Ans. ; To read a 2D-array

```
→    (defun read (m n )
     (setf ar (make-array '(m n)))
     (dotimes  (i m ar)
     (dotimes (j n ar)
     (setf (aref ar i j) (read)))))
     ; to sum its diagonal elements
→    (defun sum (m n)
            (setf sum 0)
            (setf ar (make-array)        '(m n))
                    (read (m n))
            (dotimes (i m ar)
            (dotimes (j n ar)
            (if (= i j)
                    (setq sum (+ sum aref)
                    (print sum)))))
```

Property-lists in LISP

Every symbol in LISP may have a number of properties associated with it.

(*a*) **PUTPROP function**

It is used for assigning the properties to an atom. Its syntax is — (PUTPROP object value attribute)

For example: → (putprop 'car 'red 'color)

It sets color of car as red.

(*b*) **GET function**

Syntax:

(get object attribute)

For example: → (get 'car 'color)

red (is the output)

It gets the color of car.

(c) **REMPROP function**

Syntax:

(remprop object attribute)

We are in a position to solve an example now.

Q. 1. You are given the following network regarding AI-bird, Tweety:

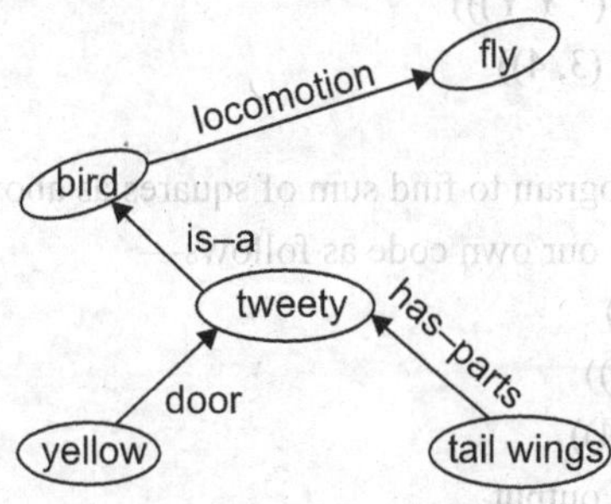

Write statements using LISP predicates to—

(a) Get color of Tweety as yellow.

(b) Get locomotion of Tweety as fly.

(c) Get parts of Tweety as tails and wings.

(d) Define Tweety bird.

(e) Remove Tweety's color from yellow to red.

Ans. (*a*) → (putprop 'Tweety 'Yellow 'color)

→ (get 'Tweety ' Color)

It gives yellow as the output.

(*b*) → (putprop 'Tweety 'fly 'locomotion)

→ (get 'Tweety 'locomotion)

It gives fly as output.

(*c*) → (putprop 'Tweety '(tail wings) 'has-parts)

→ (get 'Tweety 'has-parts)

It gives tail wings as output.

(*d*) → (putprop 'Tweety 'Yellow 'Color)

→ (putprop 'bird 'fly 'locomotion)

→ (putprop 'bird 'tweety 'is-a)

(*d*) → (remprop 'tweety 'color)

(putprop 'tweety 'RED 'COLOR)

(getprop 'tweety 'color)

It gives RED as output.

Let us write a program now.

Q. 1. Write a LISP program to simulate putprop. [Don't use putprop].

Ans. →

```
(defun putprop (obj val attr)
(self value (get 'obj 'attr))
(print value)
)
```

LAMBDA expression

A lambda expression is a function without a name.

Syntax: (LAMBDA <formal-parameters><body>)

where <formal-parameters> is a list of distinct symbols and <body> is one or more forms.

For example: (LAMBDA (X Y)
(+ (* X X) (* Y Y)))

If we call, → (LAMBDA (3, 4))

We get 25 as the output

Can't we write our own program to find sum of squares as above?

Yes, certainly we can write our own code as follows—

```
(DEFUN SUMSQ (X Y)
    (+ (* X X) (* Y Y)))
```

If we call, → (SUMSQ (3 4))

We will again get 25 as the output.

Please note that the difference between them is that lambda expression does not have a name while the function SUMSQ does.

MAPCAR function

Mapping functions apply a given function to every element of a list.

MAPCAR is an in-built function that takes as its arguments a function of n-arguments (for an arbitrary n) followed by n-lists of equal length. It evaluates to a list whose first element is obtained by applying the function to first elements of the n lists and so on for all the elements. In other words, it combines the power of MAPCAR-1, MAPCAR-2 etc into a single function.

9.2 LISP PROGRAMMING EXAMPLES

Q. 1. Write a LISP function-LEN that finds the length of a list.

Ans. →

```
(DEFUN LEN (L)
    (COND ((NULL L) 0)
        (T (+ 1 ((LEN (CDR L))))))
```

It uses recursion as follows—

1. Length of the null list is 0.
2. Length of a non-null list is one more than the length of its tail.

The 1st observation is a terminating condition. This 2nd observation allows us to write the recursive step because we have reduced the problem of finding the length of the list to that of the tail of the list.

∴ → (LEN '(7 2))
2
→ (LEN '((8, 7)))
1
→ (LEN '(8 7 (2 2)))
3

Q. 2. Define a function OCCURS-IN which takes a symbol and an object and returns true if the symbol occurs in the object.

Ans. → (OCCURS-IN 'COLOR

```
'((TABLE (COLOR BROWN))
        (CHAIR (SIZE 20))))
→ T
```

Q. 3. Write a LISP program to —

(*a*) find the last element of a non-null list.

(*b*) remove the first occurrence of atom A in list, L.

Ans. (*a*) →

```
(DEFUN LAST-ELEM(L)
   (COND ((NULL (CDR L)) (CAR L))
   (t (LAST-ELEM (CDR L)))))
```

NOTE: LAST is also an in-built function that returns the last cons-call of its argument list.

(*b*) →

```
(DEFUN REMOVE1 (A L)
   (COND ((NULL L) ( ) )
   ((EQL A (CAR L)) (CDR L))
   (T (CONS (CAR L) (REMOVE 1 A (CDR L))))))
```

NOTE: REMOVE is also an in-built function to remove occurrences of A from L.

Q. 4. Write a LISP function to linearize a list. For example,

```
→ (LINEARIZE '((THE BOOK (IS GOOD))))
  THE BOOK IS GOOD
```

Ans. →

```
(DEFUN LINARIZE (L)
   (COND ((NULL L) ( ))
     ((ATOM L) (CONS L ( )))
     (T (APPEND  (LINEARIZE  (CAR L))
                 (LINEARIZE  (CDR L))))))
```

Q. 5. Write a LISP function to count the number of atoms in a list.

Ans. →

```
(DEFUN COUNT-ATOMS (L)
      (LENGTH (LINEARIZE L)))
```

Q. 6. Write a LISP function OUR-MEMBER to check if the first argument is equal to one of the elements in the second argument list.

Ans. →

```
(DEFUN OUR-MEMBER (S L)
      (COND ((NULL L) O)
      (T (OUR-MEMBER S (CDR L)))))
```

Q. 7. Write a LISP function to find the factorial of a number, n.

Ans. →

```
(DEFUN FACTO (N)
      (COND ((ZEROP N) 1)
            (T (*N (FACTORIAL (1-N))))))
```

Q. 8. The Ackermann's function is as given below—

ack (o, n) = n + 1

ack (m, o) = ack (m – 1, 1)

ack (m, n) = ack (m –1, ack (m, n – 1)))

Write a LISP function to solve it.

Ans. →
```
(DEFUN ACK (M N)
    (COND ((ZEROP M) (1+N))
        ((ZEROP N) (ACK (1–M) 1))
        (T (ACK (1–M)
            (ACK M (1–N)))))))
```

Q. 9. Write a LISP function called SET-UNION that returns the union of two sets S1 and S2.

Ans. →
```
(DEFUN SET-UNION (S1 S2)
    (COND ((NULL S1) S2)
        ((SET-MEMP (CAR S1) S2)
        (SET-UNION (CDR S1) S2))
    (T (CONS (CAR S1) (SET-UNION (CDR S1) S2)))))
```

Q. 10. Write a LISP program to do SET-INTERSECTION. If S1 is empty set then the result is the empty set as there are no elements common to S1 and S2.

Ans. →
```
(DEFUN SET-INTERSECTION (S1 S2)
    (COND ((NULL S1) ( ))
        ((SET-MEMP (CAR S1) S2)
        (CONS (CAR S1) (SET-INTERSECTION (CDR S1) S2 )))
    (T (SET-INTERSECTION (CDR S1) S2 ))))
```

Q. 11. Write a LISP program to find GCD of two numbers—x and y. Use Euclid's algorithm as given below—

(*a*) **For positive x and y:**

gcd (x,y) = x if x = y
gcd (x – y, x) if x > y
gcd (x, y – x) if x < y

(*b*) **For non-positive x or y:**

gcd (x, y) = 0 if x = 0 or y = 0
gcd (–x, y) if x < 0
gcd (x, –y) if y < 0 ?

Ans. →
```
(DEFUN OUR-GCD (X Y)
    (COND ((OR (= X 0) (= Y 0)) 0)
        ((<X 0) (OUR-GCD (–X) Y)))
        ((<Y 0) (OUR-GCD X (–Y) ))
        (T (GCD-POSITIVE X Y))))
```
→
```
(DEFUN GCD-POSITIVE (X Y)
    (COND ((= X Y) X)
        ((>X Y) (GCD-POSITIVE (–X Y) Y))
        (T (GCD-POSITIVE X (– Y X)))))
; main program
```
→
```
(DEFUN MAIN (X Y)
    (OUR-GCD X Y))
```

Q. 12. Write LISP functions to add two polynomials.

Ans.

```
→ (DEFUN +POLY (P1 P2)
      (COND ((NULL P1)   P2)
            ((NULL P2)   P1)
            (T (CONS (MAKE-SUM (CAR P1) (CAR P2))
                     (+ POLY (CDR P1)  (CDR P2))))))
  ; funciton MAKE-SUM takes two coefficients
  ; and constructs their sum
→ (DEFUN MAKE-SUM (C1 C2)
      (COND ((AND (NUMBERP C1)  (NUMBERP C2))
             (+ C1 C2))
            (( = 0 C1) C2)
            (( = 0 C2) C1)
            ((T (LIST '+ C1 C2))))
```

∴ If S1 = (5 C (* A 3))
S2 = (3 0 (* – 3 A))
then

```
→ (+POLY S1 S2)
  (8C (+ (* A 3)  (* – 3 A)))
```

Q. 13. Write LISP functions to reverse a list of length n. Firstly, reverse the rest of the list and then append it to the first element of the list.

Ans.

```
→ (DEFUN OUR-REVERSE (L)
      (REV-AUX L ( )))
→ (DEFUN REV-AUX (REM-LIST REVERSES-SO-FAR)
      (COND ((NULL REM-LIST) REVERSE-SO-FAR)
            (T (REV-AUX (CDR REM-LIST)
                        (CONS (CAR REM-LIST) REVERSED-SO-FAR)))))
```

Q. 14. Write LISP functions that takes two strings and returns their appended string.

Ans.

```
→ (DEFUN STRING-APPEND (STR1 STR2)
      (LET ((L1 (LENGTH STR1))
            (L2 (LENGTH STR2)))
      (LET ((NEW-STR (MAKE-ARRAY (+ L1 L2)
                     : ELEMENT-TYPE 'CHAR)))
      ; COPY STR1 into NEW-STR
            (DO (( I O (+ I 1)))
                ((= I L 1))
            (SETF (AREF NEW-STR I) (AREF STR2 I)))
      ;  copy STR2 into NEW-STR following
      ;  copy of STR1
            (Do ((I O (+ I 1)))
                ((= I L2)    (NEW-STR)
            (SETF (AREF NEW-STR (+L1 I))
                            (AREF STR2 I)))))
```

Q. 15. Write LISP functions to—

(*a*) rotate a list.

(*b*) reverse a list.

(*c*) keep the first n-elements of a list.

(*d*) skip off first n-elements of a list.

Ans. (*a*) (defun rot (l)

```
        (append (last l)  (reverse (cdr (reverse l)))))
```

(*b*) (defun reverse l (l)

```
        (cond ((null l)  l)
        (t (append (reverse1 (cdr l))
        (cons (car l) nil )))))
```

(*c*) (defun keep (n l)

```
        (reverse (nthcdr (–(length l) n) (reverse l))))
```

(*d*) (defun skip off (n l)

```
        (if (= n 0) l
                (skip off (–n 1) (rest l))))
```

Q. 16. Write LISP functions to simulate on—

(*a*) Member primitive.

(*b*) Last primitive.

(*c*) Append primitive.

(*d*) nth cdr of a list.

Ans. (*a*) ; to simulate member primitive

```
→       (defun member1 (s l)
                (cond ((null l) 0)
                        ((equal s (car l)) l)
                        (t (member 1s (cdr l)))))
```

(*b*) (defun last-elem (l)

```
        (setq l2 nil)
        (cond ((null (cdr l)) (cons (carl) l2)
                (t (last-elem (cdr l)))))
```

(*c*) (defun append1 (l1 l2 & OPTIONAL l1 l2 & REST 1)

```
    (cond ((null l1) l2)
            (t (cons (car l1)
    (append 2 (cdr l1) l2)))))
```

(*d*) (defun keep (n l)

```
        (reverse (nth cdr (–(length l) n) (reverse l))))
```

Q. 17. Write LISP functions to get non-nested list from nested list.

Ans. → (defun linearize (l)

```
                (cond ((null l)  ( ))
```

```
((atom l) (cons l ( )))
(t (append (linearize (car l))
(linearize (cdr l))))))
(defun keep (n l)
(reverse (nthcdr (– (length l) n)
(reverse l))))
```

Q. 18. Write LISP program to find depth of a given list.

Ans.

```
(defun non-nested (list1)
(cond ((< max degree) (setf max degree)))
(cond ((atom (car list1)) (setf list2 (cons (car list1) list 2))
(cond ((equal (cdr list1) nil))
(t (non-nested (cdr list1)))
))
(t (cond ((equal list1 nil))
(t (setf degree (+ degree 1))
(non-nested (car list1))
(setf degree (– degree 1))
(cond ((equal (cdr list1) nil))
(t (non-nested (cdr list1 )))
))))))
(defun start nil
(setf max0
degree 1)
(print "Enter the list: ")
(setf list1 (read))
(setf list2 nil)
(non-nested list1)
(format t "The depth is ~a \n" max)
```

Q. 19. Write LISP program to find the union and intersection of two lists.

Ans.

```
; To find union of 2-sets
(defun read1 NIL
(format t "Enter your list1: ")
(setf l1 (read))
(format t "Enter your list2: ")
(setf 12 (read))
(set-union l1 l2))
(defun set-memp (e s)
(member e s))
(defun set-union (l1 l2)
(cond ((null l1) l2)
((set-memp (car l1) l2)
(set-union (cdr l1) l2))
```

```
                    (t (cons (car l1)    (set-union (cdr l1) l2)))))
            ; to find inter of 2-sets
    (defun set-memp (e s)
            (cond ((null s) nil)
                    ((atom e)    (member e s))
                            ((atom (car s))    (set-memp e (cdr s)))
                    ((subsetp e (car s)))
                    ((cond ((subsetp (car s) e) t)
            (t (set-memp e (cdr s)))))
        (t (set-memp e (cdr s)))))
    (defun read2 NIL
            (format t "Enter your list1: ")
            (setf l1 (read))
            (format t "Enter your list2: ")
                    (setf l2 (read))
                            (inter l1 l2))
    (defun inter (l1 l2)
            (cond ((null l1) nil)
                    ((set-memp (car l1) l2)
            (append (car l1) (inter (cdr l1) l2)))
        (t (inter (cdr l1) l2))))
```

Q. 20. Write LISP program called as sum-squares which uses mapcar to find sum of the squares of list of integers. The function takes a single list as its argument. (Use lambda and mapcar functions).

Ans.

```
(defun squares nil
    (print "Enter your list: ")
(setq lst (read))
(seft 1st1 (mapcar #'(lambda (x) (* x x)) 1st)
)    (sum1 1st1))
(defun sum1 (1st)
    (setq sum 0)
    (print "Sum of squares of list is: ")
(loop
        (cond ((endp 1st) (print sum) (read)))
        (setq p (car 1st))
        (setq sum (+ sum p))
        (setq 1st (cdr 1st))
        )    (read))
```

Q. 21. Write LISP program to do bubble sort on an array of size, n.

Ans. ;To sort an array-BUBBLE SORT

```
    (defun read1 nil
```

```
(format t "Enter your n: ")
(setf n (read))
(setf i 0)
(format t "Enter array elements: ")
(setq a (make-array n))
(dotimes (i n)
(setf (aref a i) (read ))) ; to read n-elements
(print a)
(sort1 a n)
(print "sorted vector is: ")
(print a)
(defun sort1 (a n)
(setf j (+ i 1))
(dotimes (i n a)
(dotimes (j n a)
(cond ((< (aref a i) (aref a j))
(setf temp (aref a i))
(setf (aref a i) (aref a j))
(setf (aref a j) (temp))
)
)
)
)
```

9.3 TURBO PROLOG AND ITS CONSTRUCTS

Programming Logic (or PROLOG) was invented by **Alian Colmerauer and his associates at the University of Marseilles during 1970s.** PROLOG uses the syntax of predicate logic to perform symbolic and logical computations. **Before we discuss the programming part of PROLOG, let us see some salient features of PROLOG:**

1. PROLOG is a declarative language: We encode the facts and relationships of the system under investigation, to make it a part of KB of the system. The user can thus query the system for information. **Please note that PROLOG resembles a database or query system.**
2. PROLOG uses the language of predicate calculus.
3. PROLOG handles lists and recursions naturally.
4. PROLOG language has in-built inference engine and automatic backtracking facility.
5. Parallelism is inherent in PROLOG.

In-built data types in PROLOG

1. **Char:** Character is enclosed between a pair of single quotes.

   For example: 'r', '%'
2. **Integer:** A whole number in the range of – 32768 to 32767. **Please note here that negative numbers must start with minus (–) sign and positive numbers may optionally start with a plus (+) sign.** For example, 1000, – 1000, 0, 1, 32767

3. **Real:** Positive or negative special character followed by digits.

For example: 999, 32768, 3.1419, 3e10

NOTE: Integers are automatically converted to real numbers whenever necessary.

4. **String:** Any set of characters enclosed within a pair of double quotes. Strings can include up to 255 characters.

Do you know? Turbo Prolog system reads strings from a file or builds up internally up to 64K characters long.

For example: "Computer Graphics".

5. **Symbol:** A sequence of letters (A to Z or a to z), digits (0 to 9) and the special character underscore (_).

For example: enrollment_number
"PM"
"Mahatma Gandhi"
u_v

NOTE: Symbols and string are treated identically within PROLOG system but are stored differently.

6. **Variables: A variable is a symbol which can be assigned different values at different stages of the execution of the program.**

Variable names in PROLOG must begin with an uppercase letter, after which there may be any number of letters (uppercase or lowercase), digits or the character underscore (_).

For example: Name, Age, Head, Tail, Father_name etc.

A variable may be **bound or free variable. In case a variable is currently assigned a value of any domain, it is said to be a bound variable. A free variable is one to which no value is assigned.**

NOTE: In-built predicates—free and bound—help to check whether a variable is free or bound.

7. **Reserved words:** PROLOG has some reserved words and must not be used in place of user defined names:

and, asserta, assertz, bound, clauses, database, domains, fail, findall, free, global, goal, if, include, not, or, predicate, readterm, retract.

Do you know? A single underscore (_) is a very special variable name and is called as an anonymous variable. It can be used in place of any other variable.

8. **Arithmatic operators and its hierarchy:** +, –, * and / are basic arithmatic operators in PROLOG. Let us see how they work—

Operand 1	Operand 2	Operator	Result
integer	integer	+, –, *	integer
integer	integer	+, –, *	real
real	integer	+, –, *	real
real	real	+, –, *	real
integer or real	integer or real	/	real
integer	integer	int division	integer
integer	integer	mod	integer

Precedence hierarchy

Rule 1: The parentheses are evaluated first.

If the expression includes sub-expressions within parentheses, the sub-expressions are evaluated first.

Rule 2: Operators *, /, div (integer), remainder (mod) are evaluated next. These are evaluated from left to right.

Rule 3: Operators + and – are evaluated next, again working from left to right.

9. Relational Operators

PROLOG uses <, <=, =, >, >= and < > or (not equal to) relational operators.

Within an expression, if there are more than one relational operator, operating are evaluated from left to right. **Please note that in PROLOG a relational expression can be a goal or subgoal** but Turbo Prolog does not permit the assignment of the result of the evaluation of a relational expression to another variable. So, the expression

digit = (x% 10) is not accepted.

Also note that the relational operator equal to (=) looks same as an assignment operator. How PROLOG distinguishes them. If the variable on the left is bound to a value, i.e., it is not a free variable then the system decides it to be relational equal to comparison otherwise assignment is done.

Structure of a PROLOG Program

Basic structure

domains

/*...domain statements...*/

predicates

/*...predicate statements...*/

goal

/*...subgoal1, subgoal2, etc...*/

clauses

/*...clauses (rules and facts)...*/

NOTE: If you don't include a goal in the program, Turbo Prolog will ask for a goal when the program is executed.

Facts have the general form as follows—

relation (object, object,...,object)

Rules have the general form as follows—

relation (object, object,..., object) if
relation (object,..., object) and
⋮
relation (object,...,object)

To be consistent with other versions of Prolog, if can be replaced by the symbol :–, and a comma (,) can be used instead of **and** and a semicolon (;) can be used instead of **or**.

For example: The following two are exactly equivalent

is_older (Person 1, Person 2) if
age (Person 1, Age 1) and
age (Person 2, Age 2) and
Age 1 > Age 2.

is same as

```
is-older (Person 1, Person 2):–
    age (Person 1, Age 1),
    age (Person 2, Age 2),
    Age 1 > Age 2.
```

Let us consider an example to understand this. The program is given and Turbo Prolog will solve the following compound goal:

likes (X, reading) and likes (X, Swimming).

```
domains
    person, hobby symbol
predicaies
    likes (person, hobby)
clauses
    likes(ellen, reading).
    likes(john, computers).
    likes(john, badminton).
    likes(leonard, badminton).
    likes(eric, swimming).
    likes(eric, reading).
```

Turbo Prolog searches from left to right in the first subgoal

likes(X, reading)

the variable X is **free** (its value is unknown) before Turbo Prolog attempts to satisfy the subgoal) but, on the other hand, the second argument, **reading** is known. Turbo Prolog will now search for a fact that can fulfil the demands in the subgoal.

The first fact is a match, so the free variable X will be bound to the relevant value in the first fact ellen.

likes(ellen, reading)

At the same time, Turbo Prolog places a pointer in the database indicating how far down the search procedure has reached.

Next, the second subgoal must be fulfilled. Since X is now bound to ellen. Turbo Prolog has to search for the "fact"

likes(ellen, swimming).

Turbo Prolog now attempts another solution of the first subgoal with X free once again. The search for a second fact that can fulfil the first subgoal starts from the place last marked (provided there are more untested possibilities).

The skill to bind variables and set them free again when backtracking and the use of pointers to mark backtracking points are substantial elements in Prolog's search strategies.

A prolog program is divided into 3 main sections—

(*a*) Clauses section.

(*b*) Predicates section.

(*c*) Domains section.

Clauses section includes all facts and rules that make up a program. Facts and rules with the same name must be placed together. **A collection of clauses defining a predicate is called as a procedure.** During execution, user is prompted to type in a goal after a goal. To find a solution for the entered goal, Prolog starts at the top of the clauses section, looking at each fact and rule sequentially as it searches for a possible match. For subsequent processing, Prolog system places internal pointers next to each clause that matches the current goal or subgoal. **A goal may in turn include two or more subgoals.** Normally, subgoals are connected with and (,) or or (;) logical operator. **If that clause fails to lead to a solution then PROLOG returns to the pointer and looks from that point onwards for another possible solution. This is called as backtracking.**

Predicates section

A predicate consists of one or more clauses. Clauses that belong to the same predicate must follow one another. In general, a predicate may be declared as—

```
predicate_name (arg-1, arg-2,…, arg_N)
```

If there are no arguments then there is no need of parentheses also. Only the predicate name is sufficient. Predicate name begins with a lowercase letter followed by a sequence of letters, digits and the special character underscore (_). A predicate name can be a maximum of 250 characters length.

Domains section

A user can use problem related meaningful names to domains even though for PROLOG they are same as in-built domains.

Usually, user-defined domain names are specified but the PROLOG system doesn't understand this. So, the user includes within the domains section information about these user-defined domain.

Lists in PROLOG

A list is a simple data structure which represents an ordered sequence of n number of elements. These elements are put in square brackets separated by commas. These elements may be integer, real, character, string or symbol.

Any list can be broken into two parts— 'head' and 'tail'. The first element is called as '**head**' and the rest of the list is called '**tail**'. The empty list is represented by [.]. In general, a list can be represented as—

[Head | Tail]

For example: [9, 10, 11, 12] →[9 | 10, 11, 12]

The tail can be further decomposed into head and tail, i.e.,

[9 | 10 | 11, 12]

Similarly, we can further decompose the list—

[9 | [10, | [11 | [12 | [ ]]]]

Many operations can be done on list..

PROGRAM 1. Write a PROLOG program to find the length of a given list.

SOLUTION. If the list is a null list, its length is zero. Else its length is one plus the length of its tail.

```
/* To find the length of a given list */
domains
    integerlist = integer*
    symbolist = symbol*
predicates
    length (symbolist, integer)
    length (integerlist, integer)
```

```
clauses
    length ([ ], 0)
    length ([ _ | Tail], N) if
        length (Tail, Nl),
        N = Nl + 1.
```

Explanation

The first clause in the clauses section translates the first line of the pseudo-code and means that in case the input list is a **null list** the resulting variable gets instantiated to zero and thus serves as a **terminating condition**. Otherwise, if it involves the predicate-length once more to find the length of the Tail of the current input list. This is called as **tail recursion**. A stage will be reached when the current input list will be a null list, the variable Nl gets instantiated to zero and for each recursion of the predicate-length one is added to generate the value of N, the output variable and thus the length of the given input list. **Please note here that integer* and symbol* are being used in the domains section. Integer*** means the domain is integer list. Similarly, for **symbol***, we mean the domain is symbollist.

PROGRAM 2. Write a PROLOG program to check if given element is a member of a given list.

SOLUTION.

```
        domains
            symbol_list = symbol*
            integer_list = integer*
            real_list = real*
            char_list = char*
        predicates
            member (symbol, symbol_list)
            member (integer, integer_list)
        clauses
            member (X, [X1 _ ])
            member (X, [ _ 1 Tail]) if
                        member (X, Tail)
```

OUTPUT

```
Goal: member (a, [a, b, c, d, e])
      Yes
Goal : member (a, [ ])
      No
Goal : member (X, [p, q, r])
      X = p
      X = q
      X = r
3 solutions
```

In goal-3, the successive elements of list are **bound** to the variable given as first argument.

The predicate **member** checks whether a particular element is present in a list or not. The predicate is defined as follows—

```
member (X, [X 1 _])
member (X, [_1 Tail]) :-
                member (X, tail).
```

How **member** predicate works?

Element E is a member of the list L if

(*a*) X is equal to the head of the list, L, or

(b) X is member of the tail of the list, L.

PROGRAM 3. Write a PROLOG program to append list L2 to list L1 and bind the result to L3.

SOLUTION.

```
includes "domains.pro" /* to add domains*/
predicates
    append (symbol_list, symbol_list, symbol_list)
    append (real_list, real_list, real_list)
    append (char_list, char_list, char_list)
    append (integer_list, integer_list, integer_list)
clauses
    append ([ ], L, L)
    append ([H1 | T1], L2, [H1 | T3]) if append (T1, L2, T3)
```

PROGRAM 4. Write a PROLOG code to find the last element of a given input list.

SOLUTION.

```
includes "domains.pro"
predicates
    last_object (symbol_list, symbol)
    last_object (real_list, real)
    last_object (char_list, char)
    last_object (integer_list, integer)
clauses
    last_object ([X], X)
    last_object ([– | Tail], X) if
                last_object (Tail, X).
```

PROGRAM 5. Write a PROLOG predicate to reverse the order of the elements of a given input list. **[MDU, BE (CSE) 6th Sem., Dec. 2007]**

SOLUTION.

```
reverse ([ ], [ ])
reverse ([X | Input_Tail], Output) if
    reverse (Input_tail, Output_tail),
    append (Output_Tail, [X], Output).
```

Goal:

```
reverse (['a', 'b', 'c', 'd'], L)
    L = ['d', 'c', 'b', 'a']
```

PROGRAM 6. Write a predicate to find the nth element of a given list.

SOLUTION.

```
nth_element ([H | _ ], 1, H)
nth_element ([_ | T], N, X) if
                N1 = N –1,
                nth_element (T, N1, X)
```

The first clause matches when the second argument is bound to an integer value of 1 and thus results in binding the head (H) of the given input list to the third argument and this serves as a terminating condition. Or else the second clause involves the predicate again, to look for (n – 1)th element of the Tail of the given list.

PROGRAM 7. Write a PROLOG program to find the area of a circle.

SOLUTION.

```
constants
      text= "Radius of circle is ="
      pi = 3.14159
      double = 2
predicates
      output (integer, real)
clauses
      output (0, _),
      output (N, R) if N > 0,
            C = 2 * pi * R,
            A = pi * R * R,
            write (text, R, "Circumference=", C, "Area =", A),
            nl,
            R1 = double * R,
            N1 = N – 1,
            output (N1, R1)
```

The constants are declared in the constants section. **But please remember the following points regarding constants–**

1. A constant cannot be expressed using itself.

   For example: length = length * 2.01

   will give an error.

2. Named constants must start with a lower letter.
3. Constants must be declared first before they are used.
4. There may be more than one constant declaration section.
5. There must not be mutiple definitions for the same named constant.

PROGRAM 8. Write a PROLOG program to find the sum of first n natural numbers, i.e., $\sum_{i=1}^{N} i.$

SOLUTION.

```
predicates
      add_upto (integer, integer)
```

```
clauses
        add_upto (1, 1)
        add_upto (N, Result) if
                        N > = 2,
                        N_1 = N–1,
                        add_upto (N_1, Res1),
                        Result = Res1 + N.
goals
        add_upto (3, Result)
                Result = 6
```

Note that the subgoal N > = 2, takes care of the situation when a user gives a negative number or even zero as the first argument.

PROGRAM 9. Write a LISP program to check if a given year is a leap year or not.

SOLUTION.

```
predicates
        run
        check_year (integer)
clauses
        run if
        write ("Enter the year"), n1,
        readint (y),
        check_year (y),
        write ("this is a leap year"), n1.
run if
        write ("this is not a leap year"), n1.
check_year (y) if
        0 = y mod 4, 0 < > y mod 100;
        0 = y mod 400.
goals :   run
        Enter the year : 1978
        "this is not a leap year"
```

PROGRAM 10. Write a Prolog program to find GCD of two positive integers.

SOLUTION.

```
predicates
        gcd (integer, integer, integer)
clauses
        gcd (M, O, M).
        gcd (M, N, Result):–
                Rem = M mod N,
                gcd (N, Rem, Result).
goals:
        gcd (6, 4, Result)
                Result = 2
```

```
goal2:
    gcd (24, 119, A)
    A = 1
```

PROGRAM 11. The LCM of two given positive integers is given by —

$$\text{LCM} = \frac{\text{multiplication of two numbers}}{\text{GCD of the two numbers}}$$

Write a PROLOG code for the same.

SOLUTION.

```
include "gcd.pro"
predicates
    lcm (integer, integer, integer)
clauses
    lcm (M, N, Result) if
        gcd (M, N, Res1),
    Result = M*N/Res1.
```

PROGRAM 12. Write a PROLOG code to find the factorial of a given number, n.

SOLUTION.

```
predicates
    factorial (integer, real)
    go
clauses
    go if
    Write ("Enter a positive integer number :"),
    readint (N),
    factorial (N, Result),
    Write ("Factorial of ", N, "is = ", Result).
    factorial (0, 1)
    factorial (N, Result) if N > 0,
                N1 = N – 1,
                factorial (N1, Res1),
                Result = N* Res1.
goals:
    factorial (6, Answer)
        Answer = 720
```

PROGRAM 13. Write a PROLOG code to find n^{th} fibonacci number.

SOLUTION.

```
predicates
    run (integer, integer)
    go
database
    f (integer, real)
clauses
    go :-   assert (f (1, 0)),
```

```
              assert (f(2, 1)), readint (N),
                     N>2, run (2, N).
    go : –
              write ("Enter a positive number greater than 2").
              run (I, N) if      I< N, I3 = I + 1,
                                 I1 = I3 – 1,
                                 I2 = I3 – 2,
                                 f(I1, A),
                                 f(I2, B), C = A + B
                                 assert (f(I3, C)), run (I3, N).
              run (N, N) if f (N, R),
                                 write ("Fibonacci", N, "is =", R), n1.
```

PROGRAM 14. Write a PROLOG code to solve Result = x^i.

SOLUTION.

```
predicates
        raised_to (real, integer, real)
clauses
        raised_to (_, 0, 1) if !
        raised_to (X, I, Result) if
                        N= I mod 2,
                        N = 0,
                        !, I1 = I div 2,
                raised_to (X, I1, Res1),
                Result = Res1 * res1;
                I1 = I – 1,
                raised_to (X, I1, Res),
                Result = X * Res.
goal
        raised_to (0, 1, L)
        L = 0
```

PROGRAM 15. Write a PROLOG code to find the maximum element of a list.

SOLUTION.

```
domains
        integerlist = integer*
predicates
        max (integerlist, integer)
clauses
        max ([X], X),
        max ([H! Tail], H):
                max (Tail, Max Tail), H>MaxTail.
        max (H! Tail], MaxTail):–
                max (Tail, MaxTail), H<=MaxTail.
```

```
goal:
        max ([1, 2, 3, 4, 5], LIST)
            LIST = 5
```

9.4 TURBO PROLOG PROGRAMMING EXAMPLES

Q. 1. Develop a mini telephone directory in PROLOG.

Ans.

```
predicates
        reference (symbol, symbol)
goal
        write ("Please type a name: "),
        readln (The_Name),
        reference (The_Name, Phone_No),
        write ("The phone no. is", Phone_No), n1,
clauses
        reference ("Albert", "01-123456").
        reference ("Betty", "01-569767").
        reference ("Card", "01-267400").
        reference ("Dorothy", "01-191051").
```

Q. 2. Write a recursive program to find the factorial of a number.

Ans.

```
domains
        n = real        /* Real nos. used for answer so answers greater
        f = real        than 32, 767 can be returned */
predicates
        factorial (n, f)
clauses
        factorial (1, 1)
        factorial (N, Res) if
            N > 1 and
            N1 = N – 1 and
            factorial (N1, FacN1) and
                    Res = N*FacN1.
```

Its working is shown now.

In the program, N1 = N – 1 should be regarded as a more readable form of the clause:

*(N1, –(N, 1))

where – is a functor. Thus N1 = N – 1 evaluates to true provided N1 is bound to the value of N – 1.

Let's investigate how factorial works when satisfying the goal

factorial (2, Answer)

Using the rule, we have

factorial (2, Res) if

2 > 1, N1 = 2 – 1, factorial (N1, FacN1), Res = 2*FacN1.

So we must evaluate the goal

factorial (1, FacN1).

Using the fact

factorial (1, 1).

the goal is satisfied by binding FacN1 to 1. In turn we now need to evaluate

Res = 2 * FacN1

which is solved with Res bound to 2 * 1, so the initial goal is satisfied with Answer bound to 2.

For a more complicated evaluation like

factorial (4, Answer)

we have the evaluation sequence

factorial (4, Res) if

4 > 1, N1 = 4 – 1, factorial (4 – 1, FacN1), Res = 4*FacN1

factorial (3, FacN1) if

3 > 1, N11 = 3 – 1, factorial (3 – 1, FacN11), Res = 3* FacN11

factorial (2, FacN11) if

2 > 1, N111 = 2 – 1, factorial (2 – 1, FacN111), Res = 2*FacN111

factorial (2 – 1, FacN111) succeeds with FacN111 bound to 1

factorial (3 – 1, FacN11) succeeds with FacN11 bound to 2

factorial (4 – 1, FacN1) succeeds with FacN1 bound to 6

factorial (4, Res) succeeds with Res bound to 24.

Hence, factorial (4 Answer) succeeds with Answer bound to 24.

Q. 3. Develop a piano using PROLOG to listen to tones on your computer.

Ans. Turbo Prolog has two standard predicates for making noises. The simplest takes the form beep and makes the computer beep. The other can be used to make more imaginative noises, and takes the form

sound (Duration, Frequency)

A note of the indicated frequency is played for Duration hundredths of second. Using the sound predicate we can turn the computer into a miniature piano, given the frequencies of various notes. In Program 1 we have done just that, using the frequencies shown in Table 9.1 and using the keys

```
   W  E      T   Y   U
 A  S  D  F    G   H   J  K
```

to mimic the normal piano keyboard layout. For example, pressing ASFGHJK (in that order) would produce a C major scale. Keys not on our pretend piano keyboard produce a high-pitched peep thanks to the clause

tone(_, 5000),

and thus only Ctrl Break interrupts the execution.

Table 9.1 The computer as piano

Note	Frequency	Keyboard Character
C (low)	131	A
C(sharp)	139	W
D	147	S

Note	Frequency	Keyboard Character
D(sharp)	156	E
E	165	D
F	175	F
F(sharp)	185	T
G	196	G
G(sharp)	208	Y
A	220	H
A(sharp)	233	U
B	247	J
C(middle)	262	K

```
predicates
        piano
        tone(char, integer)
goal
        piano.
clauses
        piano:–
                readchar(note), tone(Note, Freq), sound (S, Freq), piano.
        tone ('a', 131), tone ('w', 139), tone ('s', 147)
        tone ('d', 165), tone ('e', 156). tone ('f', 175)
        tone ('t', 185), tone ('g', 196). tone ('y', 208)
        tone ('h', 220), tone ('u', 233). tone ('j', 247)
        tone ('k', 262),
        tone (_,5000),    */all other keys squeak*/
/*Program below runs up and down a musical scale*/
    domains
        direction*up;down
    predicates
        jack_and_jiu (direction, integer)
    goal
        jack_and_jiu (up, 500),
    clauses
        jack_and_jiu (up, F):–
            F < 5000, !, sound (1, F), F1 = F + 200, jack_and_jiu (up, F1).
        jack_and_jiu (up, F):–
            jack_and_jiu (down, F).
        jack_and_ji11 (down, F):–
            F > 500, !, sound (1, F), F1 = F – 200, jack_and_jiu (down, F1).
        jack_and_jiu (down, F):–
            jack_and_jiu (up, F).
```

Q. 4. Write a Turbo Prolog program to simulate XOR gate.

Ans. Every logical circuit can be described with a Turbo Prolog predicate, where the predicate indicates the relation between the signals on the input and output terminals of the circuit. The fundamental circuits are described by giving a table of corresponding truth values (see the and_or_and not_circuit, and then check its operation with a Turbo Prolog program). The circuit is shown in Figure 9.1.

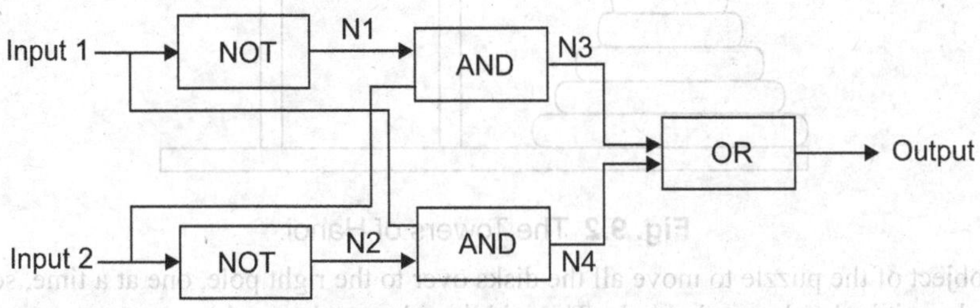

Fig. 9.1 Fundamental XOR circuit.

In program this network is described by the xor predicate

```
domains
        d = integer
predicates
        not_(D, D)
        and_(D, D, D)
        or_(D, D, D)
        xor (D, D, D)
clauses
        not_(1, 0). not (0, 1).
        and_(0, 0, 0). and (0, 1, 0). and_(1, 0, 0). and_(1, 1, 1).
        or_(0, 0, 0). or_(0, 1, 1). or_(1, 0, 1). or_(1, 1, 1).
        xor (input1, Input2, Output) if
                not_(Input1, N1) and not_(Input2, N2) and
                and_(Input1, N2, N3) and and_(Input2, N1, N4) and
                or_(N3, N4, Output).
```

Given the goal

xor (Input1, Input2, Output)

we obtain this result:

Input1 = 0, Input2 = 0, Output = 0
Input1 = 0, Input2 = 1, Output = 1
Input1 = 1, Input2 = 0, Output = 1
Input1 = 1, Input2 = 1, Output = 0
4 solutions

which verifies that the above circuit does indeed perform the task expected of it.

Q. 5. What is Towers of Hanoi problem? Write a PROLOG program to solve it.

Ans. TOWERS OF HANOI

The ancient puzzle of the Towers of Hanoi consists of a number of wooden disks and three poles attached to a baseboard. The disks each have different diameters and a hole in the middle large enough for the poles to pass through. In the beginning all the disks are on the left pole as shown in Fig. 9.2

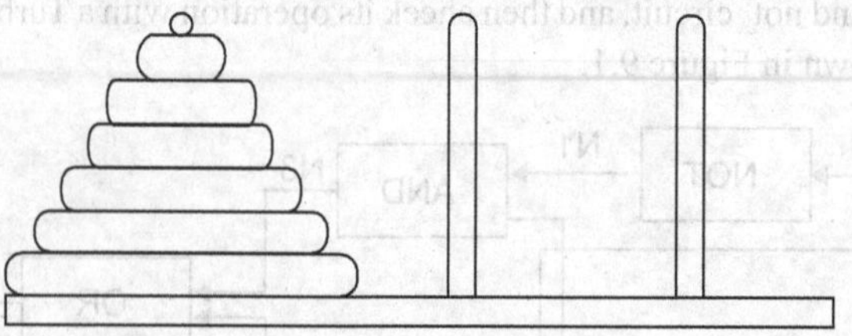

Fig. 9.2 The Towers of Hanoi.

The object of the puzzle to move all the disks over to the right pole, one at a time, so that they end up in the original order on that pole. The middle pole may be used as a temporary resting place for disks, but at no time is a larger disk to be on top of a smaller one. Towers of Hanoi can be easily solved with one or two disks, but becomes more difficult with three or more disks.

A simple strategy for solving the puzzle is—

- A single disk can be moved directly.
- N disks can be moved in three steps:
- Move N – 1 disks to the middle pole.
- Move the last disk directly over to the right pole.
- Move the N – 1 disks from the middle pole to the right pole.

Our Turbo Prolog program to solve the Towers of Hanoi puzzle uses three predicates: **Hanoi,** with one parameter that indicates just how many disks we are working with; **move**, which describes the moving of N disks from one pole to another using the remaining pole as a temporary resting place for disks; and **inform**, which displays what has happened to a particular disk.

```
domains
        loc = right ; middle ; left
predicates
            hanoi (integer)
            move (integer, loc, loc, loc)
            inform (loc, loc)
clauses
        hanoi (N) :– move (N, left, middle, right).
            move (1, A, _, C) :– inform (A, C),!
            move (N, A, B, C):–
                    N1 = N – 1, move (N1, A, C, B),
                            inform (A, C),
                            move (N1, B, A, C)
            inform (LOC1, LOC2):–
Write ("\n move a disk from ", LOC1, "to", LOC2).
```

To solve Towers of Hanoi with three disks,

We give the goal—

hanoi (3).

The output is—

Move a disk from left to right.

Move a disk from left to middle.

Move a disk from right to middle.

Move a disk from left to right.

Move a disk from middle to left.

Move a disk from middle to right.

Move a disk from left to right.

Q. 6. What is N-Queens problem? Write a PROLOG program to implement it.

Ans. THE N QUEENS PROBLEM

In the N Queens problem, we try to place N queens on a chessboard in such a way that no two queens can take each other. Thus, no two queens can be placed on the same row, column, or diagonal.

To solve the problem, we'll number the rows and columns of the chessboard from 1 to N. To number the diagonals, we divide them into two types, so that a diagonal is uniquely specified by a type and a number calculated from its row and column numbers:

diagonal = N * Column – Row (type 1)

diagonal = Row * Column – 1 (type 2)

When the chessboard is viewed with row 1 at the top and column I on the left side, type 1 diagonals resemble the "\"character is shape and type 2 diagonals resemble the shape of "/". The numbering of type 2 diagonals on a 4*4 board is shown in Fig. 9.3.

	1	2	3	4
1	1	2	3	4
2	2	3	4	5
3	3	4	5	6
4	4	5	6	7

Fig. 9.3 The N Queens chessboard.

To solve the N Queens problem with a Turbo Prolog program, we must record which rows, columns and diagonals are free and also make a note of where the queens are placed.

A queen's position is described with a row number and a column number, as in the domain declaration

queen = q (integer, integer)

to represent the position of one queen. To describe more position, we can make use of a list:

queens = queen*

Likewise, we need several numerical lists indicating the rows, columns and diagonals that are not occupied by a queen. These lists are described by:

freelist = integer*

We will treat the chessboard as a single object via the domains declaration:

board = board (queens, freelist, freelist, freelist, freelist)

freelist represents the free rows, columns and diagonals of type I, and the free diagonals of type 2, respectively.

By way of example, let's let board represent a 4*4 chessboard in two situations: (1) without queens and (2) with one queen at the top left corner.

1. board without queens

   board ([ ], [1, 2, 3, 4], [1, 2, 3, 4, 5, 6, 7], [1, 2, 3, 4, 5, 6, 7])

2. board with one queen

   board ([q (1, 1,)], [2, 3, 4], [1, 2, 3, 5, 6, 7], [2, 3, 4, 5, 6, 7])

The problem can now be solved by describing the relation between an empty board and a board with N queens. We define the predicate

placeN (integer, board, board)

with the two clauses below. Queens are placed one at a time until every row and column is occupied. This can be seen in the first clause, where the two lists of freerows and freecols are empty:

```
placeN (_, board (D, [ ], [ ], X, Y), board (D, [ ],  [ ], X, Y)):–!
placeN (N, Board1, Result) :–
        place_a_queen (n, Board1, Board2),
        placeN (N, Board2, Result).
```

In the second clause, the predicate place_a_queen gives the connection between Board1 and Board2. (Board2 has one more queen than Board1). We use the predicates declaration

place_a_queen (integer, board, board)

The core of the N Queens problem is in the description of how to add extra queens until all have been successfully placed, starting with an empty board. To solve this problem, we add the new queen to the list of those who are already placed:

[q (R, C) : Queens]

Among the remaining free rows, Rows, we need to find a row R where we can place the next queen. At the same time, R must be removed from the list of free rows resulting in a new list of free rows, NewR. This is formulated as

findandremove (R, Rows, NewR)

Correspondingly, we must find and remove a vacant column C. From R and C, the numbers of the diagonals can be calculated on which a queen in row R and column C is placed. Then we can determine if D1 and D2 are among the vacant diagonals.

The clause is shown below:

```
place_a_queen (N, board (Queens, Rows, Columns, Diag1, Diag2),
        board ([q (R, C) : Queens], NewR, NewS, NewD1, NewD2)):–
        findandremove (R, Rows, NewR),
        findandremove (C, Columns, NewC),
        D1=N + S – R, findandremove (D1, Diag1, NewD1),
        D2 = R + S – 1, findandremove (D2, Diag2, NewD2).
```

Program below is the complete program. It contains a number of smaller additions to define n queens, so we need only give a goal like

nqueens (5)

to obtain a possible solution (in this case, for placing five queens on a 5*5 board).

```
domains
        queen = q (integer, integer)
        queens = queen*
        freelist = integer*
        board = board (queens, freelist, freelist, freelist, freelist)
```

```
predicates
        placeN (integer, board, board)
        place_a_queen (integer, board, board)
        nqueens (integer)
        makelist (integer, freelist)
        findandremove (integer, freelist, freelist)
        nextrow (integer, freelist, freelist)
    clauses
        nqueens (N):–
            makelist (n, L), Diagonal = N * 2 – 1, makelist (Diagonal, LL),
            placeN (N, board ( [ ], L, L, LL, LL), Final), write (Final).
        placeN (_, board (D, [ ], [ ], D1, D2), board (D, [ ], [ ], D1, D2)):–
        placeN (N, Board1, Result):–
            place_a_queen (N, Board1, Board2),
            placeN (N, Board2, Result).
        place_a_queen (N, board (Queens, Rows, Columns, Diag1, Diag2),
                board ([q (R, C) : Queens], NewR, NewC, NewD1, NewD2)) :–
            nextrow (R, Rows, NewR),
            findandremove (C, Columns, NewC),
            D1 = N + C – R, findandremove (D1, Diag1, NewD1),
            D2 = R + C – 1, findandremove (D2, Diag2, NewD2),
        findandremove (X, [X | Rest], Rest).
        findandremove (X, [Y | Rest], [Y | Tail)):–
                findandremove (X< Rest, Tail).
        makelist (1, [1])
        makelist (N, (N ! Ret]):–
                        N1 = N – 1, makelist (N1, Rest).
        nextrow (Row, [Row : Rest], Rest).
```

Q. 7. Cryptic Arithmetic Puzzles

In crypt arith ematic problem, each letter stands for a unique digit and goal is to find that each digit such that the resulting numbers when added produce the represented result only. Constraint is that no two letters represent the same digit. An example of such a puzzle is —

```
  S E N D
+M O R E
---------
 M O N E Y
---------
```

Write a PROLOG program to accomplish the same.

[GGSIPU, B. Tech (CSE) 8th Sem. May 2010]

Ans.

```
 c3 c2 c1
  S E N D
+M O R E
---------
 M O N E Y
---------
```

From the problem, we can conclude that—

1. M = 1, sum of two unique single digits plus a carry (0 or 1) cannot be more than 19.
2. S is either 8 or 9, (S + M + c3) is greater than 9 (creates a carry digit M), M = 1, c3 = 0 or 1, (S + 1 + c3) > 9, so S + c3 > 8, if c3 = 1, S = 8, otherwise S = 9.
3. O = 0, as (S + M + c3) must be at least 10 to generate a carry and it cannot be 11, as O cannot be same as M.
4. N = E or N = E + 1, as N + E + O = E + 0 (zero). But N and E cannot have same digit, so N = E + 1. Also c2 = 1 (concluded).
5. Now for c2 = 1, (N + R + c1) > 9.or (N + R) > 8.
6. (N + R + c1) cannot be > 18, therefore E cannot be 9.

We can decide no additional constraint. From the point, we have to try all possible remaining digits, and solve the problem.

What letter we should pick up first. It is a better idea to decide a letter that occurs at most places. It is letter E in our case.

```
                         /* Cryptarithmetic puzzle */
domains
        i1 = integer*
predicates
        member (integer, i1)
        delete (integer, i1, i1)
        go
member_and_delete (integer, i1, i1)
mod_and_carry (integer, integer, integer, integer)
clauses
go if
        M = 1,
        O = 0,
        L = [2, 3, 4, 5, 6, 7, 8, 9],
        member (S, [8, 9]),
        member_and_delete (S, L, L0),
        member_and_delete (E, L0, L1),
        member_and_delete (D, L1, L2),
/* calculate possible value for Y */
        N = E + 1,
        E <> 9,
        mod_and_carry (D, E, Y, C1),
/* check that Y is one among available digits*/
        member (Y, L2),
        member (N, L2),
/* delete digit Y from the current list of digits */
        delete (N, L2, L21),
/* We know from observation that N = E + 1 */
```

```
            delete (y, L21, L3),
            member_and_delete (R, L3, _),
            N + R > 8,
            R2 = N + C1,
            C2 = 1,
            mod_and_carry (R2, R, E, C2),
            R3 = E +C2,
            mod_and_carry (R3, O, N, C3),
            R4 = S + 1,
            mod_and_carry (R4, C3, 0, 1),
            write (" ", S, E, N, D), nl, write (" ", M, O, R, E), nl,
            write (M, O, N, E, Y), nl, fail.
member (X, [X|_].
member (X, [_|T]) if member (X, T).
delete (X, [X|T], T).
delete (X, [Y|T], [Y | Z]) if delete (X, T, Z)
member_and_delete (X, L, R) if
            member (X, L),
            delete (X, L, R)
mod_and_carry (A, B, M, C) if
     S = A + B,
     M = S mod 10,
     C = S div 10.
```

Goal : go

```
  9 5 6 7
  1 0 8 5
 ---------
1 0 6 5 2
 ---------
No
```

Please note the output "No" here. "No" means that there is no more solution.

SUMMARY

LISP and PROLOG are the two main languages of AI. We learnt that LISP is procedural and PROLOG is logical and declarative programming language. The run-time system of PROLOG provides much of the services of an inference engine.

MULTIPLE CHOICE QUESTIONS [MCQs]

Q. 1. LISP stands for

(*a*) Linear Information Symbolic Processing

(*b*) List Processing

(*c*) Linear Processing

(*d*) None of the above.

Q. 2. LISP was invented by

(*a*) John McCarthy (*b*) John Mathew

(*c*) Barry Bochm (*d*) Jacobson.

Q. 3. 97 will be a

(*a*) Numeric atom (*b*) Symbolic atom

(*c*) List (*d*) Top element.

Q. 4. Quote informs the LISP interpreter that

(*a*) it should not be evaluated (b) it should be evaluated

(*c*) it should be printed (*d*) None of the above.

Q. 5. A function without a name, in LISP is

(*a*) Symbolic expression (*b*) Numeric expression

(*c*) Lambda expression (*d*) C-Expert.

Q. 6. PROLOG stands for

(*a*) Programming goal (*b*) Program logic

(*c*) Programming logic (*d*) None of the above.

Q. 7. A variable to which no value is assigned is called as a

(*a*) Bound variable (*b*) Free variable

(*c*) Numeric variable (*d*) Constant.

Q. 8. A PROLOG program is divided into 3 main sections–clauses, predicate and

(*a*) Domains section (*b*) Prolog section

(c) Body section (*d*) None of the above.

Q. 9. Named constants must start with a

(*a*) Lowercase letter (*b*) Uppercase letter

(*c*) Alphanumeric value (*d*) None of the above.

Q. 10. A predicate that inclues a subgoal which in turn invokes the same predicate again and again is called as

(*a*) Reversal (*b*) Recursion

(*c*) Backtracking (*d*) None of the above.

ANSWERS

1. (*b*)	**2.** (a)	**3.** (*a*)	**4.** (*a*)	**5.** (*c*)
6. (*c*)	**7.** (*b*)	**8.** (*a*)	**9.** (*a*)	**10.** (*b*)

CONCEPTUAL SHORT QUESTIONS WITH ANSWERS

Q. 1. Identify bound variables in the following code

```
(defun SUMSQ (P Q)
      (+ (* P P) (* Q Q))).
```

Ans. P and Q are bound variables. These get evaluated when the form gets evaluated.

Q. 2. Write a LISP code to find the roots of a given quadratic equation.

Ans.

```
→   (defun quad_roots (a b c) (( 1 3)
        (setq temp (sqrt (– (* b b) (* 4 a c))) (2 4))
        (list (/list (/ (+ (–b) temp) (* 2 a))
        (/ ( – (– b) temp) (* 2 a))))
```

Q. 3. Write LISP code to find fibonacci sequence till n.

Ans.

```
→   (defun (Fibo n))
        (cond (( = ? n 0) 0))
        (( = ? n 1) 1)
        (else (+ (Fibo (– 1)))
        (Fibo (– n 2))
```

Q. 4. Write a LISP program to find the transpose of a matrix.

Ans.

```
(defun empty_matrix_p(m)
        (null m))
    (defun add_column (column m)
        (if (empty_matrix_p (m)
            (mapcar #' list column)
            (mapcar #' cons column m)))
            (defun matrix_transpose (m)
                (if (empty_matrix_p m)
                    m
            (add_column (car m) (matrix_transpose (cdr m)))))
```

Please note here the definition of empty_matrix_p which checks if its argument is NIL.

Goal:

```
→   (matrix_transpose (list 1 2) (list 3 4))))
```

Q. 5. Write PROLOG code to concatenate two lists.

Ans.

```
append [(X | Y], Z, [X | W] :– append (Y, Z< W)
```

Goal:

```
? append ([1, 2, 3], [4, 5], A)
    A = [1, 2, 3, 4, 5]
```

Q. 6. Write a PROLOG program to find the roots of a given quadratic equation.

Ans. **predicates**

```
    run
    roots (real, real, real, real)
clauses
    run if
        write ("Enter coeff a : \n"),
        readreal (A),
        write ("Enter coeff b : \n"),
        read real (B),
```

```
                write ("Enter coeff c: \n"),
                readreal (C),
                        D = B * B – 4 * A * C,
                roots (A, B, C, D).
roots (O, B, C, _) if
        B <> O,
        write ("One root is :"),
                Root = – C/B,
                write (Root), n1.
roots (0, 0, _, _) if
        write ("Not a valid equation").
roots (A, B, _, O) if
        write ("Not a valid equation").
roots (A, B, _, O) if
        Root1 = – B/(2*A),
        Root2 = – B/(2*A),
        write ("First root is : ", Root1, "\n"),
        write ("Second root is : " Root 2, "\n")
roots (A, B, _, D) if
        D > 0.0,
        Root1 = (– B + sqrt (D)) / (2 * A),
        Root2 = (– B + sqrt (D)) / (2 * A),
        write ("First root is : ", Root1 ),
        write ("Second root is : ", Root2)
        ;
        write ("Roots are complex"),
        Real = – B/(2*A),
        Image = sqrt (–D))/(2 *A),
        write ("First root is : ", Real, "+i", Imag, "\n"),
        write ("Second root is : ", Real, "+i", Imag, "\n").
```

Q. 7. Design a medical diagnostic system in PROLOG.

Ans.

Chicken pox	–	Rash on face, mouth and throat
	–	Irritation in throat
	–	Moderate fever
	–	Rash spreads from face to limbs
	–	Center of rash is pearl-like dot
Measles	–	Severe redness of eye
	–	Breathlessness
	–	Rash on skin, face, mouth and throat
	–	High fever, redness of skin, drowsiness
Rickets	–	Deforming in chest

```
        –    Deforming in ribs
        –    Patient has fits
nowarnings
  domains
        disease, indication = symbol
        name = string
  predicates
        hypothesis (name, disease)
        symptom (name, indication)
        response (char)
        go
        loop
        go_once
  clauses
        go :–
              loop,
              go_once,
              write ("DO YOU WANT TO CONTINUE (Y/N)?"),
        go.
        loop.
        loop :–
              loop.
        go_once :–
              write ("Enter the patient name"), n1,
              readln (Patient),
              hypothesis (Patient, Disease),
              write (Patient, "has" Disease), n1,
        go_once :–
              write ("Sorry !!! I am unable to diagnose the disease"), n1.
        symptom (Patient, moderate_fever) :–                /* conclusion */
                    write ("Does", Patient," has moderate fever (y/n)?"),
                    response (C),
                    C = 'y'.
        symptom (Patient, irritation_in_throat) :–
              write ("Does", Patient," has Irritation in Throad (y/n) ?"),
              response (C),
              C = 'y'.
        symptom (Patient, rash_face_mouth_throat) :–
              write ("Does", Patient, "has rash on face, mouth & throat (y/n) ?"),
              response (C),
              C = 'y'.
        symptom (Patient, rash_spreads) :–
              write ("Does", Patient, "has rash that spreads from face to limbs (y/n) ?"),
```

```
symptom (Patient, rash_spreads) :–
        write ("Does", Patient," has rash on face, mouth and throat (y/n) ?"),
        respeonse (C),
        C = 'y'.
symptom (Patient, rash_spreads) :–
        write ("Does", Patient, "has rash that spreads from face to limbs (y/n) ?"),
        response (C),
        C = 'y'.
symptom (Patient, center_of_Rash) :–
        write ("Does ", Patient, " has center of rash that is pearl like dot (y/n) ?"),
        response (C),
        C = 'y'.
symptom (Patient, breathlessness) :–
        write ("Does ", Patient, " has Breadthlessness (y/n) ?"),
        response (C),
        C = 'y'.
symptom (Patient, severe_redness_eye) :–
        write ("Does ", Patient, " has severe redness of eye (y/n) ?"),
        response (C),
        C = 'y'.
symptom (Patient, deform_chest) :–
        write ("Does ", Patient, " has deformation in chest (y/n) ?"),
        response (C),
        C = 'y'.
symptom (Patient, deform_ribs) :–
        write ("Does ", Patient, " has deformation in ribs (y/n) ?"),
        response (C),
        C = 'y'.
symptom (Patient, has_fits) :–
        write ("Does ", Patient," has fits (y/n) ?"),
        response (C),
        C = 'y'.
symptom (Patient, high_fever_redness_eye_drowsiness) :–
        write ("Does ", Patient, " has high fever, redness in eye & drowsiness
        (y/n) ?"),
        response (C),
        C = 'y'.
symptom (Patient, rash_skin_face_mouth_throat) :–
        write ("Does ", Patient, " has rash on skin, face, mouth & throat (y/n) ?"),
        response (C),
        C = 'y'.
hypothesis (Patient, rickets) :–
        symptom (Patient, deform_chest),
```

```
            symptom (Patient, deform_ribs),
            symptom (Patient, has_fits),
    hypothesis (Patient, measles) :–
            symptom (Patient, high_fever_redness_eye_drowsiness),
            symptom (Patient, rash_skin_face_mouth_throat),
            symptom (Patient, breathlessness),
            symptom (Patient, severe_redness_eye).
    hypothesis (Patient, chickenpox) :–
            symptom (Patient, higmoderate_fever),
            symptom (Patient, irritation_in_throat),
            symptom (Patient, rash_spreads),
            symptom (Patient, center_of_Rash),
            symptom (Patient, rash_face_mouth_throat).
    response (C) :–
            readchar (C),
            write (C),
            nl.
goal
    go.
```

EXERCISE QUESTIONS

Q. 1. Explain the list manipulation features in LISP.

[U.P.T.U., B. Tech (CSE)-8th Sem., 2006-07]

Q. 2. Set up a small rule-based to advise graduates as to what courses they need to take to satisfy the requirements for an M.Sc. in Computer Science (or to satisfy the requirements for a B. Tech in Computer Engineering). It will be necessary to consult an expert advisor to get all requirements. Use PROLOG/C/C++/JAVA as the programming language. Include explanations for the user.

[GGSIPU, B. Tech (CSE)-8th Sem., May 2008]

Q. 3. Write LISP program to convert Centigrade temperature to Fahrenheit.

[MDU, BE (CSE)-8th Sem., Dec. 2006]

Q. 4. Discuss the features of LISP and PROLOG programming languages. To which generation of programming languages these two languages belong?

[MDU, BE (CSE)-6th Sem., May 2007]

Q. 5. What do you mean by flat list and association list in the context of LISP?

[**Hint:** A list of cons pairs is known as an **association list**. A property list is a flat list of even length with alternating keys and values]

Q. 6. Define a predicate: Construct a predicate using "C" language.

[GGSIPU, B. Tech. (CSE)-8th Sem., May 2011]

10 CHAPTER

TESTING AI PROGRAMS

10.0 INTRODUCTION

Testing is the process of executing the programs with the intent of finding faults. But AI programs are quite big and complicated programs. So, careful and extensive testing is mandatory.

10.1 GOLDEN (OR IDEAL) STANDARD

AI programs try to show **intelligence,** i.e., intelligent behavior. To measure an AI program, we define an **ideal or gold standard** of behavior against which an AI program can be measured. Because AI programs or ES try to automate things done by humans, so it is better that humans only test these programs. **For example,** for medical diagnosis, there are doctors that are authorities in their subfield, for students there are expert teachers and so on. Sometimes there are no single human expert but different people are expert on different pieces of a problem. We can pool their expertise.

Many humans are against their replacement by a computer unless they are rewarded. **Please understand that it is important to give the humans and the computers the same problem to work on.** Then we can **compare results** and mark any discrepancy as wrong. **Also note that if our graders do not know themselves results were by computers and which by humans and only some supervisors know then we have a double-blind test technique.** It is a good form of testing and is used in medical research. We now list some methods that require a gold (or ideal) standard and some which do not.

A. Methods requiring a gold standard

(*a*) Traces.

(*b*) Confusion matrices.

(*c*) Comparison of a near miss and example—

1. No numbers involved.
2. Composite results.
3. Numbers involved.

(*d*) Comparison of two examples—

1. No numbers involved.
2. Composite results.
3. Numbers involved.

B. Methods NOT requiring a gold standard—

(*a*) Schema for rules and facts.

(*b*) User-initiated debugging questions.

(*c*) Cooperativeness evaluation.

(*d*) A priori suitability for AI techniques.

These are the tools for testing and debugging.

10.2 TEST CASES AND CORPUS

After the establishment of gold standard, it is necessary to test an AI system in many ways or against many situations. **These situations are called as cases or test cases and a set of cases used for testing is called a corpus. Please note that the more complicated the program, the more cases we should run.** It is important to test a representative spectrum of cases. **Also note that it is desirable to have at least one test case for each major program behavior for each significant combination of inputs and for each significant kind of output.** Because this isn't always possible so judgement is required to reach a compromise. Then for each test case, we must be able to identify a clear outcome.

10.3 BUGS AND BUGS

Testing performance on a set of test cases creates two categories—

CAT 1: Cases for which the standard and the program agree and cases for which they disagree.

CAT 2: Examine program failures and try to identify characteristics that distinguish them from "successes". This helps debug our program.

Many tools also help here. One tool is **trace information** i.e., the record of reasoning done about a test case (or case). Rules that appear often in failure cases are suspect. Search problems provide partial traces in their state sequence or operator-sequence output. But ES usually give a single answer and can be considerably enhanced with the trace of what rules were used in reaching the answer. Nearly all PROLOG dialects have **in-built tracing facilities.**

Confusion matrix

It is helpful with rule-based systems. **It summarizes not only when the program went wrong but how it went wrong.**

In this matrix, **program results were grouped into categories and cross-tabulated with the gold standard. Rows** represent gold-standard categories and **columns** represent program-result categories. **Please understand that the entry in row-*i* and column–*j* is the number of times the program gave an answer in category–*j* when the standard gave an answer in category–*i*.** Thus, a confusion matrix shows which categories tend to be confused with which other categories and suggest where rule improvements are needed.

The need is to exploit pairs of similar cases. Such pairs are helpful in testing and debugging of AI programs. They can localize problems and provide generalizations.

A **critical test case pair** is when the standard and the program disagree on one case but agree on a very similar case. In other words, whenever failing cases are near misses to success then the reason for the failure then must lie in the small difference in characteristics of the two cases which helps locate the source of the bug.

> **NOTE:** (*a*) Pairs of similar cases can also suggest rule generalizations, i.e., a kind of **learning.**
>
> (*b*) Research is going on to build rule-based systems automatically from examples and non examples defining appropriate behavior. This field is named as automatic programming within AI.

If running an AI program gives a result with components then evaluating the difference between the program and the gold standard is a little more complicated. Two cases arise—

Case 1: If the pieces of the result are independent then the program and standard can be compared separately for each pieces, as for a relaxation application in which the result is separate possibility lists for variables.

Case 2: If the pieces of the result are linked in data structure then structures must be matched to establish corresponding components before comparison as for a search application in which we must match the list of program operators with the list of gold standard operators in corresponding order. In either case, only the pieces that do not match need be studied further.

For example, say, for some search problem the gold standard finds the operator sequence

[*a*, *b*, *c*, *d*, *e*, *f*, *g*, *h*]

While the program result is—

[*a*, *b*, *r*, *s*, *d*, *c*, *e*, *f*, *h*]

Please note that three things seem to be different in the program result—

(*a*) additional operators *r* and *s* have been **inserted** after action *b*.

(*b*) operators *c* and *d* have been **interchanged.**

(*c*) operator *g* has been omitted.

Also note that now we should focus our attention on the parts of the search program that affect those things. Hence, we should check the conditions controlling selection of *r* and *s* to see why they were erroneously fulfilled and check the conditions on *g* to see why it was erroneously omitted. The switch of *c* and *d* suggests a mistake in the priority of those two operators.

Actually, numbers like probabilities, evaluation functions and cost functions etc. complicate comparisons of a **program** and a **gold standard.** Three ways to handle them are:

1. We can use the numbers to pick a **"best program result"** and compare this to the gold standard.

   For example:

   (*a*) For a diagnosis ES that assigns probabilities to diagnoses, we can take the diagnosis with the **highest probability.**

   (*b*) For a **search program** that finds paths to a goal, we can take the **lowest-cost path.**

2. We can treat the numbered items as a composite structure as discussed earlier.

   For example: For an ES that concludes that diagnoses *a*, *b*, *c*, and *d* are probable with probabilities 0.9, 0.7, 0.6 and 0.3 respectively, while a gold standard rates them 0.8, 0.5, 0.6 and 0.2 respectively, we can focus the debugging on *b* and *c* because their numbers are out of order.

3. We can do **statistical analysis.**

   For example: We can take the **sum of the squares** of the deviations of the program-result numbers to measure closeness of the program and the standard.

Thus, we can now quantify any proposed program improvement by this criterion. So, it can be used as an evaluation function in a **search** for a better program.

10.4 PREVENTION BETTER THAN CURE

It is said that an ounce of prevention is worth 1.07 pounds of fixes (estimates). Hence, it is very important that an AI programming environment provide software tools to help programmer avoid mistakes. For rule-based expert systems, we can use rule frames or scripts to capture the frequently strong structural similarities between different rules.

For example., rules in car–repair diagnosis system usually go like this—

1. **Localize the problem** in a part of the car.
2. **Ask** about **easily observable symptoms.**
3. **Ask about symptoms** (if required) that take a little work to establish like opening up an object.
4. **Ask about experimental actions** that need to be done to confirm the diagnosis.

For example :

diagnosis ('dead battery'):—

electrical–prob, lights–dead, not (battery-corroded),

battery–voltage–low.

Please understand that a programmer writing a new car–diagnosis rule can be provided with this list of four things as a guide or template. Or the system could automatically find analogous rules to a new rule a programmer wants to write.

Tip: Inheritance on a hierarchy of rule–class frames is helpful here.

But please understand that a gold standard of performance for an AI program can be hard to get and costly to use. At the start of debugging process, a more creative approach to performance analysis using explanation facilities is better.

NOTE: In AI development software like ESs **packages** and **shells** this is quite common.

After a program is run, these facilities can report on what your program did, how it reached a particular conclusion or why it considered a particular line of reasoning and not another. **Please note that such explanations can be helpful even when the system is fully debugged.** They help people understand the system better, use it more effectively and have more confidence in its results. **Also note that the right answers are not the only criterion we have for evaluating an AI program.** Other things like how much user-friendly it is. The **tool** used here is very common one– **Questionnaires** for its measurement. The following issues may be considered—

Q. 1. Is the output comprehensible?

Q. 2. Can the program explain its reasoning well?

Q. 3. Does the program catch common user mistakes?

Q. 4. Does the program guess well what the user meant in a mistake?

Q. 5. Does the program use specialised jargon?

10.5 GUIDELINES FOR AI–PROGRAM SUITABILITY

AI–Testing is also not 100 per cent **exhaustive.** This is due to the fact that the number of paths in a search tree are **exponential.** Furthermore, AI techniques and programs cannot solve everything. Sometimes the problem's suitability is also unknown. **But the following guidelines can help—**

1. **A problem suitable for AI–method must be completely defined to have a clear criteria for success and failure.** Else it is difficult to tell when it's working and it is difficult to test it.

   For example : An ES could create works of art but it would be hard to evaluate as there is lot of disagreement between art experts.

2. **The desired program behavior must be sufficiently stable to permit cost-effective testing.**

   For example : An ES to recommend stock-market investments would be hard to build because investment opportunities are **constantly changing.**

3. **It must be possible to use the program routinely.** This is obvious but often overlooked.

   For example : Implementation of most of the **battle management systems** is a bad idea because it is very difficult to keep them correctly and quickly informed of everything that is happening in a battle even though the prototype implementations for artificially constructed scenarios might seem to work well.

4. **An AI–program (or a system) must NOT be a reductionist in a fatal way:**

   Reductionism is defined as the extent to which an AI–program fails to capture subtleties of human behavior it is trying to imitate. A highly reductiorist program may be safe when its users thoroughly understand its limitations but can be very dangerous otherwise.

   For example : a significantly reductionist battle management system could order troops to fire on themselves or be vulnerable to sabotage in surprising ways.

5. **AI techniques should generally not be used when processing time, storage space or calculation accuracy is critical.**

   The techniques and programs are complicated and often probabilistic or heuristic. A working AI–program can often be optimized or complied to run faster, take up less space or make more accurate conclusions. But the main idea of AI is to provide "intelligence" in computers first and efficiency later.

   > **Tip:** Humans are much more intelligent than computers as humans make computers intelligent. Otherwise a computer is just like a dead piece of hardware.

   For example : A **robot-warplane** that is an autonomous military aircraft controlled by real-time AI–software is **not** likely to work fast enough because things happen too fast in a battle. A large computer imposes a weight penalty on the aircraft.

6. **An AI–program must be sufficiently complicated but not over-complicated.** This is required if we want AI-techniques to do better than other approaches.

   For example : It is a **poor idea** to write a search program to fix flashlights because people can figure it out themselves. But an ES to replace all doctors isn't reasonable because there are millions of diseases and millions of symptoms.

10.6 TESTING PROLOG PROGRAMS

To test a PROLOG program, first of all ensure that **every clause is exercised by at least one of the tests.** If the procedure is developed by CASE ANALYSIS then testing is even simpler—

"We identify an item of test data to exemplify each case. We use the outcome of the third stage of case analysis in which we identified the processing required for each case, to predict the result of each test". **Please understand that in this process of software testing, it is essential that you identify the correct outcome before running the test.** Otherwise, it is too easy to persuade yourself that the observed result is the correct one.

> **NOTE:** Every programmer shows a natural reluctance to admit that his creations (of programs) are faulty.

We are in a position to solve an example now.

EXAMPLE 1: Consider the following PROLOG program—

```
% reduce (Input–list, count–of-output, previous–better, output-list)

    reduce (–, 4, –, []) : – ! .
    reduce ([], –, –, []) : – ! .
    reduce ([Current | Others], Count, –, Code): –
        vowel–h–w–y (current), ! ,
        reduce (Others, Count, Current, Code).
    reduce ([Letter | Others], Count, Letter, Code): !,
        reduce (Others, Count, Letter, Code).
    reduce ([Current | Others], Count, –, [Current | Code]):-
        N is Count + 1,
        reduce (Others, N, Current, Code).
        vowel_h–w–y (97)                          % "a"
        vowel–h–w–y (101),                        % "e"
        vowel–h–w–y (105).                        % "i"
        vowel_h–w–y (111).                        % "o"
        vowel–h–w–y (117).                        % "u"
        vowel–h–w–y (104).                        % "h"
        vowel–h–w–y (119).                        % "w"
        vowel–h–w–y (121)                         % "y"
```

How will you test this reduce/4 procedure of PROLOG? Develop some test cases.

Ans 1: Three recursive cases are observed—

Case 1: ?–reduce ([97, 98], 1, _, Res).

Res = [98];

no

Case 2: ?–reduce ([98, 99], 1, 98, Res).

Res = [99];

no

Case 3: ?–reduce ([98, 99], 1, 10, Res).

Res = [98, 99];

no

Let us see the test data now.

Test Case	Test Data (in a Call)	
	Arguments Input	Expected Result
1. Current letter is a vowel, "*h*", "*w*" or "*y*".	[97, 98] 1 _	[98]
2. Current letter is the same as the preceding one.	[98, 99] 1 98	[99]
3. Catch–all	[98, 99] 1 100	[98, 99]

NOTE: ASCII Codes : 97 = "*a*"
98 = "*b*"
99 = "*c*"
100 = "*d*"

The table above shows the test data for recursive clauses of the procedure for reduce/4.

Please note that in these tests, we test the second base case indirectly as the recursive cases reduce the input argument to the empty list. Also we could exercise the clause for the **first base directly** by a test such as:

? – reduce ([99], 4, _, Res).

Expected Result is: –

Res = [ ];

no

However, it is better to test it indirectly by calling the procedure with an input list for which we expect a list of the maximum length to be produced without exhausting the input. In this way, we thoroughly check the arithmetic in the clause for the catch-all case:–

? – reduce ([98, 99, 100, 102, 103], 1, 99, Res).

Res = [98, 99, 100];

no

SUMMARY

This chapter pervades on how to test a PROLOG program, how to find faults and how to describe its behavior. We learnt that the expected result of a test must be identified before the test is run. A PROLOG program should be **tested incrementally** as its component procedures are written. Many errors are due to minor typing mistakes. The procedure box model is a view of how a PROLOG program is executed. The procedural behavior of a PROLOG program is very complex. In debugging mode a great deal of information is displayed. To avoid being overwhelmed with information, firstly narrow the potential sources of a program error and then make careful use of leashed execution and of **spy–points** when running the debugging system. An **enhanced interpreter** for debugging can make fault-finding easier but is liable to ask too many questions to the programmer.

MULTIPLE CHOICE QUESTIONS [MCQs]

Q. 1. Testing is defined as–

(*a*) Process of taking inputs and producing outputs.

(*b*) Process of executing the program with the intent of finding faults.

(*c*) Process of showing intelligent behaviour of a program.

(*d*) None of the above.

Q. 2. Method requiring gold standard is–

(*a*) Traces (*b*) Schema for rules and facts.

(*c*) Cooperativeness Evaluation. (*d*) All of the above.

Q. 3. A set of test cases used for testing is called as a–

(*a*) Corpus (*b*) Torus (*c*) Porous (*d*) None of the above.

Q. 4. Which of the following is a tool–

(*a*) Trace Information (*b*) Traces

(*c*) Rules (*d*) None of the above.

Q. 5. A PROLOG program should be tested–

(*a*) Individually (*b*) Slowly (*c*) Incrementally (*d*) None of the above

ANSWERS

1. (*b*) **2.** (*a*) **3.** (*a*) **4.** (*a*) **5.** (*c*)

CONCEPTUAL SHORT QUESTIONS WITH ANSWERS

Q. 1. How is testing a deterministic procedure different from a non–deterministic procedure?

Ans. If a procedure is deterministic then we must always reject the first answer that PROLOG produces. If the procedure is deterministic then there will be no alternatives.

If a procedure is non–deterministic then one must ensure that it can indeed be called with all the patterns of arguments you envisage and that it produces exactly the intended alternative answers. Testing a non-deterministic what it does after it has exhausted the alternative answers, so test data (though it must be complex enough to exercise the procedure fully) must not be so elaborate that it is impractical for all answers to be enumerated. This is particularly important in case of procedures for utility predicates which we expect to be used to generate values.

Q. 2. What is debugging? How is it more important in PROLOG?

Ans. Debugging is the process of finding and correcting our mistakes. A characteristic of programming is the mismatch between cause and effect:–

"A small fault can make a large program produce wildly inaccurate results."

This is very true in case of PROLOG too where typing mistakes will alter the meaning of a program only, instead of giving rise to faulty syntax.

Tip: Proof-read your program carefully.

Some common errors made in a PROLOG program include—

1. Mis-spelling of functor of a structure or the name of a variable.
2. Typing."instead of ", before the last of a series of conjoined subgoals.
3. Omitting "," between arguments.

   [This mistake results in a procedure call of the wrong arity]
4. Typing a variable with an initial lower case letter. The supposed variable becomes an atom and does not match as intended.

Q. 3. What is documentation?

Ans. Documentation of a **predicate** describes the declarative view (in terms of the form of the arguments and the relationship between them). Documentation of a **procedure** states restrictions on the declarative view and describes the techniques used in writing a program.

If a procedure can be used non-deterministically, we document the order of the answers it produces.

EXERCISE QUESTIONS

Q. 1. Write a Turbo–Prolog program to find factorial of a number, *n*. Develop a set of test cases for the same.

Q. 2. Distinguish between a test case and a corpus.

Q. 3. What common errors do occur in PROLOG program that results in serious situations?

Q. 4. What additional guidelines do you follow to test AI programs?

Q. 5. What is documentation in PROLOG programming?

APPENDIX – A

GGSIPU

DWARKA

END-TERM EXAMINATION

Eighth Semester (B. Tech.) May 2008

Paper Code: ETCS 402 | ***Subject: Artificial Intelligence***

Paper ID : 27402 | ***(Batch: 2004)***

Time : 3 Hours | ***Maximum Marks : 75***

Note: Attempt any five questions including Q. No. 1 which is compulsory.

Q. 1. (*a*) What is Turing's Test. Explain its significance. **(5)**

(*b*) How fuzzy logic is better than Boolean logic in capturing uncertainty? **(5)**

(*c*) Briefly mention the components of a typical expert system. **(5)**

Q. 2. (*a*) Give an example of a real-world problem which can be effectively solved by "Hill Climbing Algorithm". Explain the items plateau and ridge. **(8)**

(*b*) Construct a semantic net representation of the following:

- Rajesh is Indian, Rajesh is a lecturer.
- Vikram lent his new video CD to his brother-in-law.

Q. 3. (*a*) Why knowledge acquisition is considered as most difficult step in Knowledge Engineering? Discuss different tasks performed by knowledge engineer. **(8)**

(*b*) Explain the significance of conjunctive normal form. Translate the following sentence into CNF: "There exists a dog which doesn't produce milk". **(7)**

Q. 4. Set up a small rule-based to advise graduates as to what courses they need to take to satisfy the requirements for an M.Sc. in Computer Science (or to satisfy the requirements for a B. Tech in Computer Engineering). It will be necessary to consult an expert advisor to get all requirements. Use PROLOG/C/C++/Java as the programming language. Include explanations for the user. **(15)**

Q. 5. (*a*) Design a learning automation that selects TV channels based on day of week and time of day (three evening hours only) based on preference of your family. (Specify the preferences of your family clearly).

(*b*) Explain the difference of genetic operators inversion, crossover and mutation. Which operator do you think is most effective in finding the optimal population in least time? **(8)**

Q. 6. (*a*) Briefly explain any of the expert system R1 (XCON) or Mycin. **(8)**

(*b*) Why it is difficult to make inferences in non-monotonic reasoning as compared to monotonic reasoning? Explain by taking an example. **(7)**

Q. 7. (*a*) What do you understand by Grammar? Explain different types of grammars. Give a parse tree for the sentence "Bill loves the frog", where the following rules are used: **(15)**

S → NP VP

NP → N

NP → DET N

VP → V NP

DET → the

V → loves

N → bill/frog

Q.8 Explain the following: **(15)**

(*a*) Different types of learning (*b*) Conceptual dependency

END-TERM EXAMINATION

Eighth Semester (B. Tech.) May 2008

Paper Code: ETCS 402 *Subject: Artificial Intelligence*

Paper ID : 27402 *(Batch: 2004-2005)*

Time : 3 Hours *Maximum Marks : 75*

Note: Q. No.1 is compulsory. Attempt any one question from each unit.

Q. 1. (*a*) If the Turing Test is passed, does this show that computer exhibits Intelligence? State reasons. **(3)**

(*b*) How declarative knowledge is different from procedural knowledge? **(3)**

(*c*) Discuss the importance of heuristics in problem solving. **(3)**

(*d*) Explain learning by induction with an example. **(3)**

(*e*) Assuming that Diabetes starts usually at the age of 40 years, construct a fuzzy set of "Young Diabetic Patients". **(3)**

UNIT-I

Q. 2. (*a*) Explain Means End Analysis with an example. **(7)**

(*b*) What do you understand by admissible heuristic? Develop an admissible heuristic for any problem of you own. **(8)**

Q. 3. (*a*) Compare uninformed search with informed search. **(7)**

(*b*) Discuss problem reduction strategy of problem with an example. **(8)**

UNIT-II

Q. 4. (*a*) Explain why these two sentences cannot be unified (i) p(x) v (q (f(x)) ^ r(y)) (ii) p(x) v (q (x) ^ r (s)). **(5)**

(*b*) Compare knowledge representation to data representation in a database. **(5)**

(*c*) Construct a semantic net representation of following: "Gopal is Indian, Gopal is a lecturer". **(5)**

OR

Q. 5. (*a*) Create a script about shopping in a super market. **(5)**

(*b*) Write down a substitution which unifies the following sentences:

(*i*) likes (homer, dinner (x)) ^ (today (A) → dinner (x)).

(*ii*) Likes (homer, dinner (cooked by (g))) ^ (today (z) → dinner (cooked_by (marge))). **(5)**

(*c*) What is slot in a frame? **(5)**

UNIT-III

Q. 6. (*a*) Discuss major advantages and disadvantages of fuzzy logic. **(5)**

(*b*) Describe ATN. (5)

(*c*) Discuss various means of handling uncertainty.

Q. 7. (*a*) How is non-monotonic reasoning different from monotonic reasoning? **(5)**

(*b*) Compare Top-down v/s Bottom-up parsing. **(5)**

(*c*) How probabilistic reasoning handles uncertainty. **(5)**

UNIT-IV

Q. 8. (*a*) Explain learning automation with an example. **(7)**

(*b*) Explain the architecture of an expert with a diagram. **(8)**

OR

Q. 9. (*a*) Can a system be developed for problem solving for which there does not exist a practically feasible algorithm? Discuss with any case study. **(8)**

(*b*) What are different types of learning? **(7)**

END-TERM EXAMINATION

Eighth Semester (B. Tech.) May 2008

Paper Code: ETCS 402 *Subject: Artificial Intelligence*

Paper ID : 27402 *(Batch: 2004-2005)*

Time : 3 Hours *Maximum Marks : 75*

Note: Q. No.1 is compulsory. Attempt any one question from each unit.

Q. 1. Give a short answer: **(3 × 5 = 15)**

(*a*) Classify the following search algorithm as intelligent/non-intelligent. Give reason of your answer: Depth first search, best first search, branch and bound search.

(*b*) How can you classify the knowledge? What is an inference engine?

(*c*) What are the merits/demerits of semantic net over semantic frames?

(*d*) What are the different steps for natural processing?

(e) List various application areas where Neural network is used.

UNIT-I

Q. 2. (*a*) Compare depth first search and Hill Climbing search procedures. **(3)**

(b) Explain the advantages of Best first search over Hill Climbing with suitable example. **(5)**

(*c*) What are the steps to solve constraint satisfaction problem? Explain them with help of crypt arithmetical problem. **(7)**

OR

Q. 3. (*a*) Explain the process to reach goal state of a search tree which is AND/OR graph. Give an example of application whose search tree is AND/OR graph. **(8)**

(*b*) Explain the Means and Analysis algorithm. Give an example of an application where it is applied. **(7)**

UNIT-II

Q. 4. (*a*) Explain the rules to unify two predicates. **(3)**

(*b*) Represent following facts as predicates and convert them to clause form, explaining the steps of conversion: **(5)**

(*i*) Any student who is intelligent or hard working will pass the exam in good marks.

(*ii*) Anyone who is passed with good marks gets a job.

(*c*) Assume that "Shiva is neither hard working nor intelligent". Using resolution prove that Shiva does not get a job. **(7)**

OR

Q. 5. (*a*) What kind of knowledge is represented by the semantic nets? Give an example of knowledge base represented by semantic nets and explain how inferences are done in semantic Nets. **(8)**

(*b*) Give an example of a game Tree. What is the purpose of Minimax procedure in game tree? What are Alpha Beta cutoff? **(7)**

UNIT-III

Q. 6. (*a*) Consider the following sentences: **(5)**

Most birds fly unless they have broken wings

Penguins and Ostrich do not fly.

Crow is a bird

Use Non-monotonic reasoning to answer "Does Crow Fly"?

(*b*) Write short notes on handling uncertainty using probabilistic reasoning. **(5)**

(*c*) Write short notes on Fuzzy logic. **(5)**

Q. 7. (*a*) What are important challenges in Natural Languages Understanding"? **(2)**

(*b*) What are the various applications of NLP? **(3)**

(*c*) Explain the various activities which are performed during Morphological Analysis and Syntactic processing with the help of following sentence: I want to see Raju's photo. **(10)**

UNIT-IV

Q. 8. (*a*) Give short description of process of learning using Back Propagation Neural Network. **(10)**

(*b*) Give a flow graph for developing a genetic algorithm **(5)**

Q. 9. (*a*) What procedure is followed for knowledge acquisition? **(4)**

(*b*) What are the various steps for development of Expert Systems? **(7)**

(*c*) What is the role of expert system tools in developing expert system? Give one example of such tool and its usability. **(4)**

COCHIN UNIVERSITY OF SCIENCE AND TECHNOLOGY

University Question Paper-1

B. Tech Degree VIII Semester Examination

October 2000

Time : 3 Hours *Maximum Marks : 100*

(Answer all questions) (All questions carry equal marks)

I. (*a*) Discuss the nature and scope of Artificial Intelligence. Why game playing problems are considered as AI problems?

(b) Explain some of the areas where artificial intelligence finds applications.

OR

II. (*a*) What is solution guaranteed algorithm? Explain it.

(*b*) Explain AO* Algorithm.

III. Write short notes on the following:

(*i*) Context free grammars

(*ii*) Transformational grammars

(*iii*) Transition nets

(iv) Natural language understanding

OR

IV. (*a*) Explain Fillmore's grammars.

(b) Discuss n Shank's Conceptual dependency.

V. If a problem-solving search program were to be written to solve each of the following types of problems, determine whether the search should proceed forward or backward.

(*i*) Water jug problem

(*ii*) Blocks world

(*iii*) Natural language understanding

VI. Consider the following knowledge base:

$\forall x : \forall y : \text{cat}(x) \wedge \text{fish}(y) \rightarrow \text{likes- to- eat}(x, y)$

$\forall x : \text{colico}(x) \rightarrow \text{cat}(x)$

$\forall x : \text{tuna}(x) \rightarrow \text{fish}(x)$

una (Charlie)

tuna (Herb)

Calico (puss)

(*i*) Convert these wff's into Horn clauses.

(*ii*) Convert the Horn clauses into a PROLOG program.

(*iii*) Write a PROLOG query corresponding to the question, "What does Puss like to eat?" and show how it will be answered by your program.

(*iv*) Write another PROLOG program that corresponds to the same set of wff's but returns a different answer to the same query.

VII. Discuss n any one of the following expert systems:

(*i*) DENDRAL

(*ii*) MYCIN

OR

VIII. (*a*) What are the main features of expert systems?

(*b*) Explain expert system shell.

(c) Explain meta knowledge.

IX. (*a*) Explain symbolic description of pattern recognition.

Choose three common objects and determine five of their most discriminating visual attributes.

OR

X. (*a*) Explain the steps to be performed in pattern recognition process.

(*b*) What is speech recognition?

University Question Paper-2

B. Tech Degree VIII Semester Examination

May 2001

Time: 3 Hours **Max. Marks: 100**

I. (*a*) What is Artificial Intelligence? How AI can be used in visual perception?

(*b*) Explain how heuristically informed procedure improves the search process.

OR

II. (*a*) Write A* algorithm. Discuss on admissibility of A* algorithm.

(*b*) What is learning?

III. (*a*) Construct a parse tree for the following sentence: "Was the boy who was sleeping wakened?"

(*b*) Give an example for a context free grammar.

OR

IV. (*a*) Give a graphical transition network grammar for English.

(*b*) Explain Fillmore's grammars.

(*c*) Explain the following with examples:

(*i*) Semantic nets

(*ii*) Misky's frames

(*iii*) Production rules

(*iv*) Knowledge base.

OR

(*a*) A problem-solving search can proceed either forward or backward. What factors determine the choice of direction for a particular problem?

(*b*) Consider the following facts:

- The members of the Elm St. Bridge Club are Joe, Sally, Bill and Ellen.
- Joe is married to Sally.
- Bill is Ellen's brother.
- The spouse of every married person in the club is also in the club.
- The last meeting of the club was at Joe's house.

Represent these facts in predicate logic.

V. Write short notes on the following:

(*i*) Expert system shell

(*ii*) Meta knowledge

(*iii*) Expertise transfer

(*iv*) Self-Explaining systems.

OR

VI. (a) Discuss the major problems facing current expert systems.

(*b*) How the inference rules of MYCIN work?

VII. (*a*) What is speech recognition? Explain the steps.

(*c*) Write short note on symbolic description.

OR

VIII. (*a*) Write short notes on machine perception.

(*b*) Find a linear decision which separates the following x-y points into two distinct classes.

(–1, 8)	(–5, –1)	(–3, 3)	(–3, 0)
(1, 3)	(–1, 1)	(0, 1)	(3, 4)
(0, 0)	(2, 3)	(– 4, –1)	(–2, 3)

University Question Paper-3

B. Tech Degree VIII Semester Examination

May 2003 (1999 Admissions)

Time: 3 Hours **Max. Marks: 100**

I. (*a*) Give the algorithm for problem reduction and explain. **(10)**

(*b*) Explain A* algorithm. **(10)**

OR

II. (*a*) Solve the crypt arithmetic problem using constraint satisfaction algorithm.

Problem:

```
  SEND
+ MORE
------
 MONEY
```

Initial state: No two letters have the same value. The sum of the digits must be as shown in the problem.

Goal state: All letters have been assigned a digit in such a way that all the initial constraints are satisfied. **(10)**

(*b*) Explain alpha-beta pruning algorithm. **(10)**

III. (*a*) Explain the syntax of FOPL. **(10)**

(*b*) What is resolution by refutation? Illustrate with an example. **(10)**

OR

IV. (*a*) Give the complete procedure to convert any wff into clausal form with suitable example. **(15)**

(*b*) Explain the resolution principle. **(5)**

V. (*a*) Explain transformational grammars. **(10)**

(*b*) Briefly explain different parsing techniques. **(10)**

OR

VI. (*a*) Explain case grammars. **(10)**

(*b*) Distinguish between Deterministic and Non-deterministic parsers with corresponding network diagrams. **(10)**

VII. (*a*) Differentiate procedural and declarative knowledge. **(10)**

(*b*) Explain the architecture of a typical expert system. **(10)**

OR

VIII. (*a*) State and explain the theory of fuzzy sets. **(10)**

(*b*) What are the main differences between scripts and frame structures? Explain with example. **(10)**

IX. (*a*) What are perceptions? Illustrate a simplified perceptron system with suitable diagram. **(10)**

(*b*) What is unsupervised learning? Explain. **(10)**

OR

X. (*a*) Explain Multi-layer perceptron. **(10)**

(*b*) Explain the Back propagation algorithm. **(10)**

University Question Paper-4

B. Tech Degree VIII Semester Examination

May 2003 (1999 Admissions onwards)

Time: 3 Hours **Max. Marks: 100**

I. (*a*) What are different types of Artificial Intelligence and explain forward and backward reasoning? **(10)**

(*b*) Explain how a production system can be used to convert 256 into Binary? **(10)**

OR

II. (*a*) Compare the time and space complexity of depth-first and breadth-first search techniques. **(10)**

(*b*) What is Means and End analysis and explain how it is useful in game playing? **(10)**

III. (*a*) Why is predicate calculus said to be "undecidable"? What is well formed formula? **(10)**

(*b*) How to prove theorems of predicate calculus by "resolution-refutation"? **(10)**

OR

IV. (*a*) Explain the method to convert a well-formula (wff) into the clausal form. **(10)**

(*b*) What are the rules used in natural deduction system for proving theorems in prepositional logic? **(10)**

V. (*a*) What are context-free grammars and context-sensitive grammars? **(10)**

(*b*) What is the function of an ATN parser and AND/OR graphs? **(10)**

OR

VI. (*a*) Explain the problems you may face in parsing Indian Languages. **(10)**

(*b*) Design an ATN for recognizing the language $\left\{a^n b^{2n} c^{3n}, \text{for } n \geq 0\right\}$. **(10)**

VII. (*a*) How to represent knowledge in a typical expert system?

(*b*) Explain statistical reasoning and non-monotonic reasoning. **(10)**

OR

VIII. (*a*) Explain the principle of Fuzzy logic and explain use of Fuzzy sets. **(10)**

(*b*) Explain a typical fuzzy rule based expert system. **(10)**

IX. (*a*) Define learning and explain perceptron training algorithm.

(*b*) Compare back-propagation algorithm with an unsupervised training algorithm. **(10)**

OR

X. (*a*) Explain Kohenen's Network and to train the network? **(10)**

(*b*) What are Neuro-Fuzzy systems and why expert systems are modeled with Neuro-Fuzzy systems?

University Question Paper-4

B. Tech Degree VIII Semester Examination
October 2004 (1999 Admissions onwards)

Time: 3 Hours **Max. Marks: 100**

(All questions carry EQUAL marks)

I. (*a*) (*i*) What is meant by Problem? Define.

(*ii*) Define Artificial Intelligence. Give the areas where AI is applied.

Explain how an unstructured problem can be structured for solution. Illustrate with an example.

OR

II. (*a*) (*i*) What is meant by Operators in state-space solutions? Explain how operators can be framed.

(ii) What is meant by Production Rules? Also explain Forward chaining.

(*b*) Solve the Problem, given below, using state space approach.

'A man comes to Bank-I of a river with his pet tiger, cow and a bundle of grass. He wants to cross the river and to reach Bank-II with all his possessions. There is a boat and is so small that the man can take with him only one item at a time. If his tiger and cow are left at any bank, without the man being there, the tiger would eat the cow. Similarly if the cow and grass are left on any bank, without the man being there, the cow would eat the grass. The man doesn't want to lose any of his items'.

Assume required operators for the solution.

III. (*a*) Explain the Breadth First Search Algorithms.

(*b*) Solve the network given below, using Dynamic programming, to find the shortest path between I and G. The figure given with each branch indicates the distance in kilometrs.

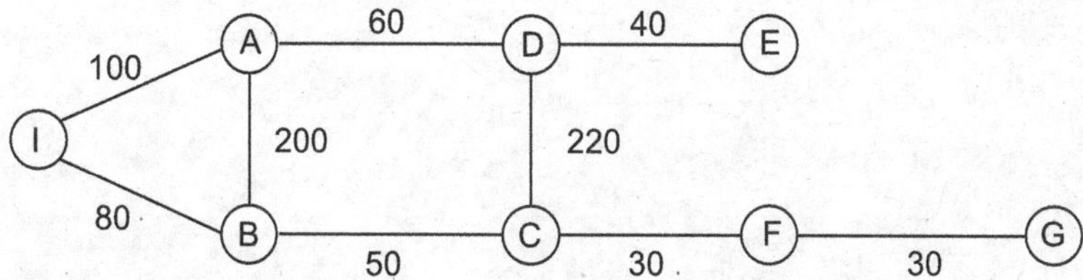

where I is the initial node and G is the goal node.

OR

IV. (*a*) (*i*) What is meant by inference rule?

(*ii*) Define Modus Ponens. Illustrate with an example. Give the complete procedure to convert any wff into clausal form with suitable example.

V. (*a*) Explain how Lexical, Semantic and Syntactic analysis are carried out in Natural Language Processing.

(*b*) Briefly explain different parsing-techniques.

OR

VI. (*a*) Using context-free grammars draw and explain a Parse tree for the English sentence. "The man bites the dog".

(*b*) Explain how can we combine Syntax and Semantic knowledge. Use language sentences, if required.

VII. (*a*) Classify and explain the different types of knowledge as far as AI is concerned.

(*b*) Draw the semantic network and write atomic formulae for the English sentence given below:

Manju is playing with a red ball.

OR

VIII. (*a*) Write short notes on the following:

(*i*) Monotonic reasoning

(*ii*) Probabilistic/Bayesian Reasoning.

(*b*) With the help of a Block Schematic diagram explain working of an Expert System.

IX. (*a*) With the help of a diagram, explain working of a simplified perceptron system.

(*b*) Explain Symbol-based learning.

OR

X. (*a*) (*i*) Explain Artificial neurons. Use necessary diagram.

(*ii*) Calculate the Logic functions 'AND' and 'OR' using McCulloch-Pitts neurons.

(*b*) Explain the Perceptron Training Algorithm.

R.T.M. Nagpur

University Question Paper-4

Artificial Intelligence
Seventh Semester Information Technology
Artificial Intelligence (Summer - 2003)

Section-A

I. (*a*) What do you mean by intelligence? What are the characteristics of intelligence? **(6)**

(*b*) State the difference between conventional software and AI software. **(6)**

(*c*) What are the domain tasks of AI? **(4)**

OR

II. (*a*) Explain various problem characteristics with suitable examples. **(8)**

(*b*) Explain hill climbing search technique in detail. **(4)**

(*c*) Give the difference between A* and AO* algorithms. **(4)**

II. (*a*) Explain the difference between procedural knowledge and declarative knowledge. **(3)**

(*b*) Represent the following sentences using predicate calculus notations:

(*i*) There is red part in the bin that has a circular shape.

(*ii*) Anant is a computer science student but not a pilot or a football player.

(*iii*) The owner of car also owns the boat.

(*iv*) All people need air. **(8)**

(*c*) Explain frame knowledge representation scheme with example. **(5)**

OR

IV. Assume the following facts:

(*i*) Manish only likes easy courses.

(*ii*) Science courses are hard.

(*iii*) All the courses in the basket weaving department are easy.

(*iv*) BK301 is a basket weaving course.

Use resolution to answer the question.

"What course would Manish like"? Also explain the resolution principle with proof. **(16)**

V. Write short notes on following:

(*i*) Uncertainty handling using probability theory. **(16)**

(*ii*) Fuzzy logic.

OR

Section-B

VI. (*a*) Explain forward and backward reasoning with suitable example of each. **(6)**

(*b*) List difference search techniques and explain any one in detail. **(4)**

(*c*) Explain non-monotonic and monotonic reasoning. **(6)**

VII. (*a*) Explain why and how AI methods are suitable for game playing. Are there any limitations? **(6)**

(*b*) What are the different ways in which ambiguity results in natural language statements? Give an example of each type. **(6)**

(*c*) Explain transformational grammar with proper example. **(4)**

OR

VIII. (*a*) Explain minimax search with reference to game playing. **(4)**

(*b*) Write short notes on :

(*i*) Non linear planning

(*ii*) Chomsky hierarchy **(12)**

(*b*) What factors must be considered in determining the suitability of problems for expert system applications? **(4)**

(*c*) Explain production and non-production system architecture of expert system. **(6)**

OR

IX. Write short notes on following:

(*i*) Knowledge system building tools.

(*ii*) Types of learning

(*iii*) Operating modes of expert system. **(16)**

ARTIFICIAL INTELLIGENCE (WINTER-2003)

Section-A

I. (*a*) With suitable examples, discuss the important characteristics of AI problems. **(9)**

(*b*) Discuss the importance of Heuristic search over Blind search. **(4)**

(*c*) Differentiate between AI. Software and Conventional Software. **(3)**

OR

II. (*a*) What is AND-OR graph? **(2)**

(*b*) Explain A* algorithm in detail. **(7)**

(*c*) Explain the method of hill climbing for solving problem. Write the difference between simple hill-climbing and steepest-ascent hill-climbing algorithm? **(7)**

III. (*a*) Construct a script for trip to a restaurant. Give the different constituents of a script. **(7)**

(*b*) Give the basic principle of resolution. Explain resolution algorithm in predicate logic. **(9)**

OR

IV. (*a*) Write short notes on the following (Any Three):

(*i*) Frames,

(*ii*) Semantic network

(*iii*) Production system,

(*iv*) Conceptual Dependency. **(12)**

(*b*) Formulate the following facts in predicate logic:

(*i*) Everyone is loyal to someone.

(*ii*) All plants require water. **(4)**

V. (a) What is forward and backward reasoning? What are the factors to be considered while choosing forward or backward reasoning techniques? **(4)**

(*b*) State whether forward reasoning or backward reasoning is applicable and why:

(*i*) Finding fault in a TV set.

(*ii*) Selecting personal computer sytesm. **(4)**

(*c*) Describe briefly how Baye's theorem can be used for uncertainty handling in AI problem. Explain it with suitable example. **(8)**

OR

Section-B

VI. (*a*) Explain the compare depth-first search and breadth-first search methods. **(7)**

(*b*) Write short notes on:

(*i*) Fuzzy logic,

(*ii*) Non-Monotonic Reasoning System,

(*iii*) Probability Theory for uncertainty handling. **(9)**

VII. (*a*) Give an example of each of the four types 0, 1, 2, 3 for Chomsky's hierarchy of grammar. **(7)**

(*b*) Explain the MINIMAX procedure with special illustration of following:

–One/two ply search

–Backing up

–Alpha/Beta cut-offs. **(9)**

OR

VIII. (*a*) Explain case grammar and semantic grammar. **(6)**

(*b*) Discuss about different knowledge levels used in language understanding. **(5)**

(*c*) Give general approaches to natural language understanding. **(5)**

IX. (*a*) Explain architecture of expert system in detail. **(8)**

(*b*) What are the main advantages in keeping the knowledge base separate from the control module in knowledge-based system? **(4)**

(*c*) Explain types of learning. **(4)**

OR

X. (*a*) What are expert system shells? What factors must be considered in determining the suitability of a problem for expert system development? **(8)**

(*b*) Give the general learning model and describe the role of each component of a general learning model and why it is needed for learning process. **(8)**

ARTIFICIAL INTELLIGENCE (SUMMER-2004)

Section-A

I. (*a*) Define AI. Outline nature of problems that led to the development of AI. Explain typical task domains of AI. **(8)**

(*b*) With the help of suitable examples, explain characteristics of AI problems. **(8)**

OR

II. (*a*) Write short notes on:

(i) Constraint satisfaction (*ii*) Means-ends analysis **(6)**

(*b*) Discuss the importance of heuristic search as compared to blind search. **(4)**

(*c*) Explain hill climbing search technique and also explain hurdles in hill climbing technique. **(6)**

III. (*a*) Discuss resolution in predicate logic with suitable example. **(8)**

(*b*) Write short note on:

(*i*) Frames and scripts (*ii*) Truth maintenance system

OR

IV. (*a*) Explain the difference between:

Predicate and propositional Logic. **(3)**

(*b*) What are semantic networks? What are properties of semantic networks? Give suitable example to explain the same. **(7)**

(*c*) Represent the following sentences using predicate calculus: **(6)**

(*i*) All people need air.

(*ii*) Raghav is a computer-science student but not a plot or a football player.

(*iii*) Some professors are scientists.

V. (*a*) Explain the difference between:

(*i*) Backward and forward reasoning

(*ii*) Breadth-first and depth-first search. **(8)**

(*b*) Write technical note on application of certainty factor and probability theory for representation of uncertain knowledge. **(8)**

Section-B

VI. (*a*) Explain non-monotonic and monotonic reasoning technique. **(8)**

(*b*) Explain various sources of uncertainty while you are developing an AI software for trouble shooting an electronic device. **(8)**

VII. (*a*) Explain MINIMAX procedure with illustration of following:

(*i*) One/two ply search

(*ii*) Backing up

(*iii*) Alpha beta cut-off. **(11)**

(*b*) Explain non-linear and hierarchical planning. **(5)**

VIII. (*a*) Explain various knowledge levels used in language understanding. **(5)**

(*b*) Explain various grammars used in natural language processing. **(8)**

(*c*) Explain chemistry hierarchy of language in brief. **(3)**

IX. (*a*) Give a general learning model and describe the role of each component of a general learning model and why it is needed for learning process. **(8)**

(*b*) What is knowledge acquisition? What are steps involved in knowledge acquisition process? **(8)**

OR

X. (*a*) Define expert system. What are its characteristic features? With the help of block diagram, explain components of typical expert system. **(9)**

(*b*) Explain the following:

(*i*) Learning by analogy

(*ii*) Learning by taking advice

(*iii*) Expert system shell. **(7)**

ARTIFICIAL INTELLIGENCE (WINTER-2004)

Section-A

1. (*a*) Analyze the traveling salesman problem with respect to problem characteristics. **(8)**

(*b*) Explain the term control strategies and what are the requirements for good control strategy? **(5)**

2. (*a*) Write AO* algorithm. **(7)**

(*b*) A farmer wishes to cross a river taking his fox, goose and grain with him. He can use a boat which will accommodate only the farmer and one possession. If the fox is left alone with the goose, the goose will be eaten. If the goose is left alone with the grain, it will be eaten. Draw a state space tree for this puzzle using left bank and right bank to denote left and right river banks respectively. **(6)**

3. (*a*) Represent the following sentences using predicate logic:

(*i*) If someone dies, then he is dead at all later times.

(*ii*) No mortal lives longer than 150 years. **(5)**

(*b*) Show a conceptual dependency representation of the sentence:

(*i*) John gave Mary a gift

(*ii*) John ate salad with a fork. **(4)**

(*c*) Construct partitioned Semantic net representation for the following:

"Every dog in town has bitten the constable". **(4)**

4. Write short notes on (Any Three):

(*a*) Truth Maintenance Systems

(*b*) Semantic Networks

(*c*) Frames

(*d*) Script **(14)**

5. (*a*) Compare depth-first search and breadth-first search and best-first search. **(6)**

(*b*) A problem solving search can proceed either forward or backward. What factors determine the choice of direction of a particular problem? **(4)**

(*c*) Explain non-monotonic reasoning system in brief with suitable example. **(3)**

Section –B

6. (*a*) Explain Bayesian Network with example. **(7)**

(*b*) Using MYCIN's rules for inexact reasoning, compute CF, MB and MD of h_1 given three observations where:

CF $(h_1, o_1) = 0.5$

CF $(h_1, o_2) = 0.3$

CF $(h_1, o_3) = -0.2$ **(6)**

7. (*a*) What are the different types of grammar used in Natural language processing? Explain each with example. **(5)**

(*b*) Explain the Minimax search procedure. Write the algorithm for minimax search procedure:

MINIMAX (Position, Depth, Player) **(8)**

8. (*a*) Derive a parse tree for the sentence "The boy ate an apple" using the following rules. Use both passing techniques i.e. Top down and Bottom up.

S → NP VP

NP → ART N

VP → V NP

N → boy | apple | fish

V → ate | flew | slapped

ART → the | a

where, S is the initial symbol for sentence,

NP stands for noun phrase,

VP stands for verb phrase,

N stands for noun,

V is abbreviation for verb, and

ART stands for article. **(8)**

(*b*) Write short note on following:

(*i*) Natural language generation

(*ii*) Chomsky hierarchy of language. **(5)**

9. (*a*) What is learning? Give its importance in Artificial Intelligence problems. Also state the difference between supervised and unsupervised learning. **(6)**

(*b*) Explain what are the criteria generally used for the selection of an Expert System problem. **(4)**

(*c*) State the difference between knowledge-base and database. **(4)**

10. (*a*) What are importance of Expert System over conventional software? **(5)**

(*b*) Explain the stability of following problems for Expert System. Justify your answer.

(*i*) Solving set of simultaneous equations.

(*ii*) Finding fault in personal computers. **(8)**

ARTIFICIAL INTELLIGENCE (SUMMER-2005)

Section-A

1. (*a*) What is an AI technique? Explain different applications of AI. **(6)**

(*b*) Why it is necessary to apply control strategies to production rule system? **(3)**

(*c*) Explain basic difference between:

(*i*) Knowledge base and Database

(*ii*) A* and AO* algorithm. **(4)**

2. (*a*) Write and explain AO* algorithm. **(7)**

(*b*) Write characteristics of AI problem. Explain each with example. **(6)**

3. (*a*) Write significance of unification algorithm in case of predicate logic.

(*b*) Represent following statements in its predicate calculus WFF's and clause forms:

(*i*) If town *x* is connected to town *y* by highway *z* and bicycles are allowed on *z*, then you can get to *y* from *x* by bike.

(*ii*) All Romans who know Marcus either hate Caesar or think that anyone who hates anyone is crazy.

(*iii*) Anything anyone eats and is not killed by is food.

(*iv*) Sue eats everything Bill eats. **(8)**

(*c*) Explain, why rule based knowledge representation is more popular than other representation techniques. **(3)**

4. (*a*) Write short note on Conceptual Dependency. **(3)**

(*b*) Design script for Trip to Restaurant. **(6)**

(*c*) Explain Truth Maintenance System (TMS) with example. **(4)**

5. (*a*) Problem solving search can proceed either forward or backward. What factor determines the choice of direction for a particular problem? Determine whether search should proceed in forward or backward direction and how for the following:

(*i*) Water jug problem (*ii*) Block world problem

(*iii*) Natural language understanding. **(9)**

(*b*) Explain Non-monotonic Reasoning System and its importance in A.I. **(4)**

Section-B

6. (a) Write short notes on:

(*i*) Application of certainty factor and probability theory for representation of uncertain knowledge.

(*ii*) Fuzzy reasoning. **(8)**

(*b*) When would best-first search be worse than simple breadth-first search? Explain it with suitable example. **(5)**

7. (*a*) Explain Minimax search procedure with respect to following:

(*i*) Backing up the values

(*ii*) Alpha cutoff

(*iii*) Beta cutoff (5)

(*b*) Discuss different knowledge levels used in language understanding. (5)

(*c*) Explain top-down and bottom-up parsing with suitable example. (3)

8. (*a*) Give the general approaches to Natural language understanding. (5)

(*b*) "Minimax Search is depth-first depth-limited search procedure." (5)

(*c*) Discuss the factors which make Natural language understanding by machine hard to achieve. (3)

9. (*a*) Draw basic block diagram for General Learning model. Explain different components of learning model. (5)

(*b*) What are the main advantages in keeping the knowledge base separate from the control module in knowledge base system? (4)

(*c*) What are the difficulties encountered in knowledge acquisition? (4)

10. (*a*) With the help of block diagram explain components of Expert System. (8)

(*b*) Write short notes on:

(*i*) Rote learning

(*ii*) Learning by analogy

(*iii*) Learning from example (6)

ARTIFICIAL INTELLIGENCE (WINTER-2005)

Section-A

1. (*a*) Discuss the importance of heuristic search over blind search. (4)

(*b*) What are the steps involved in designing a program to solve an AI program? (3)

(*c*) With suitable example, explain the characteristics of IA problem.

2. (*a*) Explain Best-first search algorithm with example. How does it differ from hill-climbing? (6)

(b) Describe a problem for which means-ends analysis can be successfully applied. Give an example of a few solution steps. (5)

(*c*) What is the difference between OR graph and AND-OR graph? (2)

3. (*a*) Formulate the following facts in predicate logic: (6)

(*i*) John likes all kinds of food,

(*ii*) All employees of the AI software company are programmers.

(*iii*) All employees earning ₹ 10,000 or more per month, pay taxes.

(*b*) Give the basic principle of resolution. Explain resolution algorithm in propositional logic. (7)

4. (*a*) Construct a script for shopping in a super market. (6)

(*b*) What are semantic networks? What are the properties of semantic networks? Explain how ISA link can be conveniently used to represent predicate logic statement. (7)

5. (*a*) Differentiate between forward and backward reasoning. What factors determine the choice of direction for a particular problem? (7)

(*b*) Explain use of fuzzy logic in representing uncertainty in knowledge representation. (6)

Section-B

6. (*a*) Write short notes on:

(*i*) Non-monotonic reasoning system.

(*ii*) Depth-first search and breadth-first search. (7)

(*b*) Explain briefly how Baye's theorem can be used for uncertainty handling in AI problem. (7)

7. (*a*) Discuss general approaches to natural language understanding. (4)

(*b*) What is meant by a 'phy' in minimax search procedure? Explain minimax search procedure. (9)

8. (*a*) Explain types of grammars used in NLP (Natural Language Processing). (7)

(*b*) What are the levels of knowledge used in natural language understanding? (6)

9. (*a*) Define expert system. What are its characteristic features? Explain with the help of block diagram, architecture of expert system. (4)

(*b*) Explain knowledge acquisition process in brief. (4)

10. (*a*) Explain the difference between rote learning and learning by analog. (4)

(*b*) Explain machine learning by giving block diagram and function of each component. Give the factors affecting learning performance. (9)

ARTIFICIAL INTELLIGENCE (SUMMER-2006)

Section-A

1. (*a*) Define AI. Explain task domains of AI. (5)

(*b*) Explain the term control strategies and what are the requirements for a good control strategy? (5)

(*c*) Give the difference between A* and AO* algorithms. (3)

2. (*a*) Explain various problem characteristics with suitable examples. (9)

(*b*) Explain hill climbing search technique in detail. (4)

3. (*a*) Represent the following sentences using predicate logic:

(*i*) If someone dies, then he is dead at all later times.

(*ii*) Anything anyone eats and isn't killed by is a food.

(*iii*) Sue eats whatever Bill eats. (6)

(*b*) Construct partitioned semantic net representation for the following:
"Every dog has bitten every constable." (4)

4. (*a*) Design a script for Trip to Restaurant. (5)

(*b*) Write short notes on (any Two):

(*i*) Frames

(*ii*) Conceptual Dependency

(*iii*) Truth Maintenance Systems. (8)

5. (*a*) Explain significance of unification algorithm in case of Predicate Logic. (4)

(*b*) Compare depth-first search and breadth-first search. (5)

(*c*) Explain non-monotonic reasoning system and its importance in AI. **(4)**

Section-B

6. Write short notes on the following:

(*i*) Fuzzy logic

(*ii*) Uncertainty handling using probability theory. **(13)**

7. (*a*) Explain Minimax search procedure with respect to following:

(*i*) Backing up the values

(*ii*) Alpha cutoff

(*iii*) Beta cutoff **(9)**

(*b*) What are the different ways in which ambiguity results in natural language statements? Give an example of each type. **(4)**

8. (*a*) Explain with an example, each of the four types 0, 1, 2, 3 for Chomsky Hierarchy of Generative Grammars. **(5)**

(*b*) Discuss about different knowledge levels used in language understanding. **(6)**

(*c*) Enlist various grammars used in natural language processing. **(2)**

9. (*a*) Give the general learning model and describe the role of each component of general learning model. **(5)**

(*b*) What factors must be considered in determining the suitability problems for Expert System applications? **(4)**

(*c*) What is knowledge acquisition? **(4)**

10. (*a*) Explain architecture of expert system in detail. **(6)**

(*b*) What are the main advantages in keeping the knowledge base separate from control module in knowledge based systems? **(4)**

(*c*) Write short notes on (any Two):

(*i*) Discovery Learning

(*ii*) Learning by Analogy

(*iii*) Expert System Shell **(4)**

ARTIFICIAL INTELLIGENCE (WINTER-2006)

Section-A

1. (*a*) What are the problems with hill climbing and how can they be solved?

(*b*) Explain the characteristics of AI problem with the help of suitable example.

(*c*) Consider Missionaries and cannibals problem. Give initial states, other states, operators, goal state, and path cost.

2. (*a*) Write and explain A* algorithm.

(*b*) Explain Means-ends-analysis search technique.

3. (*a*) Represent following statements in its predicate calculus expression:

(*i*) If the car belongs to John, then it is green.

(*ii*) Every city has a dog catcher who has been bitten by every dog in town.

(*iii*) Every Monday and Wednesday I go to John's house for dinner.

(*iv*) If student is sick, he will not attend lecture.

(*b*) Explain algorithm to convert to clause form.

4. (*a*) Write a script for "Robbing a bank".

(*b*) Represent the following sentences into semantic network:

Puss is a calico.

Herb is a tuna.

Charlie is a tuna.

All tunas are fishes.

All calicos are cats.

All cats like to eat all kinds of fishes.

5. (*a*) Give the difference between monotonic and non-monotonic Reasoning system.

(*b*) What is Dependency-Directed backtracking and how it differs from chronological backtracking?

(*c*) Explain with example backward and forward reasoning.

Section-B

6. (*a*) Write short notes on (Any Two):

(*i*) Fuzzy logic,

(*ii*) Certainty factors,

(*iii*) Bayesian networks.

7. (*a*) Explain MINIMAX search procedure.

(*b*) Write short note on STRIPS and give STRIPS operators for a block world problem.

8. Explain different types of grammars in natural language processing.

9. (*a*) Draw basic block diagram for general learning model and explain each component.

(*b*) Write short note on:

(*i*) Learning by taking advice,

(*ii*) Learning by problem solving,

(*iii*) Learning by analogy.

10. (*a*) Explain different components of an expert system.

(*b*) Explain non-production system architecture.

ARTIFICIAL INTELLIGENCE (SUMMER-2006)

Section-A

1. (*a*) Analyse following AI problems with respect to seven import characteristics of AI problems:

(*i*) Travelling salesman problem, **(6)**

(*ii*) Water-jug problem.

(b) Write and explain A* algorithm. **(7)**

2. (*a*) What is production system? What are different contol strategies for searching state space? (7)

(*b*) Differentiate between,

(*i*) AND-OR and OR graphs.

(*ii*) Simple hill climbing and steepest-ascent hill climbing. **(6)**

3. (*a*) What is the basis of resolution in propositional logic? **(4)**

(*b*) Write short note on semantic networks. **(4)**

(*c*) Design a script for trip to restaurant. **(6)**

4. (*a*) Represent following statements in predicate logic:

(*i*) All people need entertainment.

(*ii*) Prasad only likes easy courses.

(*iii*) There is a red part in the bin that has circular shape. **(6)**

(b) Write an algorithm for converting wffs into clause form. **(7)**

5. (*a*) Write the difference between:

(*i*) Forward and Backward reasoning.

(*ii*) Depth-first and Breadth-fist search. **(7)**

(*b*) What are the factors to be considered while choosing forward or backward reasoning techniques? **(6)**

Section-B

6. (*a*) Write short notes on:

(*i*) Probability and Baye's theorem,

(*ii*) Fuzzy logic,

(*iii*) Backtracking. **(13)**

7. (*a*) Explain MINIMAX search procedure. **(8)**

(*b*) Give general approaches to natural language understanding. **(5)**

8. (*a*) Write short notes on semantic grammar and case grammar. **(6)**

(*b*) Discuss the issues involved in semantic analysis of natural language. **(8)**

9. (*a*) Draw basic block diagram for general learning model. Describe the role of each component of a general model and explain why it is needed for learning process. **(7)**

(*b*) Write short notes on:

(*i*) Rote learning,

(*ii*) Learning by analogy **(6)**

10. (*a*) What do you mean by expert system shell? **(3)**

(*b*) Give different applications of expert system. **(4)**

(*c*) Discuss architecture of expert system in brief. **(6)**

ARTIFICIAL INTELLIGENCE (WINTER-2007)

Section-A

1. (*a*) Define AI. State the various task domains of AI. **(3)**

(*b*) Analyze the following problems with respect to the various problem characteristics:

(*i*) chess playing

(*ii*) water jug problem.

(*iii*) travelling salesman problem

(*iv*) 8-puzle.

(*v*) natural language understanding. **(5)**

(*c*) Explain production systems in detail. **(4)**

(*d*) State advantages and disadvantages of Breadth-First search and Depth-First search. **(2)**

2. (*a*) State AO* Algorithm. Explain with an exmaple.

(*b*) Example:

(*i*) Local Maxima

(*ii*) Plateau

(*iii*) Ridge **(3)**

(*c*) State the differences between simple Hill Climbing and steepest-ascent Hill Climbing. **(2)**

3. (*a*) Explain Truth maintenance system. Why is it needed? **(5)**

(b) Consider the following sentences:

(*i*) John likes all kinds of food.

(*ii*) Apples are food.

(*iii*) Chicken is food.

(*iv*) Anything anyone eats and isn't killed by is food.

(*v*) Bill eats peanuts and is still alive.

(*vi*) Sue eats everything Bill eats:-

(*i*) Translate these sentences into formulas in Predicate Logic.

(*ii*) Prove that John likes peanuts using backward chaining. **(8)**

4. (*a*) Differentiate between Procedural and Declarative knowledge. **(3)**

(*b*) What is goal directed reasoning? What factors decide if it is better to reason forward or backward? **(5)**

(*c*) Show a conceptual dependency representation of the sentence:

John begged Mary for a pencil.

Explain the concept of Conceptual dependency. **(5)**

5. (a) Construct a script for going to a movie from the viewpoint of the goes.

(*b*) Write short notes on:

(*i*) Fuzzy logic

(*ii*) Bayesian networks

(*iii*) Certainty factors.

6. (*a*) What are semantic nets? Explain partitoned semantic nets with example. **(5)**

(*b*) What are frames? Explain with example. **(4)**

(*c*) Explain Non-monotonic Reasoning system. **(4)**

7. (*a*) Is the minimax procedure a depth-first or breadth-first search procedure? Explain with example. **(4)**

(*b*) Explain Alpha-Beta pruning. **(3)**

(*c*) Explain Hierarchical Planning and Non-linear Planning. Differentiate between the two. **(6)**

8. (*a*) Explain Augmented Transition Networks. **(4)**

(*b*) Explain Semantic Analysis. **(4)**

(*c*) Write a note on Chomsky hierarchy. **(5)**

9. (*a*) Draw and explain the Block diagram of a learning system. **(7)**

(*b*) State and explain the various types of learning. **(6)**

10. (*a*) Draw and explain the Block diagram of an expert system. **(7)**

(*b*) What are the characteristic features of an expert system? **(7)**

ARTIFICIAL INTELLIGENCE (SUMMER-2008)

Section-A

1. (*a*) Define AI techniques and give few of them. **(4)**

(*b*) Explain different categories of Production systems. **(6)**

(*c*) Explain the term 'Combinatorial explosion. **(4)**

2. (*a*) Differentiate between Simulated Annealing and Hill climbing techniques. **(3)**

(*b*) Write and explain AO* algorithm. **(5)**

(*c*) Show how means-ends analysis could be used to solve the problem of getting from one place to another. Assume that the available operators are walk, drive, take the bus, take a cab, and fly. **(5)**

3. (*a*) Consider the following sentences:

- John likes all kinds of food
- Apples are food
- Chicken is food
- Anything anyone eats and isn't killed by is food
- Bill eats peanuts and is still alive
- Sue eats everything Bill eats.

(*i*) Translate these sentences into formulas in predicate logic.

(*ii*) Convert the formulas of part (*i*) into clause form.

(*iii*) Prove that John likes peanuts using resolution. **(10)**

(*b*) Differentiate between Procedural and Declarative knowledge base. **(3)**

4. Write short notes on (Any three):

(*a*) Frames

(*b*) Scripts

(*c*) Semantic networks

(*d*) Truth maintenance system. **(13)**

5. (*a*) Explain forward and backward reasoning with the help of examples. **(7)**

(*b*) Write and explain Baye's theorem. What is significance of probability in AI? **(6)**

Section-B

6. (*a*) Write short notes on Fuzzy logic. **(6)**

(*b*) Explain non-monotonic reasoning systems. **(7)**

7. (*a*) What are different types of Grammar? Explain each of them. **(9)**

(*b*) Develop a parse tree for the sentence "Jack slept on the table" using the following rules. **(4)**

S	→	NP VP
NP	→	N
NP	→	DET N
VP	→	V PP
PP	→	PREP NP
N	→	Jack/table
V	→	Slept
DET	→	the
PREP	→	on

8. Explain minimax search procedure. Explain calculation of α and β cutoffs. **(13)**

9. Write short notes on:

(*a*) rote learning

(*b*) learning by analogy

(*c*) learning by taking advice

(*d*) learning from example. **(13)**

10. (*a*) Give some characteristic features of Expert system. **(5)**

(*b*) Draw a block diagram of knowledge acquisition process and explain its components. **(5)**

(*c*) What are the main advantages of keeping knowledge base separate from the control module in knowledge based systems? **(4)**

ARTIFICIAL INTELLIGENCE (WINTER-2008)

Section-A

1. (*a*) Define AI. State the various task domains of AI. **(4)**

(*b*) Explain different categories of Production system. **(6)**

(*c*) Explain the term 'Combinatorial Explosion'. **(4)**

2. (*a*) State AO* Algorithm. Explain with an example. **(6)**

(*b*) Differentiate between simulated annealing and hill climbing techniques. **(3)**

(*c*) Show how means ends analysis could be used to solve the problem of getting from one place to another. Assume that the available operators are walk, drive, take the bus, take a cab and fly. **(4)**

3. (*a*) Consider the following sentences:

1. John likes all kinds of food.
2. Apples are food.
3. Chicken is food.
4. Anything anyone eats and isn't killed by is food.
5. Bill eats peanuts and is still alive.
6. Sue eats everything Bill eats.

(*i*) Translate these sentences into formulas in Predicate logic.

(*ii*) Convert the formulas of part (I) into clause form. **(8)**

(*b*) Differentiate between Procedural and Declarative knowledge base. **(5)**

4. Write short notes on (Any Three): **(13)**

(*a*) Frames

(*b*) Scripts

(*c*) Semantic Network

(*d*) Truth Maintenance Systems.

5. (*a*) Explain Forward and Backward Reasoning with the help of examples. **(5)**

(*b*) Write and explain Baye's theorem. What is the significance of probability in AI? **(4)**

(c) Explain Fuzzy logic. **(4)**

Section-B

6. (*a*) Explain Non-Monotonic Reasoning systems. **(7)**

(*b*) Explain Hierarchical Planning and Non-Linear Planning. Differentiate between the two. **(6)**

7. (*a*) What are different types of Grammar? Explain each of them. **(8)**

(*b*) Develop a parse tree for the sentene "Jack slept on the table" using the following rules:

S	→	NP	VP	NP	→	N
NP	→	DET	N	VP	→	V PP
PP	→	PREP	NP	N	→	Jack/table
V	→	Slept		DET	→	the
PREP	→	on				

8. Explain Minimax search procedure. Explain calculation of α and β cutoffs. **(13)**

9. (*a*) Draw and explain the block diagram of a learning system. **(7)**

(*b*) State and explain various types of learning. **(6)**

10. (*a*) Give some characteristic features of expert systems. **(5)**

(b) Draw Block diagram of knowledge acquisition process and explain its components. **(5)**

(*c*) What are the main advantages of keeping KB separate from the control module in Knowledge Based systems? **(4)**

ARTIFICIAL INTELLIGENCE (SUMMER-2009)

Section-A

1. (*a*) State and explain the block diagram of a typical AI system. **(6)**

(*b*) What are the problems with hill climbing and how can they be solved? **(4)**

(*c*) What do you mean by a control strategy? What are the requirements of a good control strategy? **(4)**

2. (*a*) Explain Means-Ends Analysis search technique with a suitable example. **(6)**

(*b*) State the best-first search algorithm. **(4)**

(*c*) Define the following terms in reference to steepest Ascent Hill Climbing:

(*i*) Local Maximum

(*ii*) Plateau

(*iii*) Ridge. **(3)**

3. (*a*) Represent the following sentences in predicate logic: **(10)**

(*i*) Marcus was a man.

(*ii*) Marcus was a Pompeian.

(*iii*) All Pompeians were Romans.

(*iv*) Caesar was the ruler.

(*v*) All Romans were either loyal to Caesar or hated him.

(*vi*) Everyone is loyal to someone.

(*vii*) People only try to assassinate rulers they are not loyal to.

(*viii*) Marcus tried to assassinate Caesar.

From these, answer the question "Was Marcus loyal to Caesar"?

(*b*) What are semantic networks? How can semantic networks be converted to frames? **(3)**

4. (*a*) Write a script for "Eating in a restaurant". **(7)**

(*b*) What are semantic networks? What are the properties of semantic networks? Explain how ISA link can be conveniently used to represent predicate logic statement. **(6)**

5. (*a*) Differentiate between Forward and Backward reasoning. What factors determine the choice of direction for a particular problem? **(7)**

(*b*) What is dependency directed backtracking? How does it differ from chronological backtracking? **(6)**

Section-B

6. Write short notes on (Any Two): **(14)**

(*i*) Fuzzy logic

(*ii*) Certainty factors

(*iii*) Bayesian networks.

7. (*a*) Explain alpha-beta cutoff procedure with an example. **(6)**

(*b*) Write short note on STRIPS and give STRIPS operators for a block world problem. **(7)**

8. (*a*) Explain types of grammar used in NLP (Natural Language Processing). **(7)**

(*b*) What are the levels of knowledge used in Natural language understanding? **(6)**

9. (*a*) Draw basic block diagram for general learning model and explain each component. **(7)**

(*b*) Write short notes on: **(6)**

(*i*) Learning by taking advice

(*ii*) Learning by rote

(*iii*) Learning by analogy.

10. (*a*) Explain different components of an expert system. **(7)**

(*b*) Explain Knowledge Acquisition process in brief. **(6)**

DTU (Delhi Engineering Colleges)

Computer Technology and Application

Paper-CS-602

(Artificial Intelligence)

Time: 3 Hours **Max. Marks: 100**

(Write your Roll No. on the top immediately on receipt of this question paper)

Question No. 1 is compulsory.
Answer any Four from the rest.

1. Explain the difference between the following terms:

(*a*) Knowledge and Data.

(*b*) Hill Climbing and Steepest Ascent Hill Climbing.

(*c*) Search tree and Game tree.

(*d*) Semantic Nets and Frames.

(*e*) Monotonic Reasoning and Non-Monotonic Reasoning. **(20)**

2. (*a*) Define the term control strategy and production rules. Exemplify them using the water jug problem. **(10)**

(*b*) What are the various characteristics for which AI problem should be analysed before choosing a suitable search procedure? **(10)**

3. (*a*) What are the disadvantages of Steepest Ascent Hill Climbing Search Procedure? Using a suitable search tree, illustrate that these drawbacks are eliminated in Best First Search. **(10)**

(*b*) Using a suitable example, illustrate steps of A* search. Why is A* search better than Best-First Search? **(10)**

4. (*a*) Represent the following sentence in first order predicate logic, convert it into Clause form explaining each step.

All engineering students who know programming well either get good placement or admission in some university for higher studies. **(8)**

(*b*) Using the following problem, illustrate how resolution is used to derive new facts from already existing facts:

Given facts:

- Steve Likes Computer Courses
- Computer Courses can be Software or Hardware courses
- AI is a Software Course

Derive: Steve likes AI **(12)**

5. (*a*) What do you understand by Inheritable knowledge? Give an example of this knowledge. **(8)**

(*b*) Explain the techniques to represent above kind of knowledge. Also point out merits and demerits of each scheme. **(12)**

6. Write short notes on any two from the following:

(*a*) Means-End Analysis Search Procedure;

(*b*) Minimax Search Procedure;

(*c*) Unification Procedure;

(*d*) Non-Monotonic Reasoning;

(*e*) AND/OR Search. **(20)**

APPENDIX – B

List of experiments (A.I.): (With Solutions)

1. To solve Towers of Hanoi problem using recursion.
   - **Input:** Number of disks.
   - **Output:** Goal configuration of the towers; Number of moves.
2. To implement Breadth-first search (BFS).
   - **Input:** Node to be searched.
   - **Output:** Path traversed.
   - **Constraints:** A tree.
3. To implement Depth-first search (DFS).
   - **Input:** Node to be searched.
   - **Output:** Path transverse.
   - **Constraints:** A tree.
4. To implement Best-first search.
   - **Input:** Node to be searched.
   - **Output:** Path traversed.
   - **Constraints:** A tree.
5. To find the solution of 8-puzzle problem.
   - **Input:** Initial configuration of tiles.
   - **Output:** Goal configuration of the tiles; Number of moves.
6. To find the solution of Water Jug problem.
   - **Input:** 2 empty jugs of different capacities and a reservoir containing large amount of water.
   - **Output:** Amount of water to be put in both the empty jugs.
7. To solve monkey-bananas problem.
   - **Input:** Initial configuration of monkey and bananas.
   - **Output:** Goal configuration of monkey and bananas; Number of moves.
8. To simulate a multi-layer perceptron network for XOR gate.
   - **Input:** XOR gate configuration.
   - **Output:** Goal configuration of the network.
9. To identify odd and even numbers using back propagation.
   - **Input:** Initial network configuration.
   - **Output:** Exact matching of odd and even numbers
10. To implement Hopfield neural network.
    - **Input:** Training data for the network.
    - **Output:** Hopfield neural network (with trained and tested data)

11. To solve TSP using Genetic Algorithm
    - **Input:** TSP graph depicting initial connections of all cities.
    - **Output:** Final TSP graph using genetic algorithm (non-optimal)
    - **Constraints:** Non-optimal solution.

EXPERIMENT NO. 1

AIM: WAP to implement Breadth-first search (BFS)

Program Code:

```
#include <iostream.h>
#include <conio.h>
#include <stdio.h>
#include <math.h>
struct node
{
    node * l;
    node * r;
    int d;
};
    node * root = NULL;
    class tree
{
    public:
    int count;
    tree ( )
    { count = 0;
}
    node * insert (node *, int a);
    int bfs (node *, int a);
};
    int tree :: bfs (node * root, int a)
    node * g [10];
    int front, rcor;
    front = -1
    rear = -1
    q [0] = root;
    front = 0;
    rear = 0;
    cout << cdl <" The bfs traversal is";
    while (font < = rear)
    {
      node * p = q [front];
      front ++;
      count ++;
      count << p → d << ".";
      if (p → d = = a)
    {
      return ( 1 );
    }
```

```
if (p → l ! = NULL)
{
    q [++ rear] = p → l;
}
    if (p → r! = NULL)
{ q [++ rear] = p → r
}
    return (0);
}
node * tree :: insert (node * root, int a)
{
    if (root = = NULL)
    {
        root = new node;
        root → l = NULL;
        root → r = NULL;
        root → d = a;
    }
else
    {
        if (0 < root → d)
        {
            root → l = insert (root → l, a);
        }
    else
        {
            root → r = insert (root → r, a);
        }
}
  return (root);
}
void main ( )
{
  clrs cr ( ) ;
  tree a ;
  int goal, val;
  cout << "Enter the value for tree (8 nodes): ",
  for (int I = 0; I < 8; I ++)
{
    cin >> val;
    root = a insert ( root, val);
}
  count << endl << "Enter goal";
```

```
        cin >> goal;
        int b = a.bfs (root, goal);
        if (b = = 1)
      {
        count << endl,
      }
    }
```

OUTPUT:

```
Enter the value for tree (8 nodes) : 23
998
6
56
34
89
56
45
Enter goal89
The bfs traversal is: 23:6:998:56:34:89:
```

EXPERIMENT NO. 2

AIM: WAP to implement Depth-first search (DFS)

Program Code:

```
#include <iostream.h>
#include <conio.h>
#include <stdio.h>
#include <math.h>

struct node
{
  node *l;
  node * r;
  int d;
};
node * root = NULL;
class tree
{
  public;
  int count;
  tree ( )
  {
     count = 0;
  }
  node * insert ( node * Q, int 0 )
  int dfs (node *, int a);
};
  int tree : : dfs (node * root, int a)
  {
     node * s[10];
     int top = –1;
     s [0] = root;
     top ++;
     count << cndl << "DFS traversal is";
     while (top ! = -1)
     {
        node * p = s [top];
        top – –_;
        count ++;
        cout << p → d << "–";
        if (p → d = = a)
     {
        return (1);
     }
```

```
        if (p → r! = NULL)
        {
            s [++ top] = p → r;
        }
            if (p → l! = NULL)
        {
            s [++ top] = p → l;
        }
    }
        return ( 0);
    }
    node * tree : : insert (node * root, int a)
    {
        if (root = = NULL)
        {
            root = new node;
            root → l = NULL;
            root → r = NULL;
            root → d = a;
        }
        else
            {
                if (a < root → d)
                {
                    root → l = insert (root → l, a);
                }
            else
                {
                    root → r = insert (root → r, a);
                }
            }
        return (root);
}
void main ( )
{
    clrs cr ( );
    tree a;
    int goal, val;
    cout << "Enter the values for tree (8 nodes)";
    for (int I = 0; I < 8; I ++)
    {
        cin >> val;
```

```
        root = 0 . insert (root, val);
    }
    cout << endl << "Enter goal";
    cin >> goal;
    int b = a ; bfs (root, goal);
    if (b = = 1)
    {
        cout << "OFS has found the node & root → "<< a . count
        <<" iterationo " << endl;
    }
        if (b = = 0)
        {
            count << endl <<" no node is found";
        }
        getch ( ) ;
    }
```

OUTPUT

Enter the number of discs: 2
The three towers are A, B and C
Move top disk1from begAtoB.
Move top disk1from begAtoC.
Move top disk1from begBtoC.
The number of moves: 3

EXPERIMENT NO. 3

AIM: WAP to implement tower of Henoi

Program Code:

```
#include <iostream.h>
#include <corin.h>
#include <math.h>

void tower (int n, char beg, char, aux, char end)
{
  if (n = = 1)
    { cout << "\n Move top disk " << n << "from leg "<<beg<<
    "to" <<endl << ".";
    return;
  }
else
  {  tower (n–1, beg, end, aux);
    cout <<"\n Move top disk " << n <<" from leg " << leg <<" to "" << endl << ".";
    tower (n–1, cux, leg, end);
  }
}

void main ( )
{ clrs cr ( );
  int n;
  cout <<" Enter the number of discs";
  cin >> n;
  cout <<"The three towers are A, B and C \n";
  tower (n, 'A', 'B', 'C');
  cout << "\n The number of moves";
  int a = pew (2, n) – 1;
  cout << a;
  getch ( );
}
```

OUTPUT

Number of cities = 3

Enter the distance between cities 1 and 2 = 12

Enter the distance between cities 1 and 3 = 22

Enter the distance between cities 2 and 3 = 45

Cities transversed in the order : 1231

Total distance: 101

EXPERIMENT NO. 4

AIM: WAP to solve travelling salesman problem.

Program Code:

```
#include <iostream.h>
#include <conio.h>

int l = 0;
int path [10], dist [10] [10];
int not_trav (int i)
{
  for (int k = 0; k < l; k++)
{
  if (path [k] = = i)
  return 0;
}
  return 1;
}
  int get next (int if, int n)
{
  int min = 100, pesi, posm;
  for (int i = 0; i < n; i ++)
  {
      for (int m = 0; m <n; m ++)
        {
            if (i! = m)
            {
              if {(( i = j) && net_trav (m + 1) || (m = j && net_trav (i + 1)))
            {
              if (dist [i] [m] < min)
              {
                  min = dist [i] [m];
                  posi = 1;
                  posm = m;
              }
            }
        }
  }
}
 if (posi = = j)
 return posm;
 return posi;
 }
```

```
void main ( )
{
   int i, j, n;
   clrs cr ( );
   cout <<"\n Enter the number of cities";
   cin >> n;
   int min = 100;
   for (i = 0; i < n; i++)
   {
      if (i < j)
      {
         cout << "distance between cities "<< i+ 1 << "and" << j + 1 << ",";
         cin >> dist [i] [j];
         min = min > dist [i] [j] ? dist [i] [j] min;
      }
         int flag = 0;
         for (i = 0; i < n; i ++)
         {
            for (j = 0; j < n; j++)
         {
         if (dist [i] [j] = = min)
         {
            flag = 1;
            goto here;
         }
      }
         here;
         int next;
         path [l++] = i+ 1;
         path [l++] = j + i;
         while (l! = n)
         {
            next = getnext (j, n);
            path [l++] = next + ;
            j = next;
         }
      }
         path [l ++] = path [0];
         cout <<"\n The cities transversed in the order";
         for (i = 0; i < 0; i ++)
            cout << path [i] << "\t";
         for (i = 0; i < l –1; i++)
```

```
distance + = dist [i – 1] [i];
cout <"\n Total distance; "<< distance;
getch ( );
        }
    }
}
}
}
```

EXPERIMENT NO. 5

AIM: Write a program for Water Jug Problem.

Program Code:

```
#include <isotream.h>
#include <coino.h>
int x, y;
void rule ( )
{
        if (x = = 2)
        {  x = 2;
            y = 0;
            cout <<"\n x = "x <<"y = " << y;
            return;
        }
else if (if = = 2 && x = = 0)
{
        x = 2;
        y = 0;
        cout <<"\n x = " << x <<" y = << y;
        return;
    }
else if (y = =2 & & x > 0)
{
    x = 0;
    cout << "\n x = "<< x <<"y = " << y;
    return;
}
    else if (x + y = = 2)
    {
        x + = y
        y = 0;
        cout <,"\n x =" <<x <<"y=" <<y;
        return;
    }
    else if (! y && ! x)
    {
        x = 0;
        y = 3;
        cout <<"\n x \ "<<x<<"y=" <<y;
        return;
    }
    else if ((x < 2 && !y) || (! x && y <<2))
```

```
        {
          x = 0;
          y = 0;
          cout <<"\n x =" <<x <<"y="<<y;
          return
        }
        else if (y = = 3 && x = = 3)
          {
             x = 4;
             y = 2;
          cout <<" "\n x = " <<x <<"y = <<y;
          return
        }
    else if (!y && x = = 3)
    {
        x = 3;
        y = 3;
        cout << "\n x =" << x <, "y = "<<y;
        return;
    }
        else if (x = = 3)
        {
          x = 3;
          y = 0;
          cout << "\n x = " << x << "y = " << y;
          return;
        }
        else if (y = 3 && !x)
        {
          x = 3;
          y = 0;
          cout << "\n x = " << x << "y = " << y;
          return;
          }
             else if (y = = 3 && x! = 2)
             {
                x = 0;
                y = 3;
                cout << \n x = " << x << " y = << y;
                return;
             }
             else if (y! = 2 && x = = 4)
```

```
        {
            x = 0;
            cout << "\n x =" << x <<" y = " << y;
            return;
        }
    }
    void main ( )
    {
        clrs cr ( );
        cout << " jug1 ; ";
        cin >> x;
        cout << "jug 2:";
        cin >> y;
        cout <<" \n x =" << x << "y=" << y;
        while (1)
    {
        if (x = 2 && y = = 0)
            break;
            rule ( );
    }
        getch ( );
    }
```

OUTPUT

```
jug1 : 3
jug2 : 8
x = 3y = 8
x = 3y = 0
x = 3y = 3
x = 4y = 2
x = 0y = 2
x = 2y = 0
```

EXPERIMENT NO. 6

AIM: Odd and Even classification problem.

```
echo on
clc
P = [ 0000 0000 11;
      0000 1111 00;
      0011 0011 00;
      0101 0101 01];
T = [0101010101];
Pause
s1 = 20;
[w1, b1] = init p (p, s1);
[w2, b2] = init p (s1, T);
pause
    p [0; 0; 1; 0];
    a1 = Sim up (p, w1, b1);
    a2 = Sim up (a1, w2, b2);
    pause
    echo off
```

OUTPUT:

Q2 = 0

dum squared n/w error for b epodes

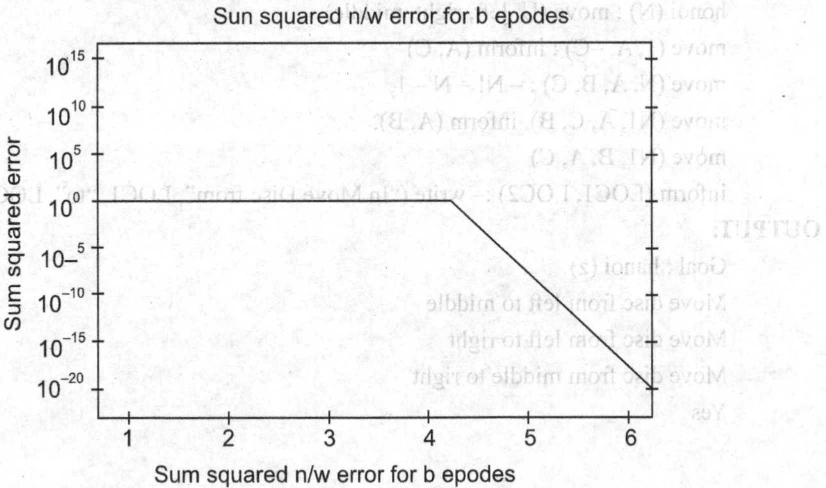

EXPERIMENT NO. 7

AIM: Monkey Banana Problem

move (state (middle, onbox, middle, hasnot; grasp, state (middle, onbox, middle, has)) move (state (p, onfloor, p, 4) climb, / clinb box, state (p, onbox, p2, H) move (state (p1, on/wor, B, H) walk (p1, p2), /walk from p1 to p2 state (p2, onfloor, B, H)

% conget (state, moves): monkey is state con get banana by performing moves

Conget (state (–, –, –, has), [ ])

Conget (state 1, [n], list] : – move (state1, state 2), conget (state 2, list)

sawe (moves): Conget (state (at door, wnfloor, at window, has not), moves)

OUTPUT:

solve (MOUSE)

MOVES (WALK (at door, at windows), push (at window, middle), climb, grasp]

EXPERIMENT NO. 8

AIM: WAP to implement tower to Honoi using Prolog.

```
domains:
doc = symbol
predicates
honoi (integer)
move (integer, loc, loc, loc)
inform (loc, loc)
clauses
honoi (N) : move (U, left, right, middle)
move (1, A, –C) : inform (A, C)
move (N, A, B, C) : – N! = N – 1,
move (N1, A, C, B), inform (A, B),
move (N1, B, A, C)
inform (LOC1, LOC2) :– write ("In Move Disc from", LOC1, "to", LOC2);
```

OUTPUT:

```
Goal : hanoi (z)
Move disc from left to middle
Move disc from left to right
Move disc from middle to right
Yes
```

EXPERIMENT NO. 9

AIM: XOR Classification

```
echo on
clc
clf;
P = [ 0 0 1 1;
      0 1 0 1];
T = [0 1 1 0]
Plot PU (P, T);
```

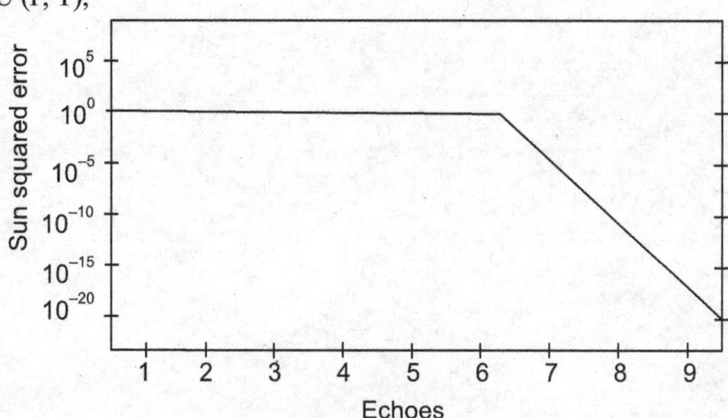

Vector to be classified

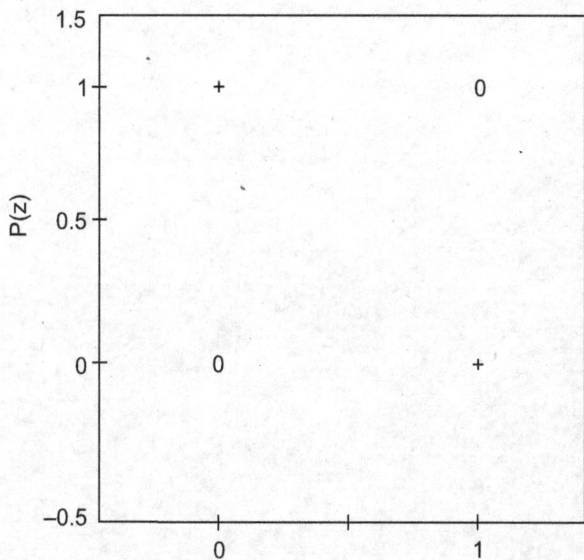

This Page has been intentionally left blank

A PROJECT ON

SEARCH ENGINE OPTIMIZATION USING KEYWORD INTELLIGENCE

This Page has been intentionally left blank

APPENDIX – C

PROBLEM DOMAIN

1. In today's world people need to retrieve a lot of information from the Web everyday. However, as there is too much text information of web, how to find what we want becomes a serious problem.
2. The following statistics reveal percentage of clicks on various pages of a search result:

First Page:

- 1st link : 30%
- 2nd link : 15%
- 3rd link : 7%
- 4th link : 5%
- 5th link : 4%
- 6th link : 4%
- 7th link : 2%
- 8th link : 2%
- 9th link : 3%
- 10th link : 5%

Second Page:

- 1st link : 6%
- 2nd link : 4%
- 3rd link : 2%
- 4th link : <1%

It is observed that if the desired search result is not on the 1st and 2nd page then in most cases the user prefers to enter a new search query than moving on to the remaining pages.

This work involves:

Modification and implementation of four algorithms that determine the keyword sets and closest keyword sets.

INTRODUCTION

If I know, I shall act, but if I don't know, I shall "SEARCH"!!

Unknown has always baffled the Mankind and search is an important rather only tool to convert the unknown to known. Effortless and smooth search can be a powerful tool in unnerving the mystery of unknown. Web searching is the activity of finding something or some one on the World Wide Web. The most common tool for searching is a SEARCH ENGINE. **The search engine is a means of finding that particular information which may be residing in the web pages in the form of documents, image, different types of files etc.** The search engine employs various searching techniques to bring about the desired search result. In the upcoming pages we discuss about this tool and various related optimization techniques.

SEARCH ENGINE: THE TOOL

Searching finds its ease most commonly through SEARCH ENGINES. Broadly, search engines can be of 3 types:

Crawler-Based Search Engines

As the name suggests, they '**crawl**' through the web and retrieve web pages. In the process of crawling they build list of words encountered. Any change in the content of the web pages is brought to their notice and a track is kept to keep the indexer updated, e.g: GOOGLE

Human Powered Search Engines

They use human power to bring about their listings and submit a description from where the searches of these search engines are preceded. Any change in the content of web pages does not make a difference to them.

Hybrid Powered Search Engines

This combines both the crawler-based human powered searching technique and chooses the best among them accordingly. MSN uses hybrid approach for searching.

WORKING OF CRAWLER-BASED SEARCH ENGINE

Here we consider the working of # 1 ranked GOOGLE search engine as with its parterns catches 70% web traffic to websites.

Crawler-based search engines are most widely used ones and following are the steps involved in their technique of searching:

Crawler

It 'crawls' through the web and retrieves web pages. In the process of crawling it builds the list of words it encounters. Any change in the information of the web pages is brought to the notice and a track is kept by visit to those web pages on a regular basis to keep their indexer updated. Website crawls are performed by main Google spider called 'GoogleBot'. The more 'popular' your website is, more often is it crawled by the GoogleBot. Highly ranked websites and sites that update content frequently like new sites, blogs etc. are crawled daily.

Indexer

It stores a copy of the web pages that the spider crawls through. The changes in the web pages that are discovered by the crawler are made in the indexer. Sometimes the changes crawled may not be indexed at the same time, it may be done after a while. Unless the changes are made in the indexer they are not available to be used. In a broader sense INDEXER is Google's database. It is a type of database in which web pages are stored.

SEARCH ENGINE SOFTWARE AND PAGE RANK

Crawling through numerous pages stored in the indexer and finding the best match according to a search being made is done by this program. Further it arranges them according to **page rank technique followed**. The pages appear in the same order as being ranked in a search. **A page ranked higher is more popular and is certain to be retrieved earlier than a lower ranked page**. Google uses a sophisticated and propriety algorithm for ranking Web sites that in turn uses over 100 different criteria in the calculation, each of which gives specific weighting which can change over time as per change in algorithm. Hence optimization is not a one time task.

Google algorithm can be broken into 2 major groups of factors:

On page (Keyword) factors: Keyword factors involve how, when and where keywords are used i.e. how well the website is optimized for your most important keywords and if those keywords appear in your content. These factors determine **page relevance**.

Off page (link) Factors: These include quantity and quality of links that point to your site. Link factors determine **page importance** and are related to PAGE RANK. Links play a VERY important role in getting high ranks for competitive market.

Google finds pages in its index that are relevant and important to search for a particular term on phrase and lists in descending order.

(a) **On page Factors and Page relevance:** Keywords are intrinsically related to search terms. When a search word is entered, Google analyses all pages in its index and lists the pages that contain, usually contains one or two keywords that are repeated more often than others throughout the site. Keywords dictate the 'theme' of the website. In addition to this other sites are also analyzed that contain links to your site. Google looks to see if text of a link points to your site and contains those keywords.

(b) **Off Page Factors and Page Importance:** Google looks for links that point to your site. It is believed that a link from website A to website B. In this way other sites add votes for your site. **Each page on a site has a page rank value**. Usually the page rank for homepage is higher than another page on your site.

The more web pages that link your site and the more important in turn those pages are, the more important Google thinks your site is and hence the higher is your page rank value.

"Sites that are highly optimized for on-page factors can outrank that are less optimized but have higher Page Rank."

Page Rank value is assigned after every page in the indexer against one another.

NOTE: Page rank does not factor in keywords or phrases used on your site.

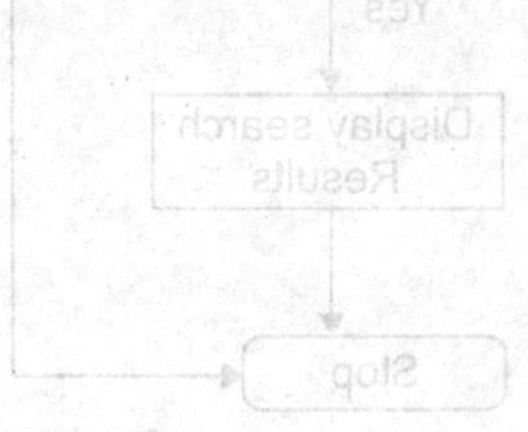

HARDWARE AND SOFTWARE REQUIREMENTS

Hardware Requirements

✧ Processor	:	Pentium III or above
✧ RAM	:	128 MB or above
✧ Disk	:	10 MB free space or above

Software Requirements

✧ Operating system	:	Windows 98 or above
✧ Application	:	MS-office 2000 or above
✧ Browsers	:	Mozilla Firefox, IE
✧ Turbo C++complier 3.0		

FLOW CHART FOR BASIC SEARCHING

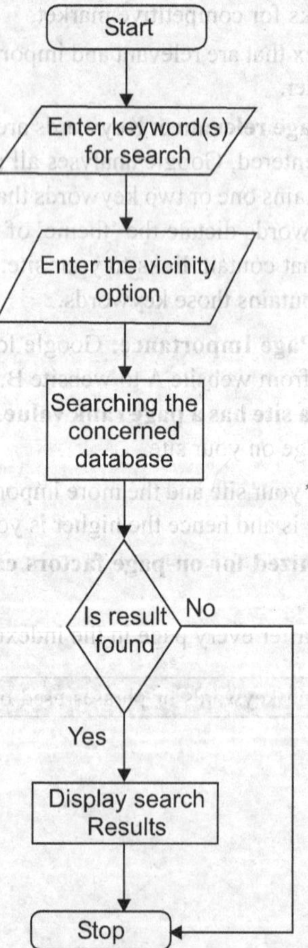

APPENDIX – D

GLOSSARY

Anonymous variable : The variable "-" used in place of an ordinary variable when the values that the ordinary variable may become bound to are of no interest.

Arguments : Collective name for the objects and variable names in a relation.

Atom : A relation, possibly involving objects or variables.

Attribute : A positive whole number that determines the characteristics of the display in a given window, including color, blinking/non-blinking and normal/inverse video.

Backtracking : The mechanism built into Turbo Prolog whereby, when evaluation of a given sub-goal is complete, Turbo Prolog returns to the previous sub-goal and tries to satisfy it in a different way.

Bound variable : A variable that refers to a known value.

Calling a sub-goal (or predicate) : An expression denoting that Turbo Prolog is now trying to satisfy a certain sub-goal (belonging to the given predicate).

Char : An arbitrary character enclosed between two single quotation marks.

Complier directives : Instructions to the Turbo Prolog complier compiler to take special actions.

Clause : A fact or rule for a particular predicate, followed by a period (.).

Compound goal : A goal containing at least two sub-goals.

Compound object : An object consisting of a functor and a list of objects separated by commas and enclosed in parentheses.

Current input device : The currently assigned write device to which standard predicates take input to default.

Current output device : The currently assigned write device to which standard predicates send output by default.

Cut (or !). The cut commits Turbo Prolog to all the choices made so far in the evaluation of the predicate containing the cut. Once the cut has been evaluated as a sub-goal, Turbo Prolog may not backtrack past it.

Database predicates : Predicates for which facts can be added to or deleted from the Turbo Prolog system during execution.

Dialog window : The system window in which external goals are given and the results of those goals recorded.

Domain. Specifies the types of values objects may take in relation.

Editor window : The window where text currently in the workfile can be edited.

Element of a list. Either an object or another list.

Expert system : A computer system that mimics the ability of an expert in a certain (usually very narrow) field.

External goal : A goal entered in the dialog window by the user and given to the program currently in the workfile.

Fact : A relation between objects. In the fact likes (john, mary) likes in the name of the relation and john and mary are objects.

Fail : A sub-goal that Turbo Prolog cannot satisfy.

Field : A contiguous sequence of character display positions occurring on the same row of the screen display.

Filename : Either a symbolic file name starting with a lowercase letter and appearing on the righthand side of a *file* domain declaration, or one of the predefined symbolic file names printer, screen, keyboard, and coml.

Flow pattern : The pattern formed according to whether the parameters in a predicate call are used for input (i.e., are known) or for output (i.e., are unknown).

Flow variant : If a predicate is associated with several different flow patterns, a separate internal implementation of the routines corresponding to that predicate will exist for each flow pattern. These different implementations are called flow variants of the predicate.

Free variable : A variable that does not currently refer to any value.

Functor : A name for a compound object.

Global : Qualifier used to allow more than one program module access to certain domains and predicates.

Goal : The collection of sub-goals that Turbo Prolog attempts to satisfy.

Goal tree : A diagrammatic representation of the possible choices that can be made in the evaluation of the constituent sub-goals of a goal.

Hand trace. A trace produced by the programmer working with pen and paper rather than by the computer.

Head of a list : The first element of a list.

Heap : That part of memory used by Turbo Prolog for building structures, storing strings and inserting facts for database predicates.

Infix notation : Writing arithmetic expressions with the operators between the two values or expressions on which they are to operate.

Integer : A whole number in the range–32,768 to 32, 767.

Internal goal : A goal contained in the goal section of a program.

Iterative method : A method that involves repeating the same basic action(s) over and over again until the desired objective is achieved.

List : A special sort of object consisting of a collection of elements enclosed in square brackets and separated by commas.

Message window : The window in which messages related to the operation of the Turbo Prolog system appear.

Module. A Turbo Prolog program with global declarations forming part of a project.

Multiple predicate declarations. Any one predicate can have several declarations, each involving different domain specifications for the argument(s) of the relevant relation.

Name. Any contiguous sequence of letters, digits and underscore characters that start with a lowercase letter or underscore.

Object : The name of an individual element of a certain type.

Operator priority : The hierarchy that determines the order in which operators are obeyed in arithmetic expressions.

Parameters : Collective name for the objects and variable names in a relation.

Pointer : The device by which Turbo Prolog keeps a record of the next place in its database of facts and rules to which to backtrack.

Predicate : Every Turbo Prolog fact or rule belongs to some predicate, which specifies the name of the relation involved and the types of objects involved in the relation.

Project : A Turbo Prolog program consisting of more than one module.

Real : A decimal number in the range ± 1.0 E – 307 to + 1.0 E ± 30.8

Recursion : The technique whereby an entity is defined in terms of itself.

Reference objects and domains : If an unbound variable is passed from one sub-goal to another, the domain containing the values to which the variable will eventually become bound must be declared as a reference domain. Elements of such a domain are reference objects.

Relation : A name describing the manner in which a collection of objects (or objects and variables referring to objects) belong together.

Repeat..fail combination : A technique that can be used to avoid tail recursion by using Turbo Prolog's backtracking mechanism instead.

Return from a sub-goal (or predicate) : An expression used to denote that Turbo Prolog has now finished evaluating a certain sub-goal (belonging to the given predicate).

Rule : A relationship between a "fact" and a list of sub-goals which must be satisfied for that "fact" to be true.

Satisfying a sub-goal : The process by which Turbo Prolog chooses values for any unbound variables (if possible) in such a way that the sub-goal is true according to the given clauses for the corresponding predicate.

Search principle : One of four basic rules that Turbo Prolog follows in attempting to satisfy a goal.

Stack : The part of memory used by Turbo Prolog for parameter transfer.

Stand-alone programs : Programs that can be run from DOS independently of the Turbo Prolog system.

Standard predicate : A predicate already defined internally in Turbo Prolog.

Standard type (of domain) : A domain containing objects of a single type chosen from integer, real, char, string, symbol and file.

String : An arbitrary number of characters enclosed by a pair of double quotation marks.

Sub-goal : A relation, possibly involving objects or variables, which Turbo Prolog must attempt to satisfy.

Sub-object : One of the objects in a compound object.

Tail of a list : The list that remains when the first element of a given list (and its separating comma) are removed.

Tail recursion elimination : Action taken internally by the Turbo Prolog system to reduce the space/time overhead of tail recursion in rules.

Term : Either an object from one of the domains of standard type, a list, a variable, or a compound term, i.e., a functor followed by a list of terms enclosed in parentheses and separated by commas.

Token : A name, an unsigned (real or integer) number, or a non-space character.

Trace : The production of a step-by-step report on the execution of a program showing all relevant details.

Trace window : The window in which Turbo Prolog can generate a trace of program execution.

Trail : The part of memory used by Turbo Prolog to register the binding and unbinding of reference variables.

Type system : The means by which all objects in a relation or all variables used as arguments in a relation are constrained to belong to domains corresponding to those used in the relevant predicate's declaration(s).

Unification : The process by which Turbo Prolog tries to match a sub-goal against facts and the left hand side of rules in order either to satisfy that sub-goal, or to determine one or more further sub-goals necessary to evaluate the original sub-goal.

Variable : A name beginning with a capital letter that can be used to represent the (possibly unknown) value of a certain object.

Variable binding(s) : The status—free or bound— of one or more variable .

Workfile : The file in which a Turbo Prolog source program text is held ready for compilation or execution.

APPENDIX – E

BIBLIOGRAPHY

1. E. Rich and K. Knight, "Artificial Intelligence", TMH, 2nd Edition, 1992.

2. D.W. Patterson. "Introduction to AI and Expert Systems", PHI, 2004

3. Saroj Kaushik, "Logic and Prolog Programming", New Age International Publishers, 1st Edition, 2002.

4. M.C. Trivedi, N.N. Jani and S.S. Sarangdevot, "A classical approach to AI", Khanna Book Publishing Co. Pvt. Ltd., Ist Edition. 2009.

5. R.P Suri, "Introduction to Prolog", Narosa Publishing, 1st Reprint, 2010.

6. Ela Kumar, "Artificial Intelligence", I.K. International Publishing House Pvt. Ltd., First Reprint, 2010.

7. S.Gupta, Jaideep Kumar, Munesh Trivedi, "Artificial Intelligence," Shubhanm Publications, 2nd Edition, 2010.

8. Neil C. Rowe, "AI through Prolog", PHI (USA Edition), 1998.

9. Rajeev Sangal, "LISP Programming", TMH, 1995.

10. S.P. Rao Borde, Sucheta V. Kolekar, "Artificial Intelligence," Tech-Max Publications, Pune, 1st Edition, 2008.

11. VVS Sarma, N. Vishwanadham, B. Yegnenarayand and B.L. Deekshatulu, "AI and ES Technologies in the Indian Context", Conference Proceedings of IIS, Bangalore, TMH, 1991.

APPENDIX – F

Some recent developments in AI and Robotics

Dated : 3rd June, 2009 **(Source: Mail Today)**

A SOFTWARE TO MANAGE YOUR MOODS

IMAGINE a software that can solve depression, sadness , anxiety and loneliness.

Software engineers and scientists in the US are using **Artificial Intelligence** to develop a software that will provide solutions to various psychological conditions.

Artificial Intelligence is the use of programs to enable machines to perform tasks which humans perform using their brains.

Experts believe most emotional challenges can be successfully met by activities such as listening to music, watching funny video, breathing exercises or yoga.

The software will use computational models to come out with solutions based on certain words keyed in by the user.

The team plans to have trials of the software this October in several universities. The scientists have also initiated the patenting process.

"All of us have emotional challenges. Most of these can be addressed by changing the mindset and distracting," said Vinay Gidwani, research affiliate, Massachusetts Institute of Technology.

The software is web-based and can provide solutions by sending text message or e-mails. The team working on the concept is setting up an independent company.

"For example, a student sends a message saying 'I am nervous for my exam'. The software will recommend solutions like stress-busting exercises," Gidwani said. The software is meant to deal with all emotional challenges including nervousness, anger and frustration.

"If the user is not satisfied with the answer, he/she can reject the response and seek more answers, " he added.

Gidwani said the technology will be more relevant in countries such as India where people are not comfortable visiting psychiatrist.

Date: 19th March, 2011 **(Source: Times of India)**

PATIENT'S WISH IS ROBOT'S COMMAND

If the brain-machine interface technology is a success, roots will act according to the thought process of paralytic patients.

Imagine a robot that can help paralytic patients perform simple tasks like self-feeding, switching on the TV or playing computer games. Scientists at the National Brain Research Center (NBRC) in Manesar, Haryana, are working on a technology called Brain-Machine-Interface (BMI) that uses electrodes to record signals from the brain and decode them in real-time to perform the tasks using a robot.

The research project is being funded by Defence Research and Development Organization (DRDO). Trials on animals will be conducted extensively, said one of the scientists. Such a technology will help paralytic patients who are mostly dependent on attendants.

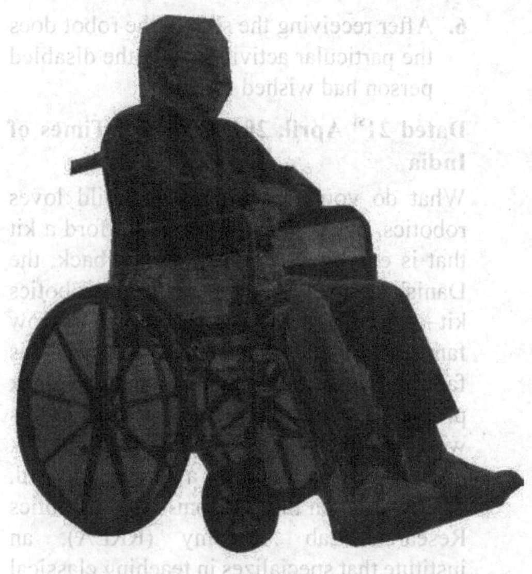

The BMI technology has three components: First, there is a system to detect and record signals from the brain. Second, a signal analyzer deciphers the recorded signal, and third, an effecter device executes the action based on the output from the signal analyzer.

Professor Neeraj Jain of NBRC, who is working on this project for three years, said they were using electrodes to record the activities of neurons in the brain.

"The toughest part is to decode the signals, and for that we have collaborated with Professor Rangarajan of the Indian Institute of Science (IISc), Bangalore, who has developed a mathematical tool, called algorithm, for the purpose. The program for the robot, to be used for animal trials, has been done by another IISc scientist, Ashitave Ghosal," he said.

Dr MC Mishra, chief of AIIMS Trauma Center, said more than 300 spinal injury patients were admitted at the centre every year and that the new technology, if successful, can help these people lead a better life. "Paralytic patients mostly live a vegetative life. They are completely dependent on family members or attendants. The new technology provides hope, but we will have to wait until it materializes in real terms," said Mishra.

The NBRC project on brain-machine interface is a first in the country. Similar researches are being carried out across the globe with limited success on animal models.

There have been human trials in which electrode arrays made from silicon have been used with some success. Experts, however, say the project is not outlandish; it can be achieved. "We have not set any time limit for completion of the project. It is an ongoing process," Jain said.

HOW WILL IT WORK ?

The technology has three parts:—

1. A system to read brain signals,
2. Signal analyzer, and
3. A robot to do the work.

1. People who suffer a spinal injury or a paralytic stroke can't move their body but they are mentally sound. Even for small chores, they have to depend on others.
2. Scientists and NBRC are developing a technology which may enable such patients to move a robot just by their thoughts.
3. Disabled person will wear a cap similar to EEG. His head will be surrounded by electrodes, which will monitor the brainwaves.
4. The activity of the brain will be converted into electronic signals and passed on to signal analyzer.
5. The signal analyzer translates these signals and interprets the patient's wishes into commands for the robot.

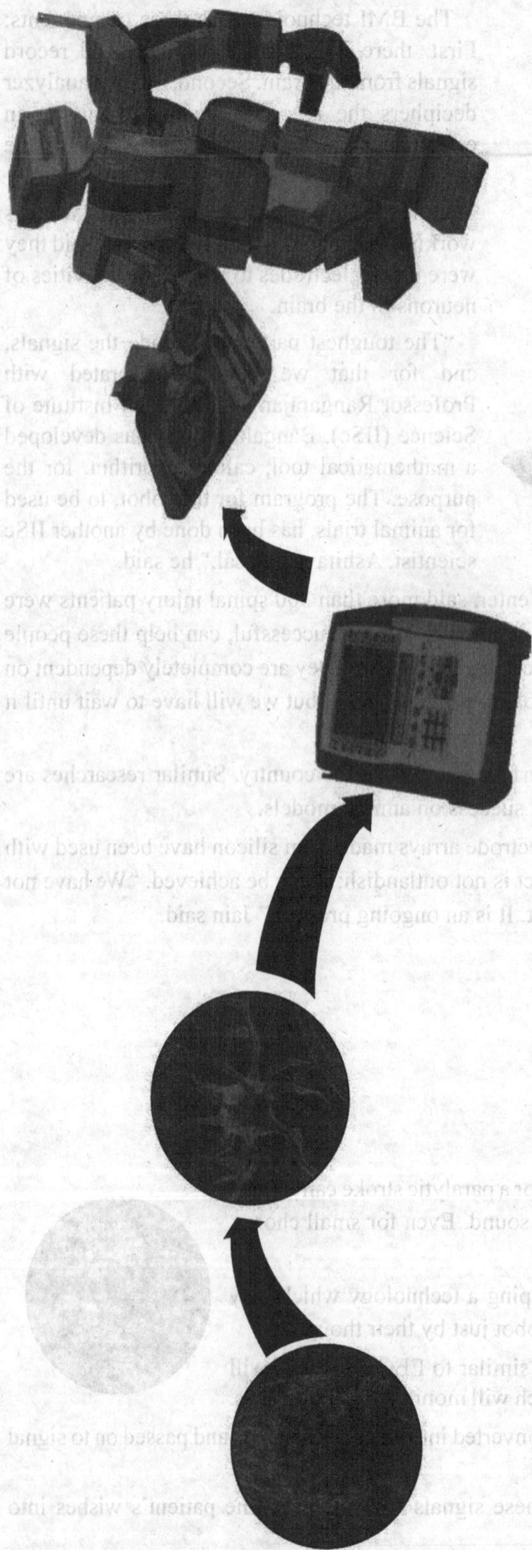

6. After receiving the signal, the robot does the particular activity which the disabled person had wished for.

Dated 21st April, 2011, Source: Times of India

What do you do when your child loves robotics, but you simply cannot afford a kit that is exorbitantly priced? Years back, the Danish company Lego introduced a robotics kit–as users built the kits, they began to grow familiar with the principles of robotics. This familiarity would eventually help them crack problem statements. But the downside of this wonder kit was the pricing Rs. 25,000 to Rs. 40,000 was too much for a parent to afford. That was when the Chennai-based Robotics Research Lab Academy (RRLA), an institute that specializes in teaching classical robotics, stepped in. PO Veejayshree, Head, Projects RRLA, says, "We focus on the robotics movement at the school level. We felt that if the kits were priced reasonably, then we would be able to embrace a wider market. So we decided to stock the kits and charge about Rs 500 per programme. That would make the prospect more affordable." The robotics movement at the school level has been hugely successful because of the interest evinced in and created by what is called Fun Robotics or Hobby Robotics. The RRLA, that has its presence in schools like Chettinaad Vidyashram in Chennai, will soon reach five schools in the next academic year by teaching the principles of robotics, in tandem with the Maths and Science NCERT syllabus. Veejayshree says, "We have structured programmes, depending on the age group. The level of complexity grows with the age group. For instance, at the lower levels, they are given a bread board that teaches them how to build circuits".

Several other factors have been conducive to the growth of the robotics movement in South India. Advanced robotics is up for the taking at the post-graduate level and for research endeavors. Robotics at the college level in Chennai is a range too. "Almost every university in Chennai has robotics lab. But there is need to upgrade the robotics systems in labs," says Veejayshree.

RAGE OF ROBOTICS

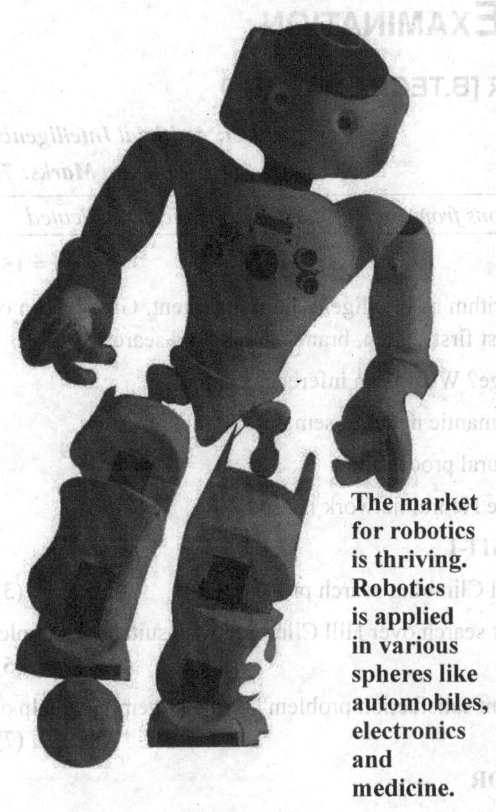

The robotics movement at the school and college levels is helping steer societies towards the age of automation, says **Anjana Raghu Ram.**

Dr G Venkatesh, Chief Mentor, Bangalore Robotics, a Bengaluru-based institute, says, "Robotics competitions are a big draw for students – they are integral to the tech fest of engineering colleges. Since they are a major draw, students rush to training centres to win competitions." While the supply sphere is demonstrated by the rage to excel in competitions and the number of people enrolling at training institutes, the requirements for students trained in robotics by the industry reflect the demand. The market for robotics is thriving – and the myriad applications of robotics in various electronics and medicine demonstrate that employment opportunities are aplenty for those interested in the field. Saranga Rajan, Head of Productions, Hyundai, Chennai, says the company recruits people with a background in robotics, "Yes robots are used in our welding shops, the painting processes, and assembly processes where precision is required. We recruit students through campus interviews. The demand for students is only going to increase. Robots perform jobs of repetitive, dirty and dangerous nature. These robots are programmed by humans. Students are thus required for programming, maintaining and trouble-shooting." But despite its scope, robotics is not a main course, like computer science or engineering. "Robotics as a course is offered by most colleges at the post-graduate level. But there is no exclusive course at the BE level. Students would benefit more if they started off at the Bachelors level itself, says Dr Madhava Krishna, from the Indian Institute of Information Technology in Hyderabad. Experts also feel robotics must be introduced in polytechnic colleges too.

The market for robotics is thriving. Robotics is applied in various spheres like automobiles, electronics and medicine.

Research in robotics is also emerging as a fertile field, what with labs mushrooming across the South to cater to the growing interest. Dr Krishna offers his perspective on robotics for research, "I see considerable interest at the level of hobby robotics. There is, however, a large gap between robotics as a hobby and robotics as a research medium. There is also a need to move to advanced-level robotics. There are enough takers for subjects like embedded robotics." He points to a vital gap in the demand-supply scene – that there are not many dedicated robotics companies in India. "Another problem is the lack of faculty," he sums up.

End Term Examination

EIGHTH SEMESTER [B.TECH.] MAY 2010

Paper Code: ETCS402 ***Subject: Artificial Intelligence***

Time: 3 Hours ***Maximum Marks: 75***

***Note:** Q. 1 is compulsory. Attempt one questions from each unit. Internal choice is indicated.*

Q. l. Give a short answer: **(3 × 5 = 15)**

(*a*) Classify the following search algorithm as intelligent/ non intelligent. Give reason of your answer: Depth first search, best first search, branch and bound search.

(*b*) How can you classify the knowledge? What is an inference engine?

(*c*) What are the merits/ demerits of semantic net over semantic frames?

(*d*) What are the different steps for natural processing?

(*e*) List various application areas where Neural network is used.

UNIT-I

Q. 2. (*a*) Compare depth first search and Hill Climbing search procedures. **(3)**

(*b*) Explain the advantages of Best first search over Hill Climbing with suitable example. **(5)**

(*c*) What are the steps to solve constraint satisfaction problem? Explain them with help of crypt arithmetical problem. **(7)**

OR

Q. 3. (*a*) Explain the process to reach goal state of a search tree which is AND/OR graph. Give an example of application whose search tree is AND/OR graph. **(8)**

(*b*) Explain the Means end analysis algorithm. Give an example of an application where it is applied. **(7)**

UNIT-II

Q. 4. (*a*) Explain the rules to unify two predicates. **(3)**

(*b*) Represent following facts as predicates and convert them to clause form, explaining the steps of conversion: **(5)**

(*i*) Any student who is intelligent or hard working will pass the exam in good marks.

(*ii*) Any one who is passed with good marks get a job.

(*c*) Assume that "Shiva is neither hard working nor intelligent". Using resolution prove that Shiva does not get a job. **(7)**

OR

Q. 5. (*a*) What kind of knowledge is represented by the semantic nets? Give an example of knowledge base represented by semantic nets and explain how inferences are done in semantic Nets? **(8)**

(*b*) Give an example of a game Tree. What is the purpose of Minimax procedure in game tree? What are Alpha Beta cutoff? **(7)**

UNIT-III

Q. 6. (*a*) Consider the following sentences: **(5)**

Most birds fly unless they have broken wings

Penguins and Ostrich do not fly.

Crow is a bird

Use Non monotonic reasoning to answer "Does Crow Fly"?

(*b*) Write short notes on handling uncertainty using probabilistic reasoning. **(5)**

(*c*) Write short notes on Fuzzy logic. **(5)**

OR

Q. 7. (*a*) What are important challenges in Natural Languages Understanding"? **(2)**

(*b*) What are the various applications of NLP? **(3)**

(*c*) Explain the various activities which are performed during Morphological Analysis and Syntactic processing, with the help of following sentence: I want to see Raju's photo. **(10)**

UNIT-IV

Q. 8. (*a*) Give short description of process of learning using Back Propogation Neural Network. **(10)**

(*b*) Give a flow graph for developing a genetic algorithm. **(5)**

OR

Q. 9. (*a*) What procedure is followed for knowledge acquisition? **(4)**

(*b*) What are the various steps for development of Expert Systems? **(7)**

(*c*) What is the role of expert system tools in developing expert system? Give one example of such tool and its usability. **(4)**

QUESTION PAPER 2011

GGSIPU Dwarka (2011)

B.TECH (CSE) (Sem VIII)

End Term Examination

Paper Code: ETCS - 402 — ***Subject: Artificial Intelligence***

Time: 3 Hours — ***Maximum Marks : 75***

Note: *Q. 1 is compulsory. Attempt One question from each unit. Internal choice is indicated.*

Q. 1. (*a*) How does the Artificial Intelligence solve problems for which no practically feasible algorithm exists? **(3)**

(*b*) Give an example of non-monotonic reasoning. What are the techniques for making decisions in non-monotonic systems? **(3)**

(*c*) How is an Expert System different from other softwares like DBMS etc? **(3)**

(*d*) Define a predicate: Construct a predicate using "C" language. **(3)**

(*e*) Why Hill-climbing is named so? Illustrate using an example. **(3)**

UNIT-I

Q. 2. (*a*) Discuss the scope of Artificial Intelligence applied to various categories of problems. **(8)**

(*b*) Discuss and compare Blind search with Heuristic based search. Which one is better? Discuss using an example. **(7)**

OR

Q. 3. (*a*) What is a Constraints Satisfaction Problem? Create a CSP from the real world and suggest some measures to solve it. **(7)**

(*b*) What is a State Space Search? Give any example of a Game which happens to be a problem of state space search and justify your answer properly.

UNIT-II

Q. 4. (*a*) Perform minimax on the following tree

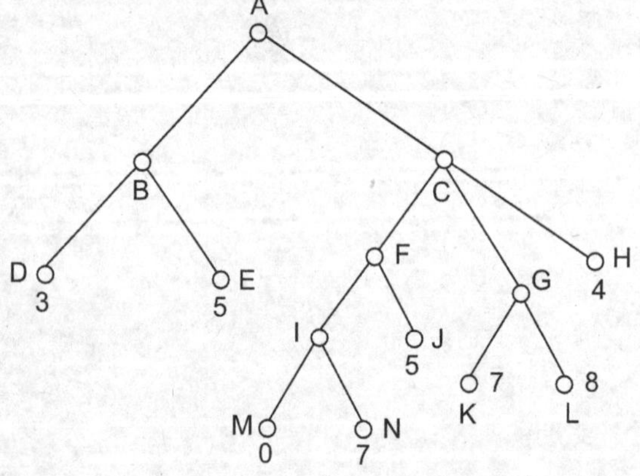

Explain each step.

(*b*) Given the following information for a database: **(8)**

A1. If x is on top of y, y supports x

A2. If x is above y and they are touching each other, x is on top of y

A3. A COUP is above a book

A4. A cup is touching a book.

(*i*) Translate statements A1 to A4 into clausal form

(*ii*) Show that the predicate supports (book, cup) is tree using resolution.

OR

Q. 5. (*a*) Create a script for "appearing for an examination". **(5)**

(*b*) A new operator ⊕, or exclusive or may be defined by the following Truth Table: **(5)**

P	Q	$P \oplus Q$
T	T	F
T	F	T
F	T	T
F	F	F

Create a propositional calculus expression using ∧∨ and > that is equivalent to P ⊕ Q.

(*c*) Explain conceptual dependency using an example. **(5)**

UNIT-III

Q. 6. (*a*) What are the different types of fuzzy membership function? What is the criteria to define a fuzzy membership function? **(8)**

(*b*) Describe Chowsky hierarchy of languages. **(7)**

OR

Q. 7. (*a*) How uncertainty is captured using probabilistic reasoning? How is it different from handling uncertainty using fuzzy logic? **(8)**

(*b*) Differentiate between Syntactic and Semantic processing. **(7)**

UNIT-IV

Q. 8. (*a*) Describe an Automation. Extend it to learning automation. **(7)**

(*b*) Pick one problem area that you feel would justify the energy required to design an expert system solution. Spell the problem out in some detail. Based on your intuition, which aspects of this solution would be most difficult to automate? **(8)**

OR

Q. 9. (*a*) What are the different types of learning? Explain with an example. **(8)**

(*b*) Why is the process of knowledge acquisition so tedious? **(7)**

Subject – Artificial Intelligence Roll No.

B.Tech (SEM VIII) April-2012

IInd Term Examination

Paper Code: ETCS - 402 *Subject: Artificial Intelligence*

Time: 3 Hours *Maximum Marks : 30*

Note: *Question* 1 *is compulsory and attempt any Two Questions from remaining.*

Part 1 COMPULSORY (Make any combination of 2 and 3 marks-questions to make it 10)

Q. 1. (*a*) Differentiate between forward Vs Backward reasoning taking example of Prolog syntax? **(2)**

(*b*) Define properties of conventional reasoning and how they differ from Non-monotonic reasoning systems **(3)**

(*c*) Explain JTMS, LTMS and ATMS. Take an example to illustrate your point **(3)**

(*d*) Contrast (a) Expert systems with Production systems, Neural Networks and Intelligent agents. **(3)**

(*e*) Define Dempster-Shafer theory making it different from Bayesian belief networks **(2)**

(*f*) Make a comparison chart between game problem and state space problem and explain pictorial Nim Game theorem **(2)**

(*g*) Explain application areas of expert system technology and limitations. **(2)**

Any Two Questions of Part 2

Q. 2. (*a*) Make a case study defining two A.I. systems, SOAR and PRODIGY, in terms of their learning mechanisms? **(3)**

Define 3 fuzzy membership functions corresponding to different (assumed) cases of organization. **(3)**

(*b*) What do you mean by default reasoning and what are two different logics to do it and also define non-monotonic reasonings that can be defined in same logics? **(3.5)**

(*c*) Explain approaches taken for reasoning under various kinds of uncertainty and explain different mechanisms where propositions are not independent of each other. Also propose techniques for representing ignorance. **(3.5)**

Q. 3. (*a*) Give steps for development of expert systems and explain inference engine using fuzzy and rule-based systems taking an example. **(3)**

(*b*) Show how a JTMS could be used in medical diagnosis. Consider rules "If you have a runny nose, assume you have a cold unless it is allergy season? Solve same problem using ATMS. **(3)**

(*c*) How is Mini-max procedure (alpha beta search) used to play tic-tac-toe? Give situation where it is better to search graph instead of game tree as normally happens in mini-max search algorithm where search proceeds always forward from current position rather than backward from goal node. **(2 + 2)**

Q. 4. (*a*) Implement candidate elimination algorithm for version space. Choose a concept space with several features (animals, books etc.) Choose a concept and demonstrate learning by positive and negative examples of concept. **(3)**

(*b*) Explain neural net learning and genetic learning. **(2)**

OR

State contributions made by people for dealing with uncertain situations with their Theorems and Laws. **(2)**

(*b*) Explain BACON data driven discovery and how it differs from analogy approach of learning. **(2)**

(*c*) Define a case study of a college where student has different learning mechanisms to solve problems. Explain mechanism with optimum satisfaction to problem. Give a short note on fuzzy logic making it different from conventional logic **(3)**

Subject – Artificial Intelligence Roll No.

B.Tech (SEM VIII) Feb-2012

Ist Term Examination

Paper Code: ETCS - 402 *Subject: Artificial Intelligence*

Time: 3 Hours *Maximum Marks : 30*

Note: *Question* 1 *is compulsory and attempt any Two Questions from remaining parts.*

Part-1

Q. 1. (*a*) Name AI is misnomer. Comment and state why AI should be a part of Computer Science. **(2)**

(*b*) What is heuristic function and what happens if by mistake it is underestimated at the node? **(2)**

(*c*) When can breath-first search be better than best-first search? **(1)**

(*d*) Differentiate good solution or optimum solution and satisfying solution. **(1.5)**

OR

Explain how conventional computing differs from intelligences computing.

(*e*) Trace the operations of unification algorithm on f(x) and f(g(y)). **(1.5)**

(*f*) A semantic net to describe household goods **(1)**

(*g*) Differentiate between procedural knowledge and declarative knowledge. **(1)**

OR

What do you mean by 'Knowledge Acquisition'?

Part-2

Q. 1. (*a*) Describe various methods you have learnt to determine useful heuristic functions. **(3)**

(*b*) Using an example show uniform cost search operation. **(2)**

(*c*) With reference to traveling salesman problem, explain what is meant by combinational explosion and what effect it has on optimal solution. **(3)**

(*d*) A O * Algorithm can be modified to work on graph which contains cycle. **(3)**

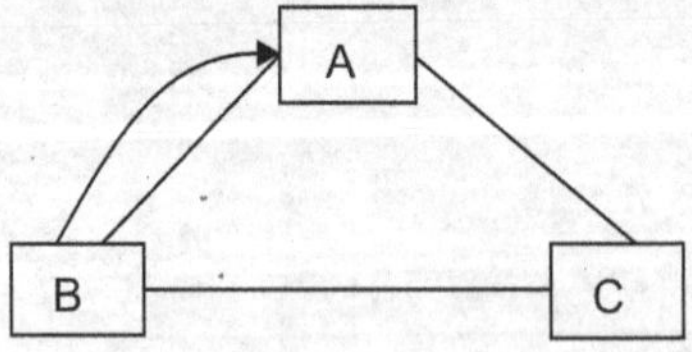

What changes must be done in the algorithm to handle this cycling procedure? so as to save efforts and also handle this situation when the cost of node C is changed.

Part-3

Q. 1. (*a*) You have 3 Jugs measuring 12 Gallon, 8 Gallon and 3 Gallon. You can fill the jugs up or empty them from one to another or onto ground. Your objective is to measure out of exactly one gallon. Give the completely state space and set of all applicable rules. **(4)**

(*b*) Consider the following sentences:

(*i*) John likes all kinds of foods.

(*ii*) Apple are food

(*iii*) Chicken is food

(*iv*) Anything anyone eats, and is not killed by is food.

(*v*) Jack eats peanuts and is still alive

(*vi*) Jill eats everything, Jack eats.

Represent these sentences in predicate logic and prove that John likes peanuts. **(4)**

(*c*) Represent the same story in a frame using associative network structure. **(2)**

Part-4

Q. 1. (*a*) Show the conceptual dependency representation of the sentence:

John begged Mary for a pencil **(2.5)**

How this representation makes it possible to answer the question:

Did John talk to Mary?

(*b*) Differentiate between semantic net and partitioned net. **(2.5)**

OR

Explain means and analysis method with help of suitable example.

(*c*) Consider the following facts: (5)

- The members of the Elm St Bridge Club are Joe, Sally, Bill and Ellen.
- Joe is married to Sally.
- Bill is Ellen's brother.
- The spouse of every married person in the club is also in the club.
- The last meeting of the club was at Joe's house.

(*a*) Represent these facts in predicate logic.

(*b*) From the facts given above, most people would be able to decide on the following truth of the following additional statements:

(*i*) The last meeting of the club was at Sally's house.

(*ii*) Ellen is not married.

Can you construct resolution proofs to demonstrate the truth of each of these statements given the five facts listed above? Do so if possible. Otherwise, add the facts you need and then construct the proofs explaining resolution.

Subject – Artificial Intelligence Roll No.

B.Tech (SEM VIII) April-2012

IInd Term Examination

Paper Code: ETCS - 402 ***Subject: Artificial Intelligence***

Time: 1.5 Hours ***Maximum Marks : 30***

Note: *Question* 1 *is compulsory and attempt any Two Questions from remaining.*

Q. 1. (*a*) What is futility cutoff in game playing?

(*b*) Briefly explain the significance of Bayes' Theorem.

(*c*) Name any two expert systems?

(*d*) What is horizon effect in game playing?

(*e*) What does Certainty Factor in a rule signify? **(2.5)**

Q. 2. (*a*) What is non-monotonic reasoning? Explain. **(5)**

(*b*) Explain various types of learning with examples. **(5)**

Q. 3. (*a*) Explain how game playing comes in the domain of artificial intelligence. **(3)**

(*b*) Explain MINIMAX search procedure giving an example. **(3)**

(*c*) Apply Alpha-Beta pruning procedure to the following tree: **(4)**

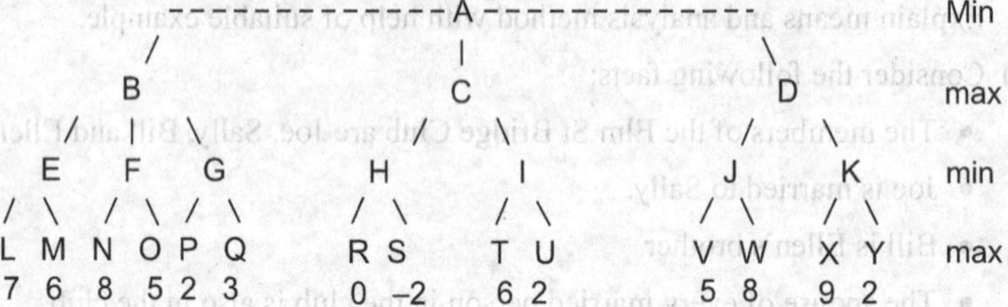

Q. 4. Write short note on any two: **(2 × 5)**

(*a*) Fuzzy Logic

(*b*) Perceptrons

(*c*) Genetic Algorithms

END TERM EXAMINATION

EIGHTH SEMESTER [B.TECH.] MAY-JUNE 2012

Paper Code: ETCS402 | ***Subject: Artificial Intelligence***

Time: 3 Hours | ***Maximum Marks: 75***

***Note**: Attempt all questions. Internal choice is indicated.*

Q. 1. (*a*) What is the turing test for AI? **(2)**

(*b*) What are the limitations of expert system? **(2)**

(*c*) What is "Horn clauses" in AI? **(2)**

(*d*) What is Agents? **(2)**

(*e*) What are different types of Blind Search? Explain. **(2)**

(*f*) Explain Plateaux. **(2)**

(*g*) What is Context-free Grammer? **(2)**

(*h*) What is LISP, WAP in LISP to append a list? **(2)**

(*i*) Perform resolution on the set of clauses. **(2)**

A: PVQVR

B: = ~PVR

C: = ~Q

D: = ~R

(*j*) What is Fuzzy Set? **(2)**

(*k*) Where CD (Conceptual Dependency) used in AI? **(2)**

(*l*) What are Research Areas in NLP? **(3)**

Q. 2. (*a*) Define Artificial Intelligence as a Science? How it was introduced? **(4)**

(*b*) Explain Production System. What is meaning of f(n), g(n), h(n)? **(5)**

(*c*) What is heuristic function? Explain hill climbing problem. **(3.5)**

OR

(*d*) Differentiate between conventional programming and AI programming. **(4)**

(*e*) Solve the problem for finding shortest path from A to Z using A* algorithm. **(6)**

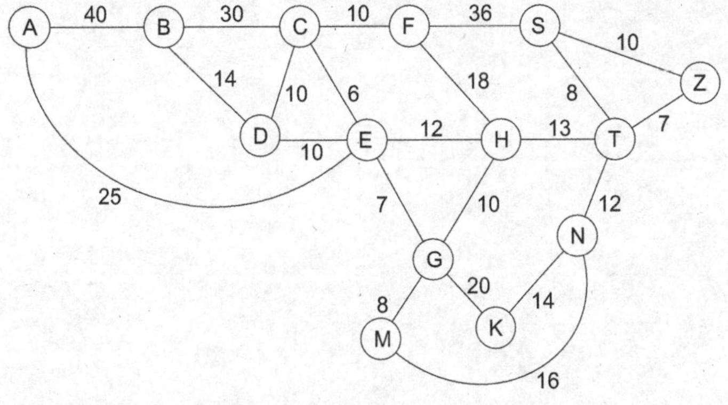

(*f*) Where Breadth first search is better than Best first Search? Explain with the help of example. (2.5)

Q. 3. (*a*) Why Game playing is part of AI? (3)

(*b*) Design Semantic Networks and frames for the banking system. (6)

(*c*) How to interpret the frames in Knowledge Representation? (3.5)

OR

(*a*) Explain Alpha-Beta cutoff in Min-Max Algo with the help of an example. (6)

(*b*) Consider the following statement:– (6.5)

"Mary likes all kinds of food. Pizza is a kind of food. Apple is a food. Anything anyone eats is a food. John does not eat chicken. Ana eats everything Mary eats." Convert these statements into predicate logic. Answer questions given below using Resolution Algorithm.

(*i*) What food does Ana eat? (*ii*) Is Mary like chicken? (*iii*) Pizza is liked by Mary or not?

Q. 4. (*a*) Differentiate between deterministic versus non-deterministic Parsers. (4)

(*b*) Define Fuzzy inference. What are the main steps in fuzzy inference process? (8.5)

OR

(*a*) What ia NLP? Explain Pragmatic Processing. (5)

(*b*) How does a rule-based expert system propagate uncertainties? (7.5)

Q. 5. (*a*) Draw and explain the architecture diagram of Rule-based expert system. (6)

(*b*) What is learning in AI? (4)

(*c*) Where forward chaining is better than backward chaining? (2.5)

OR

(*a*) What are the fundamental characteristics of Expert system and why we need an expert system? (4.5)

(*b*) What are the difference between expert system and artificial neural networks? (5)

(*c*) "Robotics is a branch of AI". Comment. (3)